HOTHOUSE

The Art of Survival and the Survival of Art at
America's Most Celebrated Publishing House,
Farrar, Straus and Giroux

BORIS KACHKA

SIMON & SCHUSTER
New York   London   Toronto   Sydney   New Delhi

Simon & Schuster
1230 Avenue of the Americas
New York, NY 10020

First Simon & Schuster hardcover edition August 2013

SIMON & SCHUSTER and colophon are registered trademarks
of Simon & Schuster, Inc.

For information about special discounts for bulk purchases,
please contact Simon & Schuster Special Sales at
1-866-506-1949 or business@simonandschuster.com.

The Simon & Schuster Speakers Bureau can bring authors
to your live event. For more information or to book an event,
contact the Simon & Schuster Speakers Bureau at
1-866-248-3049 or visit our website at www.simonspeakers.com.

Designed by Ruth Lee-Mui

Manufactured in the United States of America

3   5   7   9   10   8   6   4   2

Library of Congress Cataloging-in-Publication Data
Kachka, Boris.
Hothouse : the art of survival and the survival of art at America's most celebrated
publishing house, Farrar, Straus, & Giroux / Boris Kachka. — First Simon & Schuster
hardcover edition.
        p. cm.
Includes bibliographical references.
1. Farrar, Straus, and Giroux—History. 2. Publishers and publishing—New York (State)—
New York—History—20th century. 3. Publishers and publishing—New York (State)—
New York—Biography. 4. Authors and publishers—New York (State)—New York—
History—
20th century. I. Title.
Z473.F37K33 2013
070.509747'0904—dc23
2013003199

ISBN 978-1-4516-9189-4
ISBN 978-1-4516-9192-4 (ebook)

Endpaper and photo credits appear on page 431.

For Aron and Nora Kachka,
and in memory of Zinovy Vaysman

Contents

HOTHOUSE

Introduction

A Long and Beautiful Life

Roger W. Straus, Jr., the grandson of an ambassador, would have made a terrible diplomat. No matter the situation or his level of expertise, Straus had an opinion, and as often as not, he shared it, in public. Whenever he took a phone call from a journalist, his devoted secretary liked to hold up a sign that read: OFF THE RECORD. Straus had, however, an unusually diplomatic answer to everyone's favorite question: What was the best book that Farrar, Straus and Giroux, the publishing house he led for nearly sixty years, had ever published? Straus had to strike from the list his most competitive writers: Robert Lowell, John Berryman, Jean Stafford, Jack Kerouac, Elizabeth Bishop, Philip Roth, Aleksandr Solzhenitsyn. Picking among his closest friends— Susan Sontag, Joseph Brodsky, Tom Wolfe, John McPhee, Edmund Wilson, Isaac Bashevis Singer—would be like declaring a favorite child. It certainly wouldn't be one of his rare bestsellers, from Sammy Davis, Jr., to Scott Turow, who rather embarrassed him.

It was one of the toughest questions you could throw at Roger.

For all their great size, commercial publishing conglomerates like Simon & Schuster—a favorite Straus whipping boy—had maybe a book or two per season of lasting literary value. And besides, it would be silly to direct such a question to corporate CEOs, and not just because they rarely read their own books; these giants and their constituent imprints had changed hands so many times it was hard to tell who deserved the credit, or what the value of their logo really was from year to year. Farrar, Straus and Giroux was, and is, different. Those three angular fish stacked vertically at the bottom of a book's spine are a guarantee to critics and discerning readers: You may or may not love this book, but we do. This was as true in 2011—Jeffrey Eugenides, Péter Nádas, Denis Johnson, Thomas Friedman, Roberto Bolaño—as it was in 1968.

Straus's consistent choice of a favorite book was on its face an odd one. Though he often stood accused of chasing Nobel Prizes to the exclusion of all else, including profits, this writer was not one of FSG's twenty-five Nobel laureates (the latest being Mario Vargas Llosa, 2010). Instead he chose *Memoirs of Hadrian,* by Marguerite Yourcenar, a historical novel written in the voice of the great Roman emperor. Picked up from France via one of Straus's shady European scouts and hastily translated by Yourcenar's lover, the book had a brisk-enough sale—about forty thousand in hardcover—but sales on a work like this were, Straus declared, "caviar." *Memoirs,* which had stayed in print for decades after its publication in 1954, had "this long and rather beautiful life."

The same could be said of the twin engines behind FSG, Straus and his reticent editor-partner, Robert Giroux. The story of their lives, their publishing house, and a postwar period during which the bestseller lists teemed with brilliant and difficult work (even poetry) inevitably flirts with nostalgia. Independent publishers are largely history—FSG itself was sold in 1994 to a German conglomerate—and even books themselves, we are told, are quickly giving way to pixels and tablets. Both the art and the craft of bookmaking seem to be under grave threat.

But that's a simplistic storyline. Narratives will persist, and conglomerate-owned houses still put out excellent work. Nor was the old, independent Farrar, Straus any kind of Xanadu. It was filthy, inadequately heated and cooled, never painted, teeming with bugs and ugly fluorescent tube lights and impoverished if passionate lifers. It was also a private fiefdom under one lord, Roger Straus, a man who could be cheap, vulgar, classist, and sexist all in one gratuitously cruel remark. What really made him sell the company wasn't market forces, but his inability to cede power to his own son. Less charitable observers would say he singled out *Memoirs of Hadrian* because he himself was a despot. But whether you saw the independent FSG as an "antique spinning wheel," in the words of one detractor, or as a paradise for those who loved books above all else, the fact is that its demise was foreordained, just like that of CBGB, the League of Nations, or Scribner's bookstore. Its history, like so much of the writing it published, is fascinating and vivid but difficult to parse—and all the more rewarding for the effort.

Memoirs of Hadrian well deserved its place in Straus's pantheon, mainly because it handled vast themes with great subtlety. The fictional notes of an old man looking to the future and the inevitable end of his empire, it expresses, better than the combative and not very subtle Straus ever could, an enduring and tempered faith in the lasting works of civilization at its best:

> Life is atrocious, we know. But precisely because I expect little of the human condition, man's periods of felicity, his partial progress, his efforts to begin over again and to continue, all seem to me like so many prodigies which nearly compensate for the monstrous mass of ills and defeats, of indifference and error. Catastrophe and ruin will come; disorder will triumph, but order will too, from time to time . . . Not all our books will perish, nor our statues, if broken, lie unrepaired; other domes and pediments will arise from our domes and pediments; some few men will think and work and feel as we have done, and I venture to count upon such continuators, placed irregularly throughout the centuries, and upon this kind of intermittent immortality.

• • •

Just as breaking news is the rough draft of history, the first pass at a person's legacy is written by his eulogizers. FSG's legacy is inseparable from those of its two departed leaders, Straus and Giroux—one its restless gut, the other its quiet brain. And to understand them, it pays to begin at the end, with their memorials, each a perfectly tuned tribute to an inimitable man.

St. Paul's Chapel, at Columbia University in New York, is as spacious and soaring inside as most cathedrals, but it doesn't put on airs. Its Renaissance Revival design—redbrick outside, delicate rose herringbone tile within—mingles politely with the McKim, Mead & White brick-and-stone campus that surrounds it. A chilling, windswept rain was falling outside the chapel on December 10, 2008, as one hundred current and former employees of FSG gathered to remember Robert Giroux, who had died three months earlier at the age of ninety-four. It was a grim autumn for publishing: sales plummeting, layoffs and closings pouring down, and more on the way. A week after the service, FSG publisher Jonathan Galassi would have to announce layoffs and further consolidation with the other American holdings of Holtzbrinck, the German owners of FSG. Never before had the company's autonomy looked so precarious. The Giroux memorial was a brief, solemn respite, "the eye of the storm," as one editor put it.

Six speakers—three of Giroux's FSG acolytes, an Elizabeth Bishop scholar, a Jesuit priest, and the daughter of Bernard Malamud—attested briefly to Giroux's integrity, his editorial care, his excellent taste, his passion for opera. Then they read selections from writers, including Robert Lowell, Flannery O'Connor, and Thomas Merton—artists whose tumultuous lives the editor improved as much as he did their tumultuous work.

Giroux had lived long enough to eulogize his partner and boss of almost a half century, Roger Straus, at a service that couldn't have been more different from his own. Straus's death in 2004 at the age of eighty-seven was marked by not one but three public services, in Frankfurt, London, and New York, as well as a proper funeral at Fifth

Avenue's Temple Emanu-El, one of the largest synagogues in the world. The memorial for Straus in New York, where Giroux was one of fifteen speakers, took place in September at the 92nd Street Y, in the dark, mahogany-paneled Unterberg Poetry Center, venue of many an FSG author reading. A secular Jewish temple of literature and performance, it suited Straus—the worldly, ecumenical showman—just as St. Paul's fit the liberal, Jesuit-trained Giroux.

There had also been rain on that September day, but it had blown over by the time of the remembrance. The audience swelled to six hundred (most dressed for an evening out, though it was three in the afternoon) and included nearly every American friend, rival, and enemy who had ever crossed paths with the founder of FSG. It felt, said an editor, like "the keynote event of a publishing conference." And then the speeches began. While Straus's Emanu-El service had been solemn (some thought too solemn), this was a grander, more cacophonous affair, played at a snappy clip and in a variety of keys. At times it was wistful, but at others it was as bawdy and cutting as a Friar's Club roast.

Jonathan Galassi opened the service by recalling his first encounter with the man who would, twenty years later, hand him the keys to his kingdom. Back in the seventies, Galassi was introduced to Straus and Susan Sontag, huddled in matching leather jackets inside a banquette at an old Washington Square restaurant known as One Fifth. It turned out that Roger's wife, Dorothea, was publishing a memoir with Houghton Mifflin, where Galassi was then an editor. By way of introduction, Straus roared, in his marble-mouthed North Shore accent, "Tell your fucking copyediting department to get off their asses and fix my wife's proofs!" Then he turned back to his glamorous, long-limbed guest. Galassi's first impression: "This guy is a hood."

John McPhee, a loyal FSG author for four decades, was characteristically dry in his encomium, save for a pitch-perfect Straus imitation: "He was absolutely mahvelous! Mahvelous! Et cetera, et cetera, and so forth and so on . . ." Farrar, Straus gave him unconditional love: Every single one of his books, many of them about rocks, was accepted and kept perpetually in print. But then there was the money, or lack thereof. He'd once asked Straus if he was earning less because he didn't have an agent, and Roger answered honestly, "Oh, not a whole hell of a lot." McPhee concluded with some backhanded praise for the publisher who'd once given him a "Fuck you" in lieu of an advance. "If he kept back money that he might have laid on me," McPhee said, "I'm particularly happy about that now, because I'm sure he has it with him, and he'll need it."

Union Square Cafe owner Danny Meyer was out of town attending his own grandfather's funeral, but in a speech read by a business partner, he mused on how much higher FSG's author advances might have been if Straus had curtailed some of his three thousand meals at the restaurant. ("Danny's a good writer," an editor said with a nudge. "Somebody should sign him up.") Publisher Peter Mayer remembered his onetime mentor calling him a schmuck and hanging up on him. Czech-born children's book author and illustrator Peter Sís recalled his hesitance to enter FSG, at 19 Union Square West, because it looked like an INS office—until he met Roger, who "gave me hope that there might be a better way to live, that we might go to some bar, and have some drinks, and do other things that I don't dare talk about here." Ian Frazier compared Roger to Max Bialystock from *The Producers* and praised (but did not demonstrate) his talent for telling dirty stories. But he also recalled that Straus "enjoyed thinking about the possibility that in the year 2600 people might still be reading a book published by him." It was a trick that works brilliantly in Frazier's writing: smuggling in a sense of seriousness beneath the humor, a surprise guest at the party.

Straus's sui generis blend of vulgarity and refinement was owed partly to his upbringing. The product of two powerful families, the Strauses and the Guggenheims, he had defied his kin—Princeton-trained industrialists and politicians—by serially failing at school, forsaking the family business, and starting, of all things, a tiny publishing shop. Yet by the time he died he was, to all observers, the epitome of noblesse oblige. Thus it made perfect sense for the service's final speech to be given by Tom Wolfe, that keen observer of both class distinctions and the distinctively crass. Having come to FSG in 1964, the Man in White admiringly sketched Roger's aesthetic—ascots, broad pinstripes, custom camel-hair coats, and the prized beige Mercedes convertible. When that car pulled up across the street from old drug-ridden Union Square Park, Wolfe said, the resident junkies "would freeze, the needles in midair, the straps around the arm, and all the rest of it . . . It was a magical car, and a magical arrival, and he was absolutely immune from all of the terrors of Union Square."

But before Wolfe spoke, literary agent Andrew Wylie came to the podium. His appearance was the shock of the afternoon. Straus was not big on agents, particularly the openly mercenary types, and Wylie plays that part better than anyone else, practically twirling an invisible mustache as he poaches other agents' clients and extorts astronomical advances from publishers. (It wasn't Straus who nicknamed him "the Jackal"; he simply called him "that shit.") Moving Philip Roth away from FSG had been a mortal sin. Straus rarely spoke to Roth after that, but Wylie he had to deal with. Besides, they had much in com-mon—their haughty manner, natty attire, and reverence for capital "L" Literature. They were doppelgängers in their separate towers of the literary citadel, usually (but not always) on opposite sides of the moat. What could Wylie possibly have to say?

He began with what he'd heard about Straus before meeting him and went on to describe their strange courtship:

> He was always doing battle with one person, or he was at war with another. A good number of fights he had started. He was a prolific abuser of nicknames. His broadly reported acts of withering con-descension were exhilarating. I conspired to meet him. Naturally I was treated abysmally . . . Gradually, we came to know each other—though a bit warily at first. I studied him carefully. He was a magnifi-cent character: vindictive, raucous, willful. A wonderful man. We had terrible fights . . . He had a vile tongue. He relished obscenities. He was always curious about everything and supernaturally aware. He seemed to have a second sense about what mattered in publish-ing and what did not. He was consistently provocative for a reason. He was singular; he was superb. I will miss him for the rest of my life. I guess we all will. It's already getting very dull without him.

Some ranked it the best speech of the afternoon. Straus might have agreed. It was a barbed tangle of epithets for a complex hero, a litany read out by a fierce rival still awed by the outsize presence of the departed. Straus, who liked to issue the warning shot "Too much ego, amigo," couldn't have asked for a better testament to his own.

The strongest speech at Giroux's memorial was, like the ceremony, far more solemn. Pat Strachan, now an editor at Little, Brown, began her career as Giroux's assistant in 1971. Had things gone differently, she might have eventually succeeded him as editor in chief. Unspoken in all of her hugs and quiet exchanges with former colleagues—including Galassi, who *did* become editor in chief—was the mutual understanding that her tenure had ended badly, regretfully. But this evening wasn't about resentments, only remembrance. Strachan chose to pay tribute to Giroux as a professional mourner himself, a guardian of legacies. She had known "Mr. Giroux" as a charming but stoic presence, a man whose emotions—save for the occasional outburst over production snafus—were hard to know. But she did once see her boss break down—just once. "In the winter of 1972," she said, "Bob called me into his office, asking me to shut the door. After I sat down, he said, 'John has jumped off the bridge.' Tears began streaming down his face. His beloved poet John Berryman had taken his own life."

Strachan herself welled up at the memory. She also read from some of Flannery O'Connor's letters, noting the southern Catholic's early death from lupus. And she closed by referencing yet another untimely passing. Giroux had spoken at the 1979 funeral for his friend Henry Robbins, his immediate successor as FSG's editor in chief. At that earlier memorial, Giroux had drawn on the subject of Straus's favorite book, the legacy-obsessed Emperor Hadrian. But he didn't quote from *Memoirs of Hadrian*. Instead he recited his own rough Latin translation of the philosopher-king's best-known piece of verse, which he'd written on his deathbed:

Little soul, gentle and drifting, the guest and comrade of my body,
where will you now find a dwelling place? Poor little, naked little,
pale little soul, without your old power of joking.

It was perhaps not the happiest vision of an afterlife (surely they
didn't take cash in this nameless limbo, as they did in McPhee's more
transactional paradise). But it was appropriately wistful and, maybe,
Strachan's way of calling attention to other editors who had made
FSG what it was. She pointed out that Giroux had read those same
lines at a memorial for "yet another great and fine editor," a dapper,
slim, and devastatingly witty man named Harold Vursell. Aside from
editing *Memoirs of Hadrian,* Vursell was also at various times the managing editor, head of production, and chief of children's books.

Going back through the editorial history, Strachan seemed to be
raising the curtain on a long line of ghosts leading back to John Farrar,
whose imprimatur and inherited writers Straus had once desperately
needed. Giroux was sharing the spotlight at St. Paul's, not just with his
famous writers but also with other editors who were in danger, as he
once put it—citing Orwell's *1984,* which he'd helped publish—of being
"dropped down the memory hole."

It may have been Straus who, by sheer force of his charm and quick-
ness, managed to preserve the company that arguably set the intellectual
tone of postwar America. But it was Giroux and Robbins and Vursell
and many other underpaid strivers who advised him on what to publish,
how to promote it, how to translate it and sell it properly abroad—who,
in short, made the company worth preserving. They worked in gloves in
the winter when the heat broke down; they jerry-rigged the paper towel
roll in the ladies' room with an oversize dinner fork; they repaired their
own desks and bought their own pencils and made sacrifices in their
lives that well-born Roger W. Straus, Jr., would never have to make, all
for the freedom to publish what they loved, and little else.

At Giroux's memorial, FSG editor Paul Elie, the author of a group
biography of four Catholic authors—three of them Giroux writers—warned against false nostalgia. "It is tempting to float an analogy

between his death and the death of a certain kind of publishing," said Elie. "But the fact is that his kind of publishing was rare in his own time, and so was he."

As calculated and profit-driven as mainstream publishing has become, there was no such thing as a golden age. Both Giroux and Farrar had found refuge, in Roger's company, from a business already rife with unreasonable, callous, and daft publishers. Cofounder John Farrar had been ousted from his own firm, Farrar & Rinehart, while lying in an Algerian hospital during World War II—a predicament that left the esteemed editor on the verge of a nervous breakdown. He and Roger Straus were lucky to find each other. The Farrar name, as Roger once said, "meant something in publishing, and the name Straus meant nothing."

Giroux's break from his previous employer was even more symptomatic of the pressures put on any talented editor of literature. For fifteen years he had prospered at Harcourt, Brace and Company, publishers of Virginia Woolf, Edmund Wilson, and T. S. Eliot, all of whom he cut his teeth editing while still in his twenties—a dream come true for a factory foreman's kid from Jersey City who'd attended Columbia University on scholarship. But in the late forties the company was merged with a textbook publisher, and Giroux's generous boss was replaced with a businessman, Eugene Reynal. When Giroux requested approval to acquire *The Catcher in the Rye,* Reynal objected, "The guy's crazy," meaning Holden Caulfield. Then he forwarded it to the textbook division, which turned it down. After having to tell J. D. Salinger to take a walk, Giroux eventually did the same. He joined Farrar, Straus as editor in chief in 1955.

As with John Farrar, Straus needed his editor as much as his editor needed him. At St. Paul's, Galassi—the only person who read at both Straus's and Giroux's services—poked another bit of fun at his predecessor. Galassi read from Farrar, Straus's Spring 1952 catalog. A few titles on the list:

The Trouble with Cinderella: An Outline of Identity, by Artie Shaw
A Husband in the House, by Stuart David Engstrand

Water Wagon: Through Florida Waterways by Scow and Outboard Motor,
   by Rube Allyn
They Want to Know: Answers from Business to Questions All of the American People Are Asking, by Earl Bunting and Edward Makeer

It was funny, but there was a bit of the notorious FSG smugness in the assumption that these books were all beneath their publisher; bandleader Shaw's searching autobiography was reprinted as recently as 2001. Yet it was true that most of those early forays were eminently forgettable, and Giroux was not in the habit of doing forgettable books. "The most sobering of all publishing lessons," he had once said, is that "a great book is often ahead of its time, and the trick is how to keep it afloat until the times catch up with it." A half century later, it looked as though Straus had been keeping his publishing house afloat until Giroux could get there.

Upon leaving Harcourt, Giroux never directly asked any of his authors to follow him to Farrar, Straus. But seventeen of them did, including T. S. Eliot, Lowell, O'Connor, Malamud, Berryman, and—at least for two books—Jack Kerouac. In one fell swoop, Straus, who always advised prospective publishers to "find yourself a damned good editor," had himself a damned good house.

FSG really became itself around the time Giroux was made partner, in 1964. There was its logo, purloined from Noonday Books, a down-and-out publishing house Roger acquired on the cheap, picking up not only those three angular fish but Isaac Bashevis Singer. There was Susan Sontag, the long-haired siren of what she called, in one of her groundbreaking essays, "The New Sensibility," uniting in one person all the charisma, smarts, and unflagging energy that Roger Straus looked for in a writer and a person. There were Tom Wolfe and Joan Didion, journalists of a type no one had read before. There was the freewheeling office, a cauldron of adultery that Roger's wife called a "sexual sewer," and a place uncommonly tolerant of gay men in various stages of openness, from Vursell to Giroux to Michael di Capua, editor of Maurice Sendak and Christopher Isherwood. And there were the parties, gatherings of the New York intelligentsia at the Strauses' 70th Street town house where you might eavesdrop on Leonard Bernstein, Mary McCarthy, and Jerzy Kosinski deep in conversation with a small-waisted woman in head-to-toe black silk, a veil, and an enormous-brimmed hat: Dorothea Straus.

But you didn't have to score a party invite to know where the vital center of books could be found. All you had to do was browse the shelves of Brentano's with a discerning eye, and find yourself drawn inexorably to those three little fish. It wasn't all in a particular genre, any more than those personalities on 70th Street represented a single point of view. Literary culture, like the rest of society, shifted seismically in those postwar decades, with generations jostling for supremacy. Lowell and Wilson and Dwight Macdonald were arguing loudly with Sontag and Wolfe and Grace Paley over what art and the world should look like. In the crucible of Manhattan, culture wasn't monolithic, and that was exactly what made it exciting. Bridging those divides was Farrar, Straus and Giroux. Their method, and Roger's, was to build a culture of their own, to stand for what they genuinely believed to be the best, most beautiful books: to be aristocrats of taste in a mercenary meritocracy. Powered by ideas and glamour and just a little bit of capital, FSG was, hands down, the hottest house in New York.

And yet, even in those days, before slick agents and German bankers got into the book business, 19 Union Square West already felt a little out of place. Born of high society, Roger Straus had gone into a gentleman's profession. His path had been blazed by the heads of several "Jewish houses": the pioneering Horace Liveright; the venerable Alfred A. Knopf, whom Roger considered stiff and pretentious; Random House's telegenic Bennett Cerf; and the founders of the more commercial-minded Simon & Schuster. But by the time Roger was parading *his* house geniuses around *his* country manor in Purchase, New York, publishing no longer looked so much like the fiefdoms of flashy scions. In 1960, Alfred Knopf fell out with his son and sold his company to Random House. Five years after that, Random House was sold to RCA. Before 1960, there were no independent publishers, just publishers. Today, 50 percent of the American book market is controlled by four corporations—and soon enough there may be only three, or two. Yet even in the sixties, it was apparent that most firms would have to choose: grow and acquire, sell out to a bigger firm, or die.

Roger Straus made it his mission to find a middle way. Fueling that mission was boundless optimism, a tolerance for risk, and just enough of a personal financial cushion to keep from falling over the brink. But one thing he couldn't bring himself to do, at least for forty-eight years, was to sell his company. If survival meant losing one's identity, or ceding one's authority, then it wasn't worth the struggle.

The benefits of this approach are obvious: See all those beautiful books, and all those editors who learned their trade in an office where their talents could flower without the intrusions of focus groups or growth imperatives. One obvious cost was an almost cultlike aversion to change. Roger's FSG resisted inevitable market forces on the one hand, and the inevitable fact of succession on the other. Few companies better embodied Emerson's definition of an institution as "the lengthened shadow of one man" than Farrar, Straus. But no man can cast a shadow forever.

Giroux learned to thrive in that shadow—albeit less and less happily. Readers at the St. Paul's memorial cited his humility as a virtue inseparable from his talent. When they weren't reciting the words of his illustrious writers, they eulogized him for his turkey-sandwich-and-Jell-O lunches at his desk; for his forbearance with writers; for a dearth of personal photos that could be used at the service. "He did have a priestly aspect to his character," Father Patrick Samway, the Jesuit who spoke at the ceremony, later said. "What was so unusual about him was his utter lack of ego." In fact, Giroux had plenty of ego; he just preferred not to put it on display.

Roger, on the other hand, didn't so much mind being photographed. Every time a camera appeared, he seemed reflexively to strike a bold, Apollonian pose or, later in life, a teeth-baring smile almost as broad as his armspan, the latter fully extended to embrace everyone within the frame. Above the stage at the 92nd Street Y was a screen showing slide after slide of Straus snapshots—Roger bestowing his presence on colleagues and authors both famous and forgotten.

One of them was Giroux's successor as editor in chief, Henry Robbins, who left the company for more money after only one tumultuous year in charge. After Giroux, there was a different would-be successor every few years—until he or she was, all of a sudden, gone. The last of these was Roger Straus III, Roger's only son, who literally learned publishing at his father's knee. In the mid-nineties, "Young Roger" gave up not just his aspirations for succession but his life in book publishing. A year after his departure, his father finally relented and sold the firm. It was left to Jonathan Galassi, who'd steered his own middle course—between father and son—to take over running FSG. But he wasn't the owner, nor was his shadow anywhere near as long as Roger's.

There might have been a deeper reason than Straus's and Giroux's wildly divergent personalities for the contrast between the two memorials. In the four years between them, FSG had moved out of those cramped Union Square offices to shiny new quarters of glass and blond wood. Galassi began publishing a few more commercial books and creeping ever closer to the rest of the Holtzbrinck properties. Gone were the cubbyholes stacked with dusty manuscripts, the letters passed among editors by hand, and even Peggy Miller, Straus's secretary and intimate of more than forty years. What had felt like a cliché in 2004, during those three Straus memorials, turned out to be true in 2008: An era had ended.

Eras never last, though, and neither do people, as Yourcenar put it so elegantly and as the founders of FSG knew well. Both Straus and Giroux had been exceedingly lucky. Their company exploited a glorious middle place—geographically, culturally, and historically. Overlooking Union Square, FSG had one foot in Knopf's midtown, another in Grove Press's Greenwich Village, and both arms reaching out to Europe. Their timing was good, too. As their first catalog was going out, the G.I. Bill was flooding colleges with eager minds, American art was asserting itself across every field, and mores were changing, though not yet at a disorienting pace. These men, elitists with democratic impulses, had their pick of editors, authors, and readers.

And then . . . the world kept moving. Corporations consolidated, academia and pop culture cleaved apart, writers started making—or at least wanting—real money, and Europe stopped handing out Nobels to Americans. Dynasties survived in politics but dissolved in business. Yet it wouldn't be right to dismiss FSG as a burst bubble, protected for too long from all that was good and bad in the world. Think of it, rather, as an eddy: a place where the water flowed against the current for a while. It was fated to rejoin the mainstream eventually; the only alternative was extinction. But for a long time, this particular watering hole sustained the vibrancy and diversity of a new ecosystem, a vital piece of the intellectual life of the United States, which then fed back into the mainstream. And while its legacy was Roger Straus's great project, its unique impact in his own lifetime was almost satisfaction enough. Commenting on FSG's feat of netting three Nobel Prizes in five years, Straus once proudly said, "The best part of that is that it will never happen again."

1

An "Our Crowd" Story

The notice in the *New York Times* read like a rave review. By January 11, 1914, the Gilded Age was over and the fuse nearly lit on the powder keg of world war, yet the paper of record for New York's Jewish aristocracy was running an ebullient two-page spread, bedecked with flowery borders and florid language to match, under the banner headline GUGGENHEIM-STRAUS MARRIAGE UNITES NOTED FAMILIES.

The opening of the story, devoted to good friends of the family that owned the *Times,* set the tone: "The forthcoming marriage of Miss Gladys Guggenheim to Roger Williams Straus suggests more romance than the one conjured up by lovers of sentiment. It is a real romance . . . but it is also an old romance, inasmuch as it cements the friendships of years and unites the daughter and son of the two houses that the world over stand for all that is triumphantly successful in their vast undertakings." There was something in these undertakings that "for want of a better word must be termed epical."

The wedding the next day was as elaborate as its advance billing.

Gladys, the daughter of Daniel Guggenheim, paterfamilias of the country's wealthiest Jewish dynasty, had turned eighteen the previous summer, just after graduating from Rosemary Hall in Connecticut. A pale beauty with raven-black hair and a downturned nose, Gladys was to attend Bryn Mawr but gave up her college plans after falling in love with a Princeton senior, a friend of her cousin's, named Roger Williams Straus. Her father sent her off to Europe in order to slow things down, but at the end of the trial by separation the couple's ardor was undiminished. And so instead of preparing for her second semester, Gladys was marching across the grand marble ballroom of the St. Regis Hotel, her family's city home, in a white satin robe and a point lace veil held in place with orange blossoms, toward an ersatz Roman temple (eight columns of silver, a dome of white roses, flowering vines). There she joined her groom, who struck a stoic figure—wavy hair kept short and neatly parted, features just a little broader than those of a generic classical bust.

Rarely, outside glorious Temple Emanu-El, was so much of New York's new elite gathered in one room. Roger's father, Oscar S. Straus, had been the first Jewish member of a U.S. president's cabinet. His uncle Nathan was a partner in two department-store dynasties—Macy's and Abraham & Straus. Others in his party included Harold Loeb, the Princeton friend and Guggenheim cousin who'd introduced the couple; James Seligman II, of the family known as "the American Rothschilds"; and an actual Rothschild—Walter—who would later run A&S. Among the wider circle of guests were Mr. and Mrs. Andrew Carnegie and Mrs. Theodore Roosevelt.

"It's an 'Our Crowd' story," is how Roger and Gladys's eldest son, Roger Jr., would explain his provenance more than sixty years later, in his characteristic social shorthand. "Our Crowd" was what Manhattan's Germanic-Jewish haute bourgeoisie called themselves, distinguishing them from both the Christian upper class that still held the main levers of power and the eastern Europeans of the Yiddish ghettos downtown. Our Crowd socialized and intermarried as strategically as the European aristocracy in centuries past, and they gossiped and quarreled with a ferocity befitting the court that gave its name to the banquet chambers of the St. Regis—the Louis XVI rooms.

Fissures within the group reflected the era's divergent politics. Three years before the illustrious wedding, Harold Loeb and his future cousin Roger were walking the Princeton grounds when Roger began extolling Teddy Roosevelt's conservationist crusader, Gifford Pinchot. At the time, the Guggenheims were in a pitched battle against the forester over Alaska's natural resources.

"Did you know," Roger asked Harold, "that the Guggenheims are trying to steal Alaska?" Loeb took no offense. "Conditioned to hear the worst about the family, I merely shrugged my shoulders," he recalled in his memoir. He was inclined to take the word of one of his best friends, a precociously mature and worldly youth he'd always looked up to. "Broadened by his sojourn in foreign lands," Loeb wrote, "Roger walked with assurance in the exotic world of his elders and talked of even wider circles: of Englishmen he had known in Asia, of Turks and harems, of diplomats and countesses."

And yet in later years it was Loeb, and not Roger Straus, who would beat his own worldly path. Loeb would drink with Gertrude Stein in Paris, dodge bulls with Ernest Hemingway, and start a literary journal known as *Broom*. Among the artists and writers published in his short-lived periodical were Marianne Moore, John Dos Passos, William Carlos Williams, Picasso, Klee, and Kandinsky.

For Loeb it was an adventure, for Straus a road not taken. Two decades before Straus's own son, Roger Jr., would make a bold foray into the culture business, Loeb begged his Guggenheim grandfather to help keep *Broom* afloat. Simon Guggenheim rejected him out of hand, in 1923: "I am sorry you are not in an enterprise that would show a profit." Simon's primary assistant at the time, already a vice president with the family organization, was Harold's onetime progressive hero, Roger W. Straus.

Roger Sr.'s father, Oscar, had been a more conventional kind of pioneer. Descended from Bavarian immigrants who had founded a dry-goods business in Georgia and moved north after the Civil War, Oscar studied law at Columbia University, and at first vacillated between that profession and his brothers' expanding businesses. Finally he acceded to the advice of his father, Lazarus, and joined the family fold. But he was soon enmeshed in politics, agitating against Tammany Hall and, in 1885, leading a local businessmen's chapter that helped put Grover Cleveland in the White House. Three years later he went abroad to serve as Cleveland's minister to Turkey. Under the administrations of Cleveland, McKinley, Roosevelt, and Taft, Straus served three terms as minister to Turkey and one as Roosevelt's secretary of labor and commerce. He founded the precursor to the U.S. Chamber of Commerce.

Oscar's idol was the progressive Republican Theodore Roosevelt. Oscar believed in political moderation, abstemiousness, and pluralism. Having written a book on Roger Williams, the Puritan reformer and champion of religious tolerance, Oscar named his son Roger Williams Straus. While his social circle in New York was whittling away at gentlemen's agreements in country clubs and prep schools, Oscar defied the will of foreign governments and homegrown bigots simply by serving his country. While his son Roger was at Princeton, Oscar was running for governor of New York State under the banner of Teddy Roosevelt's "Bull Moose Party." Though he lost, Oscar got more votes in his home state than the man at the top of the ticket.

Next to the Strauses, the Guggenheims were arrivistes. Their wealth among Our Crowd came relatively late, and they never moved into "cleaner" trades like retail or finance. Their work, no matter how far removed from the daily grit, still consisted of sifting dirt. Their chief source of wealth resided in the American Smelting and Refining Company, known by the graceless acronym ASARCO. Decades before the family name became associated with arts and philanthropy, it was considered slightly disreputable. When Guggenheims married other members of the crowd, a certain contingent at Temple Emanu-El held its nose. Family lore had it that when Daniel's brother Benjamin became betrothed to one of the banker Seligmans in 1894, the latter family cabled relatives in Europe, FLORETTE ENGAGED GUGGENHEIM SMELTER, which the cable office clerk allegedly mangled into FLORETTE ENGAGED GUGGENHEIM SMELT HER. The story became a dinner-party staple.

And yet, as Roger Jr. would later tell friends and family, it was the Guggenheims who set conditions on Gladys's marriage to Roger Straus—conditions that led him down a more conventional path. "Like a lot of wealthy Jews," says Roger Straus III, "the Guggenheims preferred that their children marry something like an impoverished British lord." Gladys's father, Daniel, said he would consent to the marriage only if Roger went into his new family's business.

The reasons for this condition were eminently practical. Much has been made of the propitious fact that the Guggenheim patriarch, Meyer, had seven sons, but in the next generation there was a notable lack of willing and able male heirs. According to his son, Roger Sr. had wanted to continue his studies at Princeton and perhaps become a history professor. But he was madly smitten with Gladys. After their honeymoon, he went to work in ASARCO's personnel division, tasked with channeling his reformist ardor into the narrow course of company health and safety—thereby, not incidentally, helping to sanitize the corporation's public image.

While Gladys joined all the right committees and pursued the life of a socialite philanthropist, Roger Sr. made a go, like his father, at a dual career in business and politics. After failing in a bid for assistant secretary of state in 1931, he developed very close ties to the liberal Republican Thomas E. Dewey. On the decisive night of each of Dewey's campaigns—for district attorney and then governor (both successful) and then twice for president (both not)—the Deweys would dine at the Strauses' Upper East Side town house, allaying their anxiety with roast duck and blueberry pie. As Dewey's New York campaign manager, Straus was a devoted power broker but never a kingmaker, and he always just missed the opportunity to take in the spoils of his loyalty.

In 1949, Dewey considered him as a midterm replacement for a U.S. Senate seat, but decided against the appointment. Had Dewey indeed defeated Truman, Straus might well have followed his father into the president's cabinet. Instead, Roger Sr. settled for the role of dutiful son-in-law, rising through ASARCO's ranks. Without a doubt, he left his mark on the world, but it wasn't entirely his own: He merely ambled further along the paths blazed by the Strauses and Guggen-heims a generation before him.

In a photograph taken around 1926, Roger Straus, Jr., and his brother, Oscar, sons of Roger and Gladys, flank their toddler sister, Florence. The boys wear identical outfits—shirts with broad sailor collars and high black socks—and have nearly identical broad noses, slightly hooded eyes, and dark hair they inherited from their parents. Oscar, around eleven, jovially wraps his arm around Florence. Roger, two years younger, sits back with an intense look, an eyebrow cocked, charming but aloof. Around them is a pastoral scene that could be set at either of the compounds where the family spent most of its time.

Gladys had always preferred the countryside to the glamorous but transient atmosphere of the family pied-à-terre at the St. Regis. Her second son was born at New York Hospital in Manhattan on January 3, 1917, but almost from the beginning, Roger Jr. (Bill, to his family) spent much of his time with his grandparents. When Roger Sr. shipped off, in 1918, to meddle in the Russian Revolution with the Si-berian Expeditionary Force, Gladys followed her husband as far as San Francisco, leaving her two boys with her parents. So "Bill" and Oscar spent their first vacation together at Sands Point on the north shore of Long Island, where their grandfather, Daniel Guggenheim, had recently bought 250 acres, including two neo-medieval estates, from railroad tycoon Howard Gould. With the entire Guggenheim clan gradually trading in its New Jersey starter dachas for larger estates, Daniel decided to make his home on the Long Island peninsula that would shortly be immortalized in *The Great Gatsby* as East Egg—the old-money enclave with the green light on the dock.

Hempstead House, as Daniel renamed the manor overlooking Long Island Sound, is composed largely of granite blocks and Gothic windows, giving the windswept grounds the aspect of an Oxford quad in midwinter break. The structure was as forbidding inside as out: cold limestone fireplaces, dark wood walls, Jacobean furniture throughout its forty rooms, and an entrance hall dominated by a stone fountain. The feudal atmosphere was total: Daniel "took a poor view of any of us wanting anything that was not there on the property," his grandson Roger Jr. later remembered. A small army of staff raised and butchered Daniel's cattle, pigs, and chickens, grew fruits and vegetables, and maintained the stables and golf course and indoor tennis court and beach house, where the Guggenheim grandchildren sought to master the new family pastimes. Roger Jr. remembered a bowling alley, a ski chute, "all kinds of things for all ages and sizes—it was really quite miraculous and quite marvelous."

Roger never saw his grandfather casually dressed, even in the summer heat. His grandmother, née Florence Schloss, was heavily involved with Jewish charities easing the immigration of eastern Europeans into New York's new shtetls. But up in East Egg she was "the grand dame," according to her namesake granddaughter, Florence Straus Hart, pursuing a paradoxical dream Europe's new refugees could not even imagine: assimilation into a world built on exclusion.

As "marvelous" as all this was, Roger Jr.'s fondest memories were not formed on Long Island, which was a little too "flamboyant" for his father's modest taste. The family's true respite was an estate of a mere thirty acres that grandfather Oscar S. Straus bought in Purchase, New York, in 1914, the year Roger Jr.'s parents married. The compound's fanciful name, Sarosca Farm, combined the names of Oscar and his wife, Sarah. The main house, a long, low-slung manor in a half-timbered Tudor style, was built in 1904 after a design by Tuxedo Park mastermind Bruce Price. The architect's style marked a halfway point between the revivalist crazes of the nineteenth century and the formalist rigor of Frank Lloyd Wright. It was, in a word, tasteful—more English retreat than Loire Valley fortress. Inside were the spoils of Oscar's Oriental sojourns: a Turkish coffee table, a variety of urns, and a sedan chair with a telephone inside. Wicker furniture and Tiffany lamps clashed nonchalantly. A rug embroidered with the figures of menorahs was a nod to the family religion. Similar in style was the house Oscar had built for the newlyweds Roger and Gladys, just across the lane, complete with a stone water tower whose rough-hewn base and Bavarian turret bordered on playful kitsch. Down the hill from the manor lived Oscar's daughter and son-in-law, Aline and Leonard Hockstader.

Oscar died in 1926, when Roger Jr. was just nine. The grandson vividly remembered his visits up the gravelly circular driveway to the big house where, one day, he himself would play lord to a coterie that included Susan Sontag, Edmund Wilson, and Isaac Bashevis Singer.

In public, Oscar Straus was austere and disciplined. A portrait behind a vellum page in his stilted autobiography, *Under Four Administrations*, features a gaunt-faced man with a broad pate, intense protruding eyes, and a slightly pointed white beard: a parody of the Teutonic bureaucrat. Oscar supported Prohibition, and maintained that the greatest legacy of his father, Lazarus, lay in his refusal to default on a single penny after his business was ravaged by the Civil War. "I propose to pay my debts in full," Lazarus had said, "and leave to my children a good name even if I should leave them nothing else." Oscar must also have believed public revelation to be a sin, as his memoir neglects to mention the heroic death of his brother, department-store mogul Isidor Straus, on the *Titanic*. (Benjamin Guggenheim, another of Roger Jr.'s great-uncles, also perished there. Years later Roger would quip hyperbolically: "All my grandparents died on the Titanic!")

His grandchildren knew a different Oscar—playful, kind, patient, and doting. Roger Jr. remembered Oscar, his favorite grandparent by far, releasing his pet canaries to flit around the breakfast table. They would alight on his shoulders as he ate, and he would feed them bits of his toast—a "Jewish St. Francis." He would take Roger Jr. out on walks through the grounds, beyond the orchard and vegetable gardens, across a stone bridge over a willow-shaded brook, and on through marshland, lecturing on the natural wonders around them. He showed Roger how to grow fig trees in Westchester County; the trick was to bury them in the winter. In his grandfather, Roger Jr. observed a model of the New World baron: a self-made man out in the world, and at home not a feudal lord, like Benjamin Guggenheim, but a gentleman content with his secluded few acres.

Even in rapidly declining health, Oscar "was still working, still writing, still trying to enjoy life," Roger recalled. After he died, his study was preserved as what the family called "the ghost room," decorated with prints of the Founding Fathers alongside a photo of the patriarch, resplendent but relaxed in a straw hat and white shoes, beard full and eyes piercing, his larger wife posed on a lower step beside him. His widow, Sarah Straus, became formidable in her old age, leading two expeditions through Africa and collecting hundreds of bird varieties. She reminded Dorothea of "an ancient turtle," forever accompanied by an ornery cocker spaniel named Nero.

It was all "very cozy," Roger's sister, Florence Hart, remembers. Set amid the country clubs of Westchester County, many of which still excluded Jews, Sarosca Farm was no less contrived an assimilationist fantasy than the Guggenheim estate. But it was a fantasy of small-farm gentility rather than imperial conquest, with a dash of old-money thrift and spontaneity. To Roger Jr., it was inseparable from the family name.

Roger Sr. proved a capable and successful business executive, and he expected his children to follow the path prescribed for them by lineage and breeding. His elder son, Oscar, went smoothly down that road: Collegiate, then the Bovee School; St. Paul's, the elite prep school in Concord, New Hampshire; and on to Princeton, diplomatic service, and, finally, ASARCO. It was all very respectable and predictable.

"He was a good scholar and I was not," Roger Jr. told Louis Sheaffer, who recorded his oral history for Columbia University. "I was a good athlete and he was not. So these were the early variables between the two of us. He achieved and accomplished all of the things that my parents felt a well brought-up young boy should do, and I did just the opposite, I am afraid." The brothers would dislike each other for most of their lives—the residue of a sibling rivalry that, Straus said, "whetted my combative nature."

To Roger's sister, Florence, he was simply what was then known as a "Peck's Bad Boy," after a series of children's stories that gave us the archetype for scamps like Dennis the Menace. Up at Sarosca Farm, he might swipe an onion from the vegetable garden and convince his baby sister to take a hearty bite, which left her in tears while he laughed hysterically. He would place a wager on the flip of a coin: "Heads I win, tails you lose." "I never caught on because I adored him," Florence says, "and he was never wrong." Some summers Grandma Sarah would let Florence raise spending money by selling her back her own garden vegetables. "By the end of the summer I made quite a bit of money. Roger came and said, 'Sis, I got a hot date, would you help me out? I need a corsage.' Before I knew it, my money was gone. But I kept loaning him the money, which he never paid back." Great-grandfather Lazarus Straus would not have approved.

It was Roger's academic stumbles that raised the alarm for his parents. Some of them he later blamed, like so much else, on luck. Roger followed his brother into the Bovee School, right by Central Park, but a year before Roger was to finish, Bovee was sold and replaced with a thirty-six-story co-op (the first of the tall parkside buildings that would gradually replace the palazzos of the Gilded Age). After a year at another school, he was rejected by St. Paul's. His father suggested St. George's, in Newport, Rhode Island, which placed more weight on legacy than on grades. That's probably why, according to Straus, he was the first Jew ever to set foot on campus.

Roger Sr. felt he was living up to his namesake, Roger Williams, by cochairing the National Conference of Christians and Jews. He wanted to complete the process of assimilation—already under way economically and socially—on a political level. Never mind that Hitler was on his way to Berlin: The horrors of World War II would only deepen Roger Sr.'s faith in pan-religious solidarity as a salve to the "false gods" of science and materialism—idols that, in his view, led to fascism and communism alike.

And so he set out to make an example of his wayward son by shipping him off to a staunchly Presbyterian school—"every day to chapel and so forth and so on," as Roger Jr. put it. Whatever resentment and mutual distrust had already been hardening between father and son, St. George's set it in concrete. Roger Jr. never detailed the nature of the teasing that went on, not even to his own son, Roger III. Perhaps the humiliation was too deep. But he did say that having to take Jewish holidays off only made things worse.

The adolescent Straus read popular books of the time—he particularly adored Steinbeck—but not much of his course work. He was a very good athlete, "a minor jock," he claimed, modestly. Some believe he could have had a professional tennis career, had it been acceptable for someone of his class. His style of play certainly wasn't genteel. "Roger was a gifted but ugly tennis player," says Andrée Conrad, a former FSG editor and friend of the Strauses. "He was the king of the slices and drop shots, very aggressive and determined to get it over fast: He defended his territory, intimidated the competition, and won." The screenwriter Roger Hirson, who was his once-a-week tennis partner for fifty years, remembers playing with a pulled groin muscle and begging Straus to turn down the heat, only to be told he shouldn't be on the court if he didn't want to play. Though their friendship consisted almost entirely of tennis dates, Hirson was named a coexecutor in Straus's will. "He didn't have a lot of personal friends," Hirson says.

Roger's athleticism dampened the teasing, and he found girls easily. But his grades were bad, and at the end of his junior year, he "resigned." "Whether I would actually have been fired from St. George's is a moot question, but I suspect so, if I had given them the opportunity."

Roger told Peggy Miller there was exactly one class that had taught him anything at St. George's: extemporaneous speaking. "The teacher said, 'Get up and talk for five minutes about crystal chandeliers—or ashtrays,'" Peggy remembers. "And he said it was the only course he ever got something out of because from that moment on, you could wind him up and he would make a speech. It was extraordinary. I saw him do it many times."

Straus never earned a high school degree. After leaving St. George's, he spent a year in limbo, being tutored in New Jersey at the Warner School, "which existed for strange, indifferent children, I guess," and trying to convince his parents he should skip college and travel through Europe. In later years, the intellectuals he dined with and dealt with and slept with in Rome and Paris and Munich and Stockholm discovered to their surprise that Europe's favorite American publisher could only manage *parlez-vous* French. But glamorous Europe would have to wait, because Roger "got cold feet on that subject" and dropped his plan.

Nor did Mr. and Mrs. Straus think much of his next idea. Rollins College, in Winter Park, Florida, had no formal lectures or final exams, and professors were vetted by the student body. Depending on whom you asked, it was either a worthy experiment or an eccentric country-club resort—and a last resort—for wealthy jocks with shoddy records. A *Time* magazine writer later said its curriculum ran "heavily to tennis and horseback riding." Shortly after meeting a Rollins scout, Roger took the entrance exam at the august Century Club, answered questions that "had nothing to do with anything," and was admitted on the spot. His father wasn't too concerned until he read the course catalog, whereupon a screaming match ensued. Roger wasn't going to Rollins College to ride horses among the palms.

Roger Sr. had had enough. He called in a favor to Henry Allen Moe, the head of the John Simon Guggenheim Foundation, and Roger was admitted to Hamilton College in Clinton, New York— another way station for mediocre students of means. Roger Jr. lasted barely two years. But it was during the summers that he found his first fulfilling work, as a copy boy for the White Plains *Reporter*. At the now long-defunct paper near Sarosca Farm, the cocky teen not only earned his first salary, thirty-five dollars a week, but also got to write the occasional obituary or wedding notice—"and this turned me on."

Norton Mockridge, the boy's minder at the *Reporter*, wasn't expecting much. All he saw was "a tall, good-looking kid with dark curly hair" who knew how to make a terrible first impression. "He parked his big car in front of the office," Mockridge remembered, "bounded up the stairs with the energy of an antelope, grabbed my hand and said: 'What can I do for you, chum?'" Mockridge resisted the urge to respond to this "playboy youngster": "There's NOTHING you can do for me—except get the hell out of this office and don't bother me." By the end of the first summer, though, he concluded that the "mildly irritating know-it-all attitude" was all surface bravado. "Down under he thirsted for information, for technique, for a special kind of savvy. He had guts."

For better and worse, Straus was easily distracted without constant stimulation. He needed an occupation that "turned him on," in his words, not simply make-work at the family mining concern. How could the slow rigors of school compare with the bustle, the dead-lines, the *chase* of the news? Ironically, this was the revelation that led to his only academic degree, at the University of Missouri's journalism program. It was there, in the hinterlands ("untouched by the hand of Man," he liked to say), that the education of Roger Straus, Jr., finally took hold. He worked on the school's daily paper, a force in the local market, and helped revive a literary magazine called *The Asterisk*. Cru-cially, he was not only the editor but also the publisher, soliciting sub-scriptions and ads from Kansas City to St. Louis. One of the writers he published, who wrote book reviews for *The Asterisk*, was his wife, Dorothea Liebmann.

Roger and Dorothea met so early in their lives that neither remem-bered their first encounter; it was, again, an Our Crowd story. They had attended the same tony dancing schools in New York, but really started getting to know each other around the time Roger was toying with his first love, journalism, at the *Reporter*. She had briefly gone out with the favorite son, Oscar, and later said he was the only per-son she'd ever dated with whom she would be afraid to get into a cab alone.

The Liebmanns, heirs to the Rheingold brewing fortune, were wealthier than the Strauses but even newer to Manhattan society. Dor-othea's father, Alfred, had grown up in Bushwick, Brooklyn, learning German in a school built right into the brewing compound. But after they moved to Park Avenue he assimilated all too well. Before marry-ing late in life he'd been "a youthful dandy," in her telling, a "bachelor of the Gilded Age" who charmed numerous Ziegfeld girls with a "genuine appreciation of their sex."

Dorothea's parents stormed their way into the haute bourgeoisie, studying music with émigré princesses and rolling through Europe in luxury train cars. In childhood Dorothea adored *Alice in Wonderland;* as an adult she reread *Remembrance of Things Past* almost every year. And in romance, she found a kindred spirit to her father in Roger Straus, a connoisseur of tennis, women, and the finer points of cultivating people.

Roger and Dorothea spent the summer together in 1935, when he was at Purchase and she at the Liebmanns' summer estate nearby. The following summer he and his brother, Oscar, took a European cruise, visited Stalin's Soviet Union, and quarreled bitterly in Paris. "We couldn't stand the sight of each other any more," he said, and so they split up. Oscar, entrusted with the money wired from home, was no longer passing any along to his brother. But Roger's luck turned: Dorothea was in Paris. Their courtship blossomed along the boulevards, and in the end she lent him money to take a boat home. His lucky streak continued stateside, where he "made a big strike playing poker." He meant to repay her out of the money, but when the time came to mail his winnings, he'd already lost them again. Roger filed it away as a lively joke. "I always maintained that I married her for her money so I wouldn't have to pay off that debt."

Roger, who measured out his life in dinner parties, had a preternatural talent for talking to women he hardly knew. He would simply turn to his female neighbor and declaim, "Tell me the story of your life!" Roger Hirson remembers him as "a notorious man-about-town," and recalls the legend of Straus's twenty-first birthday party: dinner and dancing at the Plaza with six or seven guests, all of them women. Each had a turn with Roger on the dance floor. Dorothea was one of them. Three months later, to the considerable surprise of friends and family, Roger announced that he and Dorothea were engaged. Bill and Dolly, as Our Crowd knew them, set a date for June.

Dorothea was deeply attracted to Roger's bold gestures and broad-striped suits. For the daughter of urban sophisticates, the brusque athleticism that underlay his refinement stirred romantic notions of escape. She wrote of it in several memoirs in almost cloyingly lush prose, her tone somewhere between her beloved Proust and the first few pages of a Harlequin romance (the parts before the bodice is ripped). In one of them, *Thresholds*, Dorothea recounts her visit to Sarosca Farm on the day of their engagement. She and Roger "wandered hand in hand over the grounds and stretched out on the tender April grass near the tennis court between the two houses. It seemed as though our twined fingers had become the very core of our bodies, and I examined his hands, aristocratic and delicate for such a tall athletic boy, and his small-boned wrists sprinkled with dark hair, as though they held all the secrets of his being."

Could Dorothea have known then just how many secrets Roger would keep from her, how many trips abroad and trysts at lunchtime, affairs she'd alternately ignore and bemoan? Their son, Roger III, to whom she confided her suspicions, surmises that she must have accepted it tacitly. "She liked the idea of being married to an alpha male," he says, "and this was the not-so-great side of the package."

They were married on June 27, 1938, on the terraced lawn at the Liebmanns' house in Armonk, New York. Dorothea, who had just graduated from Sarah Lawrence College, was crowned with orange blossoms and dressed in ivory satin. It rained relentlessly, but bride, groom, and guests were protected by a vast canopy. Reformed ladies' man Alfred Liebmann gave her away, and she had no female attendants aside from her maid of honor, Roger's sister—no rivals for his attention. After the honeymoon, Dorothea followed Roger to Missouri, where he still had a year to go before graduating.

Now that Roger was finally settling on a profession, his father called Arthur Sulzberger, the owner of the *New York Times*. In short order, Roger Jr. had an offer to start with the Sulzberger-owned *Chattanooga Times*. Yet again, he confounded his father by turning it down. "I didn't see any future in working there," he explained: "(a) I didn't want to live in Chattanooga very much, and (b) I didn't see any good reason to work for a family group called Sulzberger."

Roger's father may have misunderstood him, and not for the first or last time. He thought his son wasn't ambitious enough. But Roger rejected the offer because he didn't want to work for a Sulzberger—nor, for that matter, did he want to work for a Guggenheim or a Straus, because what they did wasn't interesting to him. He was bred to be on top, and he wanted to get there in the business of his choosing. In the interim, he and Dorothea had two trust funds to tide them over.

Although Straus would always be a generous Missouri alumnus, the Midwest was not his cup of tea. Itchy to get back to New York, he fled before the graduation ceremony. He became a full-time journalist at the White Plains *Reporter*, handling labor and police stories, only to get impatient again. A little more than six months into his beat, he realized it was "sort of a dead end," and left to become an editorial assistant at *Current History* magazine in New York.

The magazine had Sulzberger connections, too. It had been born as a *New York Times* side project—an effort to cover exhaustively the outbreak of World War I, running more ambassadorial letters and AP witness reports than were fit to print. It had been run by Iphigene Sulzberger's uncle George Oakes, but was sold soon after he died in 1931. When Straus joined it in 1940, as the assistant to managing editor Norman Cousins, it was owned by E. Trevor Hill, "a very strange, reasonably disturbed, and interesting man," as Roger put it, a quiet type from a wealthy New York family, with "a withered arm like the Kaiser." Six years later, Hill would be working for Straus.

Roger was quickly promoted to associate editor; restless as ever, he turned his mind toward the business of the magazine. He went to Hill with the idea of forming a book-magazine partnership, of the kind that had endured for years at Harper's and Scribner's. Book publishing started out, for Roger, as a half-baked side project.

Given the go-ahead, Straus approached "an old pirate," Melville Minton, who owned G. P. Putnam's Sons. No doubt the family connections helped; in 1927, it was Putnam that published Charles Lindbergh's bestselling autobiography, *We,* which the aviator had written in a six-week frenzy at Falaise, the home of his close friend—and Roger's uncle—Harry Frank Guggenheim. It was just down the road from Hempstead House at Sands Point. Roger had met Lindbergh there as a boy, and his first time in an airplane, in 1928, had been as Lindbergh's passenger on a short flight over Long Island.

Lindbergh was by then a famous isolationist, whereas Straus and Putnam produced a book—the most successful of the three they made together—directly attacking that position. *War Letters from Britain,* a collection of dispatches written by Brits across all levels of society, offered some of the most detailed print accounts of the Blitz. Straus's real coup was to persuade Vincent Sheean, a veteran reporter and a friend of Roger Sr.'s, to write the preface. "It is difficult to believe that any other people in Europe could endure what [the British] are enduring," Sheean wrote. "They are fighting for survival, of course, as Mr. Churchill said; they are also fighting for the perpetuation of institutions which otherwise may perish from the earth."

Straus described "Jimmy" Sheean as "my boyhood hero"—a frequent visitor to the Straus home whose political memoir *Personal History* was "the greatest book I ever read." Sheean had fled Greenwich Village for Europe, gotten soused with Hemingway, and reported on the rise of Mussolini, uprisings in China and Palestine, Stalin's ascendancy, and Hitler's first acts of aggression. It was a leg up on the Westchester police beat. Nabbing Sheean for the book in 1940 was also a commercial coup; that year, Alfred Hitchcock released *Foreign Correspondent,* his film based on *Personal History.* *War Letters,* on which Straus was credited as coeditor, was "basically propagandistic," Roger conceded. Royalties went to the British-American Ambulance Corps.

Just before Pearl Harbor, *Current History* ran aground. Trevor Hill bailed out, and Straus was out of a job. So Roger set out for himself, launching a book packaging firm called Book Ideas from *Current History*'s old office space. (Book packaging was, and is, akin to outsourcing the production of a complicated book—usually the product of multiple authors or something in a specialized field.) He soon sold Nelson Algren's short stories to Harper's. That collection, *The Neon Wilderness,* was followed by *The Man with the Golden Arm,* the addiction novel that won Algren a National Book Award. Other titles were less stimulating: a guide to FDR's proliferating federal agencies, for example, and a pithy rundown of the world's proliferating ideologies (*Know Your Isms*).

Straus certainly believed in interventionism, but he didn't expect the war to come knocking on his door the morning after Pearl Harbor. That was when the government came after Joseph Hilton Smyth, part owner of the family of magazines—including *The Living Age, The North American Review, The Saturday Review,* and the defunct *Current History*—that also housed Book Ideas. Smyth happened to be an undeclared agent of the Japanese government, a conflict of interest that would earn him seven years in prison. A little shocked that he'd been paid by the Japanese, Roger was ready to enlist—so long as he could be an officer.

Only recently, Roger had had a series of medical problems culminating in osteomyelitis, a spinal infection that left him without a coccyx and disqualified him from service. Ironically, he might never have served his country if not for a wealthy connection once affiliated with the enemy-funded *North American Review.* James Van Alen, Jr., a rich dilettante from Newport, Rhode Island, had bought the *Review* in a previous incarnation as a project to keep his wife busy.

The Strauses and the Van Alens became fast friends. They shared an obsession with tennis that Jimmy would later take to extremes, lobbying the USTA to adopt a new way of tallying points. The Van Alen Streamlined Scoring System (VASSS) never took off. Among the many Jimmy stories that made him both a legend and a laughingstock: He had the angel hood ornament on his Rolls-Royce replaced with his initials: VA.

After Pearl Harbor, Van Alen played his connections to create a plum position for himself in the war effort. He went to the Naval War College, came out a lieutenant, and persuaded the navy to let him run a PR office in New York. Then he leaned on the Empire Trust Company, a bank in which his family had a lot of money, to lease the navy some office space in its flagship location, the thirty-story Empire Trust Building, at 580 Fifth Avenue. Thus was born, in 1942, the Branch Magazine and Book Section of the navy's Office of Public Information. For the day-to-day business, Van Alen turned to the civilian Roger Straus, by now an experienced packager of war books. One of their first assignments was to update a hoary field manual known as *Naval Customs, Traditions and Usage.* Straus sold the book to McGraw-Hill and edited it himself. "Every Naval officer," he said, "had to read this goddamn book. It told you how to salute when you came up in the Corps, and you know, what the fuck does any of us know? We didn't know from nothing."

In order to advance, Roger still needed a uniform. Courtesy of the navy's V-11 program, he spent six gloomy winter weeks at Cornell University, amid physically unfit specialists—some in sensitive technology—who the government decided had to pass muster one way or another. He remembered a decoder with severe hypertension having his blood pressure taken at its daily ebb, while he was asleep. They drilled in the snow in marine castoffs, learned maps, and were cleared for Naval Intelligence. Straus came out of it an ensign and spent several weeks in Washington, taking on sensitive assignments such as snooping on his superiors. There he made his first contacts with the movers in the country's intelligence infrastructure. They would come in handy later on.

Before long, Van Alen moved on to serve in England and was succeeded by Alan Jackson, onetime editor of *The Saturday Review.* Straus was in charge of placing articles in magazines and, if need be, censoring them. "We were involved in propaganda," he said, "although we didn't call it that." He did see active duty—in the sense of witnessing it from a safe distance. He was in Saipan just before the offensive at Iwo Jima, doing advance work for foreign correspondents. "We would all be together in the evening, you know, sitting around in the Officers Club and so forth, and then the boys would go out in the morning and then came a countdown, and of the 16 planes that went out in the morning maybe 11 would get home that night."

Straus's wife, Dorothea, later framed him in heroic terms. "He appeared more handsome in his blue and gold ensign's uniform, more desirable, never to be taken for granted," she wrote. In 1943 they had a son, Roger III, who would be their only child, and Dorothea felt lonely bringing him up that first year in what they considered a starter apartment, just east of Central Park on 86th Street. "I watched the baby taking his first steps and my happiness was feigned. I wanted my husband to share the moment." It was on one such solitary morning that "I made the discovery of writing. Here was the antidote to anxiety; a world I could order."

And yet, in Straus's version, there weren't all that many weeks away. To be sure, Dorothea's talent lay in investing fleeting moments with great significance. She remembered his coming home injured after one such tour. He had gotten a nasty cut from stepping on coral. He was also badly sunburned.

He might have gotten those war wounds in Bermuda, then the center of intelligence operations. On one of several trips there, Straus took along Jim Bishop, the war correspondent for *Collier's*. He served his country by joining Bishop for late nights out on the town, then propping him up on the way back to base. (Roger, by all accounts, handled his alcohol exceedingly well.) Straus would later attribute his profane streak to his time in the navy, but perhaps he learned how to throw "fuck" into every second sentence not from the grunts he seldom encountered but from the war's hard-drinking reporters, whom he befriended out of a combination of patriotic duty, natural bonhomie, and professional self-interest.

Many other war correspondents came into Straus's orbit; some of them would write the most important books of the immediate postwar era. He helped William Brinkley put together a jaunty collection, *Don't Go Near the Water*, which opens with a comic portrait of a pencil-pushing navy PR officer who uses a shell casing to hold paper clips. (Could he have been thinking of a certain navy liaison he knew?) Straus also helped sell William L. White's *They Were Expendable* to *Reader's Digest*, which in 1942 made it the first bestseller about the war.

Another author, Basil Heatter, was an acquaintance of Jimmy Van Alen's. The son of a famous radio broadcaster, he was badly wounded on a PT boat in the Pacific, but came out of it with the makings of a romance novel. He wound up writing much of it in Straus's office, along with speeches for the navy. (*The Dim View* would be one of Farrar, Straus's first books.) He and Straus—both funny, both venturesome with the opposite sex—would become lifelong friends. At a dinner party at the Strauses', Heatter met Kathleen Winsor, author of *Forever Amber*, a campy novel about a Restoration-era woman who slept her way to the top. Heatter followed her to a bond rally and disappeared for several days, until Straus forced Winsor's agent to track him down for urgent business in Washington.

Neither a fighter nor a writer, Roger spent the war preparing—without knowing it—to be a publisher. He wanted to be near the action, but not in it. He loved spreading stories, but not writing them. He couldn't make the art, but he could make the deal. By doing so he could serve the writers he admired as much as he was serving the war machine that employed him.

By 1944, Straus was fully in charge of the Magazine and Book Section. He was sitting pretty—literally, feet up on his battered desk—when a lieutenant named Robert Giroux walked into his office. Giroux, hair prematurely white at age thirty, outranked the handsome, grinning twenty-seven-year-old flack. He'd just witnessed heavy combat on an aircraft carrier. Yet Straus was the figure of awe and mystery at the meeting—the one who, Giroux had heard, was among "the few junior officers who had a direct line to the Navy Department in Washington."

Giroux wasn't doing so badly himself; on combat leave, he had a position waiting for him as an editor at Harcourt, Brace. But he also had ambitions to write, and he had come to the Empire Trust Building with a story to sell. Giroux had been on an aircraft carrier during the Battle of Truk Lagoon, and witnessed the daring rescue of a downed pilot bobbing in the atoll's choppy waters. "We did not have a war correspondent on board," Giroux explained in the piece, "so I gathered the details while they were fresh in the minds of the men involved." Giroux told the story like a pro, specific and structured, leavened with humor. Straus read it and promised him that he could get him major money at a major publication, and he delivered to the tune of $1,000. "Rescue from Truk" ran in the May 13 issue of *Collier's* with a fat cover line. Giroux would remember the meeting most vividly, but he clearly made a strong impression on Straus as well. The next time they'd meet, Straus would be doing the courting.

Even before he was out of uniform, Roger knew he wanted to work in publishing. He had no problem getting offers from among his many contacts, but nothing appealed to him. Paul Palmer wanted to tap him for *Reader's Digest,* and the money was good, but Palmer was a right-winger, perhaps even anti-Semitic. Straus also considered a job at 20th Century Fox, but decided he was far more interested in print. He took more seriously an offer from a casual friend, the publisher

Stanley Rinehart, a partner in Farrar & Rinehart. The Strauses and the Rineharts had dined and played bridge together (though Dorothea didn't know the game, so Roger played both hands). There was a shake-up at Farrar & Rinehart around that time—which Straus knew nothing about—and suddenly they were looking for fresh editorial talent.

It was thanks to his father, indirectly, that Straus broke through the fog. One day, when he happened to be visiting his parents, an old *Times* buddy of Roger Sr.'s stopped by. Charles Merz was the editor of the paper's editorial page, and he was eager to advise the young navy man. In the course of the conversation Roger Jr. let slip a presumptuous notion: He was considering starting his own publishing house. His friend Jimmy Van Alen had already promised $150,000, most of the nut they'd need to start Van Alen & Straus (or maybe Straus & Van Alen). Merz thought it made sense, if he could get the money together. But Straus needed more than money: He needed talent.

"Do you know John Farrar?" asked Merz. Strangely enough, Straus didn't, even though Farrar was Rinehart's partner and, as far as Straus knew, the editorial head of the firm. "I think you ought to meet him," said Merz. "It's rather a nasty story."

2

Furor, Stress

People write novels for many reasons. John Chipman Farrar started one because he was bitter and had little else to do. A High Episcopalian editor with an owlish aspect, wire-rimmed glasses, a quick temper, and plenty of red left in his hair, Farrar was on an involuntary hiatus from publishing. The company that bore his name, Farrar & Rinehart, had greeted him on his return from Algeria with the news that he'd been forced out. So he spent the year 1945 in a rented "office" in Parlor O of the Murray Hill Hotel, winding down his work on the army magazines known as *Victory* and *America,* teaching a publishing course at Columbia, and writing a novel that would never be published.

Near the beginning of "Private Relations," which he was writing under the pseudonym John Donaldson (his father's middle name), Farrar writes: "I'm an editor not working at the job. That's one of the reasons I'm writing a novel . . . This is to be a novel about a bitch."

And then he gets into it: "What I'm really talking about here is what happens to a man who expects to walk back into the place where he's parked his fanny for a long while . . . And then a Vivian Blake says: 'You can't come here anymore.'" Perhaps "Vivian" is Mary Roberts Rinehart, the bestselling writer whose books had underwritten Farrar & Rinehart—and the mother of the two Rinehart brothers, Farrar's erstwhile partners and best friends. Farrar felt betrayed by Mary Rinehart, but her direct involvement in his ouster has not been documented. Most likely, Vivian is a noir-tinted composite, a misogynistic projection of the worst betrayal of his life.

By Farrar's own account, he had "no sense of humor and a vile temper." The statement somewhat contradicts itself—obviously he had a sense of irony—but descendants and former colleagues vouch for the latter. "Johnny used to have temper tantrums, which he could almost do on command," said Roger Straus. Joyce Johnson, who worked for him at Farrar, Straus & Cudahy while romancing Jack Kerouac in the late fifties, called him "a sweet, neurotic, tweedy old man . . . left over from the Twenties." Johnson's dismissive assessment wasn't too far off (Farrar declined rather rapidly), but she couldn't be aware of how bright his heyday had been.

Farrar was born in Vermont in 1896 to an old-line WASP family with little money to show for their pedigree—especially after his father died. His Yankee neighbors had deep connections within the eastern establishment, but he still needed a scholarship to attend Yale. There he met Stephen Vincent Benét, already a published poet, and the two became best friends. They were the first generation to go to college after the onset of a world war.

"We were, believe it or not, convinced that it was a war to save democracy," Farrar wrote in a published reminiscence. World War I delayed Farrar's graduation but also provided him with his first publishing experience of a sort: issuing confidential pamphlets in France for the air corps's intelligence division. After Yale, Farrar quickly established himself in New York. After covering "crime, mysticism, opera, and the effulgence of Metropolitan life" for the *New York World,* he was chosen at age twenty-four to edit *The Bookman,* a critical review owned by George H. Doran's publishing company. Insiders derisively called him "Bookboy," but Farrar rose quickly, writing regular book reviews for *Time* and cofounding the Bread Loaf Writers' Conference in 1926.

Stanley and Frederick ("Ted") Rinehart joined Doran's company around the same time Farrar did—it was their mother's publisher—and they became close colleagues. After the company merged with Doubleday, in 1927, he and the Rineharts plotted to start a new house where they could call their own shots, with Farrar as editor in chief. Two years later they left for a tiny office on East 41st Street, taking dozens of writers with them—including Mary Roberts Rinehart, Benét, and a poet named Hervey Allen who was hard at work on an epic novel.

The split from Doran was amicable enough; after all, Stan Rinehart was married to Doran's daughter. Family feeling prevailed, too, at the new firm. Farrar's wife, née Margaret Petherbridge, had already enriched one publishing house, Simon & Schuster, with her crossword-puzzle books. (She went on to found the *New York Times* crossword puzzle in 1942.) She was a Farrar & Rinehart board member, part-time employee, and close friend of the Rineharts.

Hervey Allen became an editor after the company published his novel *Anthony Adverse.* The 1,224-page historical swashbuckler sold well over a million copies in 1933, allowing a company founded in 1929 to weather the Depression. Stephen Vincent Benét, the company's principal reader, had pushed Farrar and then Stanley Rinehart to publish the doorstop. In 1937, Farrar wrote, "The publisher's greatest luck is what partners pick him and in that respect I have been extremely lucky."

But Farrar was discovering a new passion. Having already risked his life for democracy, he was very concerned with what was going on in Europe, incensed by the arguments of American isolationists. He joined the Council for Democracy along with his best friend, Benét, bringing them even closer. (Farrar had published all of the poet's work, including the Pulitzer Prize–winning epic poem *John Brown's Body*.) Then, in 1943, Benét died suddenly of a heart attack, at age forty-four—a devastating blow to Farrar that seemed to sink him only deeper into the war effort. Still grieving, he took a post as chief of the Office of War Information's Overseas News and Features Bureau.

Farrar soon took a leave of absence to serve overseas. He spent several months in the Mediterranean, where, as the Allies advanced on Italy and North Africa, he took charge of Psychological Warfare. Based in Algeria, Farrar produced a radio broadcast that helped secure the surrender of the Italian navy. He described his job as "a battle of words . . . shooting them as though they were bullets"— sometimes literally, as Farrar saw his leaflets packed into artillery shells. Against them were "enemies with years of experience in how to use words to trick and to deceive, to muddle our thinking, to confuse our action." Farrar recalled all of this in a speech before an upstate New York private school. He implored his audience to remember that "many a man has been sent to his death by a badly constructed sentence."

Farrar's own demise at Farrar & Rinehart was engineered swiftly and silently (save for a few bad sentences) while he was enduring four operations on his ankle in Algiers, writing deliriously romantic letters to Margaret. His wife, meanwhile, was made an unwitting accomplice in the Rinehart coup. She protested in March when Stan Rinehart hired an interim editor in chief, Philip Wylie; she complained even more vehemently when her husband's vote was removed from the board in absentia. Stan dismissed her complaints: "This is no squeeze play."

That was exactly what it was. Farrar finally returned to New York, on short notice, on July 16, 1944. That Sunday, he reunited with his family and then took a moment to call his partner Stan Rinehart. Surprisingly curt on the phone, Stan told John to pay him a visit the following day—not at the office but at Stan's apartment. It was there that he told Farrar he had already been ousted. It turned out that he had never been a full financial partner. "My father was many things," says Farrar's son, Curtis, "but he was not a businessman."

In a letter she wrote to Hervey Allen but never sent, Margaret

Farrar expressed the personal nature of the hurt: "How can it happen that John, who is a great and gallant man, can come back from the war to find that his three oldest and closest friends . . . have prepared for him a reception as ethical—yes, as brimming with integrity—as a miniature Pearl Harbor?" It may or may not have been true that editors at Farrar & Rinehart were badmouthing him all over town. But the "nasty story" had obviously gotten around to Charles Merz at the *Times,* who then told it to young Roger Straus.

Farrar told colleagues he was only taking a break from publishing. During his year in Parlor O, he'd been counting up the pros and cons of fighting to get his name back from Farrar & Rinehart, knowing he might need it for a new venture. He was understandably leery when a man in his twenties, still in his navy uniform, came calling on his office at the Murray Hill. At first the cocky young lieutenant just talked publishing in general. Then he got to the point. He and his dilettante friend Jimmy Van Alen were going to start their own publishing house. Farrar could be editor in chief, or possibly chairman of the board. He wouldn't have to contribute much to the enterprise aside from his hard work, authors, and expertise. Farrar was gracious and helpful, but "he said no," Straus remembered. "He really didn't have the stomach for it, and he didn't want to start all over again, he felt too badly battered and shaken and so forth and so on."

But Roger's offer wasn't so easy to shake. After all, what other options did Farrar have? The following morning, "practically before I got out of my apartment," said Roger, a call came in to the navy office for Mr. Straus. It was Mr. Farrar. "I'd like to talk to you again. I think I am changing my mind. I might like a crack at this. What do you really have in mind?"

"The first list of a new publishing house is always an adventure." So begins a short note at the front of the Fall 1946 catalog of Farrar, Straus and Company, Inc., nineteen titles long. The "adventure" is meant to be the reader's, but for the people who crafted the first list, it was something more visceral: the adrenaline rush of bagging a new writer; the sprint to the bank for another loan; the sharp jolt of a kneecap cracked on a desk three inches away from your own; the hunger pangs of living on twenty dollars a week, or the heartburn of a potentially company-ending lawsuit. "Roger's Raiders," as publishers derisively called the new firm, felt all of it. The underlings adopted a nickname of their own: "Furor, Stress."

Across the city and the country the engines of war were being repurposed for peace and profit. At the former navy press office in the Empire Trust Building, it was just a matter of changing a couple of signs. Roger W. Straus, Jr., and John C. Farrar had drawn up the incorporation papers for Farrar, Straus and Company on November 21, 1945, back in Parlor O of the Murray Hill. Only after Straus shed his uniform could the team move into the decommissioned Empire Trust headquarters, in a prime location above Brentano's bookstore.

You'd never guess that the grand Art Deco classic, designed by the architects of Grand Central Station, could house an office suite as cramped and beaten-up as the two-and-a-half-room headquarters of FS & Co. In the bare entryway sat a switchboard operator named Patsy MacLaughlin, who was also in charge of subsidiary rights and office cleaning. Just beyond that was a small room filled with navy surplus shelves and two ancient desks. Behind one of them was a tall, restless twenty-eight-year-old man with slicked, wavy hair, a lopsided grin, and a little stock in his build, who just days earlier had traded his uniform in for a bright bespoke number from Knize, a Viennese outfitter that catered to barons. Beside him was another desk manned by a bespectacled middle-aged editor with a distracted air, rolled-up sleeves, and a half-chewed cigar in his mouth.

In the next room, if you could make it there—the joke was that only one person could pace the floor at a time—sat the de facto junior editor, Arthur Orrmont, a recent G.I. Bill graduate of Cornell who lived in the West Side Y on thiry-five dollars a week. Adding insult to penury, Orrmont was forced to share his office with an absurdly rich dilettante, favoring Peal & Co. shoes and chalk-striped Savile Row suits, who used his own private phone line to call Douglas Fairbanks, Jr., for unfathomable reasons. Mercifully, Jimmy Van Alen was around only an hour or two a day.

Finances were handled in another space not directly connected to the office—a "back-office" operation from the very beginning. An unwieldy adding machine known as a comptometer dominated this cubbyhole, its wide carriage blocking access to the room as it swung out, so passage through the space would have to be perfectly timed. This was the domain of E. Trevor Hill, who had invested in his former employee's risky endeavor in return for the title of treasurer. He and "Mr. Farrar" were the publishing veterans in the office, but the one in charge was the twenty-eight-year-old in the ascot, and he just went by "Roger"—or, as another nickname had it, "Rajah."

Despite the mock title, it was less a kingdom than a constitutional monarchy. Straus had been forced to rely on a few too many shareholders for his taste. Not long before John Farrar came aboard, Van Alen had sheepishly brought to lunch the news that his mother, Daisy, the source of his guaranteed $150,000 investment, "took a poor view of this thing, of his having a partnership with somebody called Straus." Embarrassed by his mother's anti-Semitism, Van Alen committed $50,000 but said his name couldn't be involved. They had both believed about $200,000 (Van Alen's investment plus $50,000 from Straus) would be enough to set them up as proprietors; instead they would have to beat the bushes for cash and become a corporation with a board.

Van Alen secured the help of Julius "Junkie" Fleischmann, heir to the Fleischmann gin and yeast fortune and cousin of Raoul Fleischmann, who had cofounded *The New Yorker*. Another investor was Barry Bingham, publisher of the Louisville *Courier-Journal* and a wartime friend of Straus and Van Alen. Farrar, too, found shareholders: Charles P. Taft, of the political family, and the lawyer and Broadway producer Messmore Kendall, a former Farrar & Rinehart investor indignant at Farrar's dismissal. Taft and Kendall, not coincidentally, would also publish books with the company. Straus cousins and Our Crowd associates rounded out the board.

Roger managed to squeeze out of his wary parents an investment of $60,000, an advance on his inheritance. Was this relatively modest sum a character-building exercise or simply a hedged vote of confidence? Either way, Roger didn't buy the nobility of bootstrapping:

"I would not have tried to prove it so hard on my own if anybody had decided to lay some more money on me." All told, $360,000 went into the new firm—a tight sum for a fledgling publisher even then, but more than they'd originally banked on.

As soon as the papers were signed, the Rineharts threatened to sue in order to deny Farrar the use of his own name. It was left to Patrick Sullivan, a Yale friend of Farrar's at Whitman, Ransom & Coulson, to browbeat Farrar & Rinehart into withdrawing their request for an injunction. He succeeded, and by January 1, 1946, Farrar's name was his own again.

"A new imprint on a book gathers character through the years," read the first sentence of that first Farrar, Straus catalog, calibrating expectations to take in the long view. "Our list will be a general one . . . We shall shun neither the realistic nor the romantic." Accordingly, the first list included a posthumous poetry collection by Stephen Vincent Benét, an anthology of war stories from *Yank* magazine, a work on psychoanalysis, a survey of the United Nations, a historical novel, and *Francis,* David Stern's charming debut about a surprisingly articulate army mule. (Guess which one sold the best.)

Straus would dine out for the rest of his life on his favorite review of what he claimed was the house's first published book, the August release *There Were Two Pirates,* by historical novelist James Branch Cabell. "'There were three pirates,'" as Roger would say, quoting the review from the Chicago *Sun-Times.* "'James Branch Cabell, who wrote this book, and Farrar and Straus, who published it.'" In fact, Straus confessed in his oral history that Cabell was the second Farrar, Straus author. The first product was an interior-decorating how-to called *Inside Your Home,* a vanity project brought to Farrar by the daughter of a good friend and probably financed by the author. Straus tended to elide that fact, he said, "for snobbish reasons."

He needn't have hedged; there were baubles to be proud of on the list. Besides the Benét collection, there was *Powerful Long Ladder,* collected poems by the African-American poet Owen Dodson, an important member of the post–Harlem Renaissance generation. Two years later, they published William Gardner Smith's *Last of the Conquerors,* a scathing—and largely forgotten—account of a black G.I.'s tribulations both on the front and at home.

Everything of quality was brought in by John Farrar. Reminiscing about his five years at Farrar, Straus, Arthur Orrmont remembered just missing out—by three days—on the chance to acquire Dylan Thomas, whereupon Farrar offered cold consolation: "Just be grateful you lost your big fish so early in the season." Farrar's catch included his friend Edison Marshall, whose exotic adventure stories were almost guaranteed bestsellers. Marshall's nonfiction collection on the 1946 list didn't do that well, but it was what Straus called "a holding operation," securing Marshall while he worked on a big swashbuckler. The same turned out to be true of Theodor Reik, a psychoanalyst who'd trained with Freud and developed a following of his own—which nonetheless couldn't boost sales of a book as dense as *Ritual: Four Psychoanalytic Studies*. But his *Listening with the Third Ear*, published in 1948, would sell for decades. Farrar had met Reik through his own longtime psychoanalyst, a devoted Reikian who had counseled him through his novel-writing days in Parlor O.

"The abilities of Roger Straus were more attuned to commercial than literary publishing," Orrmont recalled years later, when such a statement would sound surprising. But in the late forties, it would never have occurred to Straus to pretend otherwise. The goal was survival, then maybe growth. Deciding whether to tilt his lance at Alfred A. Knopf or Simon & Schuster was a luxury he couldn't yet afford. That doesn't mean he didn't know what a good book was, or at least what everybody thought a good book was—what would bring prestige, respectability, and potentially a long life of steady backlist sales.

That was why, in 1947, he called up Diarmuid Russell and Henry Volkening, two hard-drinking, chain-smoking literary agents whose firm, Russell & Volkening, represented the blue chips of midcentury publishing. He took them to an East Side restaurant once frequented by legendary editor Maxwell Perkins (who had in fact encouraged Russell and Volkening to start the agency before "the damned women take over the entire business"). Roger watched them down their "three or four or five martinis" but kept his own head. "I've always been nervous about drunks," he later said. "Two martinis is my limit, I can fake through a third and maybe pretend to have a fourth, but when you have five martinis at a crack that's out of my thing."

At long last, they got to the coffee, and Roger made his point. "Listen, fellows, the reason I am here is I am the newest one on the block and you are the best literary agents in town, and we are not seeing anything coming from your agency." After a long pause, one of them made the fair point that they knew nothing about him. "If we get a book that we like, why in the world should we send it to you? Why shouldn't we send it to Scribner's or to Harcourt, Brace, or Houghton Mifflin?" Straus conceded that, but added, "I expect to be around a long time, and I hope that once in a while, when you have perhaps an experimental novel that you care to lay off in a hurry, you'll think of us."

So instead, Roger went abroad—or so he allowed future profilers of the company to believe. In this short, tidy story, our dashing hero, locked out of polite American literary society, conquers Rome, single-handedly engineering a renaissance of postwar Italian literature in translation. "Like a GI carrying chewing gum," wrote Ian Parker in his *New Yorker* profile of Straus, "Farrar, Straus could cut a greater dash in Europe than at home. Straus traveled to Italy, where, looking for a good book, he found a classic."

It was a common tic of a Roger Straus story: the Royal "I." In fact, Roger didn't leave the country for the first twelve years of his firm's existence. "Maybe my peanut stand would have blown up or evaporated while I was away," he explained in his oral history. He had certainly never met Carlo Levi, an Italian-Jewish doctor, painter, and novelist, by the time word was getting out that Levi had written the classic Parker would allude to. Based on Levi's Mussolini-era banish-ment to a village so remote that its inhabitants claimed Christianity had never reached them, his novel was translated into English as *Christ Stopped at Eboli.*

In fact, though Straus heard of Levi from two scouts he knew, it was an old friend of John Farrar's, Elma Baccanelli, who first sent the manuscript. (In fact, she'd mistakenly sent it to Rinehart & Co., which forwarded it to Farrar, Straus.) And it was Farrar who took it seriously, on the basis of Levi's work for the Resistance. "These associations cannot lightly be thrown away," he wrote to Levi. The house, barely off the ground, was already looking for translators by February 1946.

Levi, a future Italian Communist senator, was no pushover in negotiating with a firm he'd never heard of. When Baccanelli passed on Levi's complaints over Straus's chintziness, Straus blamed the disagreement on Baccanelli: "I wrote a long letter to the gal in Italy who is fussing about the Levi thing, in an effort to quiet her down," Straus wrote to Sanford J. Greenburger, the U.S. representative for Levi's Italian publisher, Einaudi. Farrar urged another of Levi's proxies, Max Ascoli, to "assure Levi that he has forward-looking and honest publishers who are not trying to play games with him."

The partners walked a tightrope, flattering Levi personally while playing rough with his middlemen. Even after the contract was signed, Levi was still insisting Farrar, Straus shouldn't have any stake in motion picture rights. Greenburger had by then soured on Levi. He wrote Roger that summer that Levi was "probably the most conceited man I have ever met and we both met some lulus." Straus held firm and the contract was unchanged, but unlike Greenburger he managed to stay on Levi's good side. In later years the publisher "never went to Italy without seeing Carlo"; Levi would take the Strauses everywhere, from the Jewish ghetto to the Via Veneto. "He looked like everything that Rome should look like," Roger said. "He was Rome to me." The author painted a portrait of the Strauses in his signature Fauvist style. As Straus described it in his oral history, "I look a little bit like a mafia chief and Dorothea looks very well." Roger's god-given charm overcame the resentments that tended to arise when a hungry intellectual and a scrappy publisher fought over scarce resources.

The relationship with Levi—and Einaudi—paid enormous dividends. Italians tumbled like *pagliacci* into Farrar, Straus's catalogs: Dino Buzzati, Cesare Pavese, Romualdo Romano, and, most crucially, Alberto Moravia, whose books came to epitomize Italian style as Rome crept toward the age of Fellini. Jean-Luc Godard and Bernardo Bertolucci filmed Moravia's work. *The Woman of Rome,* his first novel with Farrar, Straus, would be published in 1949. Eleanor Blow, one of the scouts who'd tipped Straus off to Levi, wrote a trend-defining essay in the *New York Times Book Review* in 1947, describing the Italian movement as "virile, fresh and even exuberant," especially when compared to the "defeatist spirit" of most other postwar Continental literature.

It's highly likely that one or more of these go-betweens were feeding intelligence to the American government. Just after the war, the CIA was gathering information all over Italy on the potential spread of communism. Straus admitted two years before his death that, early on, he was visited by a man in U.S. intelligence who asked if he could provide cover for two operatives abroad. (In his oral history, Straus identified the visitor as an old friend from Naval Intelligence who'd joined the CIA.) The two agents would work as scouts for the firm while executing missions for the government. "I thought it was my patriotic duty to say yes," Straus explained. It wasn't bad for the firm, either. Since he could barely afford to pay scouts, the federal subsidies helped.

Several sources have identified one of these scouts as Silvio Senigallia, a Jewish Italian from a prominent military family who was officially working for Voice of America. He proved immensely helpful as a liaison with Levi and Moravia—two prominent leftists he may well have been reporting on to the spooks in Washington. Another scout was identified, but he is still alive, and while he admits knowing Roger through a mutual friend in Naval Intelligence, he denies having worked for the Agency.

Straus thought (or rationalized) that these men gathered "pretty thin soup" for the government. Agents set up a separate phone line in Roger's office with a large black phone, meant purely for his CIA contact. (Later, he kept the line for emergencies and calls to women.) His secretaries needed to get security clearance from the government. In one instance the CIA called a future assistant's mother even before she got home from the interview.

Straus's final secretary, Peggy Miller, says that she was given a secret number to a separate phone line, but was never vetted for a security clearance. That may be because FSG's cloak-and-dagger days were largely over. By the time Straus met these scouts in person—he and Senigallia would become good friends—they were probably no longer working for the CIA. Senigallia became Farrar, Straus's official subagent in Italy, as well as Roger's Continental partner in tennis and carousing.

Did the goal of publishing high-minded, socially conscious writers justify the means of collaborating with their Cold War opponents? The irony might have been less amusing than it is today, when such stratagems are safely relegated to spy fiction. Straus always thought that political agnosticism was a publisher's best course. But he did feel privately uneasy about it, especially as his later writers suffered the consequences of dirty wars and CIA-funded coups. Like those vanity projects of the early years, it was a blot on his honor, an aspect of publishing that he didn't like to discuss.

Published in April 1947, *Christ Stopped at Eboli* was well reviewed across the country. The Book-of-the-Month Club took ten thousand copies for a $3,000 advance, and within a year all editions had sold close to thirty thousand copies. Still, other books had to bolster the bottom line. Roger's buddy Basil Heatter's war novel *The Dim View* did well, along with *Francis,* about the talking donkey, and an adventure book, *Yankee Pasha,* the swashbuckler Edison Marshall finally wrote.

In its first year of business, Farrar, Straus made a respectable $190,000 in sales—not bad for only half a year's worth of books. When the lease expired on the Empire Trust Building, they moved into a very cheap suite in a brownstone at 53 East 34th Street, which afforded not much more space and what Straus called "crazy quarters." Technically, they had a second floor, but it was really a mezzanine under an enormous skylight. This upper-deck hothouse was closed during the summer, but the rest of the office wasn't much cooler. Stray fabric from a neighboring umbrella manufacturer littered the elevator, and construction work next door would interrupt meetings in sharp, staccato blasts.

Like his friend Van Alen, Straus benefited from a cozy business relationship with a bank that also held his personal finances. There was a trust fund in his name at the local branch of the Central Hanover Bank & Trust Company. Business loans of roughly $25,000 every six months or so kept Farrar, Straus churning, against the collateral of the personal Straus account. Once, when his banker hesitated, Roger visited the branch to set him straight on the vicissitudes of publishing. "You know," began his lecture, "the phone could go right now and I could be getting a telephone call from my office saying we have a book-club selection, and I wouldn't have to be talking to you." Minutes later—"It was like a movie," he recalled—his secretary was on the line. Guy McCrone's *Red Plush,* a doorstop Victorian family saga, had become their second major selection for the Book-of-the-Month Club. "I picked up my hat and said, 'Thank you, fellas,' and left."

Not wanting to rely on the rare hits, Roger experimented with strategic expansion. The publisher who would one day take an almost perverse pride in having no textbook division tried one out at the very beginning. The industry-wide move to schoolbook publishing was already in the wind. Where it was adopted, as at Harcourt, Brace, it became by far the most lucrative profit center. Straus quickly set up a joint imprint with Walter Hendricks, the eccentric founder of Marlboro College in Vermont. With the help of student labor, Hendricks published about twenty or thirty books a year. "Hendricks House–Farrar, Straus" was, in the end, doomed by Hendricks's own inefficiencies and perhaps Straus's own lack of time, passion, and attention. Another problem was the simple lack of capital. "We didn't know what we were doing in the first place," said Straus, "and we didn't have the money to pile into it . . . in order to establish a proper kind of textbook house." By his estimate, they lost $100,000 before cutting Hendricks loose.

He also tried teaming up with movie studios—first 20th Century Fox and then MGM—to cut first-look deals on promising young authors. Such nickel-and-dime synergy netted only a few books. Straus also teamed up with a film executive to launch the 20th Century Fox Fellowship, whereby a lucky debut writer would get an advance straight from Fox and the studio would get an exclusive option.

Nothing came of it but a few free books, but every little bit of cash flow helped keep Farrar, Straus going until other sources of income could be found.

Every step forward was followed by a stumble—as was the case, physically, in the cramped obstacle course of an office. At one point a newspaper misprinted the firm's name as Farrar, Straus, and Cox. It became an office joke; every time someone bungled a printing or missed a deadline—or that one time Roger left his car parked outside with the keys in and the engine on—it was blamed on the fictional third partner, Colonel Cox.

The "holding operation" ended near the turn of the decade. For the first but not the last time in the history of Farrar, Straus, two big sellers brought untold riches, unimagined opportunities, and unforeseen complications. The first boost came in the form of a health nut with a perfect movie-star physique, a dubious past, and an even more dubious-sounding name.

Gayelord Hauser held himself up as the ultimate proof of his expertise. His muscled torso and unlined face attested to the power of yogurt, brewer's yeast, powdered skim milk, wheat germ, and blackstrap molasses to heal all wounds. His faith in his own message didn't, however, always translate to book sales, and for this he tended to blame the publisher (when he wasn't publishing himself). Lately he'd become fed up with Coward-McCann, which had sold about 85,000 copies of his book *Diet Does It*—maybe impressive to some, but not to the self-styled national celebrity. So the news came to a scout for Farrar, Straus & Co., Lowell Brentano, in the late spring of 1948, that Hauser was looking around.

Having worked with the diet-pusher for years, Brentano was no longer starstruck. Farrar, Straus editor John Meyer relayed Brentano's advice to Straus in a memo: "Either you or John Farrar better see him—with or without me as Mr. H. rather fancys himself & deals only with the top—He sails for Europe June 21—Monday—so it's rush! Rush!" Hauser demanded a high royalty and a collaborator willing to do most of the work: "We must be aggressive with him and be after him as he is lazy." Moreover, "He is a snob & name dropper, according to Mr. Brentano—and insists upon being kowtowed to."

Two days later, Straus met with Hauser and Frey Brown, Hauser's lifelong companion and business manager. Hauser had come to Hollywood from Germany, via Chicago, and met Brown in the twenties when both were chorus boys. Hauser ingratiated himself with William Randolph Hearst after his concoctions (potassium broth, diabetic tea) healed the eyesight of a "sob sister" (as Hearst's lady columnists were known). Hauser and Brown soon met Greta Garbo, and the happy trio invested in the Beverly Hills land boom, buying up chunks of Rodeo Drive. As Hauser's empire grew, Brown coordinated the intertwined businesses—radio shows, a syndicated column, the books, and part ownership of a health-food distributor called Modern Food Products. Brown was "much smarter than Gayelord—he was the brains," says Peggy Miller, who came to know the couple well. By the time they met Straus, they were probably as wealthy as he was. "Roger rather enjoyed rich authors," says the French publisher Ivan Nabokov, "because he didn't have to pay huge advances."

The following Monday, the day of Hauser's departure for a summer in Europe, Straus sent Brown a contract for the book provisionally titled *Live Longer, Look Younger,* with an attached note reading, "All of us here look forward to a long and profitable arrangement together. The book sounds swell and we are all very keen on it."

A ghostwriter was quickly rustled up, though her thousand-dollar advance had to be doubled after Hauser's delays stretched three months of writing to ten. Publication was pushed to February 16, 1950, as Farrar's wife, Margaret, the crossword-puzzle creator and sometime editor, raced through the draft. Roger came up with the idea of reversing the title, to *Look Younger, Live Longer;* his informal market research—known in the pre–focus group era as "asking the ladies"—had led him to the conclusion that "the female of the species would prefer to look younger than to live longer." It was his best cover decision since ditching the original title of that first book-club selection, Guy McCrone's *Red Plush* (formerly *Wax Fruit: An Antimacassar Trilogy*).

The first two weeks' sales were healthy, but not good enough to keep Hauser and Brown from questioning Farrar, Straus's advertising strategy. Their constant letters kept Roger busy; he considered it "uncivilized" to leave correspondence unanswered, and made a morning habit of opening and answering all his mail. He wrote back to Hauser and Brown with friendly but firm reassurances. Soon he was writing with genuine excitement, as sales went up and up: two thousand copies, three thousand copies, and, by June, four thousand copies per week. Fifty years later, these would still be very happy numbers.

Look Younger, Live Longer became America's bestselling title of 1950 (aside from picture books) and one of the biggest nonfiction titles of the decade. Including a revised edition the following year, the book sold just about half a million copies.

Still, Brown complained: "We are watching with great interest your program behind 'COURTROOM.' We are sorry that you did not see fit to put the same kind of promotion behind 'LOOK YOUNGER LIVE LONGER.' As it is, we figure that the success of the book to date is largely due to Dr. Hauser's own efforts." Straus's patience never ran out; again and again he proved he could maintain friendships with authors he was battling over money. "I'm sorry about the lawyers, etc.," he once wrote a ghostwriter for Sammy Davis, Jr., who was suing him over a disputed contract at the time. "But I trust that you understand and I hope we can keep it between them—yours and ours—and let's us concentrate on lunching and laughing."

Courtroom, the target of Hauser's jealousy, was the other big bestseller of 1950. Its subject, the judge and former defense attorney Samuel S. Leibowitz, had defended everyone from Al Capone to the wrongly convicted Scottsboro Boys of Jim Crow Alabama. Leibowitz had only one thing in common with Gayelord Hauser: Straus ranked him "high on the top 10%" of the vainest people he'd ever worked with, "if not the top 1%." Now Leibowitz was a Brooklyn judge, nicknamed "Sentencing Sam." A mutual friend told Straus that he was ready to write a memoir. By January 1949, after "one damned good dinner" together, Leibowitz was on board.

After a few dead ends, Straus lucked out with a coauthor: Quentin Reynolds, whom he landed after sweet-talking Bennett Cerf at

Random House, Reynolds's regular publisher, into lending him out for one project. It was a package deal with Leibowitz, executed by Reynolds's legendary agent, Irving "Swifty" Lazar. (Reynolds carried a jewel-encrusted cigarette case inscribed with the phrase LAZAR IS MY SHEPHERD.) The appeal of *Courtroom* lay in Reynolds's chapter-by-chapter pileup of sensational, often gruesome, cases. It was published just a month after Hauser's book, and before long the two were chasing each other "up and down the bestseller list," according to Straus. Sex, violence, and the promise of eternal youth launched Farrar, Straus, however tentatively, into the age of postwar prosperity.

Straus made aggressive efforts to keep the profits coming in. Arthur Orrmont may have seen him as "a swordless Saracen intent on the conquest of Gentile publishing," but Roger was well armed: He seemed to possess countless sensitive social tentacles. He also had a keenly developed sense of quid pro quo—or, as he took to calling it, "You blow me, I'll blow you." When Judge Leibowitz engineered a controversial judgeship for a favorite underling, Straus sent the crony an effusive telegram—a rare note of praise that the crony brandished up and down Brooklyn's Sixth District—"on the theory that this pigeon might come home to roost some day."

He did, not much later, when Straus read in the morning paper that the legendary bank robber Willie Sutton had been arrested in Brooklyn. He was the one who'd supposedly told a reporter he did bank jobs "because that's where the money is," and whose penchant for prison escapes and sharp disguises had earned him the nicknames "Slick Willie" and "The Actor." But Sutton was ready for retirement, and giving valedictory interviews to anyone with a notebook. Straus used his inside man, the judge he'd strategically flattered, to ferry a message to the inmate: "You can't sell it and give it away at the same time." Of course, the judge also vouched for this obscure publisher's bona fides.

Straus reenlisted Reynolds as coauthor, much to the consternation of Bennett Cerf. A few days before *I, Willie Sutton* was published, the hyperliterate bank robber sent a message to Straus: He asked for the *Publishers Weekly* review, and added, "Is there anything I can do to be helpful?" Straus suggested a jailbreak on publication day. He was only half joking, and couldn't help checking the news every morning to see if Sutton followed through. "I couldn't figure it out," he said, "because I knew Willie was a real trier." A week later he got a visit from a shady associate of Sutton's, who explained apologetically that Sutton's arthritis had made a break impossible. Maybe it was the lack of a well-timed escape, but the book didn't do nearly as well as *Courtroom*. Quentin Reynolds's advance of $10,000 was never earned out.

Cash outlays like that soon began piling up, threatening to undo the good fortune of 1950. One crisis was almost completely out of the firm's control. (*Almost*, because Straus knew what he was getting into.) In March 1951, food-and-drug inspectors fanned out across the country, photographing displays of *Look Younger, Live Longer* in health-food stores. They made a federal case against Hauser, his publishers, and Nature Food Centre of Rochester, New York, claiming that the book, when sold alongside Plantation Blackstrap Molasses, constituted false advertising. (It was unlikely, as the book claimed, that the sticky stuff would add five years to your life and forestall menopause.) Patrick Sullivan fought the case for Farrar, Straus and lost. The damage was limited, since the book could still be sold. But the legal fees totaled $50,000. Though Hauser was contractually on the hook for them, he refused to offer his next book to Straus unless the publisher covered the legal expenses. Roger eventually buckled.

Keeping Hauser on board was priority number one, but the production of his eagerly awaited sequel, *Be Happier, Be Healthier*, was a minor debacle. Donald Porter Geddes, paid $6,000 to ghostwrite, spent months trying to get Hauser to deliver the raw material in time for Farrar, Straus's carefully coordinated publicity schedule. Straus and Frey Brown schemed behind Hauser's back to fly Geddes out to their hilltop redoubt in Taormina, Sicily—a journey with five connections at a cost of $868 (split fifty-fifty by Brown and Farrar, Straus). Geddes got there in late August 1952 with publication still planned for November.

The pace was glacial at first: three hours of work and a dip in the Mediterranean, followed by a long lunch, then into town to talk "business"—which, Geddes reported to Straus, "consisted of telling me how everybody but you was trying to exploit him." There were boozy dinners, canapés with Truman Capote. Eventually, Hauser left Geddes alone to finish, and the work came in just under the wire. The firm had "desperately overspent" on promotion. The Farrar, Straus edition sold a little more than 25,000 copies over the next two decades. Thus was another lesson learned: No amount of publicity, by itself, can boost a book that isn't moving in the first place.

Another author who made Farrar, Straus take a bath was Harry S. Truman; in later years Straus liked to joke that the only two authors who ever doubled-crossed him were Sutton (for not breaking out of jail) and the thirty-third president of the United States. Thanks largely to Straus's navy-era media connections, names such as Stalin and Eisenhower had begun to grace the young list—albeit largely in photo-heavy as-told-tos and diary excerpts. *Mr. President,* by William Hillman, brought together the White House correspondent's writings with Truman's position papers and sixty-two glossy photos. It was a coup—the first officially quoted words of a living president in book form—and all for a modest advance and no money to the president. There was a great deal of respectful press. Sales were another matter.

Because of the expense of production, the publisher had to print one hundred thousand copies of *Mr. President* and charge a then-exorbitant five dollars apiece. Straus had occasionally consulted with Truman over the book, which the president was managing personally. Truman liked to call him "Young Roger," and once showed him the cabinet seat grandfather Oscar had occupied. (Could this be where Roger got the nickname for his own son?) Just before the publication date, Roger was granted a private meeting with Truman. Having already gone to the extreme of insuring the book against the president's death, he wanted to know if Truman was going to run for a second complete term. If he were to drop out too soon, Straus told the president, "I might have to eat 100,000 copies of this book, and they are going to be highly indigestible at five dollars a pop." Truman smiled and promised to give him fair notice. The book was published and sixty thousand copies had been sold to stores when, a couple of weeks after publication, Truman announced he wouldn't run. "And just like that," said Straus, "the book stopped dead." Only the sale of syndication rights to the *New York Times* and *Reader's Digest* prevented an all-out disaster.

The early fifties, those years of heady success followed by a fall to earth, taught Straus a great deal. He'd succumbed to a publishing trap that seems obvious but turns out to be very hard to resist. One very successful year leads to excess cash, which is then plowed into ever-larger advances buoyed by excessive confidence. But today's best-seller is tomorrow's dud, and today's star writer tomorrow's dejected alcoholic. Linear growth is very hard to achieve—never mind the exponential kind—and the headiest times call for the greatest excess of caution. Years later, Straus summed up the state of play in the fifties: "Success almost bankrupted me once." He'd emerge from it a more conservative publisher, one who focused less on his company's growth than on its identity—less on market share than on a market niche.

Colonel Cox was given the boot in December 1950, when Farrar, Straus became Farrar, Straus & Young. Stanley Preston Young, "a tall, springy man," as Dorothea described him, "with a shock of tawny hair and a virile, ruddy pioneer's face," hailed from Indiana by way of Harcourt, Brace & Co., where he had worked with Robert Giroux. Young was also a writer and playwright, but his second wife, Nancy Wilson Ross, was a better-known author, writing on everything from Zen Buddhism to the all-female "WAVES" division of the U.S. Navy. It was through the latter work that she had come to know the Strauses during the war. The Youngs lived in a gatehouse by the grace of the wealthy Straight family (relatives of the Whitneys), on the edge of a vast Long Island estate. The Strauses and Youngs had many long evenings together, stocked with personalities at the intersection of money, power, and culture. Dorothea later described a typical scene: Young would read from his poems, especially his epic, *America, My America*, while his wife, "dressed in diaphanous Indian gauze of turquoise and gold," wiped away tears.

Young had done good work at Harcourt, but the place began to change when its Anglophile visionary, Frank V. Morley—Giroux's great mentor—went to England after the war. Giroux would stick it out for nearly another decade before succumbing to the lure of Farrar, Straus. Young made the leap, though, and became a founding shareholder in the fledgling firm. He had little money of his own but was an incredibly well-connected fund-raiser, bringing in tent-pole investors. He was also an important strategy man, scouting both new books and other publishers to acquire.

It was Young who masterminded the company's first large buyout of a smaller firm. One of the more mystically inclined friends of the Youngs owned a small publishing company called Creative Age Press, which by the late forties was bleeding money. Flush from *Look Younger* and *Courtroom,* Straus bought it for less than $30,000, a tenth of Creative Age's annual sales. Its hidden value lay in its backlist—writers like James Reynolds and the poet Robert Graves—and if Straus had to pick up the bathwater with the baby (*What Is Hypnosis?; Conditioned Reflex Therapy*), he saw little harm in it. There was a clear economic advantage in taking over a firm, eliminating overhead, and using its list to expand on the cheap. "One of the easier ways to grow," Straus said, "is that you take over a publishing house even if it's losing money." The big fish eat the little fish, Roger knew; it would become his vocal complaint in later years. Farrar, Straus & Young may have floundered on occasion, but now it was eating rather than being eaten.

One staff member Straus kept on from Creative Age was its managing editor, Harold D. Vursell, a tall, lean, stylish man with a thin Clark Gable mustache. Vursell proved to be the best thing about the Creative Age acquisition, a jack-of-all-trades who could move fluidly from production to copyediting to acquisitions (John McPhee was among his later finds). He also had a sharp, acid wit, an asset in any office. Vursell was worldly and well traveled, and his fluent French made him a natural editor for Marguerite Yourcenar's first novel with the firm, *Memoirs of Hadrian.*

Yourcenar's fictional autobiography of the legendary Roman was such a passion project for Roger that when the Book-of-the-Month

Club failed to take it, Roger told them, "in no uncertain terms," that their decision was "absolutely stupid." It would be taken by other book clubs, padding its roughly forty-thousand-copy hardcover sale on the way to that "long and rather beautiful life" Roger bragged about decades later. After acquiring Yourcenar on another tip from Eleanor Blow, Roger handed her off to Vursell, honoring Yourcenar's request that her companion, Grace Frick, do the translating. Yourcenar and Vursell understood each other at least on one level: Both spent decades with same-sex partners, and they collaborated happily on a book that treated gay themes with refreshing gravity, openness, and lack of judgment.

Vursell also helped shepherd the revival and retranslation of the entire oeuvre of Colette—which Straus had acquired after making a rare and expensive long-distance phone call to her British publisher, Secker & Warburg. He convinced them to break an option put down by Blanche Knopf, then busily acquiring European writers on behalf of her husband, Alfred A. Knopf. Poaching from them was a big-league play, already a long way from that boozy lunch with Russell and Volkening.

With a larger staff in tow, Farrar, Straus made its third move, into an old loft building at 101 Fifth Avenue at 17th Street—trading in the perks of being in midtown, near all the publishers and bookstores, for cheaper rent hard by New York's derelict former theater district.

Along with the physical move came some overdue staff changes. Arthur Orrmont was the first of the old guard to be asked to leave. Treasurer E. Trevor Hill also left, to be replaced with yet another man down on his luck. Robert Wohlforth was a West Point graduate and former *Daily Telegraph* reporter who had ended up employed as an economist at the Department of Justice. But as the McCarthy era picked up steam, Wohlforth was dismissed for his lefty associations (his friends included Paul Robeson). Straus met him at an Our Crowd function and offered him the job virtually on the spot.

Wohlforth had literary interests but an accountant's mind. He was not universally liked. Hal Vursell called him "shit-for-brains." Others laughed at his office memos, like one that allowed staffers to leave fifteen minutes earlier in the summer if they could take forty-five-minute lunches. Another lamented the "picnic atmosphere" of the office.

Wohlforth also hired Rose Wachtel, the manager of supplies, a prematurely elderly-looking woman who went to extremes of thrift. The office's frequent early name changes never fazed her; she'd just cross out the old partner's name on the letterhead and write in the new one. She bought toilet paper and envelopes in such great bulk that thousands of rolls and reams would be found in the warehouse decades later. (The warehouse was itself a bargain: the former Rheingold Brewery, courtesy of Dorothea Straus.) Before paying the commissioned salesmen's travel expenses, Rose demanded they hand over all their stolen hotel soap for use in the Farrar, Straus bathrooms. There was nothing she loved better than running over to the massive S. Klein department store on 14th Street in the eternal hunt for the cheapest pencils around. The story goes that if you needed a new pencil, you had to come to Rose with your old one, to prove you'd worn it down to the nub.

Wohlforth and Wachtel played bad cops to magnanimous Straus, taking the blame for an institutional chintziness of which their boss actually approved wholeheartedly. John Peck, Edmund Wilson's editor, wrote his mother about the talented publicity director, Carolyn Wolf, who resigned in 1955 because she couldn't stand Wohlforth. She had told Straus she was going to Mexico:

> Straus asked her how she was going to get down there, and she said she would drive, if she could pick up some second-hand car. "Well, you can have my station wagon," said Straus, and he thereupon gave it to her as an outright gift, not as something to borrow. It is hers to keep. This means little to Straus, who is stuck with a Cadillac or two, but don't get the idea that he is an easy touch, or that he has the rude shortcomings of a wealthy benevolent office despot. He is none of these things. He is not mean and stingy, nor does he intend to be played for a sucker. He is genuinely kind, very fond of Carolyn, and has the knack of making quick decisions that are dramatic and also sound. He realizes that Carolyn is intelligent enough not to

labe [*sic*] him one way or the other just because he gave her a Chrysler station wagon during a moment's idle conversation.

Was Peck, a practical joker around the office, being a little facetious? Probably not. Carolyn Wolf died suddenly in Mexico City a year later. Wohlforth and Peck, on the other hand, worked at Farrar, Straus for the rest of their lives.

Stanley Young had other ideas. Two years after his name was put on the door, Young and his wife took a five-month trip to Europe, Cairo, and the Far East. Although he visited with Moravia, Levi, and other writers, he and Nancy spent the bulk of their trip in Asia, where she was researching a book on Buddhism. The couple returned in May 1953, and six months later, Stanley took a year's leave. He tried to negotiate with Straus to keep his job part-time while he worked on his writing, and promised he would remain a shareholder. Roger rejected the plan (but of course accepted the continuing investment). The company was too young, and its hard-driving founder too demanding, for divided loyalties. But it was a sensible decision, leading to what Roger liked to call "an amicable divorce."

It wouldn't take long for the constantly shorthanded Straus to remarry, and this time it was a better fit. Sheila Cudahy's family history was a Catholic midwestern version of Roger's, though darker and more tortuous. Her grandfather Edward A. Cudahy had emigrated from Ireland to Chicago in the nineteenth century and worked his way up from office boy to co-owner of Armour and Company meatpackers. By the time Edward's son married Sheila's mother, heiress Margaret Carry, the owners of Cudahy Packing were a society-page staple. The couple had a beautiful Gold Coast home, a private railcar, and five automobiles, including a Rolls-Royce. Sheila's elaborate coming-out party was headlined by Count Basie. According to her son, Ed Pellegrini, it was a deeply unhappy home, "a pathological upbringing of alcoholism and neglect." Mother was dependent on booze and possibly drugs (Sheila remembered seeing the butler carry her supine body upstairs). She died mysteriously in 1942, when Sheila was twenty-two. But even before that, Cudahy was left to her own devices.

She was shuffled off to boarding school in Virginia, where, according to her son, her family never visited.

Sheila's father, the only son of the company founder, was not up to the job of succeeding his father. The Depression hit the industry hard. Sheila stayed east and escaped into academia, falling in love with Italian literature. "She sought refuge in the world of horses and poetry," says her son. Sheila wound up at Columbia University and, while studying Romance languages, met a fellow outcast at the school's Casa Italiana. George (né Giorgio) Pellegrini had grown up in a prominent Italian military family but fled the Fascists, and he was studying economics at Columbia while working the elevator at Casa Italiana.

If Sheila's marriage to the stateless Pellegrini, in 1943, was meant as an act of rebellion, it only partly succeeded. Her father, resigned to the match, offered Giorgio a job heading the research division of Cudahy Packing. He hated it, and after the war the couple decided to start their own publishing house, Pellegrini & Cudahy, along with a children's imprint called Ariel Books. Their education and European contacts brought a list that rivaled Farrar, Straus in its Continental prestige: Giovanni Guareschi, whose "Don Camillo" books blended humor and pathos in the voice of a provincial friar, and the Nobel Prize winner François Mauriac, whose Catholicism-infused novels would inspire Flannery O'Connor.

The firm and its founding family soon moved to New York, living happily in Greenwich Village and running their publishing house out of office space shared with the prestigious tiny publisher New Directions. Cudahy and Straus met through a mutual friend and discovered shared preoccupations: Italian publishing; gossip and the art of the witty put-down; an inborn sense of privilege constantly at war with an urge to revolt. Straus and his colleagues would later make inside jokes of Cudahy's upper-class thrift, as well as her twisted observations. "Wouldn't publishing be wonderful without all those wretched authors," she liked to say, and once while visiting the Strauses in Purchase: "I hate the country; all those trees eat up the oxygen!" Bob Giroux often told of bringing T. S. Eliot to cocktails at Sheila's house, where not a single hors d'oeuvre was served, forcing the great editor and the great poet to hit a hot-dog stand on the way to the opera.

Straus, though, was fond of her intelligence and spirit, and the two families spent long evenings together. The Pelligrinis eventually moved to bigger digs on Park Avenue, and for a while it looked like their little lark, with its thirty-odd books a year, might get off the ground. Then, in September 1952, a year after the couple's only son was born, George Pellegrini had a bad bout of the flu. Sheila "said he would be out of the office for a few days," Roger remembered. He knew George had high blood pressure, but thought nothing more of it. Then the flu became bad pneumonia. "The next thing I knew, he was dead." George was thirty-nine, Sheila thirty-two.

He had a grand funeral at St. Patrick's Cathedral. A month or two later, Sheila met Roger for lunch and asked what she should do with the publishing house. Straus told her to bide her time. He spent a day or two a week over the next few months essentially managing the firm from Pellegrini's old desk, giving Cudahy space to consider her options. It's possible he himself was figuring things out, knowing the firm would be a good fit for Farrar, Straus, but not quite able to afford a deal. Company finances were stretched in the post–*Look Younger* era.

Within six months, the two arranged a purchase and stock transfer. Roger's mother came through with the needed capital, agreeing to lend him money against his inheritance. Pellegrini & Cudahy was absorbed into the company in April 1953. Roger kept the Ariel Books imprint—the beginning of Farrar, Straus's long and profitable relationship with juvenile books. Hal Vursell, despite his other duties, took over Ariel a year later. For the second time in the very short history of his publishing house, Straus had saved a foundering publisher, an unlucky loser in the postwar publishing scramble, from near-certain ruin. In the process, he had also improved his own prospects. Roger's combination of lordly benevolence and canny calculation was well suited to an era when the publishing business stood poised, like a middle-aged gentleman, between its old-money roots and its corporate destiny.

•   •   •

Announcing the merger, the Chicago *Tribune* declared confidently that Farrar, Straus & Young "now assumes a leading role in the publishing business." That may have been premature; there were giants up in midtown, both financial (Simon & Schuster, Doubleday) and cultural (Alfred A. Knopf and Harcourt, Brace). But Farrar, Straus was catching up on both counts. Even in the early fifties, the firm could boast of publishing Martin Buber, André Gide, and the young Shirley Jackson. Its publisher proved every bit as canny in nurturing the seedlings of a literary list as he was in sowing potential bestsellers. In fact, he was getting better at the former than the latter.

Alberto Moravia's *The Woman of Rome* was one book by which Roger schemed to achieve both. Moravia's character study had the depth of Carlo Levi along with some popular appeal, thanks to the sympathetic and industrious prostitute at its center. Aiming for spectacle, Farrar, Straus hired an ad agency, which came up with the idea of plucking a lingerie salesgirl out of obscurity, slapping her figure on the book's cover, and promoting model and novel at the same time: "Who is the woman of Rome?" was the slogan of the campaign. More than thirty thousand copies were sold over the next six months, and the Italian publisher's next edition used the American photo.

But Straus couldn't live forever on Italians; he needed to cultivate the intelligentsia closer to home. Straus had a friend, a cousin by marriage, named Louis Kronenberger, who was a theater critic for *Time* magazine. Together with Kronenberger he dreamed up the Great Letters Series. Prominent people like Lionel Trilling, a close friend of Kronenberger's, would edit and introduce the selected letters of long-dead writers. First Trilling edited Keats, then Mark Van Doren introduced the letters of William Cowper. Jacques Barzun treated Byron and Lillian Hellman did Chekhov. "This was another ploy," as Roger explained—the idea being not to sell many books, which they didn't, but to aim for the "entrapment of authors." It met with limited success in that sense, too, but it was part of the long game—the highbrow equivalent of making nice with a toady judge and winding up with a prison memoir.

It was at Kronenberger's house that the Strauses first got to know

Philip Rahv, the cofounder of the leftist, fiercely intellectual journal *Partisan Review*. The couple would become closest to Rahv and to Lillian Hellman, scoring invitations to literary soirées where young writers like William Styron and Philip Roth practiced their social networking. Soon the Strauses became formidable hosts in their own right. Rahv would show off Straus's Purchase estate to other writers like a Bavarian tourist trap. (Rumors spread that Straus and Rahv teamed up on sexual adventures.)

Their new friends brought the Strauses into a social circle that led back to Roger's old friend Robert Giroux. It was a loose conglomeration of writers—many published by Giroux—who made up New York's motley intellectual core: old Southern Agrarians like Allen Tate, Caroline Gordon, and Peter Taylor along with acolytes like Randall Jarrell, Dwight Macdonald, Delmore Schwartz, Robert Lowell, Jean Stafford, and John Berryman, as well as the mostly Jewish editors of the *Partisan Review*, which eagerly published their work. Edmund Wilson, Mary McCarthy, Hannah Arendt, and Alfred Kazin were some other key members. The critic Irving Howe theorized that what united these circles was their status as "semioutsiders": mostly Jews and Catholics and Confederates manqué on the fringes of *Time*-reading Protestant America.

Dorothea limned the circle's characters in her memoirs, and Straus became an adviser to *Partisan Review*, fund-raising for the magazine and picking up its writers. Intellectual heavyweights Lionel and Diana Trilling became informal advisers to Farrar, Straus. And, of course, the more critics Roger knew intimately, the more inclined they'd be to review his books. This was "the whole theory of the Letters," Straus said, "to become involved with the people who were being useful in the literary world."

A year after meeting Rahv, Straus lucked into an even more direct cultural pipeline. Robert Linscott, a senior editor at Random House and the father-in-law of a secretary from Straus's old navy office, called him in frustration. Edmund Wilson, the eminent critic and bane of all publishers, had long moved on from Robert Giroux and Harcourt, Brace and was now falling out with his latest "printer" (which is what he called his publishers). Random House head Bennett Cerf refused to publish to his specifications. Wilson controlled everything about his books, down to their narrow size and thin paper (in emulation of France's classic Pléiade editions). His essay collection would have to go somewhere else. Would Roger like to have it?

Straus later claimed that *Axel's Castle,* Wilson's influential study of turn-of-the-century literature, was "the first book I read that really straightened me out when I was in college." Surely he was also familiar with a book more attuned to both his commercial aspirations and his pungent turns of speech. Wilson's story collection *Memoirs of Hecate County* had become a bestseller in 1946 before being suppressed as pornography by the state of New York. In any case, Straus was awed by Wilson and his reputation.

He met Wilson at the Princeton Club and found a ruddy, sharp-nosed Yankee bulldog: a canny negotiator who never used an agent (an even lower life form than publishers) and who wasted no time before asking, "How much are you going to pay me?" Straus recalled being haggled up $500, but he paid only $1,500 for what would become *Classics and Commercials,* the first of Wilson's omnibus collections of literary criticism. In the contract, Roger struck out the option clause, forfeiting the publisher's customary right of first refusal on the next book. "Mr. Wilson, I understand that you're death on publishers," Straus said. "If we don't get along, you're not going to give me the next book anyway, and I'd just as soon not have the option." Wilson appreciated the sentiment, and Straus followed suit by meeting all of Wilson's production demands.

Neither *Classics and Commercials* nor Wilson's play *The Little Blue Light,* both published in 1950, sold very well. But publishing every last bit of a middle-aged icon's work, even though his best books were behind him, was no mere gesture of charity or respect. By now the Strauses and the Wilsons were exchanging dinner parties in New York and at the Wilson house on Cape Cod (left over from Wilson's disastrous marriage to Mary McCarthy), but theirs was a friendship between savvy *machers,* each supporting the other's great social and financial needs. Straus's end of the bargain was entrée into a world

beyond his parents' circle, a foundation upon which to build a prestigious house. In 1957, he participated in a panel on publishing and
was asked what form of publicity he would use if he had only one.
His first choice: "For Edmund Wilson to give a dinner party for about
eighteen or twenty friends" in order to talk up a book on the Farrar,
Straus list. Second choice was a front-page piece in the *New York Times
Book Review.*

Wilson was the publishing house's first writer-confidant, a consultant as important as any editor. Susan Sontag, Carlos Fuentes,
Tom Wolfe, and Joseph Brodsky would join this elite group in later
years. Along with Wilson, they were often asked for advice, received
financial support far beyond standard contracts, and had their books
published indiscriminately, as a matter of course.

The Wilson connection even earned Straus a first look at Vladimir
Nabokov's *Lolita*. Despite Wilson's contempt for the tale of a professor
and his preteen lover, his wife, Elena, sent the book to Straus. Roger
confessed to being "somewhat ambivalent," but suggested they might
publish it anyway. He later claimed he'd demurred because Nabokov
insisted on anonymity, which he thought would make a legal defense
impossible. Nabokov's wife, Vera, disputed this account, claiming
Roger rejected it outright. Straus's correspondence with Mary McCarthy—whose theater criticism he was about to publish, and who'd also
read *Lolita*—reveals the fullest range of his feelings. "It is the damned-
est book," he wrote, "and as I walk down Madison Avenue I can now
see a nymphet or a juvenile nymphet or an overage nymphet at least
three blocks away." But the Americana-steeped second half bored him,
and all of it scared him. "I agree with you that nobody will dare touch
this, leaving out its literary merits or demerits."

The further inside Straus maneuvered himself, and the more help
he had from rich intellectuals like Cudahy, the more peripheral John
Farrar, middlebrow and middle-aged, came to seem. He had found
himself, again, less a full partner than an employee, with a set salary of ten thousand dollars and limited rights to his own name. The
company became Farrar, Straus & Cudahy in February 1955, just two
months after Stanley Young's name was taken out. With the money

and the will to find and visit foreign authors, Cudahy was allowed to nurture the sense of being number two. She pursued her own, sometimes lucrative initiatives as well. Her Catholic series, Vision Books—simple lives of saints and martyrs for children—proved "an absolutely marvelous way of making money," according to Roger, and opened up an entirely new religious field for the house. They would publish seventy Vision Books in all through 1967—by which point Cudahy would be long gone.

Straus would later date the onset of John Farrar's decline to the early fifties. Accounts vary of his physical and psychological state as the years wore on. Certainly by the late sixties he was suffering from advanced arterial sclerosis and dementia, but family members say he was lucid and relatively healthy up until then. A doctor did write him in 1953 about hypertension so serious it caused severe nosebleeds and required medication. On top of this, he drank. Some veterans of the firm thought he had a problem, and though relatives deny that he was an alcoholic, his daughter Janice Farrar Thaddeus once wrote a grateful letter to Straus about a night when Johnny had come home looking like a mugging victim—but actually just very drunk—and Roger had to come over and put him to bed. Hal Vursell and his production assistant, Dorris Janowitz, poked fun at Farrar's growing irrelevance, laughing over what he'd frequently say to the switchboard operator on his way out to lunch at the Century Club: "The Century and home!"

Farrar, Straus had thus far fulfilled the first dictum of the introduction to its catalog: Every year, every rise and dip in finances and staff and the acquisition and production of books good, bad, and mediocre, had been in some sense an adventure. What wasn't there—what couldn't be there without a vital, commanding editor in chief—was *character.* The list was a hodgepodge. Novelists well past their prime jostled for space with gardening columnists, diet gurus, and a smattering of geniuses. Then Sheila Cudahy had an idea. It turned out that she was also friendly with Robert Giroux, by then arguably the most talented young editor in publishing. She ran into him one night at a party, and he shared a litany of complaints about his employer, Harcourt, Brace. He was unhappy, and he didn't mind if Sheila told Roger about it.

3

The Golden Boy of Publishing

The most remarkable thing about the partnership of Straus and Giroux is that their paths crossed at all. Even if, as children, they spent a year or two walking the same blocks of the Upper East Side—the Jewish prep school jock and the Jersey City Jesuit on scholarship—they were odd boys out in very different ways.

No national paper announced the wedding of Arthur Giroux and Katharine Lyons—a factory foreman from Quebec and an Irish-American schoolteacher. Their one brush with local fame, in 1927, came on the heels of two breathless nuns from St. Aloysius Parochial School racing through Jersey City's West Side Park, just before the Friday-evening dinner hour, to the coal-fired row house where the Girouxs lived. One of them clutched a piece of paper bearing the news that Bob Giroux had become the school's first student ever admitted to Regis High School on Manhattan's Upper East Side, several miles and a universe away. Arthur and Katie must have been just as surprised as the nuns—must have thought, if only for a moment, "Where did this kid come from?"

Robert Giroux loved a good mystery. Both of the books he wrote were mysteries of a sort, though hardly genre fiction: *The Book Known as Q*, on the possible origins of Shakespeare's sonnets; and *A Deed of Death: The Story Behind the Unsolved Murder of Hollywood Director William Desmond Taylor*. Giroux was intensely curious, too, about his own family history. If Roger Straus seemed to come into the world a known quantity, Bob Giroux was the opposite: a cipher at birth, hungry for both knowledge and acknowledgment. He was, despite this, private about his own life—his childhood, his faith, his very brief marriage, and his lifelong companionship with a man. There were practical reasons, of course, for his reticence, preferences a self-made professional could not afford to share. Yet it was consistent with his avowed philosophy: A good man, like a good Catholic, should be known and judged by his works.

Giroux's works—the books he published—were more than just vehicles for art; they were objects in which he took a craftsman's pride. This, if nothing else, he inherited from a long line of weavers going back at least to his first New World ancestor, the seventeenth-century sailmaker Toussaint Giroux, and ending with Arthur in a mill in Paterson, the heart of New Jersey's manufacturing base. The Guggenheims and their ilk were hardly buying clothes off the rack, but the growing American middle class depended on the labor of the ethnic tanners and sewers of Newark, Flatbush, and the Lower East Side.

Giroux's mother had been a schoolteacher but, after her children were born, settled for occasional piecework as a seamstress. (The Girouxs kept a loom in their basement.) Even before the Depression and, years later, a deeper neighborhood decline, money was scarce. Arthur made things worse by drinking and gambling. Bob's four siblings always felt he was Katie's favorite, the object of her doting protection. His eldest brother, Arnold, was institutionalized in Secaucus for emotional problems. The middle brother, Lester, would become an electrician and, like his father, an immoderate drinker. One sister, Josephine, ran off to California with a man who'd been boarding in their house, only to return with him later and live across the street. Giroux's life would distance him from his family—no one else graduated from college—but he was a good son: quiet, devoted, polite, and sharp.

Regis, which still offers New York's best Jesuit education and among the city's best in any category, was founded as a free institution in 1914, the year of Giroux's birth. Close by Central Park on East 84th Street, just seven blocks south of the Straus brownstone, the handsome stone campus bred in its students a uniquely Jesuit blend of elitism and civic-mindedness. It was here that Giroux first tasted the liberal strain of Catholicism that he would share with many of his authors, from the pacifist Trappist Thomas Merton to the civil-rights activist John LaFarge to the pseudonymous Vatican II chronicler Xavier Rynne. Giroux took Latin, Greek, and his father's native French. He was an obedient student, but flashes of insouciance shone through, like the slightly toothy smirk he wears in a yearbook photo, slim and ruddily handsome in a cheap-looking tie.

Giroux attained a superb education even as the Depression cast its pall (though not on the likes of Dorothea Straus, who wrote, "Prohibition and the Crash meant no more to me than rubber pants and those patient apple venders on the streets of New York"). Bob's sister Estelle, a keypunch operator at Colgate Palmolive, gave him some change for the daily fare on the train across the Hudson. The rest he made up by working at the *Jersey Journal*. Roger Straus had done his stint as a teen journalist at the White Plains *Reporter* mostly for fun; Giroux needed the money. Nonetheless, it was an important experience, during which he interviewed eminent writers like Pulitzer Prize winner Zona Gale and biographer Emil Ludwig.

Two months before graduation in 1931, Giroux left Regis to work at the *Journal* full-time, believing it was his only option. "Jobs were hard to find," he told a reporter fifty-seven years later, when he was finally awarded his (honorary) Regis diploma. "I needed one and if I didn't take that one in April I wouldn't have gotten it at all." It was Giroux's editor at the *Journal*, Lillian Hull, who set him straight, insisting he get a high school degree and go to college. After he finished up at Dickinson High School, she helped him secure a scholarship to Columbia University.

"The times were serious and so were most undergraduates,"

Giroux wrote of Columbia in the thirties, introducing the fiftieth-anniversary edition of his college classmate Thomas Merton's *The Seven Storey Mountain*—the first bestseller Giroux would edit. But Columbia was also a cauldron of passionate, callow strivers. Giroux and his fellow students read and wrote intensively and juggled part-time jobs. Yet they found plenty of time to see W. C. Fields flicks, jazz gigs on 52nd Street, and burlesque shows at the Apollo ("tit shows," as Giroux's classmate the future poet John Berryman called them). They danced scandalously close to Barnard girls at "tea dances" under the not-too-watchful eyes of the deans. While on "strike" (i.e., cutting classes), they bellowed with all the ferocity of their elders at the Communist-sponsored John Reed Club, which was just at that moment planning the first issue of *Partisan Review.*

Before transferring to Columbia, Thomas Merton, the future monk, had been expelled from Cambridge University after fathering an illegitimate child. Of Columbia, he wrote in *Mountain,* "There was a kind of genuine intellectual vitality in the air—at least relatively speaking." Its students were the spiritual forefathers of the SDS sympathizers who would take over Columbia's copper-roofed halls thirty years later. One *Mountain* passage captured the scene wryly:

> The *Spectator* was always starting some kind of a fight calling for mass-meetings and strikes and demonstrations. Then the fraternity boys, who elected to play "Fascist" in this children's game, would get up in the classroom buildings and turn the firehoses on the people who were standing around the Communist speaker. Then the whole thing would come out in the New York *Journal* that evening and all the alumni would choke on their mock turtle soup down at the Columbia Club.

You couldn't say there was a "counterculture" per se (a word Giroux would disdain decades later), but the seeds of the Beats who would attend Columbia just a decade later were already being sown. Giroux, though, ranked art high above politics. He rightly predicted that Merton had too much of a sense of humor to join the

Communists, and in the spring of 1934 he responded vehemently to the campus paper's derision of a poetry reading for indulging in "eccentric fantasies." In a long published response, he wrote sarcastically, "Come the revolution and the subsequent cooperative commonwealth, there will still remain the problem of how poetry may best be read to an audience."

Giroux's several part-time jobs kept him well in touch with proletarian realities. One early job cured him for good of an unhealthy habit: distributing samples of Philip Morris's products in return for ten dollars a week plus two free cartons. After bartering some cigarettes and trying to smoke the rest, he quit smoking in disgust. He was also a press agent for the Cinéma du Paris, a movie house on 13th Street devoted exclusively to French films—a product he indulged in to more lasting and salubrious effect. His income was soon supplemented with a more rewarding gig, writing film reviews for *The Nation*. That job came his way thanks to a man who embodied the Platonic ideal of the word "mentor": Columbia professor Mark Van Doren.

"Mark was the great teacher in my life," Giroux once recalled, "an influence I can never forget." Van Doren, a generalist, taught Shakespeare as well as American literature and various colloquia, all of which Giroux attended. He was also the literary editor and a sometime film critic at *The Nation*. If not for his long tenure there, we may never have heard of Giroux, or Berryman, or the minimalist poet Bob Lax, or, for that matter, Jack Kerouac and Allen Ginsberg. Again Merton is most affecting on the subject: "For a man to be absolutely sincere with generation after generation of students requires either supernatural simplicity or, in the natural order, a kind of heroic humility."

"Mark's unusual technique," Giroux said, "was to treat every student as his intellectual equal"—whether or not they were. And, just as important, with the academy already beginning to swing from one ideological fad to the next, he endeavored to preach no point of view, whether political or methodological. The professor's business was the novel, poem, or play before the class, the work taken "as a human whole," not as a dead object autopsied in search of some fatal flaw.

His kind of analysis was ideally suited to aspiring editors and artists, because what he taught, more than anything, was taste.

Giroux and his circle likewise made a strong impression on their teacher. Van Doren later wrote:

> If anyone supposes that the depression produced only bitterness in students, and savagery, and wrath, such cases as Berryman and Merton and Lax refute the supposition . . . There were bitter cases, granted; though again there was Robert Giroux, whose nature was as noticeably sweet as that of Merton or Lax, and as modest and as charitable. Giroux . . . thought then that he would never be interested in anything but movies. He saw all the films, and made sure that I saw the best of them; scarcely a week passed without his coming in to tell me of one I must not miss.

Van Doren was soon farming out *Nation* reviews to his movie-mad acolyte.

There was also Professor Raymond M. Weaver. Described by a critic as a "dandy with a bishop's voice," Weaver liked to tell the story of how he helped tranform Herman Melville from a forgotten dead novelist to a fully vested member of the American pantheon. Obsessed with *Moby-Dick,* he wrote the first biography of Melville in 1921. During his research, Weaver had uncovered Melville's final work, *Billy Budd,* lying in the same room on East 26th Street where the dying author had finished it thirty years earlier. Weaver had done more than just explicate great works: He had found one. This distinction was not lost on Giroux. "I thought how great it would be to discover a literary masterpiece," he later recalled, "and that sort of directed me toward publishing."

Giroux met John Berryman in Van Doren's Shakespeare class. Already a rising poet on campus, Berryman cut a colorful figure, with a slim, square face, a perennially cocked eyebrow, and a penchant for bow ties, pipes, and high-flown insults. As sophomores, he and Giroux found their way to the fourth floor of John Jay Hall and the offices of the *Columbia Review.* Berryman exempted Bob from his characterization of *Review* staff members as "drips." By the spring of 1935, Giroux was coediting the literary magazine with Robert Paul Smith, but most often he consulted with Berryman.

The poet had spent much of his first two years drinking and working hard to bed as many Barnard girls as possible. Eileen Simpson, Berryman's first wife, gave Van Doren full credit in her memoir, *Poets in Their Youth*, for turning him around. "It was as Mark's student that John had developed his lifelong passion for Shakespeare. It was Mark who introduced him to Stephen Crane, Mark who encouraged him to become a poet, Mark who tried to keep him in line."

The studious Giroux reinforced the bond, sometimes serving as liaison from mentor to student. Together they advanced Berryman's "Pauline conversion," as Giroux called it—the frantically productive final year during which the poet shed the accoutrements of the "preppie, interested in campus politics and fraternities." Giroux, thanks to Berryman and others, also changed. Bob wasn't born a bon vivant, a natural connector like Berryman. The poet, along with a few lesser-known writers like Leonard Wallace Robinson, "helped me bridge a gap" at a time when he "felt 'outside' and isolated at Columbia." Giroux learned to get along in the world, to make connections to people as well as ideas—to compete in a world of John Berrymans and Roger Strauses.

By 1936, Berryman and Giroux were running the *Review* together. Berryman was the showman—"more or less the star on *Review* that year," Merton recalled. Giroux was the inside man, the steady operator who perfected the prose and the layout. Merton described the fourth floor of John Jay, where all the magazines were produced, as an extension of the campus rabble, "seething with the exchange of insults from office to office." Giroux stood out simply by not standing out: "A Catholic and a person strangely placid for the Fourth Floor. He had no part in its feuds and, as a matter of fact, you did not see him around there very much." He did socialize with Merton, whom he found "better educated than most of my classmates"; they shared a taste for slapstick (W. C. Fields, the Marx Brothers), and both adored Van Doren. Merton was strong, stocky but muscular, with fair features and thinning blond hair. He played jazz piano and had a record collection; Giroux found him "a terribly interesting fellow."

In their senior year, Giroux and Berryman reinvented the *Review,* modeling their issues on the legendary Harvard quarterly *Hound & Horn.* Appearing in late 1935, the new *Review* featured Berryman's first published poem, "Elegy: Hart Crane," as well as his gushing review of *The Dog Beneath the Skin,* a play by W. H. Auden and Christopher Isherwood. Berryman was delighted with the whole package—"everyone in sight says this is absolutely the best issue ever," he wrote to a friend. He also said Giroux had done everything, including the layout.

A month before graduation, the staff of the *Review* outdid themselves in the final, double issue. Giroux et al. had persuaded Van Doren to review R. P. Blackmur's latest book, while Blackmur himself reviewed essays by Allen Tate. Berryman invited Blackmur to attend that year's presentation of the annual poetry prize of the Boar's Head Society, which Berryman won. He had already won, in January, the Euretta J. Kellett Fellowship, which provided for two years of study at Cambridge University on a stipend of two thousand dollars a year—this despite the fact that Berryman barely had the grades to graduate. What he apparently did not know was that Van Doren had first offered the prize to Bob. Giroux told friends he had stepped aside in the mistaken belief that the fellowship would obligate him to enter academia, when he already knew he wanted a publishing job.

After graduating, Giroux also declined the chance to become a full-time film critic at *The Nation* (again over Van Doren's objections). He insisted, instead, on working in books. But all his interviews—like one with John Macrae, the elderly head of E. P. Dutton, whom he described as the spitting image of Colonel Sanders—came to naught. Publishing, the gentleman's profession, was still in large part the province of the well born, and even a stellar college record couldn't hold a candle to the right clubs and relatives. So Giroux eventually gave in and went to work in a newer medium, radio, at the Columbia Broadcasting System.

The job, PR and market research, was "very steady and unexciting," he reported to Berryman. "But I am really grateful to have the job." It seemed like a placeholder, dull and ordinary, but the times were hardly that. Over in Europe, CBS's correspondents were reporting on Hitler's first incursions, from the annexation of Austria to the invasion of the Sudetenland. Giroux produced two special-edition books for CBS on the topic. His first compilation was a short supplement about the *Anschluss*. Then came September 1938. Hitler was after Czechoslovakia, and on the ground were the cream of CBS: Edward R. Murrow, William Shirer, H. V. Kaltenborn, and others. The stories culminated in Chamberlain's appeasement at Munich and the eradication of another democracy. Giroux layered the reports in documentary style for a gripping hardbound book simply titled *Crisis*. The opening copy, probably written by Giroux, reads: "Here, as the world heard it hour by hour for twenty crucial days, is the sound of Europe tearing up its maps."

The war united many strivers of disparate backgrounds, and it was already binding Giroux, Farrar, and Straus—though they didn't yet know it—to a common cause. Along with Straus's *War Letters to Britain* and Farrar's ardent interventionist letters, Giroux's coffee-table compendium was forcing a country bent on isolation to pay attention to the conflagration abroad. And it was drawing both him and Roger deeper into the world of books, that vital center of Western culture.

Giroux's books, which he compiled anonymously, soon drew the attention of Frank V. Morley, head of the trade division at Harcourt, Brace and Co. Barrel-chested and imposing—Ezra Pound called him "the Whale"—Morley had spent his youth in England cavorting with a clique of expat American writers. He ended up at Faber and Gwyer (later Faber and Faber), a start-up publishing firm cofounded by the expat T. S. Eliot that quickly became one of the most prestigious in Britain. In 1939, Morley returned to the States at the behest of Donald Brace, who had cofounded Harcourt in 1919. The Anglophile firm had published John Maynard Keynes under extremely generous terms, sacrificing short-term profits for long-term rewards: Thanks to Keynes's loyalty, it had become the American home of the Bloomsbury Group.

Morley wanted CBS's *Crisis* for the Faber list, but CBS refused to give up the rights. So Morley decided to hire its editor. Giroux gladly accepted a pay cut and moved into Harcourt's offices just up Madison Avenue on January 2, 1940. The Jersey City scholarship kid who'd felt "outside" at Columbia, until the conversation turned to literature, found himself among kindred Anglophiles and Columbia alumni. The founders of the firm, Alfred Harcourt and Donald Brace, had worked together as classmates on the *Columbia Spectator,* a team of opposite personalities just like Giroux and Berryman.

Giroux was very lucky to start his career in a house where junior editors were assigned to the best writers (since they required the least editing). One of his first charges was Edmund Wilson, with his massive and intellectually exacting paean to Lenin, *To the Finland Station,* which would sell poorly for decades before being hailed as a classic. (By then it would be an FSG book.) "He needed no editing," Giroux remembered of Wilson. "My only function was to praise the writing."

Another very early assignment came directly from Donald Brace. Naturally, the reticent Giroux was closest to Brace, "the silent partner, who watched from the sidelines the more colorful antics of Alfred Harcourt." Giroux was astounded when Brace assigned him the British proof of Virginia Woolf's latest novel, *Between the Acts.* Brace, whose smiles were rare but "miraculous," was solemn on the late March day in 1941 when he called Giroux into his office and handed him a letter he'd just received from Woolf's husband. Virginia had filled her pockets with stones, walked into the River Ouse, and drowned. For the first time but certainly not the last, Giroux felt the undercurrent of many an editorial friendship: the fear that it could one day end, suddenly and senselessly.

Brace's lessons were often more explicit. Once, Giroux reported on a manuscript he didn't like but believed to have bestseller potential. "Bob," Brace said, "a book needs every support it can get and if you, the editor, like it, it starts out with one real friend. That's important. And that's a good reason never to take on a book if *you* don't like it."

Giroux took the advice seriously, and he didn't let friendship sway him. Thomas Merton submitted four manuscripts to Harcourt via Naomi Burton, an agent Giroux had cultivated. When he received the first two, in 1940, he didn't even make the immediate connection between "Thomas James Merton," the writer of *The Straits of Dover,* and the Tom he'd known in college. He agreed with a first reader that it didn't meet his basic criterion of narrative: "Certainly in those days I felt a novel should have a beginning, a middle, and an end." He rejected it, but over lunch Burton told him, "You didn't seem to realize the author was your classmate, Tom Merton!" After Merton's fourth submission, in 1941, Giroux "now knew that Merton was not a novelist."

Shortly afterward, the young editor was browsing during lunchtime at Scribner's bookstore when Thomas Merton startled him with a tap on the arm. "I hope you're still writing," said Giroux. Merton had just left a *New Yorker* meeting; they wanted him to write about Gethsemani, a Kentucky monastery where he was making a retreat. Merton had demurred; it was too personal. Giroux was surprised Merton had any religious leanings at all. The next Bob heard of his suddenly pious friend was from Mark Van Doren, who called to say Merton had sent him some poems, burned the rest, and joined the Trappists in Kentucky. Van Doren sent the poetry to James Laughlin and his young, highbrow press, New Directions, which published it in 1944.

New Directions also beat Giroux to his great friend John Berryman's work. Berryman had met Laughlin through Dylan Thomas and soon signed with him for a small advance. Laughlin also wanted to anthologize Berryman in a collection along with four other promising young poets. But by then Giroux had become an editor—and Berryman's best shot at a stand-alone collection.

Back in the States after his Kellett fellowship, Berryman was prey again to personal problems. Languishing in a teaching post in Detroit but hoping to reunite with an English girlfriend, Berryman had gotten Giroux interested in his scheme to fly to Blitz-torn Britain in the summer of 1940 and write a book on "the death of our kind of life." He gave up on the plan after France fell, and instead sent Giroux fifty poems. When Giroux complained this wasn't the book his bosses were waiting for, Berryman countered that he only wanted advice from a trusted source: "You were one of the first persons to take an intelligent interest in the verse." Giroux finally responded, "I'm ready to battle for you to the bitter end. I'm delighted to; it will be the first occasion since I've been here that I really wanted to see a book published." Nonetheless, he advised Berryman to stick with New Directions, as he didn't know if his bosses would approve. Berryman heeded his advice. He was not to be on the illustrious list of Giroux's debut discoveries.

The first name on that list would be Jean Stafford. Giroux's recollection of first encountering her work was, like his editing, polished and selective. A piece he wrote years later for the *New York Times Book Review* has him meeting her after reading her manuscript, then titled *The Outskirts,* on his boss's recommendation, having plucked it randomly from his briefcase on a train bound for Morley's house in Connecticut. "I was so enthralled . . . that I rode past my stop and returned to reality only when the conductor yelled 'New Haven!'"

It fits the pattern of thousands of editors' testimonials hyping manuscripts that kept them up all night, shirking their worldly responsibilities while sparkling prose carried them off to literary Nirvana. It has all the makings of a myth, much in the spirit of Maxwell Perkins, the Scribner's editor who was already legendary in Giroux's Columbia days for corralling Hemingway, Fitzgerald, and Thomas Wolfe. It also happens to be the truth—mostly.

In fact, Giroux already knew Stafford. Jean and her husband, Robert Lowell, young and promising talents embraced by Giroux's peers, came to his attention via Berryman and his contemporaries—those "semioutsiders" Irving Howe celebrated. Stafford and "Cal" Lowell moved to New York in late 1941, having recently married and converted to Catholicism (Lowell more avid though more inconstant on both fronts). They first had Giroux over to dinner that October and, as Stafford recounted, "it came as a complete surprise to him . . . that I was anything but a quiet talented mole working year after year on a novel down on 11th St."

So Giroux's curiosity had already been piqued months before

Morley dropped Stafford's manuscript in his office with an attached note that read: "It is well written in a way that creeps on relentlessly, giving the interior life of its heroine, Sonie. I found that it kept hold of me; but will it keep hold of a public? Opinions on this—RG, please?" This is not to say that he was fully prepared for the manuscript that made him miss the Morleys' stop in Riverside, Connecticut. Stafford's narrative of Sonie Marburg's rise and fall—from poverty into the clutches of a Boston Brahmin named Miss Pride—combined the class concerns of Dickens or *Gatsby* with a Proustian interiority and symbolic richness. Stafford had sublimated her own bruising experiences with Lowell in Boston: his disapproving mother; a drunk-driving accident with Cal at the wheel that left Stafford permanently disfigured. Giroux, whose own status had risen so quickly, would favor such narrative arcs as a publisher—stories with a beginning, middle, and end.

Giroux persuaded Morley it would "keep hold of a public," and in April 1942, Stafford's first book contract, for five hundred dollars, was signed in the Princeton house of Allen Tate and Caroline Gordon, where the editor and the Lowells had stopped by on their way to hear a lecture by Randall Jarrell. Gordon made a ritual of it, a séancelike candlelight ceremony. Giroux set to work editing the novel, soon to be retitled *Boston Adventure*—but navy service interrupted his first great project.

Giroux's posting in North Carolina would cause him to miss another milestone, John Berryman's first wedding. Giroux had become fast friends with Berryman's fiancée, Eileen Mulligan. She remembered that the editor "seemed more adult than John's other friends, perhaps because of the dark business suit he wore and the air of authority he already had." During the summer of 1942, while Berryman was off teaching at Harvard, she passed many an evening with Giroux and his friend Charles Reilly, a chatty Irishman he'd known since grade school. "Bob and Charlie were waiting to be called into the service," she wrote. They often came up on leave in full uniform. At one boisterous party thrown by Russian émigrés, Giroux's crisp white navy officer's hat was nearly used for a vodka toast. Giroux had expected to be granted "compassionate leave" in order to serve as Berryman's best man. But as the day of the October wedding approached, it became clear he wouldn't be getting away from base. Mark Van Doren served in his place.

When Giroux went overseas, his colleague Lambert Davis took over *Boston Adventure* at Harcourt. Published in September 1944, while Giroux was still in the Pacific, it became an immediate bestseller: four hundred thousand copies printed within seven months. In his absence, his reputation only grew. By the end of the war he was able to jump right back in. It also seemed that, with England at peace, his mentor Frank Morley might be going back to his London life, which could leave Giroux in charge of the trade department.

This may have already been percolating by late 1945, when Roger Straus took Giroux out to the Ritz "to have a drink and discuss life," as Straus put it. "I'm starting a publishing house," Straus told Giroux, "and I'd like very much for you to come in with me as the chief editor, Bob, under, or alongside of—or however you want to phrase it—John Farrar." Farrar was top-notch, but he wasn't sniffing out fresh talent; Giroux could be the dynamic lead man in editorial. But Bob demurred. He was already on track to become editor in chief of an established literary publishing house, and couldn't risk bringing himself and his major authors into a start-up. Straus conceded the fact but asked him to please think of the firm if circumstances changed.

From every angle it was the right decision at the time—a conservative one, to be sure, but Giroux wasn't an entrepreneur. At Harcourt he had the freedom and the resources to gather up the most promising writers of his generation. So long as he had autonomy, respect, and stability, he preferred to remain loyal even at some risk to his ego. Only when these privileges were threatened would he reconsider.

Who knew T. S. Eliot loved show tunes? Certainly not Robert Giroux, in the spring of 1946, when Frank Morley stepped into his office and said, "Mr. Eliot wants to take you to lunch." The poet had arrived from England that morning on a Cunard liner expecting lunch with Morley, but the editor had already made other plans. Giroux later compared the invitation to "having to shake hands with the statue in

Don Giovanni." Eliot was perhaps the first modernist poet to make the full transformation from rebel to member of the arch-Establishment. He also had a reputation as a recluse, and possessed a "rather sad and lonely aura." He was fifty-eight to Giroux's thirty-two, and the latter must have been grateful for his prematurely white locks.

They crossed the street to the Japanese-themed courtyard restaurant of the old Ritz-Carlton. The hotel's bar was a famous haunt of Giroux's hero, Scribner's editor Max Perkins, whom Bob often spied having his afternoon martinis. Henry Volkening had already introduced the two, but Giroux never found the nerve to approach Perkins on his own. And here Bob was, hosting T. S. Eliot. Tiny ducklings wading in the courtyard's pond "seemed to embody the improbable quality the occasion had for me." The poet, also a longtime editor at Faber and Faber, broke the ice just as they were sitting down. "Mr. Giroux, tell me—as one editor to another—do you have much *author trouble?*" Giroux laughed, and Eliot asked him to call him Tom (it took a year for Giroux to do so). By the end of lunch Giroux had asked him—from one editor to another—a question both audacious and self-effacing: Did he think it was true that most editors were failed writers? Tom supposed it was, but then, so were most writers. "There was something about the way he said it," Giroux recalled, "that made me realize he considered himself among the failed writers, in the sense that he hadn't done all he may have intended or wanted to do."

Giroux became Eliot's stateside editor, which involved little editing per se. But he found other ways to help the poet. Once, after a shaky reading Eliot gave before a black-tie crowd at the Metropolitan Museum, Giroux counseled him to take longer pauses between poems. He gave this advice over drinks at the Oak Room in the Plaza Hotel, where Eliot promptly displayed his performance skills. Seeing a plaque above their table dedicated to classic American composer George M. Cohan, he began reciting, in that ominous voice normally reserved for the apocalyptic visions of his verse, the complete lyrics to "Yankee Doodle Dandy," "Over There," and "You're a Grand Old Flag."

Not much later, Giroux engineered a paid recital for Eliot at the

92nd Street Y, not far from his own apartment. (That was where Eliot met John Berryman and Robert Lowell.) Giroux soon became Eliot's unofficial, unpaid local booking agent. After Giroux settled into his long-term apartment, a two-bedroom in a whitewashed row house on East 66th Street, Eliot would stay there whenever he was in New York; while Giroux was at work, Eliot passed the time by reading, playing solitaire, and lunching alone across the street in Longchamps, on the ground floor of the iconic white-brick Manhattan House.

Eliot had, Giroux said, "a liveliness of spirit, a humor, and an attitude wholly unlike the solemn pontifical manner that was generally ascribed to him." They had a similar wit—dry, erudite, refined, and yet affectionately corny. Eliot surely found Giroux and his more outgoing partner, Charles Reilly, a charming pair, all the more appealing for their slight awkwardness. "There was a lot of Catholic stiffness in them, they didn't relax easily," the editor Jason Epstein says of Giroux and Reilly, having passed numerous cocktail afternoons with them in those years. One of Eliot's private jokes, Giroux told Epstein, was to put Charlie's name into his Tony Award–winning play *The Cocktail Party*. Henry Harcourt-Reilly, the play's mysterious psychoanalyst and deus ex machina, combines the name of Giroux's firm and his lifelong partner.

Giroux visited Eliot in 1948 at Princeton's Institute for Advanced Study, where he mapped out plot points for *The Cocktail Party* on a blackboard in playful imitation of his Institute colleague Albert Einstein. It wasn't the only thing Eliot and the physicist had in common: That year Eliot won the Nobel Prize. In November, Giroux accompanied the poet to LaGuardia Airport on his way to Stockholm. He later gave Charlie a snapshot of him and Eliot out on the tarmac, with a jet's enormous silver wing glinting in the background. Both stand in profile, wearing suits, black overcoats, and fedoras, leaning back and gazing upward, perhaps toward a plane taking off. Giroux, ruddy and round-cheeked, wears a slight, dazed smile. He himself isn't going to Stockholm—not yet.

Giroux and Eliot became closer in much the same way that Straus and Edmund Wilson did: Publishers who began as servants became loyal friends and protectors. What really built Giroux's reputation, though, was literature of his own generation. In March 1946, just before he met Eliot, Giroux had gone up to Cambridge, Massachusetts, to sign book contracts with both Robert Lowell and his wife, Jean Stafford. Jean was working on her second novel, *The Mountain Lion*, while "Cal" was putting together the collection that would become *Lord Weary's Castle*. Lowell, at the urging of his southern mentor Allen Tate, had sent his first sixteen poems to the tiny Cummington Press; his *Land of Unlikeness* was relegated to the smallest of literary circles.

After Lowell finished the poems in *Castle*, Philip Rahv at *Partisan Review* offered him a copublishing contract with Dial Press. The two firms were planning a partnership, but it fell apart in January, and Rahv rushed the manuscript over to Stafford's wartime editor, Lambert Davis, at Harcourt, Brace. Giroux, who had already seen many of the poems in progress, plucked out the manuscript and saw them perfectly formed. Collectively, they indicted Lowell's Puritan roots from a Catholic perspective. Their violent imagery burst through tightly controlled meter. Giroux loved both the power and the point of view. He quickly convinced Morley and Brace it should be published.

The sales of *Boston Adventure* had earned Stafford enough to buy a white clapboard farmhouse in idyllic Damariscotta Mills, Maine. There she worked through the winter, fighting the isolation and frozen pipes, to revise *The Mountain Lion*. Out came a fresher, rawer product than her first novel—more painful and more powerful. Giroux praised the new version and its sharpened focus on the central brother-sister relationship, which closely tracked Stafford's family past. "The ending comes off beautifully," he wrote upon receiving the draft. "Those weeks at Lord Weary's Castle have been really profitable."

For the Lowells, though, success bred contempt, and the summer they spent in the house would become the stuff of dark midcentury legend. Stafford would memorialize it, as thinly veiled fiction, only in the last year of her life, in her 1978 story "An Influx of Poets." It begins, "That awful summer! Every poet in America came to stay with us." Jealousy boils over among hosts and guests alike; the narrator suffers headaches and nausea; by the end of the summer a marriage is destroyed, and the darling kittens born early in the story have been drowned in the beautiful lake. Lowell and Gertrude Buckman, Delmore Schwartz's ex-wife, spent unsavory amounts of time together on their way to an affair. Jean was drained from dredging her past for *The Mountain Lion,* while Cal was dictatorial, puffed up on his newfound calling as the Catholic savior of poetry. Stafford confided to Berryman's wife, invoking Lowell's college nickname, "I fell in love with Caligula and am living with Calvin."

Giroux was a well-meaning bystander. He brought Charlie up to visit the Lowells that summer, just missing his old friend Berryman by an hour. Charlie took a photo of Giroux standing with the Lowells in front of their clapboard house. His too-crisp white shirt, high-waisted khakis, and slight middle thickness look out of place beside the rumpled Bohemian Brahmins, well-born waifs with their cigarettes dangling languidly.

Stafford's split from Lowell led to a protracted, rum-soaked nervous breakdown. Giroux was one of her most helpful friends. He recommended Dr. Carl Binger, a psychiatrist who published with Harcourt, Brace and who prescribed sobriety and institutionalization. She wasn't ready for either course but soon entered a Detroit facility on another therapist's advice. It felt like a prison, and a panicked Stafford barely managed to secure her own release. She made it to Chicago and a branch office of Harcourt, Brace, where—upon Giroux's authorization—she was given a small advance. When she returned to New York, Giroux found her yet another therapist, a friend and Melville scholar named Henry Murray. He had time for only one conversation, on a three-hour walk through Central Park. "I wish he were our father," Stafford wrote her sister. "He makes me see reasons for living." That day, she got a letter from Lowell demanding a divorce. By late November she had gained the courage to check herself into Manhattan's Payne Whitney Clinic. A month later, when Harcourt, Brace published Lowell's *Lord Weary's Castle* to a crescendo of acclaim, she was still there.

Giroux, having visited his brother in Secaucus frequently, was no stranger to asylums; over the coming years he would have a full national tour. He saw Stafford often, bearing copies of *The Mountain Lion* along with rave reviews. He probably wasn't the one to bring her *The Nation,* which on March 21 ran a poem by Lowell, clearly about Stafford, called "Her Dead Brother." She wrote Lowell that the poem "passes beyond dishonor and approaches madness." A month later, Lowell won the Pulitzer Prize. His fame now surpassed Stafford's, and her bitterness soon threatened to overwhelm whatever gratitude she felt for her editor. In 1949 Giroux had the chance to acquire a story collection by Mary McCarthy, who not only was Edmund Wilson's ex-wife—the survivor of a marriage as abusive as the Lowells'—but was now leaving Robert Linscott, the same editor Wilson had abandoned for Roger Straus. A week after he signed McCarthy's book, Giroux told Stafford about it over lunch. "Well, you're not going to be *my* editor if you're hers," she told him. Giroux felt "as if I'd been hit with a wet fish." He gave her over to a subordinate, Denver Lindley.

Lowell, who (like Stafford) had been staying in fleabag New York hotels, was suddenly beset with prizes and job offers. A movie producer phoned Giroux after seeing Lowell in a *Life* magazine spread and asked if the poet was interested in acting. Lowell eventually turned down a plum offer to teach in Iowa in order to become a poetry consultant at the Library of Congress.

During his time in Washington, DC, Lowell took Giroux to see Ezra Pound. The poet had been detained in Italy for making pro-Fascist broadcasts during the war, was judged criminally insane, and now resided at St. Elizabeths Hospital on the Potomac. During recreation hour on the lawn, Lowell introduced Giroux as Eliot's publisher, and Giroux ingratiated himself with an initially hostile Pound by declaring, "I came to pay homage to a *poet.*" He regretted his obsequiousness after Pound began ranting about "Franklin Rosenfeld," "Weinstein Kirschberg" (Winston Churchill), and the Jewish worldwide banking cabal. He recommended a book to Giroux, which turned out to be the anti-Semitic ravings of a treasonous World War II admiral. If Giroux had had any illusions about the romance of poetic madness, they evaporated on those leafy grounds.

The following year, Lowell had his own public crack-up on a

Chicago street and was taken to a Massachusetts hospital. He refused to see his mother, but allowed Giroux to visit his leather-padded room. Giroux tried to convince him to let Mrs. Lowell in, but when he refused, Giroux didn't object. "Even people locked up in cells have rights," he decided. He later blamed some of Lowell's and Berryman's troubles on "problem mothers, who caused difficulties greater than their sons' illnesses."

Just as the first reviews were coming in for *Lord Weary's Castle*, Giroux received an unexpected manuscript—Thomas Merton's autobiography. Monks at Gethsemani, the abbey where Merton was now permanently ensconced, were bound to silence and only did work assigned to them. But the abbot, knowing Merton's talent, ordered him to write his memoirs. Giroux read the spiritual confession overnight, just before Christmas, with "growing excitement." It began with a four-page "sermon-essay," as Giroux called it, "an example of misplaced 'fine' writing," a prolix definition of the "soul." But then it improved, evoking all the bold acts and missteps that had led Merton to the abbey—his follies at Cambridge (but with his love-child scandal deleted), the scene at Columbia, and the ambitions that he'd left behind for his calling. Giroux took the manuscript immediately to Donald Brace. (After Frank Morley returned to Britain, Brace was in charge of the trade department.) "Do you think it will lose money?" Brace asked. "I'm sure it will find an audience," said Giroux, though he doubted his own objectivity and asked Brace to have a look. "No, Bob, I'll read it in print. If you like it, let's do it."

Shortly after Christmas one of the fathers at the abbey handed Father Louis (as Merton was now known) a telegram: MANUSCRIPT ACCEPTED. HAPPY NEW YEAR. Nothing was said about the editing required, but Merton himself wrote his agent two days later that Giroux had "a free hand." The first thing the editor did was cut the opening; he asked Merton to let readers know "who *he* was, where he came from, and how he got there." Merton nailed the real opening after several tries: "On the last day of January 1915, under the sign of the Water Bearer, in a year of a great war, and down in the shadow of some French

mountains on the borders of Spain, I came into the world." Giroux
retained an imagined conversation with God that closed the book,
but persuaded Merton to cut it in half—increasing its power and, as
elsewhere, reining in Merton's grandiloquence. The monk wrote to a
friend that Giroux "did a very good job . . . I am perfectly satisfied to
see anything go out of a book."

After the editing, the final Catholic censor refused to release the
book because the prose was too colloquial. Giroux advised Merton to
appeal directly to the head of the Cistercian Order (as the Trappists
were officially known) in France. The abbot general had no objections, and the censor acquiesced. Giroux then solicited quotes from
a targeted audience of Catholic eminences—Evelyn Waugh, Clare
Boothe Luce, and Graham Greene. Each came through with a blurb.
Waugh not only wrote that it "may well prove to be of permanent interest in the history of religious experience," but also went on to edit
Seven Storey Mountain for British publication.

No one expected *Mountain* to be a bestseller. But even before it
was published, in October 1948, the print run had to be increased—
after its adoption by three book clubs—from 5,000 copies to 25,000.
During the week between Christmas and New Year's, exactly two
years after Giroux had read that first meandering manuscript, sales
exploded: 31,000 in December. The *New York Times* refused to list it as
a bestseller because it was a "religious book," so Harcourt ran a March
ad in the paper giving the sales figures. Giroux reserved copy number
100,000 for a special leather edition to be given to Merton during his
ordination in Kentucky, but by that time, in May 1949, more than
600,000 copies had been sold.

Giroux's best explanation for Merton's unforeseen success was
that it "appeared at a time of disillusion, following the Second World
War, when another war—the cold war—had started and the public
was ready for a change from disillusion and cynicism." In *The Life You
Save May Be Your Own*, a masterful study of four Catholic American
authors, Paul Elie attributes it partly to an Anglo-American "Catholic
moment." Blueblood writers like Lowell, Stafford, and the Tates all
joined the fold, preferring the denomination's metaphors and martyrs

to the secular Protestant mainstream. As Elie emphasizes, it was a new brand of Catholicism, rugged and individual, a wave that would crest during the Second Vatican Council fifteen years later. Giroux, Catholic but very much sui generis, was drawn toward the center of this loosely defined movement.

Both professionally and personally, Giroux often found himself at odds with the Church. When he wasn't fighting censors, he had to face his own ambivalence. He'd soon ask Merton's advice about his complicated personal life. In the early fifties, Giroux began a relationship with Carmen de Arango, a daughter of Cuban aristocrats who split their time between Havana and Greenwich, Connecticut. She served as an adviser to the Vatican delegation to the United Nations. She'd arranged benefits at the Metropolitan Opera, of whose club Giroux was a member, and she'd once been engaged to one of Giroux's old Regis friends.

On August 30, 1952, Giroux and de Arango were married at St. Mary's Roman Catholic Church in Greenwich, with Merton's abbot, Dom James Fox, officiating and Charles Reilly serving as best man. The reception was held at the Arango estate nearby. Giroux's niece Katherine Mulvehill was a flower girl, and remembers being instructed by the bride on the use of finger bowls and the importance of going to college. It was a lavish ceremony, especially by Jersey City standards. Among the guests were the Skakels, parents of the future Ethel Kennedy.

Within a few months, the marriage was essentially over. Giroux's family remains confused about the doomed union; the official story is that Carmen had refused to seek treatment for severe epilepsy. Correspondence from the time accords with family lore. By January 1953, Thomas Merton had already come to know that "something had occurred to spoil things between you and Carmen." A month later he wrote Giroux: "Medicine cannot perhaps do much and maybe she has found that out by experience. But anyway it doesn't seem much to ask that she try it again." He promised to pray for both husband and wife.

The marriage was annulled, according to the family, but de

Arango kept Giroux's name, and the divorce was not made official until 1969. Perhaps they both had something to gain from being officially married. A *New York Times* notice of her death in 1999 listed her as Carmen de Arango Giroux. Giroux's family never saw her again, whereas Charlie became a permanent summer fixture at gatherings on the Jersey Shore. Giroux and Reilly would live next door to each other, buy a country house together, and move together to the same assisted living facility in central New Jersey. Reilly would die a few months after Giroux, in 2009, and Reilly's nephew Hugh McKenna executed both of their wills. Late in his life, Giroux found greater solace in religion, attending church every Sunday. Father Patrick Samway, a Jesuit priest, professor, and biographer of Walker Percy, became one of his last trusted friends. He holds some of Giroux's letters and arranged for the editor's papers to end up at Jesuit-run Loyola University in New Orleans. In death as in life, Giroux and Catholicism have a complicated but permanent relationship.

By 1949, Robert Lowell's patriotic Catholicism was acquiring a manic tinge. He was railing against alleged Communists at Yaddo, the writers' colony where he was a resident. He was also telling anyone who would listen that a Yaddo colleague, a young Catholic writer named Flannery O'Connor, was an actual saint. (Some thought O'Connor, for her part, was in love with Lowell.) In February of that year, just as Harcourt was racing to meet demand for its surprise hit Catholic memoir, Lowell brought O'Connor to meet his editor. As was usually the case with new authors, Giroux had more than one lead on O'Connor; Alfred Kazin, another Yaddoite who was also a scout for Harcourt, had tipped him off about her novel-in-progress. In person, Giroux was blown away; somehow he knew he beheld a genius.

"Lowell was of course vocal and full of interesting phrases, a great talker," Giroux told O'Connor's biographer Brad Gooch. "But she had electric eyes. Very penetrating." Elsewhere Giroux said merely that he "had a hunch" about her, and that "her demeanor, her reluctance to theorize about the book, her integrity impressed me." Unfortunately, O'Connor was committed to Rinehart & Company. They had a firm option on her novel-in-progress, *Wise Blood*—a condition of her $750 Rinehart-Iowa Fiction Award. O'Connor walked away from the Giroux meeting with nothing more than a copy of *Seven Storey Mountain*, which she'd specifically requested.

As it turned out, *Wise Blood* wasn't a novel Rinehart had the stomach to publish. It remains, even today, a delightfully twisted piece of work, centered on a southern preacher named Hazel Motes who strives to establish a blasphemous Church Without Christ. It is religious yet existential, episodic but taut, both hilarious and bleak, and O'Connor was fully confident of its rightness. But Rinehart's editor, John Selby, was sitting on her first nine chapters. Giroux, on receiving them, immediately offered $1,500. Selby finally suggested serious changes in order to soften the "aloneness" in the novel. He added that he assumed she was a "straight shooter"—which she found condescending. "The letter is addressed to a slightly dim-witted Camp Fire Girl," she wrote her agent, suggesting they break with Rinehart. "I am not writing a conventional novel," she wrote Selby. "The finished book, though I hope less angular, will be just as odd if not odder than the nine chapters you have now."

While O'Connor spent the next year revising tirelessly, her agent worked to secure a release from Rinehart. Selby granted one on the condition that Harcourt accept the full manuscript. He also called O'Connor "stiff-necked, uncooperative and unethical." Through most of 1950 O'Connor took up residence in the Connecticut home of Robert Fitzgerald, soon to become a famous translator of classical works, and his wife, Sally. Giroux had known the Fitzgeralds since editing Robert's translation of *Oedipus at Colonus*. That year, when their daughter Maria was christened, Giroux and O'Connor presided jointly as godparents. The final corrected galley of *Wise Blood* didn't come in until the end of 1951, but the delay was understandable. By then, O'Connor had been hospitalized several times, and diagnosed with lupus.

Wise Blood was, by Giroux's own account, "a flop," selling poorly in the wake of baffled reviews that "all recognized her power but missed her point." Yet he recognized that O'Connor could build slowly. The stories she began churning out in the mornings back in Georgia, where she'd moved back in with her mother, were increasingly celebrated. Given the leeway to acquire what he liked, Giroux had moved far beyond Harcourt's legacy books. He and O'Connor were ahead of their time.

Giroux's commercial hits notwithstanding, he needed to be able to take bold risks on debut flops like *Wise Blood*. Under Frank Morley and Donald Brace he had the perfect balance of freedom and responsibility: not only the latitude to follow his own taste but the duty to choose wisely for the house. Occasionally he was too cautious, especially when friends were involved. He had paused before publishing Merton and missed out once on Berryman's work. In 1947, Berryman wrote Giroux that another editor was offering to publish his first book of poetry. Giroux waited too long, making Berryman an offer ten days after the other editor's deadline—once again letting his old friend slip through his fingers.

Giroux became Harcourt, Brace's editor in chief in 1948, at age thirty-four. True to Van Doren's lessons, he was a keen mentor who also learned from his underlings. There was Giroux's elder Denver Lindley, who would soon be editing Stafford, and then the up-and-comer Catharine Carver. Carver had started out as a fiction reader at *Partisan Review*, tipping off Giroux about new authors, before coming to Harcourt, Brace full-time in 1950. A very enthusiastic supporter of O'Connor, Carver would become Giroux's lifelong friend and confidante. Alfred Kazin, a year younger than Giroux but destined for the pantheon of the New York intelligentsia, also scouted for Harcourt. It was Kazin who brought Giroux the manuscript of Hannah Arendt's *The Origins of Totalitarianism*, which had already been rejected elsewhere. As Kazin wrote in his memoir *New York Jew*, Giroux "immediately recognized its quality, went through the enormous manuscript in all-night bouts of enthusiastic reading, and published it. Hannah was launched."

Kazin and Carver both told Giroux, independently, about Bernard Malamud. Giroux sent the writer a warm letter commending his Jewish stories (one, "The Magic Barrel," was about to be published in

Partisan by Carver) and was surprised when Malamud replied that he had a baseball novel in the works. As with Merton, he chanced upon a book with popular appeal. This time it was less to his taste. "It wasn't something genuine, that came from the heart," Giroux told Malamud biographer Philip Davis of the jocky milieu of *The Natural*. But he suspected that "Bern needed a success and wanted a theme which would be successful." As a publisher as well as someone with similar roots— both born to modest means in 1914, both with brothers in mental institutions—he understood the source of that ambition. "Malamud wanted success for himself . . . His beginnings haunted him as they did me when I was trying to make a living."

As they shook hands in Giroux's office in 1951, Giroux said, "I greet you at the beginning of a great career." "Emerson to Walt Whitman," Malamud replied, clocking the reference. *The Natural* was published in 1952 to mixed reviews but relatively brisk sales. On its publication, Giroux told Malamud, "We prefer to publish a writer, rather than a book." It was an odd thing to say on the heels of a *successful* novel, sounding more like consolation than congratulations. But considering Giroux's misgivings about *The Natural,* he may have meant to encourage Malamud to write something less blatantly commercial—to consider the long arc of his career, rather than the next royalty check.

Eugene Reynal, Giroux's new boss in 1948, didn't know much about that philosophy. A New York Social Register aristocrat, a graduate of Harvard and Oxford, he was nevertheless no intellectual. After Harcourt, Brace acquired Reynal & Hitchcock in late 1947, cofounder Reynal became the head of Harcourt's trade department. His credentials didn't impress Giroux for very long. "Terrible snob," he thought. "This man has had one of the best educations possible—why hasn't it done something for him?" Almost simultaneously, a banker type named Spencer Scott replaced the seventy-four-year-old Donald Brace as president of the company. "His background was textbooks, which usually meant trouble," Giroux recalled. A few years later, Donald Brace showed Giroux the company's financial figures going back to 1919: It was in 1947 that textbook sales surpassed trade sales for the first time.

The newly minted editor in chief found his stature growing but his autonomy shrinking. His uncharitable assessment of his two bosses arose not out of envy or personal animus, but from bitter experience. This was the tag team, after all, that cost him *The Catcher in the Rye*.

Just as Reynal and Scott were getting settled, Giroux read with excitement "A Perfect Day for Bananafish," a short story published in the January 31, 1948, issue of *The New Yorker*. Two more stories by J. D. Salinger ran in the coming months, and "everyone was talking about them"—so Giroux typed up a letter to Salinger in care of *New Yorker* head William Shawn. He insisted that he would happily publish the short stories first, rather than push for a novel (novels, then as now, invariably sold better). He didn't hear back and assumed Salinger was making other plans. But several months later, one of his desktop lunches was interrupted by a visit from a Jerome Salinger. It only gradually dawned on him that the tall, dark, shy stranger, who made Giroux think of Hamlet, was J. D. When Salinger insisted he didn't want to publish stories first—he had a novel in the works—Giroux smiled and said, "You're a born publisher." They made a handshake agreement for the novel.

The manuscript arrived in late 1949. Giroux couldn't believe his luck. Holden Caulfield had a genuinely fresh voice, sharp and brave, but also intimate, colloquial—irresistible to anyone who'd ever felt alienated, including Giroux and potentially lots of readers. Giroux sent a rave internal review to his new boss—and didn't hear from him for two weeks. Finally, he strode into Reynal's office. "I think the guy's crazy," Reynal said, meaning Holden Caulfield. He had sent it over to Spencer Scott's beloved textbook division, which turned the novel down. As he often did, Giroux held his tongue. "I felt like saying, 'You son of a bitch,'" he later recalled. Reynal had done far worse than simply make a stupid decision; he had forced Giroux to renege on an agreement with a writer. Giroux appealed to Donald Brace, but the old bookman said he couldn't overrule his trusted hire. The long leash he gave his subordinates, such a boon to Giroux in the early years, now looked to the editor like weakness and surrender.

Giroux revised and polished this nugget in later years: "That's when I decided to leave Harcourt, Brace," he told George Plimpton for a *Paris Review* interview in 2000. He said he handed in his resignation to Brace shortly afterward. Giroux's timing, however, is way off. Little, Brown published *The Catcher in the Rye* in July 1951, four years before Giroux left Harcourt. In fact, he continued to edit brilliant works in the face of growing resistance. When Giroux was editing the American edition of George Orwell's *1984,* he had to cringe silently as Spencer Scott stood in his doorway, shaking his head and declaring, "Bob, love and rats don't mix." Fortunately, Frank Morley had committed to a two-book deal with Orwell, so they had to publish the book. Giroux almost lost E. M. Forster after Scott sent the author a form letter suggesting a royalty cut. Only Giroux's abject apologies kept Forster from leaving.

Giroux's second great miss of the early fifties—*On the Road*—had more to do with the editor than he would later admit. Perhaps he wanted to downplay his own doubts, and his own squareness, in the face of Jack Kerouac's very strange second novel. Or perhaps he was embarrassed by his own impotence.

Mark Van Doren was now mentoring a new generation of Columbia alumni, and it was partly thanks to him, in 1948, that urbane Robert Giroux met the dropout John Kerouac. Van Doren had read Kerouac's first manuscript at the insistence of one of his star students, Allen Ginsberg, and called Giroux to recommend it. (Kazan, Kerouac's teacher at the New School, had already sent the editor a copy.) Van Doren later blurbed: "John Kerouac is wiser than Thomas Wolfe, with whom he will be compared." The day after Van Doren's call, Giroux was surprised to be visited by Kerouac himself, manuscript in hand. In a dark suit and tie, Kerouac came off a "very sober, neat-looking fellow." Over lunch, they discussed their shared French Canadian ancestry as well as the difficult upbringing of Jean-Louis (as he called himself) in Lowell, Massachusetts. Giroux signed him up for a thousand-dollar advance. Kerouac, already rejected by Little, Brown, signed an ecstatic letter to a friend: "BET-A-THOUSAND KEROUAC."

The manuscript that would become *The Town and the City* stretched to 1,100 pages, and indeed reminded Giroux (and Kerouac) of Thomas Wolfe's *Look Homeward, Angel.* It was lyrical, autobiographical, and loose, but would prove to be the founding Beat's most conventional work. "In that period Jack saw himself as [Thomas] Wolfe . . . and me as Max Perkins," Giroux later wrote a friend. The Scribner's editor, who died in 1947, had spent unending days and nights carving Wolfe's meandering reams into publishable chapters. Giroux was flattered if slightly abashed by the comparison. "I don't believe there was as much editorial work as the Perkins-Wolfe team experienced," he wrote a graduate student. But he did cut more than a few windy, pseudointellectual dialogues, mostly from the beginning. Each did their bit to play up the Wolfe-Perkins routine. Giroux once lost track of an original copy of a Kerouac story, then realized "I had put it, symbolically no doubt, in my copy of the Max Perkins letters." Kerouac wrote a long dedication to Giroux for *The Town and the City,* in the spirit of Wolfe's grandiose public notes to Perkins. Harcourt policy forbade such dedications, so Kerouac settled on "To R.G." But he had two special copies made with the full note inside, one for himself and one for Giroux.

The Perkins-Wolfe jokes were a way of smoothing a slightly uneasy relationship. Kerouac brought Giroux home to see his mother, who worked in a shoe factory on Long Island. She said he looked more like a banker than an editor, meaning it as a compliment. "Jack," she told her son, "you stick with him and keep away from those bums you're hanging out with"—meaning William Burroughs, Neal Cassady, Allen Ginsberg, and Lucien Carr. (Cassady thought Giroux looked more like a private detective.) In July 1949, Giroux flew to Denver to meet Kerouac, ostensibly to correct galleys but really to get to know him better and, as he wrote the author, just to get out of the office. In Denver he and Kerouac hitchhiked for half an hour—the very idea of which so confounded Giroux's secretary that she nearly crossed out his reference to it in a letter. Kerouac bragged to his hip buddies that the "Golden Boy of Publishing . . . hitch-hiked with me in my wilderness." That summer he urged Ginsberg to submit his poetry to Giroux. "He knows you. He agreed dead eyes see," he wrote, bizarrely, of his editor. But Kerouac reminded him "that he is also a big businessman . . . a stockholder in the company, editor in chief, and member of the Opera Club (with the Rockefellers.) Be smart, now, and don't shit your pants."

Giroux embodied the straight world, a place Kerouac respected, feared, and loathed all at once. He told Giroux that the editor's New York skepticism resonated with the writer's calming, logical side: a superego, in so many words. "He quite sensibly told me that the laurel wreath is only in the moment of writing," Kerouac wrote in his journal. And yet Jack considered the bearer of this lesson—art for its own sake—a flawed messenger: "I had seen that my being a published writer was going to be merely a sad affair—not that he intended to show me that. I saw how sad he was, and therefore how the best and highest that the 'world' has to offer was in fact empty, spiritless; because after all he is a great New Yorker, a man of affairs, a success at thirty-five, a famous young editor."

In New York, Giroux took Kerouac, in his rented tux, out to the ballet, where the handsome wunderkind was fawned over by male artists like Gore Vidal. "Giroux was sort of in love with him," says Kerouac's onetime girlfriend Joyce Johnson, who published a memoir about the writer in 2012. "It was common knowledge among his friends." Neither she nor others who were close to Kerouac knew if Giroux had ever made any blatant admissions or propositions. He must have known that Kerouac experimented with men, yet Giroux was incredibly discreet. At any rate, their correspondence makes clear that they regarded each other with strong but complicated affection. Their first rift was over *The Town and the City*'s low sales. Kerouac's friends disapproved of Giroux's cuts to *The Town and the City*, as well as his wining and dining—calling the Harcourt office "the rose bushes." Kerouac himself began growing skeptical once the novel was published, to disappointing sales; he complained that Giroux hadn't done enough to promote it.

In Denver, Kerouac had shown Giroux a few journal notes for the book that would become *On the Road*, but he wasn't ready to share manuscript pages. In April of the following year, after several false starts, Kerouac spent twenty days writing nonstop, hopped up on what he insisted to Neal Cassady was little more than coffee. He was still angry with Giroux over his handling of the first novel but convinced that his brilliant new manuscript would turn things around. Giroux told George Plimpton his version of what happened next:

> Kerouac phoned one day in great excitement, saying he had just typed the last sentence of his new novel and wanted to come over right away. The word *stoned* was not yet in use but there was something hyped up and frantic about his condition, and I thought him drunk. He soon stood in my doorway with a big roll of paper under his arm, as fat as a kitchen paper-towel roll. He held one end and tossed it across my office like a long string of confetti, yelling, "Here's my new book!" Instead of congratulating him and taking him to a bar to celebrate, I foolishly said, "Jack, don't you realize you'll have to cut this up for the printer. We'll need separate pages for editing, too." He became red with rage and bellowed, "The hell with editing! Not one word is to be changed. This book was dictated to me by the Holy Ghost!" Over my protests he rolled up the paper and stormed out of the office and, I thought, out of my life.

Kerouac went begging to other publishers, and by the time Viking put out *On the Road* six years later, it was greatly changed. "All the biographers claim I rejected *On the Road*," Giroux added, "but the fact is that I never read it until [Viking editor Malcolm] Cowley sent me an advance set of proofs." Kerouac's letters, some of which were in Giroux's possession, tell a more complicated and plausible story. Kerouac spent the next two months revising the scroll, which—whatever he may have said in the heat of epiphany—was never meant to be the finished copy. A letter to Cassady in June has Kerouac "waiting for the word from Giroux" on a revised version; two weeks later he writes to Neal: "Giroux says HE likes the book but is sure the President of the company and the Sales Manager won't—even tho it's 'like Dostoevsky' (he says) they don't even read Dosty and don't care about all that shit and bums etc. Giroux says Harcourt expected me to write

AGAIN like Town & City and this thing so new and unusual and controversial and censorable (with hipsters, weed, fags, etc) they won't accept." Johnson, herself unsure of the absolute truth, says Kerouac told her much the same thing. Nor does she fault Giroux: "A lot of people were very disconcerted with *On the Road* when they read it, including people like Allen Ginsberg."

Kerouac's letter implies Giroux might not even have shown the manuscript to Reynal or Scott. Perhaps, by 1951, he knew how they would respond. Perhaps he was providing cover for his own reservations. He had already declined Kerouac's offer to look at William Burroughs's *Junky*, writing, "If I thought there was any chance of our offering Mr. Burroughs a contract for his book about drug addicts, I would ask to see the manuscript." As late as 1952, a Kerouac friend offered to pay off his unearned Harcourt balance if the publisher would accept *On the Road*. Giroux wrote back flatly refusing: "It would be a disservice to him and his future literary career." He added, "John's feelings about the second book are very strong, however, and who knows if he is right and we are wrong?"

As it happened, the next publisher to look at *On the Road* was Farrar, Straus & Young. FSY wanted revisions, but Kerouac withdrew to make his own extensive changes. He was still casting about for a publisher in 1954 when he wrote a long, maudlin letter to Giroux. Kerouac thanked him for his work on the first novel, something "I guess I never formally told you." By this point, he was "some kind of unpublished freak." He wondered, "What has happened to our friendship or was it just based on business?" And near the close of the letter he wrote, "Maybe I've gone crazy but by God I like to remember the times when we talked about Yeats and watched pigeons."

Even setting aside "freaks" like Kerouac, Harcourt, Brace seemed increasingly indifferent to its best writers. If George Orwell, E. M. Forster, and Edmund Wilson were feeling disrespected, what chance was there to hold on to new talents like Hannah Arendt and Randall Jarrell? Jarrell, a poet, critic, and key figure in Lowell's circle, went with Harcourt for his first book, then Dial for his second and back

to Harcourt—and Giroux—for his third. But by 1949 he was court-
ing other publishers. To New Directions' James Laughlin he wrote,
"Harcourt always seemed to me grudging and dreary—they made me
feel that publishing the poems was a minor cultural duty." The gentlemanly Laughlin asked Jarrell to explain himself first to Giroux. He did,
the following February, with a litany of complaints, concluding, "This
isn't the way an *ardent* publisher behaves." Giroux talked him into staying, but two years later, Jarrell went to Knopf.

The day after Alfred Kazin heard about Jarrell's departure, he
wrote Giroux with a sense of alarm. "What has happened to turn
Jarrell against H.B. and Co.? Can anything be done to salvage the
situation? . . . Jarrell is the sort of writer we have always taken great
pride in publishing; his future is of the greatest promise. Another such
writer is Hannah Arendt." Oxford University Press was pursuing her,
and Kazin feared she would be next. "Can nothing be done to keep
Hannah at Harcourt?"

It's difficult to tell exactly what drove Jean Stafford away. Giroux
patiently endured broken deadlines, and when she scrapped a novel
in favor of the one that would become *The Catherine Wheel,* he simply
wrote the new title into the old contract. It was published in 1952, followed by a story collection, *Children Are Bored on Sunday,* in May 1953.
Reviews for both books were strong. But in between, she balked at the
next contract. Giroux drove her to a ship leaving for the Virgin Islands,
where she was to divorce her second husband, Oliver Jensen. The editor brought along a new contract and she signed it—only to write him
from the boat asking to cancel it. A few months later, Stafford had a
dispute over the sale of British rights to *Children* and left for good. She
described tensions with Harcourt as "a narrative that has been unfold-
ing for eleven years." She considered a handful of other publishers
before settling on Random House and the renowned editor Albert
Erskine. One of the highest bidders, offering ten thousand dollars, was
Farrar, Straus & Young—already going after Harcourt, Brace refugees.

In 1954, William Jovanovich replaced Spencer Scott as Harcourt's
president. He had also come up through the textbook division, but
he was self-made, and more concerned with maintaining Harcourt's

cultural clout. He cultivated friendships with writers like Mary McCarthy and Hannah Arendt, thereby keeping them at the firm. Giroux never disparaged him in public as he did Scott and Reynal. In fact, he took pains to deny that they ever had personal tensions. But years later he allowed some bitterness to filter into a letter he wrote to Kazin, in reference to a profile in which Jovanovich "has announced his 'personal' editing of Hannah Arendt, Charles Lindbergh, and Mary McCarthy . . . Read it and weep." He later told an FSG staffer about another perceived outrage, one that helped him decide to leave. Jovanovich had had the temerity to suggest that editors should be going out to bookstores in order to persuade buyers to order their books.

Jovanovich's ascension did nothing to improve Giroux's life. He remembered putting out E. E. Cummings's collected poems "in the face of Reynal's indifference," and only by appealing to Brace did he manage to publish his last enduring masterpiece at Harcourt—and perhaps the most difficult work of his young career—William Gaddis's *The Recognitions.*

Just as it was being published, Giroux got one of several calls from Roger Straus, following up on Sheila Cudahy's tip. Over the next few weeks they hammered out his departure from Harcourt to become the editor in chief of Farrar, Straus & Cudahy. On March 25, 1955, he announced his resignation. One of his last encounters with Donald Brace, the "inside man" with the rare smile, took place in Giroux's office, six months before Brace died. The retired chairman handed Giroux a cable from London. T. S. Eliot had written: "Dear Don, Bob tells me he is leaving and I want you to know I'm offering him my next book." Giroux recalled being "so moved that I could say nothing." Neither could Brace, who left without speaking a word.

4

Protestant, Catholic, Jew

One of the first works that Bob Giroux brought over to FSC's offices at 101 Fifth Avenue was a drawing. Behind his desk he placed a three- by four-foot framed illustration by James Thurber, from Harcourt's 1942 collection *My World, and Welcome to It.* The *New Yorker* humorist's pencil sketch featured a pair of classic Thurber hounds. One dog bounds through a meadow toward the other one, which bays soulfully (perhaps haughtily) at the moon. Giroux named the drawing "Author and Publisher," which amused Thurber, and he gave his editor the original—one of his last. Presumably the publisher is the pouncer, the author the aloof beloved.

In the first few months of his new job, Giroux had to restrain his puppy love for his authors. He needed to bring over as many of his Harcourt discoveries as he could, without appearing to. He believed strongly in the honor code that forbade the poaching of authors from rival houses, but these were *his* authors. The test of his staying power and that of his still-green employer, with the literary world watching, was his ability to coax as many authors over as subtly as possible—to play the distant pooch but pounce when necessary.

Giroux claimed personal offense at form letters, whether sent by publishers or politicians or Con Edison, but his responses to the letters of congratulations that poured in from friends, rivals, and authors were virtual carbon copies. "I am more grateful than I can say for your good wishes," they began almost invariably. "I find my new duties stimulating and challenging," they went on, playing it cool. On occasion he did add a gleeful note: "I feel like a new man," he wrote to Houghton Mifflin editor Anne Ford in early April. "Thomas Merton has received an official release," he added. "There will be others too."

The next writer to come was Paul Horgan, a prolific novelist-historian and bon vivant (Edmund Wilson thought him "an endearing and slightly ridiculous figure"), whose study of the Rio Grande, *Great River,* had just won the Pulitzer Prize. He and Giroux, bachelor Catholics who moved in similar circles, got along instantly.

A month later, Robert Lowell sent Giroux a note that teased, "Please give my best to that young author you are launching, Mr. Eliot." He also apologized for delays in "my plan to take leave of Harcourt Brace, at least for my prose at that time . . . I have no doubts and can't imagine that HB will try to hold me. What do you advise me to do about my verse? Shall I come to Farrar for the works, my works?" He wanted to know whether he should immediately sign a contract and try to transfer previous work. Giroux marked up his copy of the letter in red pencil, underlining "the works, my works," and writing a big, circled "YES" in the margin.

Not every author came so readily, nor was every publisher or agent as gracious about Giroux's move as Anne Ford was. He wrote to Peter du Sautoy, by then head of Faber and Faber in England, to inquire into the availability of Louis MacNeice's *Collected Poems,* and was refused. He only found out much later that du Sautoy had strongly advised Eliot against leaving Harcourt. He also had lunch with Malamud's agent, Diarmuid Russell.

"I'm not going to let Malamud leave Harcourt," Russell said of his client.

"I've never asked Malamud or any other author to leave," Giroux answered.

Russell groused, "You editors are always playing musical chairs."

"Diarmuid," Giroux said, "I've been at one place for fifteen years, and I intend to spend the rest of my life at the other."

Giroux had in fact rejected Malamud's second novel, *The Man Nobody Could Lift*, in 1953, while still at Harcourt. The decision wasn't ultimately his, but he largely agreed with the first reader, advising Malamud: "In terms of your career, I hope you will put it aside." But then, a year after Giroux's departure, Harcourt declined *The Assistant*, Malamud's most autobiographical novel and possibly his greatest. Harcourt's reader did not believe it to be "a step upward" from *The Natural*. He knew it might mean losing Malamud, "and this I regret." Russell had also submitted it to Viking Press, whose rejection was less equivocal: "I see no sales, and I don't believe it would get favorable critical attention."

Russell may have been holding out on Giroux, because it was Malamud who told the editor about their rejections. Giroux's first reaction was shock, followed by "muted elation that we would be reunited." When he read *The Assistant*, he knew his elation was justified; here was the real culmination of those Malamud stories, something—unlike *The Natural*—rooted in lived experience. Over the next two decades, *The Assistant* would sell well over a million copies. The next book, *The Magic Barrel and Other Stories*, won the 1959 National Book Award.

In the matter of Flannery O'Connor—whose career-making book of stories, *A Good Man Is Hard to Find*, was nearing publication—Giroux acted in good faith but also served his own best interest. He left O'Connor in the hands of his protégé at Harcourt, Catharine Carver, telling her Carver "did all the work anyhow." But in June, just as *A Good Man* came out, they had tea to talk over his new situation and her new contract. "He looked better than when I saw him in the fall," she wrote the Fitzgeralds. He advised her to add a clause requiring a renegotiation if Carver left Harcourt. Carver did, within a year (something her good friend Giroux may already have known). After that, O'Connor amended the contract to state that she would leave if Giroux's successor Denver Lindley departed as well. She made these changes only after Giroux promised he'd take her on if she left Harcourt.

Condemned to a short, sickly life and confined to her mother's house in Georgia, O'Connor preferred stability to uncertainty in her practical affairs, and stayed with Harcourt as long as she felt she could. But she would not go down with a sinking ship. Robert Lowell, much closer to the New York scene, wrote to Elizabeth Bishop about the atmosphere at Harcourt. He'd gone to a dinner party at Denver Lindley's, only to find everyone "in a state of mute gloom." Lindley's wife, he recalled, had spent more than an hour ransacking her bookcase, "obsessed to prove" that Edmund Wilson, another Harcourt refugee, "was a bad stylist."

Lindley left Harcourt, Brace in April 1958, while O'Connor was still laboring over her second novel. Harcourt's editors beat a path to her Georgia farmhouse to have "tea" and convince her to stay, and when she asked her agent, Elizabeth McKee, what she should do with them, McKee suggested she poison the tea. Instead, O'Connor signed up with Giroux.

During the three years it took for O'Connor to take up "where I left off," Giroux not only lassoed Merton, Eliot, Lowell, and Malamud; he closed in on virtually every member of the Lowell-Stafford circle. Elizabeth Bishop, the poet who perfected a deceptively natural, plain-spoken style, carried on a long-distance relationship with the circle while living in Brazil. She tested her editors at Houghton Mifflin by proposing they publish her translation of the sixty-year-old diary of a poor Brazilian teenaged farm girl. Houghton Mifflin, which had never been interested in her prose, declined—in spite of the fact that their 1956 Bishop collection, *Poems: North & South/A Cold Spring,* had just won the Pulitzer Prize. Giroux accepted the diary for Farrar, Straus on the condition that he could become her regular publisher. He would have to wait years to secure her release from Houghton Mifflin as a poet, but he earned her loyalty in the interim.

Bishop distrusted publishers, Farrar, Straus included; she complained about the design and cost of corrections for the book that became *The Diary of Helena Morley*. She knew, however, that Giroux cared for all her work regardless of status or sales potential, a fact of which Lowell (though he mocked Bob from time to time) reminded her. In the summer of 1957, just as Bishop was haggling over jacket copy with Giroux, Lowell wrote that he'd run into Houghton Mifflin's Paul Brooks, "who said breezily to me, 'It seems absurd that I should have to ask you the address of our own author, Miss Bishop.' All the age-old author and publisher rifts began to widen in me and I said, 'But isn't she a Farrar and Straus author.' Then I said something about how much I admired your stories [the stories they'd rejected], and we parted rather coldly."

Giroux called his old friend John Berryman immediately after arriving at FSC. Berryman had published parts of a long poem, *Homage to Mistress Bradstreet*, in *Partisan Review* and anthologies, but not as a stand-alone book. He was also bound to Viking Press for a stalled biography of Shakespeare. By the end of April, Giroux had secured Viking's release on the condition that Farrar, Straus repay its $1,000 advance—which they did, as part of a $2,000 contract for both *Bradstreet* and the Shakespeare book. At long last, Berryman was with Giroux. "I really think I'm going to die of happiness and excitement," the poet wrote to his mother the day he got the contract.

Giroux gained far more than an old buddy; *Bradstreet* was Berryman's first major work. His imagined dialogue with a historical female Puritan poet was muscular, daring, and dramatic, climaxing in a bravura childbirth scene that stunned readers of both genders. Giroux, sending Berryman the galleys a year later, was "struck again by its power and beauty. How marvelous that we are publishing it!" A month after that, in July 1956, he cabled Berryman the news that Edmund Wilson, "who rarely gives quotes," had provided a blurb: "*Bradstreet* seems to me the most distinguished long poem by an American since *The Wasteland*." Giroux concluded, "Bravissimo."

The finished book, with Expressionistic illustrations by Ben Shahn, was a masterpiece of both poetry and design. Berryman inscribed a copy for Giroux with a personal dedication:

To Bob

—to whom the physical existence of this thing is due, and after 20 years
of unbroken friendship, & more particularly: I was dying, not in brain but
in heart & spirit, when you rescued me with this—so that I can hope to
do some more—

w. admiration & affection
John   (15 July 56)

The Edmund Wilson quote was indeed a feat, coming from an author even Straus almost never had the temerity to solicit, for fear of getting one of his notorious postcards in reply: "Edmund Wilson Regrets That It Is Impossible For Him To:"—followed by a list of twenty-one tasks beginning with "Read manuscripts." But Wilson's antipathy to publishers seemed to have softened, at least when it came to Roger Straus.

Wilson's long and promiscuous life with publishers (prior to his late-blooming monogamy at Farrar, Straus) had meant at least a glancing familiarity with nearly every major editor of the twentieth century. He had worked with Maxwell Perkins for years before one of his legendary fallings-out. Giroux had, of course, edited—lightly— Wilson's *To the Finland Station*. But he only met the great critic for the first time at a party at Jason Epstein's on New Year's Eve 1955. Giroux told him about his new job, and Wilson startled him with his intense, owlish glare. Then he said: "Inspire Roger! That's what the house needs, inspiration."

No one knows exactly when Straus and Giroux made their pact never to truly retire, but they did it early in their collaboration. They shared the attitude that the firm in which they eventually became near-equal partners (as near as Roger could allow) was the cause and devotion of their lives.

For Roger, this was another point of rebellion against his father. Roger Straus, Sr., didn't like people overstaying their welcome. He thought his elders had held on too long at American Smelting and Refining, forcing him to wait until 1947 to take over as chief executive. When he finally did, Roger Sr. instituted mandatory retirement at age sixty-five. Making an example of himself, he stepped down from ASARCO five months after his sixty-fifth birthday, in April 1957. There was plenty to keep him busy into his old age: the National Conference of Christians and Jews; the state Board of Regents, of which he was elected chancellor; the Guggenheim foundations; and the family's hunting and fishing grounds in the Catskills.

In his fishing lodge that July, Roger Sr. suffered a massive heart attack. His son Roger Jr. got the call in the middle of the night, and it was he—not Oscar, the favored son, or Florence, a wealthy housewife in Chicago—who made the drive up to the local hospital to see his comatose father just before he died.

Roger Jr. returned to his corner office at Farrar, Straus & Cudahy in shock. He seemed "lost," remembers Helen Weaver, who worked in the production department at the time. "He looked much younger, like a little boy—vulnerable, which is a word you wouldn't think of applying to Roger Straus. That cocky, sometimes arrogant mask simply disappeared. We all noticed it." Roger's frequent foil, his cold fish of a father, was gone, and resentment gave way to regret.

Roger brooded on a couple of things in the wake of his father's death. For one, there was no longer any opportunity to prove his worth. His mother would come around to recognizing his redemption, but his father would never get the chance. "My father was 'the fuck-up,'" says Roger Jr.'s son, Roger III. "And as often happens in those family situations, that stuck long after he stopped fucking up." Roger Sr.'s last big piece of advice to his son was that he should sell Farrar, Straus to *Reader's Digest*.

Straus's other preoccupation was the link between retirement and death. It wasn't just Giroux but the entire firm that absorbed his ethos. Employees who stayed with Farrar, Straus were never dismissed for old age. They might be sidelined, shoehorned into smaller offices, sometimes even openly mocked, but never fired. Farrar would be the first in a long line of diminished gray eminences stalking the halls or napping on their fainting couches. For Roger Jr., this quirk—in fact, all his rebellions—sprang from a kind of filial love, a determination to redeem the perceived mistakes of his father. He believed Roger Sr. had been stifled by family expectations, so he defied them. He believed his father had been killed by early retirement, so he foreswore it.

Roger Jr.'s safari-going grandmother, Oscar's widow Sarah, had died just before the war ended and Farrar, Straus was founded. Her son, Roger Sr., had long preferred the Catskills grounds to the Purchase, New York, estate where his mother lived, and he put the latter property up for sale. Roger Jr. told Peggy (but no one in his family) that, one day, a wealthy South American had taken a helicopter over Westchester County in search of a house grand enough for his country quarters. The manor house on Sarosca Farm—the one grandpa Oscar had loved so much—caught his eye between the trees, and he decided to buy it. Before the sale could go through, however, Roger Jr. tracked him down and explained how much the house meant to him. He retracted the offer and Roger scrambled to get the money together, so that he could pay his own father for the property. (Much of it came from his wife's Rheingold Brewery fortune.) Roger only bothered to tell his sister, Florence, about it a couple of years before his death. All along she thought Roger Sr. had passed it on. "Come on sis, don't be so naïve," he'd shot back. "I bought it."

Roger moved into the manor, and like everything in his life, it became an extension of the publishing house. Downstairs and out at the pool, visiting author-dignitaries would be received and entertained in high summer-villa style, with cocktails at the appointed hour, cold salads and ripe peaches newly plucked from the garden, followed by a dip in the pool. (Roger would change quickly, dive in, start on his backstroke, and shout, "Ah, it's good to be rich!") Only those who ventured upstairs, perhaps to use the extra bathroom, would register the private counterpoint to the boss's public finery: Straus's bare, almost Spartan bedroom, with nothing but a few books and manuscripts lying around. The agent Candida Donadio compared it to a monk's quarters, and told a friend it convinced her that "beneath all this crap is this rather pure idea of the value of literature."

In other areas, Roger wound up hewing surprisingly close to his father's attitudes. He came around, for example, to the assimilationist ideals espoused by the National Conference of Christians and Jews. Though he had resented Roger Sr. for bundling him off to a gentile boarding school just to prove the religions could mix, Straus sent Roger III to Choate, which was still quite restrictive in the fifties. "I'm not sure he disapproved of the fundamental philosophy" of assimilation, says Roger III. "He wanted to both affirm his sense of class and show the goyim that we didn't have horns." Roger III calls boarding school "the worst four years of my life," and to this day he thinks to himself in his lowest moments: "At least I'm not at Choate." Once, on a home visit, he arrived in tears, only to be reprimanded: "Toughen up and get used to it. You're a Straus and that's part of it."

If any publishing house could mirror the ideals and demographics of the National Conference of Christians and Jews, it would be Farrar, Straus & Cudahy. In a field divided between WASPs (Doubleday) and Jews (Knopf), FSC had one representative of each group, plus a Catholic for good measure. Thanks to Cudahy and Giroux, it already had a strong Catholic reputation; its tenth anniversary was celebrated in Catholic publications. It wasn't just Flannery O'Connor, Thomas Merton, and the Vision Books: Humanitarian doctor Tom Dooley, Jesuit thinker John LaFarge, and Catholic historian-novelist Paul Horgan all published with FSC in the late fifties. The "Catholic moment," as Paul Elie called it in *The Life You Save May Be Your Own,* was after all Giroux's moment; three of the four writers in Elie's book were Giroux writers.

The sociologist Will Herberg, in his late-fifties study *Protestant Catholic Jew,* defined an era when American culture was growing more secular and more religiously identified at the same time. Religion, Herberg argued, was the true melting pot, boiling dozens of nationalities down into only a few self-identified classes. Thus could the Irish and Italians come together under one distinct American identity; thus could the Germanic Strauses embrace Yiddish stories and eastern European mysticism as a part of their culture.

Third-generation groups were rediscovering affiliations their parents had forsaken—and this was especially true of Judaism in the wake of the Holocaust. Herberg was himself a Jewish writer published by Farrar, Straus (*Judaism and Modern Man*, 1951). "Serious works dealing with Jewish faith and destiny began to find interested readers precisely among the most American segments of the Jewish community," he writes of the time period. A footnote lists six of the most influential works, four of them published by Farrar, Straus (the fifth was by a writer frequently published by FSC and the sixth was for Schocken, which FSC distributed). Not on that list was Rabbi Philip Bernstein's *What the Jews Believe*, published by FSC in 1951, which sold more than one hundred thousand copies over the next five years, helping Roger weather the post–Gayelord Hauser slump.

The most important of these authors, at least to his publisher, was Abraham Joshua Heschel. Straus's father had been a donor to the Jewish Publication Society, which ran a book club of roughly ten thousand members. One of its board members introduced Roger Jr. to Heschel, a Polish-born philosopher-rabbi descended from Hasidic gentry. In 1950, Farrar, Straus collaborated with the JPS to publish Heschel's second English-language book, *Man Is Not Alone*.

Straus's partnership with the JPS lasted a decade, until it cooled in the late sixties over a dispute about who deserved credit for "discovering" Heschel. (Indeed, many of Straus's fallings-out resulted from seemingly trivial fights over credit.) In 1957, Straus and the JPS collaborated on a juvenile line called Covenant Books, a Judaic answer to Sheila Cudahy's Vision Books. Rather than lives of the saints, they featured Jewish heroes ranging from Albert Einstein to Myer Myers, "Silversmith of Old New York." It was a miserable failure, which Roger later gave a slightly anti-Catholic gloss: "I suppose as a Jew I should have realized that the business of selling a sort of chintzy juvenile literature to the Catholics was a little bit different than selling chintzy juvenile literature to the Jews."

Heschel, on the other hand, was both fairly successful—his next book, *God in Search of Man*, was a breakout—and an object of great reverence. Straus addressed him in letters as "Dr. Heschel" for decades, something he did for no one else. After Roger Sr.'s death the Strauses would attend Heschel's earnest but leisurely Passover Seders every year. (The rabbi would also officiate at Roger III's bar mitzvah.) His daughter, Susannah, says her father "found the religious side in Roger that other people would say didn't exist." Part of it was also a reverence for his grandfather Oscar. Heschel was a vocal advocate for fellow European theologian Martin Buber, and with Heschel's help Straus published a long lecture by Buber. Roger met Buber once, at the Jewish Theological Seminary where Heschel taught, in 1953: "There was this little man, tiny, white haired, and he looked so much like my grandfather Straus it almost knocked me down."

If the Strauses were following the path designated by Herberg, moving closer to a unified notion of Jewish identity in the wake of the Holocaust, it was not Heschel but Isaac Bashevis Singer who finally led them into the promised land. The novelist and story writer, who came to Farrar, Straus in 1960, was a serial blasphemer and adulterer, but a very spiritual one, with the added value of being a literary genius and, as Straus once put it, "the most marvelous little gnome I've ever seen in my life."

Like Heschel, Singer was a Polish refugee descended from shtetl rabbis. But he and his older brother, Israel Joshua, had answered the calling of literature rather than religion. Israel had become a minor star after Knopf published the translation of his Yiddish novel *The Brothers Ashkenazi*. But he died young, in 1945, leaving Isaac to carry on alone in the new family profession, largely in the pages of the Yiddish *Daily Forward*. Isaac's grief—over Israel's death and over the Holocaust—was poured into his novel *The Family Moskat*. Singer re-created on its vast canvas a complete lost world of characters, both archetypal and irreducibly unique, hurtling collectively toward the oblivion of World War II. Alfred Knopf published the novel in English in 1950, but insisted on cutting out roughly two hundred pages. Singer thought Knopf had torn its heart out and vowed never to publish with Knopf again.

It was a short story titled "Gimpel the Fool" that first caught the attention of New York's literati. Saul Bellow translated the fable in 1953 for *Partisan Review*. After hearing it read aloud at a party, an editor named Cecil Hemley, who ran a small intellectual publishing house called Noonday Press, signed Singer up. Jealous of Bellow's increasing fame, Singer never let him translate another story; instead he relied on rough translations by his nephew, Joseph, Israel Singer's son. It was left to Hemley, his wife, Elaine, and his assistant, Elizabeth Pollet, none of whom knew Yiddish, to craft Singer's work into polished English. Together they produced *Gimpel the Fool and Other Stories* and a novel, *Satan in Goray*. Another novel, *The Magician of Lublin*, was about to go to press just as FSC acquired Noonday in 1960.

Singer's Yiddish-inflected sweetness clashed endearingly with his gargoyle features, to say nothing of his rigid routines and irrepressible womanizing. He also appealed to Roger as a specifically Jewish author. Singer shared more with Heschel than a similar history: Both writers presented the United States with a corrective to the rationalist Germanic culture that had dominated the American Jewish literary elite. The ghosts of the Holocaust had everything to do with the popular appeal of the dybbuks, or demons, in Singer's supernatural stories. It was right there in the jacket copy of Farrar, Straus's 1965 reissue of *The Family Moskat* (with all of the Knopf cuts restored), which described the book's subject as "the civilization that vanished into the gas chambers twenty years ago."

Dorothea would become even closer to Singer than her husband was. (She was also a closer reader of Heschel—but then she was a closer reader of almost everything.) Her book *Under the Canopy* is devoted to her and Singer's friendship and the ways it awakened her Jewish identity, building a bridge between her wealthy secular roots and the deep spirituality of the shtetls.

One of Dorothea's essays, "Singer's City," immortalizes his visits to the Purchase manor. Dorothea had explained to Singer that Oscar S. Straus's former study—now an extra bedroom festooned with heirloom photographs, mounted butterflies, and a Victorian bed—was called "the ghost room." Singer insisted on visiting the room alone, hoping to encounter the shade of beloved Oscar. "Well, Isaac," Roger asked when he finally came down, "did you see Grandfather's ghost?" "No, I did not," Singer answered, then explained that ghosts showed themselves most often to skeptics. He said this while looking at "cosmopolitan, intellectually sophisticated" Hal Vursell, who was also visiting. A letter from Vursell to Singer confirms the encounter, and also Vursell's little conversion. "I must hurry to tell you, in all seriousness," writes Vursell, "that at about 1:00 last night I woke up to find a poltergeist in my bedroom."

As Singer's English improved he would become his own first translator, collaborating mostly with non–Yiddish speakers to produce the finished work. Many were young girls whom he flirted with or seduced; others were just friends—including Dorothea. She would visit his building on the exotic (to her) Upper West Side and watch Singer read aloud a spot translation straight from the Yiddish *Forward*. Occasionally he would ask for synonyms. At the end of the session he would pay her $71.03, sometimes saying, "It's a pleasure for me to make a check out to a rich woman." In "Singer's City," she noted the oddity of the two of them working so closely together. "We are like remote cousins with contrasting nationalities and family customs . . . Singer and I never cease to marvel inwardly at our difference at the same time that we recognize our kinship." She would, of course, join Roger a decade later when they flew to Stockholm to watch Singer accept the Nobel Prize.

The Jewish and Catholic strains of FSC came swirling together at the turn of the sixties, as Straus, Heschel, and Giroux became embroiled in the Vatican's Second Ecumenical Council, known as "Vatican II." Pope Pius XII had reigned during World War II and been criticized for not standing up to Hitler. John XXIII succeeded Pius in 1958 and almost immediately called for Vatican II in order to "update" the church in myriad ways. One of these was to address, and perhaps erase, the Catholic charge that the Jews were responsible for killing Jesus. Abraham Joshua Heschel, as house theologian for the American Jewish Committee, went to Rome and cultivated close ties with the official in charge of redrafting Catholic doctrine on the Jews, the elderly Augustin Cardinal Bea.

Vatican II was convened in October 1962 and concluded in late 1965. During that time, it was intermittent front-page news, but the best accounts of its internal machinations were published by *The New Yorker* and Farrar, Straus. There was intense speculation about the identity of the author of "Letters from Vatican City," known only as "Xavier Rynne." The pseudonymous cleric's rambling but juicy reports treated the conference for what it really was—political jockeying among a rabble of all-too-human bureaucrats. He depicted a Pope intent on reform but stifled by a powerful group of conservative advisers, the Curia. The Holy See may as well have been the Kremlin.

The man behind "Xavier Rynne" was only publicly revealed decades later (though his identity was an open secret): a priest named Francis X. Murphy. And behind Murphy was the editor who brought his groundbreaking coverage to light, Robert Giroux. Giroux first heard of him through a Catholic editor named John Chapin who did workman-like FSC compilations like *The Treasury of Catholic Reading.* Murphy had shown Chapin a rough draft of his insider reports, and Chapin had decided, instead of reaching out to a Catholic magazine, to phone Giroux. "It will make a book," Chapin told Giroux. "It might even make a piece in the *New Yorker.*" Giroux agreed and asked Chapin to put it "in *New Yorker-ese.*" Numerous "Letters from Vatican City" ran in that magazine, and the four volumes Straus and Giroux published became bestsellers. In order to boost the international impact of Murphy's books, Straus enlisted his friendly scout, the ex-spy Silvio Senigallia, to distribute them among influential journalists stationed in Rome.

Late in the game, as the Vatican examined the question of the Jews, Heschel and the American Jewish Committee made intense behind-the-scenes efforts to influence official opinion. They enlisted a mysterious Jesuit, Malachi Martin, to help them. By some accounts, including Straus's, they were secretly paying him. In any event, Martin, an Irish priest and Biblical archaeologist who knew many Semitic languages, was sympathetic to the cause. He was helping Cardinal Bea draft the proposed *schema* absolving the Jews of deicide. Or so he claimed; it was sometimes difficult to know exactly how close Martin was to the centers of power. "In each of his yarns, he always found a good role for himself, perhaps too good," wrote Robert Kaiser, who covered Vatican II for *Time.* "Invariably, he was the sleuth and the hero of each tale, a black-cassocked Sherlock Holmes." (The book in which Kaiser wrote these impressions, *Clerical Error,* focused largely on Martin's seduction of Kaiser's pregnant wife. Kaiser cast him as a serial seducer in contempt of his priestly vows.)

After Pope John XXIII died and was succeeded by the weaker Paul VI, a new Jewish doctrine looked greatly imperiled. So in 1964, Heschel asked Straus for a big favor. The rabbi believed a book by Malachi Martin, written and published quickly under a pseudonym, could perhaps spur the Vatican to act. Roger trusted Heschel and, of course, agreed with his ultimate aims. He rushed the publication of *The Pilgrim,* by "Michael Serafian," in an unprecedented (for Farrar, Straus) six weeks. He persuaded British, German, and Italian publishers to translate and rush copies through as well, so that they could be distributed to Council participants high and low.

Heschel's biographer Edward Kaplan considers the book's revelations to be "a treacherous blend of fact, overstatement, and invention." The Pope is portrayed as benevolent but weak—a plausible enough picture, though Martin/Serafian also included less plausible anecdotes to which he was the only witness. Malachi Martin was eventually laicized and persuaded to leave Rome. He spun Straus vague tales of mysterious plots against his life in order to explain his flight to the United States (omitting rumors of his seductions and double dealings). To his later regret, Roger was enamored of the dashing archaeologist. He compared Martin to a dear friend of the Strauses, the influential renegade priest-paleontologist Pierre Teilhard de Chardin. Teilhard, a suspiciously close friend of Dorothea's cousin Rhoda de Terre, had frequently stayed with the Strauses in New York before his death in 1955. He was Roger's kind of cleric, a charismatic figure who spoke his mind and always had something to say. So was Martin.

Shortly after leaving Rome, Martin sought Straus's help in getting established in New York. Roger not only pleaded successfully with his uncle Harry Guggenheim for a study grant; he paid for Martin's airfare. The result, years later, was *The Encounter,* a fat volume condemning the modern shortcomings of all three monotheistic religions. Among its inaccuracies was a misquote, hastily corrected in the second printing, that had Heschel calling the Pope a Nazi. His next book would be rejected outright, on grounds that it was incoherent and anti-Semitic. He'd have to publish his increasingly paranoid books elsewhere. It would have been no great loss, except that Lila Karpf, FSG's talented subsidiary rights director and Martin's devotee, would follow him out the door. It was the rare example of Roger's instincts leading him far astray.

Shortly after Martin arrived in the States, Roger invited him to a dinner party at East 70th Street. The "extra woman" at dinner was Kakia Livanos, the ex-wife of a shipping magnate. She and Martin got along very well. Martin had found a new advocate and benefactor. The following morning Livanos called Dorothea to say that Martin had come home with her. She had one question for Dorothea: "Is he a devil or is he a god?"

A few years after Heschel died, his daughter, Susannah, wrote Straus that she was shocked to find a French cookbook in the Farrar, Straus catalog. "We must have a long talk," he wrote back, "but let me make a point—had I not published certain books (now hold your breath) like Gayelord Hauser's LOOK YOUNGER, LIVE LONGER, Quentin Reynolds' COURTROOM, and let us say a novel or two by Frances Parkinson Keyes, I could not have afforded to publish your father and several other distinguished poets, philosophers and novelists."

That may be true, but publishing a few bestsellers on their own wouldn't have been enough. Farrar, Straus could never have afforded a list on which nine-tenths of the books bled money. Just as often, what shored them up was the kind of steady trickle of income that a stellar backlist, accruing over time, can provide on the strength of its prestige: orders for college reading lists; foreign sales; permissions fees; the possibility that a *Christ Stopped at Eboli* or an *Homage to Mistress Bradstreet* will continue to sell copies every year for more than a generation.

One easy way not to lose money on such work—particularly poetry—was to win the Nobel Prize. In the late fifties, armed with international contacts and a sensitive ear for gossip, Straus began to chase Nobels in earnest. His Spanish agent, Carmen Balcells, tipped him off in 1957 about an obscure Spanish poet named Juan Ramón Jiménez, and the company churned out a collection just before he won the Nobel. Two years later, Sheila Cudahy, on one of her Italian sojourns, reported a rumor that the aging poet Salvatore Quasimodo was due for a Stockholm surprise. They put together selected writings with what Roger called "malice aforethought," and by the time the book was published, he had already won. Even Giroux's T. S. Eliot, late in his career, could be considered a token Farrar, Straus Nobelist. The 1956 tenth-anniversary FSC catalog devoted a full page to announcing its first Eliot title, *The Cultivation of Christmas Trees*. It was hardly *The Wasteland*.

Decades later, Jason Epstein dismissed Straus by saying "he wanted nothing but Nobel Prize winners." Never mind the oversimplification: Epstein implied that commerce and prizes are incompatible. But for a scrappy publisher like FSG (as opposed to Bennett Cerf's Random House, Epstein's long-term employer), a prize like that is a major financial boon. The Nobel also furnished authors with substantial financial security, making it that much easier for them to accept low advances from a publisher who was friendly, accommodating, and lavish in other ways.

Of course there were other shortcuts to success. One was to court a little controversy, without quite tarnishing the brand. Farrar, Straus was no Grove Press—eager defenders of D. H. Lawrence and Henry Miller in court—or even Random House, which fought the 1930s ban on *Ulysses*. But, religious leanings notwithstanding, it wasn't exactly backing away from the vanguard, especially when moving forward could bring in a few extra dollars. That tenth-anniversary catalog yielded two bestsellers along such lines. Alec Waugh's *Island in the Sun,* a skillfully executed interracial Caribbean romance, outsold the abstruse *God in Search of Man* ten times over. *Reader's Digest* paid an unprecedented $100,000 to condense it, and the launch party, held on the SS *Santa Rosa,* was sponsored by a cruise line, a leisurewear clothing line, and 20th Century Fox, which bought film rights.

The second bestseller, Nelson Algren's *A Walk on the Wild Side,* reunited Straus with one of his prewar book-packaging clients. Algren documented the sensational low life of New Orleans's Storyville neighborhood in the 1930s with a flair Straus couldn't resist, giving the world such one-liners as "Never eat at a place called Mom's." Cudahy, having acquired Algren through Chicago connections, assisted Straus in "editing" the book—a process that consisted of finding a suitable euphemism for every anatomical reference in the novel. "The thing was up to here in 'cocks' and 'cunts,'" Straus remembered, clearly more comfortable with the words than his Catholic partner.

Straus said Algren was just fine with watering down his salty language if it meant selling more copies or avoiding lawsuits. By this point, it may not have made a difference. *Lolita,* rejected by Straus, was published by G. P. Putnam's Sons in 1958, leading to phenomenal sales and nary a court challenge. Meanwhile, Roger had spent four years trying to overturn New York State's injunction against Edmund Wilson's unexpurgated *Memoirs of Hecate County.* Wilson's indictment of upper-class suburbia had been banned decades earlier for its insufficiently euphemistic depictions of sex ("portals" that "made things easy for the entrant with a honeysweet sleek profusion," etc.). Trusted FSG attorney Patrick Sullivan had discouraged Straus from pressing the case; Wilson believed it was because Sullivan was Catholic. In 1956 they retained a different lawyer to plead with the Manhattan district attorney's office. Straus predicted success, only to get, as he wrote Wilson, "the back of their hand."

Both Straus and Wilson were motivated by profit as well as conviction. Wilson's first two books with Farrar, Straus sold fewer than four thousand copies combined by 1951. In the ensuing years, Farrar, Straus released a succession of mostly repackaged Wilson books: two more volumes of literary criticism to follow *Classics and Commercials,* two reissues, and a collection of five plays. Together they left Wilson in the red, despite modest advances. The only Wilson book that made money in the fifties was *Scrolls from the Dead Sea,* and that belonged to Oxford University Press, which had shelled out five thousand dollars—above Roger's limit.

Wilson needed a hit even more than Straus. He had neglected to pay taxes for several years, and the IRS caught up with him in 1958. His debts were set at almost $70,000, and both his book income and his modest trust fund were threatened with government garnishment. *Hecate County* could help in a big way. Straus happened to know the district attorney, Frank Hogan, who had succeeded Roger Sr.'s political hero Thomas Dewey. Hogan intimated to Straus that he could go ahead and release *Hecate County*—"Just don't rub my nose in it." This meant it wasn't to be published, sold, or advertised in the state of New York. The only way Farrar, Straus could do that was to exploit the company's latest acquisition—"the best buy we ever made"—L. C. Page & Company, conveniently headquartered in Massachusetts.

In May 1956, during his customary morning scan of the papers, Straus came across the capsule obituary of Lewis C. Page. Page had founded the Boston publishing house L. C. Page & Company in 1896. By the time of his death, at eighty-seven, L. C. Page had a backlist of roughly a thousand titles, including the *Anne of Green Gables* and *Pollyanna* children's book series as well as the classic *Extraordinary Popular Delusions and the Madness of Crowds*. Page was as old-fashioned as his list, abhorring "sophisticated" publishers. Straus inquired into the firm, and found out that Page had made no plans other than to sell the company (along with its Boston town-house headquarters) and split the proceeds among his beneficiaries.

Straus and his treasurer, Robert Wohlforth, engineered a layaway plan, a down payment followed by payoffs from subsidiary rights. The Boston town house was part of the package, so they hired a broker to resell it within six hours of the purchase, and in short order Farrar, Straus nearly doubled the number of titles under its control. It was a costly plan (FSC posted a loss in 1958), but it gave Roger a backdoor way to publish *Hecate County* out of state. Boston's L. C. Page, little more than a shell corporation, was its official publisher. Gayelord Hauser had subsidized the publication of Edmund Wilson; now Pollyanna was doing her part. The cheery, anodyne fare favored by Lewis Page had made it possible for scenes of graphic, adulterous mutual orgasm to infiltrate the nation's bedside tables.

By the early sixties the IRS was threatening to throw Wilson in jail. What Roger did next would enshrine him as one of those rare publishers who advanced the art by saving a writer from certain ruin. It also set a pattern in his dealings with the closest of his writers.

With the intercession of Pat Sullivan, the Wilsons worked out a repayment compromise. Straus helped out by securing the sale of Wilson's papers to the Beinecke Library for $30,000 and offering $20,000 for the writer's gossipy diaries—not a bad deal, because today the five-volume set is perhaps our most complete (and certainly most entertaining) chronicle of northeastern intellectual life in the twentieth century. It contains sections at least as graphic as *Hecate*'s sex scenes (Wilson lifted some almost word for word). The diaries would be vetted to ward off not censors but libel suits. The advance was structured as a low-interest loan. Roger frequently "prepaid" advance money to meet Wilson's IRS deadlines—$10,000 in March 1960—and would vouch personally, from his private funds, for several other bank loans to Wilson throughout the sixties. Over time, some loans were converted into advances for reissues or new books.

Wilson's tax neglect was partly ideological—a principled refusal to pay for foreign entanglements such as Vietnam. (He covered this in Farrar, Straus's 1964 volume *The Cold War and the Income Tax.*) But negligence played the dominant role, putting the lie to Wilson's persistent self-confidence in business affairs. Roger implored Wilson to hand over the foreign rights to his books. "You are making a silly decision in handling your own major foreign rights," Straus wrote him in 1960. "Frankly, the fact that you have no French public is simply absurd . . . God knows the commission we ask for handling these foreign rights is not considerable." Wilson resisted at every turn: "You are mistaken, by the way, in thinking that anybody else would do better than I can in selling my books abroad." In a few cases, he finally relented—particularly for British rights on the journals that helped pay off some of those bank loans. After Straus's key subsidiary rights director, Paula Diamond, managed to make a French deal three years later, Roger couldn't help gloating: "Damn it—I knew it would work, as well it should!" Straus may have been indebted to Wilson in countless intangible ways, but when Wilson died, in 1972, Roger was one of his creditors.

5

Not a New Look but a Nice View

Everything changed in 1960, for publishing and for Farrar, Straus &
Cudahy. The first of three major shifts at FSC wasn't even in the
office; it was the renovation of the Strauses' town house at 171 East
70th Street. Naturally, it was written up in the *New York Times:* "One
evening last spring," wrote Rita Reif in the April 9 edition, "Mr. and
Mrs. Roger Straus Jr. were lamenting their party-giving problems,
common to many New Yorkers, to a painter friend, Francis Scott Bradford." The tall, narrow building—elegant but rather dark—had been
a bargain back when the Third Avenue El rumbled less than a block
away. Now its Victorian quirks were impeding the flow of crowded
literary soirées the Strauses were hosting almost weekly. Nothing had
to be done with the private areas of the house: the second floor with
his and hers bedrooms (his spare, hers gauzy); the third, which Roger
III had to himself; and the top floor, where the servants lived. Only the
parlor floor, the public floor, needed work.

Roger and Dorothea put their full faith in the imposing man they called "Brad." A well-known painter in certain circles with a specialty in murals, Bradford immediately mastered the art of interior decoration. He designed modular benches that could double as chairs; he replaced leaded windows with sheets of clear glass; he knocked down the wall between living and dining areas, tore up fussy moldings, built bookshelves that seemed to float in midair, replaced a banister on the curving staircase with brass poles and gold ropes. The finishing touch was a pale-toned Bradford original filled with geometric avian forms, a sort of domesticated Kandinsky. "The whole project," Bradford told the *Times,* "was put together in one throw of the dice, win or lose." The Strauses felt they'd hit snake-eyes.

Bradford was a jack-of-all-crafts. He was also Dorothea's lover. The two met at a party and, a few days later, Bradford's wife called and asked Dorothea to sit for a portrait. The couples became friendly and frequented each other's houses. (The Bradfords split their time between an Upper West Side studio and a farmhouse in Cornwall, Connecticut.) Dorothea wrote an essay about Bradford:

> His face was rather small and he had a snub nose with sensual nostrils, a long upper lip and a round deeply cleft chin. Despite his age, his face often reminded me of the young Charles Lindbergh. His eyes were deep set and small and of undetermined color, as though their intensity had burned away their original hue leaving only spark and depth. Near them other eyes looked blind. And at times their light was more than human. Prometheus must have had such eyes.

Bradford was born in Wisconsin—a "Fourth of July American," Philip Rahv called him—and was destined for law school until he was shot in the head during World War I. From that point on he devoted himself to painting, especially murals. He often complained to Dorothea that murals had gone out of fashion; he might have been the best muralist in the United States, but "we are all dinosaurs." He couldn't have been more different from Roger.

The relationship was not a secret, even to an adolescent Roger III. "I have a feeling that the important part of her relationship with

Bradford was cerebral," he says. "They were both passionate about philosophy; they would read stuff and talk about it together." Bradford, who had severe heart trouble, died only a year after completing his work on East 70th Street, never to see it resonate with the contentious exclamations of Susan Sontag, Tom Wolfe, or Joseph Brodsky. Years later, Dorothea noted, a Mozart symphony would summon up the Bradford studio smell of turpentine, wood shavings, and paint—a pungent remembrance of things past for the Proust addict. Roger worried, his son remembered, that "my mother would be lonely, because [Roger] knew that Bradford was this intellectual guy. My father was many things. He wasn't an intellectual."

Nor were his affairs quite so cerebral. Though Roger's literary taste was far more conservative than that of, say, Barney Rosset, who published and defended *Naked Lunch* at Grove Press, he was not exactly sexually repressed. By the early 1960s, he was probably sleeping with three of his female employees. At the very least, there were a switchboard operator and a publicity director. They were opposite physical types, but that didn't seem to matter. "Roger would fuck a snake if you held it down," says one employee from that time period. These two women, who were good friends, went shopping together and bought Roger matching bathrobes so that their boss would feel equally at home having "lunch" at either of their apartments. The rumor went that the man who delivered fresh towels in the office on Fridays—a long tradition at Farrar, Straus—also provided Roger with fresh sheets. Giroux would make sideways remarks about his partner's returning with wet hair in the afternoon. The work liaisons lasted through the seventies.

Roger and Dorothea surely had some kind of understanding, something like the district attorney's warning over *Hecate County,* Wilson's chronicle of upper-class adultery: "Just don't rub my nose in it." They led the kind of lives that fifty years later we call "compartmentalized." That doesn't mean it was easy, or fair. Dorothea kept a list of women she suspected him of sleeping with. Open with her son to a fault, she once told him—he was maybe ten years old—that she hadn't had more children because another pregnancy might make her less desirable. Even Straus would occasionally feel guilty about what he put women through. One weekend, Roger camped out at his Westchester country club, brooding over whether he should leave Dorothea for another woman. According to a friend, he concluded, "It's not worth it," and came home.

"The three of us led fairly separate lives," says Roger III. "Both of my parents retired early so we went to our separate rooms fairly soon. I wouldn't have been privy to what was going on, but I always felt that the public world, which for them was Farrar, Straus, was more important than whatever was going on between the two of them."

In this arena, Mrs. Straus definitely made her mark. Roger, who gave credit where it was due but rarely enough of it, told his oral historian that his wife would occasionally advise him on a French novel or "a Virginia Woolf type book" where, "to say something rather chauvinist, a woman's eye might be useful." This notion that Dorothea was nothing more than a sounding board on "female" issues, like an ad exec's wife putting in her two cents on a lipstick campaign, was a convenient fiction for husband and wife. "My mother always said that she had nothing to do with Farrar, Straus," says Roger III. "That was really preposterously inaccurate." In fact, Straus called Dorothea "my Heschel specialist"; he confessed to Giroux that he didn't always understand the rabbi, and that Dorothea read whole manuscripts before he did (if he did). Heschel was not "a Virginia Woolf type"—whatever that meant.

Straus was smart enough not to engage his writers on turf that would diminish him or undermine their confidence in the worldly publisher. But how deeply, and how perceptively, did he read? The most common theory, especially among those who saw him lug manuscripts up to Purchase for the weekend, is that he didn't so much read books as "read in" them, as he sometimes put it—enough to get a nose for them, like fine wines. One former editor, Susan Sontag's son David Rieff, makes a plausible observation: "He was an autodidact," says Rieff, "the reader's equivalent of someone who listens to music and is pitch perfect. He just knew the difference between the real stuff and the fake stuff, which is the real difficulty."

Dorothea's primary duty, in any case, was not reading but hosting. "Dolly," in her wide-brimmed Mr. John hats and delicate veils, frequently clad in black dresses of indestructible silk sewn by a Russian exile who went by the name of Countess Jora, was as much a conversation piece as a conversation maker. ("I think my mother saw an Aubrey Beardsley drawing when she was young and never recovered from the experience," says Roger III, referring to the Art Nouveau illustrator.) But her talk was always of the highest order, filling in exactly those gaps left by Roger's spotty book learning. Edmund Wilson discussed with her the hidden merits of Dickens; Francis Steegmuller and his wife, Shirley Hazzard, asked her thoughts on Jean Cocteau. Roger, meanwhile, would tell them how he was going to make them money, keep their books in print, and get them into Swedish libraries—all with a broad smile, a "baby," a pat on the back, and a bit of filthy gossip thrown in for good measure.

The charm of a Straus gathering lay partly in the anachronisms. The Bradford décor may have been contemporary, but the rules hadn't changed much since the Belle Epoque. Even at more intimate dinners, the attire was black tie. There were many small courses, like medallions of duck in plum sauce. Dorothea would "turn the table," forcing guests to switch the conversation from the guest on the right to the guest on the left. After the fruit and cheese were served, the women went up to Dorothea's quarters, while the men stayed downstairs with brandy and cigars.

Dorothea's friends were more prevalent at dinner. Some authors who published few if any books with Farrar, Straus—Lillian Hellman, Philip Rahv, Jerzy Kosinski, Charles Jackson—were at least as close to her as they were to Roger. Farrar, Straus had rejected Kosinski's *The Painted Bird*. Although Straus loved it, Bob Giroux and a few other editors didn't like its queasy blend of fact and fiction, and he let their decision stand. (Later he came to regret "the whole business of democracy at an editorial meeting.") But Kosinski remained a close friend of Dorothea's until his suicide in 1991.

Charles Jackson, who had written *The Lost Weekend* for John Farrar at Farrar & Rinehart, published two story collections with Farrar,

Straus, but then went elsewhere with a novel they rejected. Yet the Strauses were loyal friends through the depths of his drug and alcohol addiction. He even spent some evenings at 171 East 70th Street. On one such night, he attempted suicide, and had to have his stomach pumped. An early memory of Roger III's is the sight of Jackson vomiting in their house. He wrote many letters to Dorothea, half-jokingly flattering her self-image as the modern incarnation of a Belle Epoque society lady. "*Chère* Mme. Straus" was his standard salutation—referring to Geneviève Straus, the Parisian salon hostess and dear friend of Marcel Proust.

On the whole, though, the Strauses came as a package. "They were Fred Astaire and Ginger Rogers," says Roger III. "If there were a better host and hostess than the two of them, I've certainly never seen one—in part because they had a sort of yin-yang effect. My father was very warm and personal and welcoming, and my mother was rather cerebral and intellectual. And so between the two of them they took care of the whole person."

The space in which this intricate dance was staged—set design by Francis Bradford—sometimes seemed to belong more fully to Farrar, Straus than it did to its occupants. "It was like a museum," says a European publisher who visited only once. "Sometimes you go into a house and you feel nobody lives there." Roger III compares the town house on a night without a party to "an airport runway waiting for the plane to come in. The main function wasn't being performed; the landing field was there but it was waiting for the plane."

Though Roger III had his own interests, especially photography, he was quickly drawn into his parents' orbit. "My parents thought they were hot shit," he says, "and I thought they must be right." He doesn't remember his father coming to his baseball games. Instead he'd attend his father's tennis matches—as the ball boy. "So it was warm, but it was warm on his turf." That turf was usually the business.

"Rog" or "Young Roger," as most took to calling Roger III, began working for his father around the age of fifteen, riding in a station wagon through New England with the firm's sales director, John

Purtell. The golden age of the independent publisher was also the era of local bookstores, and maintaining relationships with them meant racking up a lot of miles. "I'd take an inventory and give them a list of the books that they had in stock, and then you'd do backlist orders," says Rog. He joked that he was a canny hire: "There is a certain shock appeal in being so young. Buyers might have worried that if they didn't take my books I would cry."

While Farrar, Straus was finding its sea legs as a family firm, another was on the rocks. Alfred A. Knopf, a wealthy and sophisticated German-American Jew, had founded his eponymous firm in 1915 and built it into the powerhouse literary publisher of the century. Alfred and his wife, Blanche, had plundered Europe for writers and returned with books by Mann, Kafka, Freud, Joseph Conrad, and D. H. Lawrence. They were a formidable family but a fractious one. Their son, Alfred Jr., known as Pat, was expected to take over, but in 1959 he defected to establish his own company, Atheneum. That same year, a more commercial-minded Jewish firm, Random House—founded in 1927 by Bennett Cerf and Donald Klopfer—had come to its own crossroads, and decided the best way to keep growing was to place their fate in the hands of the stock market. Random House's public offering left them overflowing with cash but beholden to stockholding strangers. In April 1960, Alfred A. Knopf sold his firm to Random House. The latter then also acquired Pantheon, an equally esteemed house founded by European refugees Kurt and Helen Wolff. A wave of mergers and public offerings would follow across the industry, not least of all RCA's takeover of Random House in 1965.

Straus was, by this point, as frequent a European traveler as the Knopfs; finally feeling free to roam, he and Dorothea made annual semi–business trips to Rome, Paris, and London. Mary McCarthy wrote him in 1960 to thank him for insisting she lunch with Silvio Senigallia in Rome, and also for sending her the work of the Nobelist poet Salvatore Quasimodo. "Have you got the corner on Italian books?" she teased. "Is it a move to becoming the Alfred Knopf *de nos jours*?" Straus knew Knopf; they were neighbors in Purchase and dined together a few times. But he found Knopf's Teutonic seriousness and his obsession with wine exhausting and pretentious. Roger didn't collect wine or anything else—except authors. He wrote McCarthy back that he resented being pigeonholed as "the poor man's Knopf or the smooth version Knopf or the thin Knopf."

In fact, in the same letter he announced to McCarthy a move to emulate Knopf—the second major change of 1960. "And now a bit of news from the undersigned," he wrote. "We have officially taken over Noonday Press . . . It means, of course, that we will enter the quality paperback field and I hope with a bit of muscle."

Five years before leaving, Alfred Knopf's prodigal son had convinced his parents to start the Vintage line, entering a new field just beginning to be known as quality paperbacks. These were larger than mass-market paperbacks, and weren't always bestsellers. They looked, felt, and read more like hardcovers. Mass-market paperbacks, the stuff sold in airports and department stores, had been around for a long time, but in the wake of World War II and the G.I. Bill, as college populations exploded and high culture began merging with mass culture, it became clear that a new category of books—highbrow but affordable—could occupy a powerful niche. The pioneer of the field was Jason Epstein. In his memoir *Book Business,* Epstein explains the genesis of his big idea:

> When I became a publisher it was my undergraduate encounter with books that I wanted to share with the world. I believed and still do that the democratic ideal is a permanent and inconclusive Socratic seminar in which we all learn from one another. The publisher's job is to supply the necessary readings. But in 1951, publishers were not performing this function well, and Anchor Books seemed to me an obvious corrective.

Epstein's brainstorm was as business-savvy as it was high-minded. Anchor Books could be sold in both airports and university bookstores; they could replace cumbersome and expensive cloth volumes in libraries. Their potential market was broad and untapped. And they could be run under the umbrella of a hardcover house—in Anchor's case, Doubleday.

This wasn't the way things had worked up until now. Mass paperbacks were so different—in terms of manufacturing, sales outlets, size of printings, and target audience—that no hardcover publisher short of a vast conglomerate could efficiently make and sell them. The way it would usually work—and the way it would work for Farrar, Straus for the rest of the century—was that a hardcover publisher like Knopf or Doubleday would contract a writer for all rights. Then the hardcover publisher would turn around and license the rights, which it owned, to an exclusively paperback house—Pocket Books, Bantam, Avon—for a fixed term of seven years or so. The profits and royalties from the sale would then be split between the hardcover publisher and the author, usually fifty-fifty, often helping to offset the hardcover publisher's advance. At Farrar, Straus such income made up the bulk of subsidiary rights, which also included foreign sales, serial rights, and permissions. (Agents would come to handle more and more of these rights over time.) The "subrights" portion of Farrar, Straus income in 1960 was roughly 10 percent, which meant the difference between profit and loss. Such divisions of labor later came to seem byzantine, but they were the status quo, and the status quo was only just beginning to wobble.

Because he didn't do paperbacks, Straus had to share Edmund Wilson with Anchor's Epstein, who was even more faithful to Wilson's demands. (Roger called him Wilson's "number one boy Jason the Ep.") This was the kind of publishing Straus thought he could handle on his own. He often spitballed such business ideas with a salesman named Harry Wolff, who worked for his father at H. Wolff & Company, Straus's printer. Harry Wolff, Sr., was generous to Roger, extending a line of credit and tolerating missed deadlines. Harry Jr., meanwhile, gave Roger free advice. FSC, he said, needed to "adjust their spread"—in other words, to diversify: a beefed-up juvenile department, a paperback house, perhaps even a textbook line. Roger had tried some of these before, and he did indeed sell children's books. But Harry had a concrete suggestion. A small, high-quality paperback house known as Noonday was just about to go under. Even generous H. Wolff had stopped printing their books due to unpaid bills. If Roger wanted to adjust his spread into paperbacks, he could do worse than to buy Noonday.

Noonday-Meridian had been run in much the same way Farrar, Straus was. There was a financier, Arthur Cohen, and a literary mind, Cecil Hemley, and together they occupied a niche somewhere between New Directions and the more mainstream FSC. Hemley and Cohen parted bitterly in the mid-fifties, with Cohen taking Meridian and Hemley holding on to Noonday. Hemley published magazinelike collections of new work, and popularized such foreign writers as Boris Pasternak, André Gide, Knut Hamsun, and Hermann Hesse.

The son of a wealthy New York lawyer, Hemley took money for granted and had no idea how to hold on to it, never mind how to make more of it. Which isn't to say he was frivolous with it. He ran a gallery in Provincetown that helped launch Abstract Expressionism in 1949. He was also a poet and novelist of small renown. But by the late fifties he could barely support his family, much less Noonday. Selling was the only option, and FSC the only suitor. Straus made the usual layaway deal for Noonday—it was cheaper than L. C. Page—and hired Cecil Hemley and his assistant, Elizabeth Pollet.

Noonday wasn't the only growth strategy Roger considered. Immediately, he redoubled efforts to bring in new investors to beef up his shiny new paperback line. One potential stockholder, playwright and journalist Harvey Breit, was asked for $70,000 and declined. Straus then entangled himself in a complicated scheme involving exactly the sort of big corporate deals he would later decry. He heard that Thomas Tilling, a British bus company, was looking to unload a group of literary publishers known as Heinemann. Straus enlisted Frank Manheim, a banker whose son was a close friend of his son, Rog, in a plan to have textbook giant McGraw-Hill buy Heinemann—a rare intercontinental takeover. Roger envisioned Farrar, Straus becoming the trade division of some kind of consortium. The real prize in the deal would have been an instant backlist for Noonday. Anchor and Vintage had succeeded because they had access to the entire backlists of old, established parent publishers. Noonday had only fifteen-year-old FSC. Maybe Heinemann's collective riches were the ticket.

Straus and Manheim arranged and attended meetings in London and New York, but the Heinemann board backed off, and the deal fell apart. A few years later Straus tried another middleman scheme, also via Manheim: They'd get the giant conglomerate Gulf+Western to buy E. P. Dutton. Dutton would then want to unload the backlist of Everyman's Library . . . right into Noonday's coffers. This plan, too, was aborted.

After Gulf+Western acquired Simon & Schuster a decade later, Straus would rail against the damage conglomerates were doing to publishing. Around that time, the details of that first Heinemann deal came out, too, and Roger felt compelled to deny publicly that he'd planned to be "taken over" as part of the acquisition. It was a moot point, as Farrar, Straus's role in both deals had been left vague. Whatever the case, such machinations would have given the company breathing room at some cost to its independence. It remains somewhat a matter of luck, good and bad, that this wouldn't happen for another thirty years.

Facing dingy, overgrown Union Square Park, 19 Union Square West, which Farrar, Straus & Cudahy made its headquarters in September 1960, wasn't much of an improvement over 101 Fifth Avenue. A rabbit warren of partitioned spaces squeezed into every available nook of the fourth floor, their new home afforded only two or three offices with decent views and abundant light. One of them was Roger's corner perch, with windows facing both the park and East 15th Street and enough space to accommodate a long conference table inherited from Gladys Guggenheim Straus. The new neighborhood's distinguishing features were a grungy green swath, grungy discount stores, and discount rent—$2.75 per square foot, Roger liked to brag. "The new address reflects not a new look but a nice view," Roger told one of his authors.

The clutter of the office stopped at Roger's door—he was fanatical about a clear desk—but the grimy blue-and-white-checked linoleum

floor tiles did not. Over the next half century, while giant corporations uptown clad their trophy imprints in blond wood, frosted glass,
and floating shelves, there would be precious few cosmetic changes at
Farrar, Straus: replacement floor tiles in varied clashing colors, a paint
job every other decade in an office here and there, and thick glass at
reception, seemingly to guard against armed robbery. The office was
a common subject of clever mockery from writers and editors alike.
Roger liked to say it signaled that Farrar, Straus spent its money on
authors, not overhead.

Into these shabby quarters shuffled the new hire, Noonday's Cecil
Hemley, an editor as rumpled as his new surroundings. "Cecil looked
like an unmade bed," says Roger III. "His hair was all over the place.
But he was a brilliant editor." Hemley's head left a distinctive black
smudge where it touched the wall behind his swivel chair.

Far sleeker was Hemley's great aesthetic contribution, the Noonday logo, which still defines Farrar, Straus today. Straus's style team,
led by Hal Vursell, had played around with various colophons, from a
pop-colored "FSY" in an oval to a series of rods and joints forming an
atomic-style folding screen. Finally, they decided to steal Noonday's:
three fish stacked head to tail, one atop the other, each comprising
three clean triangles and a dot-eye slightly north of center. While lack-
ing the curvy grace of Knopf's leaping wolfhound, it had a balanced,
versatile geometry all its own. But it was also slightly odd, as a publicist noted. "You have to look at it correctly," she said. "When you turn
it on its side you get two goys shaking down a Jew." She meant Farrar,
Cudahy, and Straus, respectively. Eventually, Roger bought a ring en-
graved with those distinctive three fish. Chunky, square, and gleaming
gold, it bore a vague resemblance to a papal ring—or maybe that of a
mafia don.

The Farrar, Straus logo is so engrained in the consciousness of
savvy readers that seeing it on sixty-year-old Noonday compilations
provokes cognitive dissonance. To say that FSC simply appropriated
the logo is not enough. What Roger Straus and his company did,
with the logo as well as with its defining editors and writers, was to
absorb them into its DNA. It's something very few corporations are

able to do, whether they're buying a rival, a book, rights to a film, or any other kind of widget. Just as Roger turned a few lucky turns into a life mission, he had a preternatural gift for turning the components of Farrar, Straus into a coherent culture—from which, if things were working right, its employees and authors and logos and cover designs became inseparable.

He also had a drive to matter—and a drive for his authors to matter—that Cecil Hemley did not. Even Hemley's great friend and best writer, Isaac Bashevis Singer, knew that. As Singer's tireless translator, Hemley was beloved by the author, who sometimes implored Straus to treat the editor better. On the other hand, Singer later called Noonday "the poorest publisher I ever heard of—it reminded me of a Yiddish publisher." He did not mean this as a compliment. Hemley's son Robin has written, with fondness, of his father's lack of ambition: "I can't say that my father knew how big Singer would become; in some ways, he probably didn't care."

Straus had a different outlook. He set out to make Singer famous. Subrights director Paula Diamond made herculean efforts to sell him abroad. Singer's work—including *The Magician of Lublin,* which came out in 1960, and the story collection *Short Friday* in 1961—sold well and earned mostly rave reviews in the States, but he was still unpublished abroad. Where he was known, he was confined conceptually to the very ghetto from which he had escaped. FSC's Paris scout, Herbert Lottman, urged Diamond to take a very low French offer on *Satan in Goray* because many publishers had already declined: "Yiddish writers have no significant public in France." Diamond shot back: "Of course he's a Yiddish writer but he's also one of the finest and most original writers anywhere . . . Singer's books will never reach the people they are meant for until publishers stop boxing him in with definitions."

The French publisher, Stock, reluctantly raised its offer from $200 to $250. In 1963 they paid $350 for a short novel, the next book in the Singer program at Farrar, Straus. Soon afterward, they finally took up a long-standing option on *The Magician of Lublin,* which they hadn't been particularly keen on. *Magician* went on to win France's Prix du Meilleur Livre Étranger, the national prize for best foreign novel of 1964.

Singer didn't trust agents, but unlike Edmund Wilson he had little interest in foreign-rights negotiations. He never seemed to complain about advances as low as $500 per book. He was so prolific (with a backlog of untranslated work) and had such low expectations that money was not a problem. When Straus advised him to cap his annual salary at $20,000 for tax purposes, Singer thought the notion of making that much was absurd. Within three years the ceiling was raised, then raised again. Singer was unsparing in his praise for "Mr. Straus," letting him know, in one letter, "how much I appreciate all this, what you are doing for me in making my works known and also financially. Since I am connected with you, I am, thank God, going up and I know that it could happen only because of your talents and because of your good will. It is the first time in my life that I can say that I am happy with a publisher."

Cecil Hemley was still a crucial part of the operation. He also had a calming influence in the office. Fellow Singer translator Elizabeth Pollet happened to be the ex-wife of the troubled poet Delmore Schwartz. One day Schwartz came barging into 19 Union Square West, raving that he was determined to kill her. He disappeared into Hemley's office. One worrying hour later, they emerged, arm in arm, Schwartz's homicidal impulse long forgotten.

At the same time, Hemley was buckling under the pressure of a publishing hothouse. He and his wife, Elaine Gottlieb, ran themselves ragged churning out Singer translations, especially the epic novel first known as *The Manor* and then split into two healthy-size volumes, *The Manor* and *The Estate*. In 1963, he left Farrar, Straus to run Ohio University Press, but continued to work on Singer translations. He pleaded for fair pay, which Roger only grudgingly coughed up. In return, he demanded that Hemley speed up the translations, lest they miss "the moment juste" in which to publish Singer. Hemley, who had moved partly because of health problems, died of a heart attack in 1966, at the age of fifty-one. *The Manor* was finished by other translators.

His ambitions growing with every critical triumph, Roger became less and less tolerant of his more casual junior partners—wealthy aesthetes whose work ethic failed to match their financial pull. Sheila Cudahy was one of them. Around the time of FSC's move to Union Square, she took what turned out to be two years of paid leave in London. There she conducted office business but spent most of her time with one of her writers, Zsolt Aradi, a Catholic Hungarian émigré and another Vatican II press veteran ("a clean Malachi Martin," Roger joked), who wrote FSC books on the Popes. In the spring of 1962, Cudahy reported from London that Aradi had cancer, and wavered on whether to return. Roger flew to London that June, went to Wimbledon with Sheila, and thought he came away with a deal to retain her full-time. She was to receive the same annual salary he did—$15,000— as well as a car and driver and expense account. It turned out not to be enough, even after Roger offered the same deal for thirty hours a week.

That October, Farrar, Straus & Cudahy announced that its name was changing back to Farrar, Straus & Company. The friendship deteriorated quickly, with Straus and Cudahy clashing over what went wrong. Roger thought her entitlement and paranoia had ruined the friendship. Sheila told her son that Roger was only after her shares in the company—an 8 percent stake she still held two years later. She would portray Straus as a "grand manipulator," her son recalls, "and either you were kicking his ass or he was kicking your ass." Roger just seemed wistful. "She was an absolutely perfect partner and publisher and editor," he would recall, "and we got along extremely well, until the divorce. All those things go extremely well until the divorce."

One day in 1957, Hal Vursell's production assistant, Helen Weaver, walked into Giroux's office and told him Jack Kerouac sent his regards. Giroux, surprised to see an employee involved with his old writer, shook his head and repeated the Story of the Scroll. But he began writing Kerouac more regularly, congratulating him on Viking's publication, at last, of On the Road. During those six long years, Kerouac had written several autobiographical novels, which he grouped together as the Duluoz Legend, and Giroux had rejected those sent to him by Kerouac's agent. The editor simply wasn't interested in the

fruits of "automatic writing." But after *On the Road*, Kerouac was a celebrity, a commodity, and suddenly those works were being published
at the rate of one or two a year.

Giroux acquired *Big Sur*. Appropriately enough for the straitlaced
editor, it was Kerouac's most contrite, contemplative book, about battling alcohol and the "Beat" label at Lawrence Ferlinghetti's cabin near
the lush Pacific coastline. It was published in 1962, followed a year
later by *Visions of Gerard*, a sad veiled memoir about Kerouac's older
brother, who'd died at age nine. In a handwritten postscript to a letter,
Giroux wrote him: "Only remember that I have never ceased being
your friend & admirer & brother, mon ti Jean, And it is good to be
your editor again." Kerouac was full of plans, suggesting the order in
which to publish new parts of the Legend. His letters, though, could
be unhinged, if brilliant at times, uncorrected and full of run-ons.

Straus theorized that Kerouac's relationship with Helen Weaver
kept him coming to the office to tap away at his manuscripts, but he
and Helen had long since stopped being an item. In fact, by sheer coincidence, Jack dumped her in 1957 for another FSC employee, Joyce
Glassman (the future Joyce Johnson). Weaver's work team—Vursell
and Dorris Janowitz—knew all about it and, as Weaver wrote in her
memoir, "pretended to dislike Joyce out of loyalty to me. Hal started
calling her unflattering names like Pudding Face and the Unbaked
Muffin." Tensions dissipated when Glassman left her job to go on the
road with Kerouac.

Weaver stayed on through the move to 19 Union Square West. "In
my last two years at Farrar, Straus I was so bored I made Hal's poor
life a living Hell," she wrote. To keep her occupied, Vursell would
ask her to report on manuscripts from the slush pile. By then he not
only handled production but oversaw the juvenile division as well. Of
all the manuscripts Helen picked up, there was only one she couldn't
put down: a science-fiction novel swirling with alternate worlds, near-
death experiences, and Swiftian allegories. *A Wrinkle in Time*, by Madeleine L'Engle, popularized an entire young-adult genre and crossed
over into the adult literary market as only members of a rare breed
of books (*Alice in Wonderland*, *The Wizard of Oz*, *Harry Potter*) ever do.

Published in 1962, *A Wrinkle in Time* won the Newbery Medal the following year and sold three hundred thousand copies over the next decade. It was the foundation stone of a great children's book program.

Kerouac was respected for the glimmer of self-criticism displayed in *Big Sur*, but would never again attain the sales achieved by *On the Road*. In retrospect, his "recovery" novel only heralded the beginning of the end. His personal rapport with Giroux deteriorated, and all on one side; he not only missed a lunch Giroux had planned for Kerouac's fortieth birthday, but forgot the birthday itself. Instead, he'd gone to court and then had a massive bender, gotten thrown out of a hotel, and stayed up all night with assorted friends and strangers. "I drink and drink like a maniac," he wrote to Giroux in apology. Kerouac promised to make it up by hosting his editor in Florida, "like you done to Denver"; Giroux could drink peacefully, read Boswell, and listen to mockingbirds. He didn't go. The damage was done.

Giroux was busy shepherding his other writers over the summits of their lives, or—in the case of the aging Eliot or the dying O'Connor—managing their physical decline. He made the pilgrimage to visit O'Connor in her Georgia farmhouse, marveling at her peacocks (his car nearly ran one over) and doing his best to charm her obstreperous mother. "Mr. Giroux, why don't you get Flannery to write about *nice* people?" she asked him. His outings with Eliot were much more relaxed. He and the poet and the poet's young wife, Valerie, flew to the Caribbean, donned linen and shorts, and took dips in the still blue waters. On Emerald Beach in Nassau, a woman ran up to shake Eliot's hand. She turned out to be Joan Crawford.

The firm was renamed a final time in September 1964, becoming Farrar, Straus and Giroux. When Rose Wachtel refused to order new stationery with Giroux's name on it until the old letterhead was used up, Bob secretly stole a few reams and threw them away. Both O'Connor and Eliot died that year. A few months after O'Connor's death, Giroux would publish her first story collection, *Everything That Rises Must Converge,* whose motley brilliance, amplified in the public mind by the tragedy of her short life, would finally cement her reputation. But the first book published under the imprint bearing

Giroux's name was Robert Lowell's elegiac, politically charged *For the Union Dead*.

John Berryman was also on that first FSG list, despite a years-long rift between poet and editor. Berryman had accused Giroux of withholding royalties and—more important—of relegating *Homage to Mistress Bradstreet* to the remainder bin without informing him. He wrote a long, nasty letter that Giroux could neither forgive nor answer. It wasn't as though Berryman hadn't broken his own promises, such as the Shakespeare biography that never came to be. But then, in 1963, Berryman was ready to publish what became *77 Dream Songs*. A departure from classical form, clotted with dashes and minstrel slang, the series took the shape of a long narrative about a tormented protagonist named Henry. Suddenly in need of a publisher, Berryman had a change of heart. "Let's make an end to the long estrangement," he wrote in February 1963. "I have felt bad about it a thousand times." He then repeated his various publishing gripes.

Giroux wrote that "we may indeed now together stand easy. I have never had any but the most affectionate feelings, arising from our most ancient and longstanding friendship, from the days of your white tie and tails, my hound-and-horns, and our common Mark." He left the publishing argument for another day, and accepted the Dream Songs gladly. *77 Dream Songs* won the 1965 Pulitzer Prize for poetry. The news only depressed the unstable Berryman, already in and out of the hospital for various ailments related to alcoholism and mental illness. "Real fame must be intolerable," he wrote. Giroux tried to cheer him up by appealing to his ego, noting that the Pulitzer had given him a sales boost so big that he'd outsold Lowell that week.

Berryman was mercurial, but his long history with Giroux strengthened their professional bond. Lowell, more famous and esteemed and more stylistically in sync with Giroux, nevertheless had a cooler relationship with his editor. Colleagues remember Lowell, in his wobblier moments, dismissing Giroux as his "printer," or an "old maid." He rarely expressed it in writing—at least the writing that's been released—but he did once report to Elizabeth Bishop that he had discussed her career with "Roger Straus, much more on the move than old Bob, now on a honeymoon with the TS Eliots in Nassau." It was an unfair comment, but not a wholly inaccurate assessment of the stark contrast between editor and publisher.

It also laid bare, in its way, the harsh reality of an editor's life. Giroux had been working for twenty-five years. During that time, his acquisitions and his painstaking editorial work had helped to shape the American intellectual landscape. At FSG he was just beginning his tenure as the final arbiter on all editorial decisions (except, of course, for Roger). But though he was still approaching the peak of his professional power, he was no longer, if he ever really had been, at the vanguard of taste. By the sixties, even the Beats—most of them too radical for Giroux—were old hat. The boundaries of the culture were shifting, and literary borders cracking and reforming right along with them.

Even in times of great stability, and even in industries that don't need to adapt as quickly as publishing to cultural changes, the fact remains that generations must be replenished. Every book house needs to pump new blood continuously; hungry, young new editors must rise up beneath those advancing toward complacency, and eventually displace them. Roger Straus had found one in Giroux, and finally acknowledged his importance on the letterhead. Now he had to find another.

6

The New Sensibility

Just as Betty Friedan was finishing *The Feminine Mystique* for another publisher, two women met Roger Straus who were both determined, in very different ways, to avoid the fate of the anesthetized American housewife. Susan Sontag and Peggy Miller would each find the answer partly in Roger Straus, and each would change his life in turn.

Bob Giroux met Susan Sontag before Roger did. According to him, the striking young writer walked into his office in 1961, presented him with the partial manuscript of a convoluted dream narrative, and said, "Jason Epstein told me you're the only editor in New York who will understand my novel." Giroux summarized this encounter two decades later in a letter to Sontag contradicting her own account. She had told friends and interviewers that she'd gone to a bookstore, figured out that Farrar, Straus published more of the books she loved than any other publisher, and dropped off her manuscript in a typewriter box addressed to "Fiction Editor." Straus separately confirmed Jason Epstein's rejection and the rough outline of Giroux's version. Epstein doesn't remember turning it down, but finds the story perfectly plausible, since he didn't like her first novel.

They all agree that Sontag's first editor was not Giroux but Cecil Hemley, that hapless Noonday publisher whose taste had exceeded his ambition. Giroux remembered "admiring enormously" *Dreams of Hippolyte*, whose disassociated hero wanders an unnamed city (clearly Paris) determined to make his life align with his sadomasochistic dreams. (The title was soon changed to *The Benefactor*.) Its two main characters resembled André Gide and Jean Genet, and its themes, if not its cold style, owed something to Gide's *The Immoralist*. Giroux, unsure whether it was worth the commercial risk, asked Hemley for a second opinion. "He absolutely flipped for it," Giroux recalled, "and was so enthusiastic that he asked if I would let him be the editor. My function as Editor-in-Chief was to encourage genuine enthusiasm and of course I agreed." Hemley sent Sontag a hundred-dollar option on the partial manuscript in June 1961, against an eventual advance of five hundred dollars.

Straus probably met the dark, striking twenty-nine-year-old author before he encountered her vigorous but abstruse writing (which *The New Republic* called "translator's English"). On April 30, 1962, he reported to "Miss Sontag" that he had read eighty pages of the novel: "I think it is a wonderfully inventive work which should be great fun to publish." That spring, he began inviting her to parties at the town house. At one such soirée, she began her career as an essayist by walking up to William Phillips, cofounder of *Partisan Review*, and wondering aloud, "How do you write a review for *Partisan Review*?" "You ask," he said. "I'm asking," she said. He said that would be fine. "I do not know whether it was the whiskey or the fact that my guard was down or that there was something immensely attractive and impressive about Susan," Phillips recalled in a memoir. "I prefer to think that I was open to new talent." She had something ready for the summer issue.

The subject of Sontag's first piece in *Partisan Review* was an all-FSG production: a review of Isaac Bashevis Singer's new novel, *The Slave*. Placing the book within the context of the "post-classic novel," Sontag praised *The Slave* for its "power of sensuous evocation" and its absence of Freudian cliché. Straus, who had years ago declared his ideal form of publicity to be a dinner party thrown by Edmund Wilson, couldn't have asked for better synergy. Sontag managed, simultaneously, to sell Singer to the intelligentsia and to develop her own critical voice. She fit like a key into the culture of FSG, which operated best as a full-blown intellectual apparatus—a one-stop shop of literary greatness. Come for the parties; stay for the book contract; give back by reviewing our other authors or talking them up at the next party.

She quickly made deep inroads on the social front, often as Roger's guest. In his journal, Edmund Wilson noted "evening dinner at the Strauses" on March 20, 1962. In attendance were Dwight Macdonald, old Jimmy Sheean, and "a handsome girl from California who is one of Roger's new writers." Having possibly missed her name, he certainly learned it six months later. Just as *The Benefactor* was published in September (to baffled reviews and feeble sales), Sontag appeared on a panel with Macdonald, arguing that a new generation of critics and authors would sweep aside the outdated hierarchies and politics of Lionel Trilling and friends. Edmund Wilson, she declared, was "overrated." Years later, after a night at the opera with Sontag, Giroux, and the Strauses, Wilson wrote, "Roger can't quite forgive me because I am not impressed with her."

Neither was Wilson's ex-wife, Mary McCarthy, whose collected *Partisan Review* drama criticism Straus published in the same month as *The Benefactor*. Sontag was originally meant to fill McCarthy's influential slot as *Partisan Review*'s drama critic—which is what must have prompted McCarthy to gripe—so the story goes—that Susan was "the imitation me." (She had only recently called Straus the imitation Knopf.) The first time they met, at the Lowells', McCarthy told Sontag she must not be from New York because she smiled too much.

In literary circles as in politics, Straus was a professional nonpartisan, even if he leaned one way or the other, favoring Rahv over Phillips when they split over *Partisan Review* and Hellman over McCarthy during their famous libel suit. Though he would have strongly denied that Sontag was imitating anyone, the firm promoted her by drawing comparisons to McCarthy and Elizabeth Hardwick, both sometime FSG authors. Roger knew that, whatever the substance of the argument, controversy would be good for Sontag and for Farrar, Straus. He also saw in Sontag's fierce opinions the seeds of literary notoriety, despite her ambition to prove herself as a novelist. Just after *The Benefactor* came out, and a full year before the publication of "Notes on 'Camp'" in *Partisan Review* made her famous, he worked hard to persuade Sontag to make her next work a book of criticism. Published in 1966, *Against Interpretation* sold five times as many copies within the next year—more than ten thousand—as *The Benefactor* did in its first four years.

"Camp" was not invented by Sontag; it was outed. The arch aesthetic, the subject of her groundbreaking essay, had been associated with gay subculture for years, and was all too familiar to silent-film buff Bob Giroux and natty, catty Hal Vursell (who looked a little like John Waters). But they'd never have articulated it. Roger, though obviously tolerant, wasn't exactly keen on the new openness. He wrote to a friend that he considered a 1966 exposé on Somerset Maugham's love life "revolting" and "badly homosexual"; "let all the little queers do all their little lip smacking," he concluded. Michael di Capua, hired as an editor in 1966, never bothered to conceal his homosexuality, and Straus taunted him for it. But on the broader playing field of gender relations, Sontag, a semi-open bisexual, had a salutary effect on Roger. Not long after she began attending Straus dinners, Sontag refused to go upstairs with the women. "And that was that," Dorothea recalled. "Susan broke the tradition, and we never split up after dinner again." Susan also made her concessions to Straus's antediluvian—perhaps even slightly campy—manners. "You're the only person in the world," she told Roger, "who can call me 'Baby' and get away with it."

Farrar, Straus's "care and feeding" of Sontag (to use a common Roger phrase) did not—at first—differ greatly from his treatment of Singer or Wilson, or of prize Giroux writers like Malamud, Berryman, and Lowell. Like Singer, she was sold aggressively abroad. Paula

Diamond pushed for coordinated publishing programs rather than one-off sales, and pitched Sontag's essays to foreign magazines of all sizes in order to build her reputation. It was an expert FSG push: First build relationships, then build buzz, then build the perfect book, and then—if you're lucky—the sales will eventually follow.

Like Wilson, Sontag also had an open account from which advances could be drawn "on demand." (She also received $1,000 above the initial $500 for *The Benefactor* just before publication and a separate $1,000 loan in 1964.) Straus touted her, like other favorites, to important friends like Arthur Schlesinger, John F. Kennedy's court historian, to whom he wrote, "I can't remember when in the last fifteen years I have sent you a novel which I hold in such high esteem."

By 1965, however, Sontag was in a category of her own. When she swept into those grimy offices to work on a manuscript, "everything had to stop for her," says a former copy editor. "We would put aside whatever else and we would work with her." During the long stretches Sontag spent in Europe, FSG received and sorted her mail, looked after her apartment, and paid her bills—sometimes even her rent and Diners Club card (charging her "general account," to be repaid out of royalties). Sontag was fiercely loyal in turn. She answered a soliciting telegram from Prentice-Hall editor Gladys Carr with a high-handed rebuke, which she proudly forwarded to Roger with a note: "This may amuse you. I've probably scared the shit out of poor Miss Carr—Love, Susan." Another time she playfully reassured him: "I don't do nuthin' wif' nobody else, unless you wants me to, boss." From the start, she read manuscripts for Straus and tipped him off to European writers he'd never heard of, such as Walter Benjamin in 1963. To ease her passage in Europe, FSG treasurer Robert Wohlforth wrote a general letter confirming that she was "regularly employed as a consultant to our Editorial Department."

Concerned about the inherent conflict of interest in acting as Sontag's agent—and also a little overwhelmed—Straus advised her to seek her own representation. He sent her to one of the best in town, Candida Donadio, but when it came time to renegotiate her contract for *Against Interpretation,* she went directly to Straus anyway. They couldn't help themselves. Roger would negotiate with foreign publishers on Susan's behalf and then instruct Donadio to follow up. After two years or so, they decided Donadio's work wasn't worth the 10 percent cut.

Sontag asked many people for personal help and intervention throughout her life, but few delivered as regularly, at least on a professional level, as Roger. Some stress was inevitable, particularly when Sontag's output failed to keep pace with her demands, or when she would fall out of touch. But then she would finally write pleading for patience: "My loyalty to you, my gratitude to you, and my love for you, Roger, are absolutely unchanged." On this occasion he quickly replied, "Dearest, Dearest Susan . . . Please don't brood about us. Everything should be so good." When Edmund Wilson died, she wrote consolingly, calling Roger "my good angel." She added a highly un-Sontagian sentiment: "If they're keeping a list of your good deeds in heaven, the secretary must be getting writer's cramp."

Roger liked to tease her about her ardent fans. "Your mail isn't as interesting as it used to be," he wrote in 1966. "Are you slipping, love?—only one veiled proposition in three days." Neither Straus nor Sontag was naïve about the utility of their friendship, but they seemed genuinely to adore each other. "I think she reminded him of Dorothea, or of what Dorothea could have been," says FSG novelist Larry Woiwode, who was close to the Strauses. "Both these dark Jewish New York intellectuals. But she was writing things that Dorothea couldn't write." And what did Susan see in someone who couldn't sit through an entire play? Both were preternaturally vital, social, and restless. They loved gossip and actively sought out people who were brilliant or beautiful, preferably both. Out on the town at One Fifth or the Brussels, in matching leather jackets, they were a power couple. The question of whether or not they were ever an actual couple still divides industry gossips today.

In all likelihood, no living eyewitness could confirm an affair. But at least one woman who was involved with Roger says he told her that he slept with Sontag early in their relationship. "I don't think it was ongoing," says this former FSG employee. "I think it was part of their bonding." Another staff member—who had in fact sent Sontag her first FSG check—lived near the office and hosted Roger for the occasional lunchtime frolic. She also lent him her apartment for other nooners and would come home to find long black hairs on her pillow, which she firmly believed were Sontag's.

In any case, the rumor took on a life of its own that even its subjects seemed to relish. The first former employee, also a friend of Sontag's, once joked to her, "Roger is such a lesbian." Sontag laughed and said, "That is truer than you know." ("As I get older, only a smaller percentage of dykes dig me," Straus mock-complained to a colleague in 1964). Roger loved to joke that Susan's son, David Rieff, was "probably my illegitimate son," even though he and Sontag didn't meet until David was nine years old. It says something about their bond that at least one friend of many years nevertheless wondered if Roger might be serious.

Straus later said he and Sontag were "best friends in a way," while conceding that *her* best friend was really David Rieff. Sontag was always conflicted about the roles of guardians and children, male and female. Her father died when she was five years old, and she felt estranged from her mother. She entered the University of Chicago at age sixteen, married the professor Philip Rieff shortly after that, and divorced him at age twenty-four. Almost from the moment she took sole custody of David, she treated him as an adult, alternately taking him to cocktail parties and leaving him in others' care for months on end.

Freedom is an obsession in Sontag's first two books. As Sigrid Nunez wrote in her recent memoir, *Sempre Susan*, "to her, security over freedom was a deplorable choice." Yet Sontag allied herself with older men of authority—first Philip Rieff, then Roger Straus. She also adored and relied on the *New York Review of Books* editor Robert Silvers. Roger's relationship with his authors—especially Susan—was primarily paternalistic. A foreign publisher who loved Straus nonetheless sounds exasperated on this subject: "Susan Sontag is sitting on his lap saying, 'Roger, father, friend, this publisher is not offering enough money for the new book of essays.'" The reality was not so cartoonish; Roger anticipated Susan's needs and fought to make reality match her expectations. Knowing she hated lecturing but needed money, he negotiated increasingly higher rates regardless of an institution's prestige. He set up a complicated FSG trust in the name of his "illegitimate son," David.

Straus wasn't personally tending to every Susan Sontag bill and fan letter that crossed his desk. That was the job of "Perfect Peggy" or "Perfect P.," as Susan and Roger liked to call her. Peggy Miller, the second woman to come into Roger's life in 1962, was not much older than Sontag, and her father had also died when she was young. From there, the paths that brought them to Straus diverged.

Miller was raised on the Upper West Side, among the Jewish middle class. She remembers, as a child, riding in the family car past the private town houses along East 70th Street—including the one the Strauses would soon inhabit—as her father wished aloud that they could afford to live there. "That was his idea of Heaven," she says, "to have one of those houses." Her father died suddenly in 1944, when she was seventeen and just about to graduate from high school. Unable to afford college, Peggy applied to become a stewardess with Eastern Airlines—it was the only carrier that took girls under twenty-one—but was, she says, disqualified for being too tall. In the fall she settled on secretarial school, and slowly moved up the ranks in three offices: first the American Federation of Arts, then a television syndication company, and finally the Lasker Foundation, working for Mary Lasker, the wife of a wealthy advertising pioneer who'd devoted his riches to health-care advocacy. Soon, she was ready to move on.

"I had gotten up to executive vice president, so by then I would only work for the head of a company," she says. Today, her bearing is as composed as ever: ramrod-straight posture, coiffed white hair, implacable eyebrows. Her Atlantic accent, larded with Rogerisms ("blood on the floor," "that was the end of the joke," "extr-awdinary"), is a living homage to Straus, though easier to parse. A quick glance around the apartment she bought with her mother in the fifties—peach walls, Deco-accented midcentury furnishings, Viennese art posters—reinforces her explanation for almost turning Straus down. "I'd always worked in fashionable, attractive offices," she says. "You can't believe what this office looked like. The reception room was archaic. There was this ancient settee. And then this very attractive, well-dressed man came out to get me. And we had a very nice interview and I had a very good résumé and everything was fine and we agreed we'd think over the weekend and I told everybody I knew I wasn't taking the job."

Straus, who'd had a succession of bad secretaries, called her on Sunday to make a special plea. "He said he'd throw a little more in the pot to entice me," she says. "Well, nobody had ever done that for me before." She came in for a probationary period, and stayed for forty-two years. Not long after she arrived, Peggy returned from a vacation and told her boss she couldn't stand the look of his office. She hired a decorator who replaced the "terrible drapes" and repainted. "The treasurer didn't talk to me for a year because I hadn't asked his permission." But, as Wohlforth well knew, anyone who had Roger's ear and his say-so didn't have to ask permission from anyone else.

Soon after Peggy started, Roger gave her the number of his extra phone line—the one that had led to his intelligence contacts but which he was, by now, primarily using to set up lunchtime encounters. "He told me, 'Sometimes the phone might ring or somebody might come in and you don't know anything.' I said to him, 'I'm a sphinx.' If I know something I'm not supposed to know, I don't know it. This goes back generations in my family." Before the FSG files went into the New York Public Library, she was allowed to throw away whatever she considered inappropriate.

Peggy refuses to answer questions about whether she and Straus were romantically involved. She did tell one FSG writer, a friend whom Straus saw a lot of in London, that it was Roger who "courted" her. "There was already a big friction in the marriage," the writer says. "But she was quite surprised, she told me, that he wanted her." Even a couple of Roger's biggest fans believe he used sex to cultivate loyalty among willing female employees, and encouraged office affairs for the same reason. It was simply part of the office culture. But his relationship with Peggy, whatever its particulars, was real and enduring. Every day he would pick her up on the drive down to work, and, after opening the office together, the two would spend the next hour or two answering all the mail. She did the letter-opening and the typing; he handled the dictating and the off-color commentary. It was a sweet, almost banal morning routine, and maybe *that* was the transgression: finding as much intimacy at work as at home—maybe even more. As Roger once told another woman, "Peggy is perfect. No one would ever think."

"It seems to me that once more the face of publishing in America is going to change," Straus wrote in June 1964, by way of explaining why he could no longer afford a British scout's services. "There are four groups who have more money than good sense eagerly and impatiently attempting to grab up a trade publisher," he continued. Then he offered a template for the future of his company in such an environment:

> Farrar Straus intends to remain healthily independent, but it is perfectly obvious to me that in order to do so, we must expand somewhat beyond our present area of approximately 90 books a year and approximately two million dollars worth of trade sales. In short, we must be prepared, I feel, to take advantage of what is becoming a more and more unique position in the American trade, i.e. medium-sized independent, which is as we both know a rather attractive breeding ground and home for the truly creative artist. I do not believe that a number of the first rate writers now being published under the Random House complex or some of the other non-independent publishers are going to stay there, and I am hopeful that our house is going to look more and more attractive to that kind of writer.

Having seen Knopf sell out, and knowing that Random House and others were in full-on expansion mode, he had already decided to hew a middle course—to stave off acquistion by the big fish not by becoming one, which was probably impossible anyway, but by getting a little bit bigger and prettier. He believed, not unreasonably—though not entirely correctly, that Random House and its ilk would go the way of Harcourt, Brace and Houghton Mifflin, driving away quality in their dogged pursuit of the bottom line. Those authors would want to go somewhere smaller and more focused, somewhere with a reputation for treating writers with deference and dignity. And yet it wasn't just care they needed, but feeding; FSG had to be big enough to afford them and stable enough to assure them, amid all the shake-ups, that they weren't moving into a house of cards. FSG needed to scale up, without losing—to paraphrase a recent acquisition, John McPhee—a sense of what it was.

To this end, Straus explained, resources had to be corralled to pump in new blood. More often than not, it was Giroux and not Straus who knew where to find talent that would fit in at FSG. First of all, a company that dealt more and more in foreign rights, sometimes in opaque Eastern Bloc countries, had to have an expert in copyright law. "You need someone like Margaret Nicholson," Giroux told Straus, referring to Macmillan's copyright expert. They put an ad in *Publishers Weekly*, and who answered it but Margaret Nicholson herself? She was sick of Macmillan and would be happy to come over, in spite of the look of the place and its paltry salaries. She became an FSG lifer.

Giroux also knew of a talented young editor, Michael di Capua, who'd gone from Macmillan to Pantheon in search of a place willing to deal with his quirks and demands. In fact, he'd always had his eye on FSG. Di Capua had Giroux's sensitivity and obsessive editorial care along with a genius for children's books—something Giroux never cared much about. He had become close with one of Giroux's lost writers, Randall Jarrell, and showed a Giroux-level dedication to nursing Jarrell through illnesses and creative blocks. He threw the poet a lifeline by suggesting he write children's books. Jarrell's second, *The Bat-Poet*, about a sensitive bat who decides to go out during the day, was illustrated by a young talent di Capua knew well: Maurice Sendak. The year before di Capua joined FSG, Jarrell was fatally struck by a car (Lowell and others thought it was suicide). But as a result of their relationship, FSG managed to publish his *Complete Poems* in 1968, and worked closely with his estate thereafter.

What FSG really needed, though, was a dynamo in tune with the next generation, the new Lowells and Malamuds. Giroux knew just the man. Giroux had noticed Henry Robbins at the very beginning of his career, when he was a temp at Harcourt, Brace. "It was soon clear to all of us that he could have a very promising future in publishing," Giroux recalled. Philadelphia-born, Harvard-bred, Robbins had then gone back to Cambridge for an advanced degree, but found academia rife with politics and backbiting. Returning to publishing, he spent nine years at Alfred A. Knopf before becoming editor in chief of Dial Press, the forward-thinking house that published James Baldwin, among others.

If Robbins thought academia cynical and corrupt, what did he expect from publishing? "Henry went from out of the frying pan, into the fire, then into the grate," says Christopher Lehmann-Haupt, the longtime *New York Times* book critic, who worked for Robbins briefly at Dial. After nine years at Knopf, Robbins left, not long after it was sold to Random House and the whole company went public. He lasted only nine months in his next job, as editor in chief of Dial, which had just been acquired by paperback giant Dell. Robbins's acquisitions met with constant resistance from publisher Richard Baron, particularly when it came to an attention-getting group of writers who were coalescing around *Esquire* and Clay Felker's Sunday supplement to the *New York Herald Tribune* (the future *New York* magazine). These post-Beatnik latter-day Algrens, probing youth insanity and socialite hypocrisy with a novelistic flair, were soon classified as practitioners of the New Journalism. "Henry had his eye on the whole *Herald Tribune* crowd, always trying to bring them to Dial," says Lehmann-Haupt. "Baron was not cooperative."

Hired as a senior editor in the summer of 1964, Robbins worked a little more aggressively than Giroux had to get his authors over to Farrar, Straus. The Catholic satirist Wilfrid Sheed came easily, then John Knowles (author of *A Separate Peace*) and about a half dozen others. He also brought in Carmen Gomezplata, who would be FSG's copy chief for decades. Like Giroux, Robbins earned his writers' and colleagues' loyalty through his taste and a tender protectiveness that was equal parts teddy bear and grizzly bear. He had a ruddy, round face and was "soft-spoken, quick to smile and sympathize," as his obituary put it. "He'd get teary-eyed talking about his authors and their work," says Lehmann-Haupt. "He was a mama's boy, to put it crudely." "Henry was a crier," seconds Peggy Miller. "He'd be the first one to tell you he would cry for any reason." He'd cry while reading Marjorie Kellogg's *Tell Me That You Love Me, Junie Moon,* which would become his first big hit with FSG in 1968.

At the same time, "it was all you could do to prevent him from fighting duels with your reviewers," Wilfrid Sheed once said. He'd spar tactlessly with book review editors at the *Times* or even friendly operations like the *Tribune.* Straus would apologize in his wake: "I've told him again and again you've got to roll with the punches." And he had no patience for publishers with a purely commercial mind-set. Former Simon & Schuster head Michael Korda, in his memoir *Another Life,* called Robbins "a man who took himself and literature seriously (he was inclined to confuse them) . . . He did not compromise. Reasoning with him, as Churchill complained about De Gaulle, was like trying to reason with Joan of Arc." Nonetheless, he had some of Straus's instincts for publishing, rather than merely editing. "He knew what to do with a book, he knew what reviewers to call, he was dogged," says Lehmann-Haupt. Obviously, he also had some of Roger's flair for combat. "Henry was hot-headed," says the agent Lynn Nesbit. "But he was hot-headed about the right things."

While at Dial, Robbins had written to Nesbit, a young agent building a powerful career, about Tom Wolfe, one of the stars of the *Tribune* and *Esquire* in their salad days. Robbins expressed the excitement of discovering this writer's "exact, exuberant prose" for the first time. Wolfe was not only a voracious processor of subcultures, most recently the cult of custom-car racing, but also a reckless alchemist of language. The title of his first book, *The Kandy-Kolored Tangerine-Flake Streamline Baby,* was an abridged version of the title story's 1963 headline in *Esquire:* "There Goes (Varoom! Varoom!) That Kandy Kolored (Thphhhhhh!) Tangerine-Flake Streamline Baby (Rahghhh!) Around the Bend (Brummmmmmmmmmmmmmmmm. . . . .)." By the time the book was on the block, Robbins was at FSG, and Nesbit gladly favored the house in her negotiations. A month after adding Giroux's name, thus enshrining an editor who helped define fifties high culture, FSG paid $12,500 for a collection and a novel by Wolfe, an author who wanted to explode all those midcentury conventions.

There was no way to translate *this* writer into *"New Yorker*-ese." Southern accent, foppish white suit, and Yale Ph.D. notwithstanding, Wolfe tilted against New York's polite literary society from the moment he arrived. His two publications of choice were *Esquire,* the un–*New Yorker;* and the *Tribune,* the anti–*New York Times.* If anyone doubted where Wolfe stood, he clarified things in April 1965—just as Henry Robbins was soliciting blurbs for *Kandy-Kolored*—with a two-part piece in the *Tribune's New York* supplement headlined "Tiny Mummies! The True Story of the Ruler of 43d Street's Land of the Walking Dead!" It began: *"Omerta!* Sealed lips! *Sealed lips,* ladies and gentlemen! Our Thing! We are editing *The New Yorker* magazine, Harold Ross's *New Yorker.* We are not running a panopticon. Not exactly!" Wolfe's mammoth write-around hit piece depicted the magazine as a cult of genteel mediocrity that had missed the boat of every new literary trend. The "Ruler" in question, whose assorted phobias were viciously mocked, was William Shawn.

Straus was in a tight spot. Shawn was not just a friend but also a close collaborator in literary patronage; he supported Elizabeth Bishop and Isaac Singer with first-look deals and published every word of FSG's latest star, John McPhee. (Like Singer, McPhee was signed up by another editor, in this case Hal Vursell, but quickly became Straus's personal ward.) So long as a writer didn't mind the *"New Yorker*-ese," it was a nice setup for FSG. Straus wouldn't need to shell out as much in support of his writers—as much money or as much editing. It was almost a pooling of resources, in the way book publishers like Scribner's and Harper's used to run magazines earlier in the century. It was the next best thing to academic tenure—or the Nobel Prize.

Wolfe's piece "almost irreparably damaged my very good relationship" with Shawn, Straus said. Shawn pleaded with Roger not to include "Tiny Mummies" in the collection that followed *Kandy-Kolored.*

Wolfe made the final decision to keep it out, at least according to both men, fearing reviews of the book would be a referendum only on that very divisive piece. It was divisive enough on its own: Dwight Macdonald, scourge of Sontag, this time attacked Wolfe as "a para-journalist with a reading block" in a lengthy two-part takedown in *The New York Review of Books.* He also wrote, tellingly, that Wolfe catered to the twin modern neuroses of "a masochistic deference to the Young" and "a guilt-feeling about class." Macdonald thus set himself up as an old fogy on the losing side of a yawning generation gap.

Straus was diplomatic but not exactly neutral. He thought the piece "very funny," and went with his strongest instinct, which was to defend his writer as far as he could without fatally offending people he needed. He loved to tell the story, years later, of how Leonard Bernstein's wife fled a dinner party rather than eat next to the publisher of Tom Wolfe. The writer had very recently savaged the couple's Black Panther soirée in his famous story "Radical Chic."

Straus feted Wolfe and *Kandy-Kolored* on June 29, 1965, at the Huntington Hartford Museum at 2 Columbus Circle. (There was an essay in the book about the museum's wealthy namesake.) Would-be gate-crashers jammed the FSG phone lines for last-minute invitations. Giroux called it "the first literary mob scene I ever experienced." Days later, Wolfe flew to San Francisco, where he was following Ken Kesey around in pursuit of a blockbuster story on the drug subculture. He wrote Roger, in his characteristic foppish fountain-pen calligraphy, a note of gratitude: "First, you gambled on me in the first place, and a lot of people told me at the time that you were out of your mind for doing so. And second, when the heat was really on in that incredible New Yorker thing, you stood by me in a very personal way, and that is something I will never forget. A lot of people with a hell of a lot less to lose than you were jumping ship like a lot of fluttery tachycardiac nutballs, and the hell with them."

It seemed that Wolfe was becoming a "Roger author." By the mid-sixties, both Isaac Singer and Susan Sontag had made the leap from belonging to their editors to belonging to Roger. (Sontag, for one, was impressed by Giroux but bored by his disquisitions on silent film.)

Though Tom Wolfe liked Henry Robbins very much, he sized Roger up as a peer: a man of style, brio, and ego.

Wolfe, for all his cynical *now*ness, had a romantic view of the world and especially of New York. It was partly the distance between his Technicolor dreams and drab reality that gave Wolfean writing such hyperreal frisson. Roger's outsize and outmoded personality attracted him from the start. Wolfe later remembered that when he arrived in New York in 1962, "the picture I had of the city was based on a book that turned out to be quite out-of-date." He envisioned, for instance, a publisher like the storied Horace Liveright, "a man with 300-watt eyeballs that bulged quite a bit, a man who would give parties in which he would wear 'Le Smoking' in velvet with elaborate frogging on it, and all of the guests would be drinking sidecars. What I actually found when I got here was that every man you saw had on a black raincoat and one of those stingy-brimmed, little dark gray hats. Their chin would always be dug into their clavicle, and they'd be scuffling along the sidewalk, kicking their heels at the cracks, and saying, 'Aw, hell.'"

Robbins may have pushed Straus to take *Kandy-Kolored* without demanding a novel first, but Straus happily let him do it. And it was Roger who fed Wolfe's imagination as well as his stomach. "Your splendid dinner Friday really did RESTORE my soul," Wolfe wrote him after perhaps his first meal at the Straus home. He pressed Roger on where he'd gotten his bootleg Cuban cigars—Montecristos—and Roger replied that he couldn't give up his source in writing: "I will have to lead you there by the hand and give you the secret password voice to voice."

"He transmitted a kind of warmth and energy that I think everyone felt," Roger III says of his father. "If I've met someone with a bigger ego than his I couldn't readily come up with a name, and with other publishers, mostly that gets in the way of your relationship with writers. But somehow, his towering ego and their ambitions became fused into a single unit. Two towering egos beating as one."

What a big ego craves above all is recognition. Kurt Vonnegut's verdict on *Kandy-Kolored* in his *Times* review was: "Excellent book by a genius who will do anything to get attention." Wolfe got it, selling tens of thousands of hardcover copies and hundreds of thousands in paperback, but both towering egos wanted more. Vonnegut had called Wolfe, in another nicely ambivalent phrase, "the fastest brilliant writer around." And yet, while the prose was propulsive, Wolfe's productivity slowed as his ambitions swelled. One story he'd been readying to include in his forthcoming collection, *The Pump House Gang*, kept getting bigger and bigger. It was a bravura mind-reading satire about Ken Kesey's hippie Merry Pranksters—what would come to be known as *The Electric Kool-Aid Acid Test*—and Wolfe thought it was approaching greatness. Robbins suggested he leave it for later and do the collection first, but Wolfe wasn't satisfied with the slow build.

"I can't bring myself to put out a book that announces to the world, well that's all the farther I'm going," he wrote to Robbins about the collection. "I sometimes get the feeling that you feel this book is bound to be something of a let-down, aesthetically, after the extraordinary excitement over the first book—in other words, an aesthetic failure—and that it is best just to get that over with, since it is inevitable, and get on with something else. Well, I am willing to risk aesthetic failure—but not in a tepid, aw-hell manner . . . I intend to dazzle, startle, delight—and win on every level. I can do things no other writer can do or has ever done—and there is no earthly forgiveable [sic] reason why I shouldn't do them in this second book."

Not only did Robbins and FSG relent; they published both books on the same day. They put more energy and more advertising behind *Acid Test*, perhaps cannibalizing sales of *Pump House Gang*. But for FSG it was just another opportunity to blitz the review pages and generate hype. In fact, subsidiary rights director Lila Karpf audaciously forwarded Wolfe's tantrum-manifesto to the head of the Literary Guild, hoping to net a big book-club deal. She closed on an effusive note of her own: "While Tom is not the kind of writer that Susan Sontag is, we have a strong feeling here that it is writers such as these two who are in the process now of forming the literature of the late 60's and early 70's."

•   •   •

For all of Wolfe's big talk, he didn't have the one thing the Literary Guild and everyone else was waiting for—a novel. FSG, which wound up paying $21,000 for it, would wait twenty-three years for any fiction from Wolfe. He sold decently but wasn't laying any golden eggs; in fact he was what Straus called "egg-bound," like a constipated hen.

And then, just in time, a better egg dropped into Roger's lap, the kind of project FSG finally had the clout to pull off. FSG was almost out of the celebrity business by the sixties, but what if Roger could find just the right moneymaker—perhaps a problem book, a challenge to publisher and reader alike? Straus was very friendly with the literary agent Carl Brandt, the son of an agent and MGM script-reader Roger had worked with in the fifties. Brandt's clients included the dapper leftist Mexican Carlos Fuentes, whose groundbreaking novel *The Death of Artemio Cruz* had just been acquired by FSG. Brandt, whose projects went directly to Straus rather than to his editors, decided—why not?—to pitch him the autobiography of Sammy Davis, Jr. "He was a very special character," says Brandt, "and it occurred to me—what could be more interesting than to take Davis and Roger and put them together? It would add a great deal of cachet to Davis." And it might give Straus a Hauser-level blockbuster. "It just made me laugh. It also, I think, made Roger laugh."

A columnist named Burt Boyar and his wife, Jane, had become very friendly with the African-American Rat Packer. Davis had married a white woman, incurring the wrath of both races, and personally desegregated many an entertainment venue by dint of his celebrity. His story—defiant but integrationist—dovetailed nicely with the mood of the country just as the civil-rights struggle kicked into high gear. The Boyars had been taping Davis in marathon interview sessions and joining him in all-night drinking sessions. They had the makings of not just a kiss-and-tell bestseller but a document of racial struggle—especially Sammy's awful experiences in the army. And yet, as Burt Boyar remembers it, publisher after publisher declined. McGraw-Hill and Doubleday made five-figure offers, only to change their minds. "Harcourt, Brace was offended by even having it offered to them," Boyar says. (Brandt doesn't recall offering it anywhere else

before Farrar, Straus.) Big publishers would want to avoid the controversy, while edgier ones would shy away from budget-busting celebrity bios. Only a midsize publisher with a gambling habit might take a
chance. And Roger was an avid gambler.

The Boyars, Brandt, and Straus met at the Lotos Club, and perhaps Roger overcompensated for the highfalutin atmosphere, because the Boyars were initially appalled. "We were kids, and we were
square," says Boyar, who, mind you, was good friends with Sammy
Davis, Jr. "Roger used 'fuck' and 'shit' just as easily as you and I say
'good morning.' Jane and I were horrified—we were ready to walk
away. In fact I very stupidly asked him what he published. I was a
Broadway columnist and knew nothing about the book world. Roger
turned to Carl and said, 'This is what I worked twenty years for!?'"

Straus let the perceived slight pass. After he read some of the 1,500
manuscript pages they turned in, he was diplomatic, minimizing the
editing work needed as nothing more than "a plumbing job" that required little input from them. "Don't worry about it," Boyar remembers Roger saying. "Go swim around somewhere." What Roger really
felt, he later said, was that "it was just a very, very good, colorful story,
but the material was really in a terrible mess."

Straus and Giroux decided it needed an outside editor. The man
they hired made it into a third-person narrative the Boyars found
"corny" and "dreadful." The second one was distracted by personal
troubles and attempted suicide. Then it went to copy editor Robin
Pitchford, who smoothed out Sammy's jargon. The Boyars scrapped
him, too. Henry Robbins was next at bat. "We learned a lot from
Henry and he helped us a great deal," Burt wrote years later. But
according to Boyar, Robbins wanted to change key scenes in which
Sammy failed to fight back against brutal racist soldiers. It's plausible that Robbins—who had worked with James Baldwin and in 1970
would publish a debut novel called *The Life and Loves of Mr. Jiveass
Nigger*—considered shuffling, cowering Sammy Davis, Jr., a bit of a
throwback. But both Peggy Miller, who is still friendly with Boyar, and
Carl Brandt, who emphatically is not, say that the editors were not the
issue. "Every editor would say, 'I can't work with these people,'" says

Peggy, and according to Brandt: "Let me simply say that the Boyars were the problem."

There was only one person the Boyars would listen to—Roger Straus—and he wound up editing *Yes I Can*. Every week they'd meet and go over about a hundred pages of manuscript. "From then on it was an absolute joy," says Burt Boyar. "His taste was impeccable, his judgment was absolutely flawless in my opinion, we accepted anything he commented on and agreed with him." Also, it didn't hurt that "I loved the guy." Peggy just thought Roger "got away with it because he was the head of the company."

Straus didn't have many one-on-ones with Sammy himself, and when the Boyars took him to see his show at the Copacabana, he was a fish out of water. But he loved the entertainer's style, and he asked who Sammy's tailor was. From then on, just like Sammy, he went to James Carroll on Madison Avenue. The Boyars also sent him the hippest gifts. To honor their friendship and Roger's impressively foul mouth, they had a few of his most colorful phrases immortalized as stamps. One stamp was embossed with the firm's logo and the phrase FUCK YOU VERY MUCH. Others read GREAT MOMENTS IN LITERATURE, HORSE-SHIT PIE, and IT'S JUST A PIMPLE ON THE PRICK OF PROGRESS. Straus would occasionally use them in actual correspondence. More often they were reserved for circulating mail. (Almost from the beginning, Roger decided to circulate public correspondence to all department heads—keeping everyone in the loop, soliciting advice and arch commentary, and spreading wonderful gossip.)

Yes I Can, brought down to a manageable six hundred pages or so, was published in September 1965, its title emblazoned in big blocky yellow and red letters. Straus's editing was adequate, though the book pulled some punches (unlike a sequel twenty years later), and later he wished he'd cut fifty more pages. But it was far from a lark. To Straus's thinking, it was counterprogramming. In the hands of Simon & Schuster, *Yes I Can* would have been just another celebrity tell-all, subject to no more marketing than any other book in the genre. Farrar, Straus, on the other hand, had enough muscle to produce and market a book this big (if only one per season) and yet enough cachet to attract highbrow attention for almost any book on the list. A publisher's imprint may have meant nothing to the casual book browser, but it meant a lot to established critics, especially those who went to Roger Straus's parties. Sammy Davis may not have known it, but the culture of mid-sixties FSG had a lot to do with the respect he earned (not to mention the money) through his cowritten memoir.

It worked in every sense. The book reached number one on the bestseller list and earned a front-page review in the *New York Times*. Although it was mixed ("often absorbing, often unsatisfying"), it was written by historian Martin Duberman and ran to almost two full pages. Unfortunately, a massive newspaper strike hit the first week of publication; several cover stories and splashy ads went straight into the trash bin. It's a testament to the timeliness, juiciness, and easy colloquial flow of Sammy's book that it thrived despite the timing. Some credit is due to Roger's editing; he had a good ear for informal language and the good sense to preserve it. Dick Schaap, in *Newsweek*, called him a "marvelous editor." "Since when?" wrote the scout Silvio Senigallia to Roger, noting his own responsibility "to deflate your ego."

As for the actual editors, there was now a deep bench at Farrar, Straus—which the Davis success made a little roomier, physically. Michael di Capua's new office was carved into space made available when accounting operations were moved upstairs, to the tenth floor—part of a bona fide expansion. And the tag team of Giroux and Robbins kept FSG on high churn. In 1967, Bernard Malamud won a National Book Award for what some consider his masterpiece, *The Fixer*. Two more finalists—Wilfrid Sheed's *Office Politics* and Walker Percy's *The Last Gentleman*—were FSG books, adding up to half of all the finalists.

Walker Percy was a true Giroux-Robbins team effort. The intense New Orleans Catholic's debut, *The Moviegoer*, was a deeply American novel of alienation, though it wore both its existentialism and its Catholicism lightly. Robbins had been at Knopf when it was published there, and had some input into Stanley Kauffmann's heavy editing of the manuscript. And it was Giroux's friend Jean Stafford, on a National

Book Award committee in 1962, who convinced her fellow judges to look at the book, even though Alfred Knopf had not submitted it for consideration. Knopf, who'd fired Kauffmann, had resolved not to support the novel. He rooted vocally for the year's other Knopf finalist, William Maxwell's *The Chateau*. When Percy won, Knopf abruptly left the ceremony. Naturally, Percy began looking elsewhere. Giroux, wooing Percy through his agent, Elizabeth Otis, played up his relationship with Stafford and also with Robbins, who, he implied, was being groomed as his successor. Robbins followed up, insisting FSG was really the only logical choice. Soon they had Percy for a $5,000 advance. He would stay there for the rest of his career.

There was an eschatological urgency to Percy's work, both fiction and nonfiction, which also pervaded other specimens of what Lehmann-Haupt and others would call a "Henry Robbins writer." Joan Didion had that sense of foreboding, alongside a diffident but razor-edged first-person presence—New Journalism of a stealthier kind. With her oversize sunglasses and cool, ambivalent malaise, she was constructing an image as carefully as Wolfe in his all-white suits. "Writers," she wrote, "are always selling someone out."

Like Sontag, Didion had begun her career with a novel but built a larger following in nonfiction. A fan of her work for various magazines, Robbins flew to California in June 1966 and took Didion and her husband, the writer John Gregory Dunne, out to dinner at the Bistro in Beverly Hills. "The three of us laughed until two in the morning," Didion later wrote, in the title essay of her collection *After Henry*. "In short, we got drunk together, and before the summer was out Henry Robbins had signed contracts with each of us, and, from that summer in 1966 until the summer of 1979, very few weeks passed during which one or the other of us did not talk to Henry Robbins." In short order, for a total of $12,000, she was signed for a novel, which became *Play It as It Lays*, and a collection of reportage, *Slouching Towards Bethlehem*. She insists she wouldn't have done either book without Robbins's encouragement. "He enabled me to do *Play It as It Lays* by just telling me I could," she says now.

Two years after Robbins signed up Didion and Dunne, he learned

from Lynn Nesbit that Donald Barthelme was looking for a new editor. Barthelme wrote short stories at once absurdist and wry—topical,
often politically inflected, but elusive and somehow also lots of fun.
The pieces in his first FSG collection, *Unspeakable Practices, Unnatural
Acts,* range from "The Balloon," in which the title object floats over
New York inciting widely divergent reactions, to "The Indian Up-
rising," which is hard to follow but concerns a Comanche attack,
Vietnam, consumerism, and a dissolving relationship. Barthelme had
devoured *Against Interpretation,* and he and Sontag would become
good friends. Later he influenced his friend Grace Paley's decision to
sign on with FSG.

As with "Giroux authors," the writers in Robbins's orbit knew
one another and were devoted to some common spirit of the times,
yet were also fiercely unique. In fact, it was newness and oddness that
bound them together. Sontag, though not a Robbins writer, articulated the same sense of both mission and ambition. *Against Interpretation* begins with the insistence that her work "is not criticism at all,
strictly speaking, but case studies for an aesthetic, a theory of my own
sensibility," and ends with the essay "One Culture and the New Sensibility." Many of FSG's young sixties writers felt this yearning toward
a unified theory of themselves. Didion's *Slouching Towards Bethlehem*
takes its title from W. B. Yeats's famous apocalyptic poem "The Second Coming," which Didion reprints in full at the front of her book.
For all of her distrust of generalization, it was a broad, sweeping gesture. Like Wolfe, she was straining (more quietly, more precisely, but
just as boldly) to say something new.

7

King of the Book Fair

Roger III might have been committed to publishing from a very young age, but he knew that FSG was not a typical publisher, and he wanted to learn things about the industry that his father couldn't teach him. So Rog spent one precollege summer working at Harper & Bros., and there he met book salesman Peter Clark. A bit of a wild child with no college education and a bottomless capacity for martinis, Clark nevertheless had a killer instinct for selling books. Rog convinced his father to let Peter join the sales team at Farrar, Straus. In 1964, when Rog was still at Columbia, Peter returned the favor by referring him to a young FSG intern. Peter had made a move on Nina Pelikan, a Bennington undergrad and acolyte of Bernard Malamud. "She didn't pay any attention," says Rog. "So he called me up and he said, 'There's a pretty good-looking woman here, and she's too serious and square for me but she might be just right for you.'" During a visit to the office, Rog came up to Nina's tiny desk and interrupted her mundane filing. He introduced himself and, almost immediately, said,

"Would you like to go out to dinner with me?" "He was the boss's son," Nina says now, "and handsome and tall and charming and of course I would not say no."

As their romance grew more serious, Malamud joked that he should get a matchmaking fee for finding her such a high-class catch. Nina's pedigree, meanwhile, had its own romance. Her father, a Czech-American engineer, had gone to Russia after the Revolution to work on a project. There he met her mother, whose father had been shot by the Bolsheviks. Together they eventually escaped through Latvia and came to the States. The Strauses were pleased with Nina. "Roger liked pretty girls, I was a pretty young thing, and he knew that I was one of Malamud's favorite students, so he was very welcoming and warm to me," Nina says. "Dorothea looked me over, and she thought that I was a bluestocking, an intellectually pretentious young thing." She quickly got over it.

Rog and Nina were married in June 1965, just after he graduated from Columbia and just before he came to work full-time at FSG. The Strauses gave them a shady piece of land on the Purchase estate, and Rog soon figured out what to do with it. He and Nina befriended an FSG staffer, Emily Gwathmey, whose husband, Charles, was fresh out of Yale architecture school and just beginning to make his name in the field. Rog and Nina were planning a trip to the Hamptons, on eastern Long Island, and Emily insisted they see the house her husband had built for his parents there. They were dumbstruck. Rog, who'd learned all about Bauhaus and Le Corbusier at Columbia, enlisted Gwathmey to collaborate on a new addition to the Straus estate: a stark white assortment of cylinders, triangles, and rectangles that somehow came together to form a home. The typical early Gwathmey was a cheeky rebuke to the mock-Tudor Straus manor up the hill, a break from tradition safely cosseted within the compound. Rog's father said not a word about the design. "He loved the idea of us being on the land," says Nina.

Straus also loved the idea of his son's finding a permanent place in the office. One of the things that most surprised Rog when he started full-time was that no one called his father Bill. When they yelled for

Roger, "I thought they were talking to me," says Rog. "People who know me from Farrar, Straus still refer to me as Rog, but they're the only ones who do. I didn't like being Roger Straus III. I've always felt that if nothing else, everyone deserves their own fucking name."

His too-similar name didn't make things any easier with the office wife. Peggy "made it clear that I didn't have any special access to the president's office just because we had the same initials. In fact, she even lopped off one of my initials." In interoffice memos, "Peggy decided I'd just be R." In person, it would be impossible to confuse the young editor with the man in the big office. Rog had a scruffy beard and favored simple white shirts without so much as a tie—never mind a different ascot every day of the week. He was warm and energetic like his father but not domineering, an overgrown Lab to Roger's sinewy wolf, and he sounded more like a therapist than an aristocrat. Whereas Roger Jr. had a fierce singles tennis game, Roger III took up deep-sea kayaking. The isolation and monotony (and lack of competition) would have driven his father crazy.

And where Rog's father had turned down a tennis book—the Boyars' ill-fated follow-up to *Yes I Can*—Rog pursued commercial books about his hobbies and enthusiasms. His two big gets in those early years were memoirs by Apollo 11 astronaut Michael Collins (the one who *didn't* walk on the moon) and race-car driver Jackie Stewart. His father "wasn't particularly interested in them," Rog says of the books he acquired. "But they usually did reasonably well. They weren't really Farrar, Straus books but what the hell."

One of Rog's enthusiasms did result, indirectly and belatedly, in a classic—though it's no surprise he hasn't gotten credit for it before. Rog met Michael Collins through NASA's publicist, Julian Scheer, who convinced Rog to set aside his liberal antipathy to the space program and come watch Apollo 9 take off. Rog was "completely hooked on the experience," and he was pretty sure Tom Wolfe would get a kick out of it, too. He called Wolfe shortly before the moon landing. "You've got to come down here," he told Wolfe. "It's a subculture of religious fanatics." Wolfe watched Apollo 11, was soon hooked as well, and set out to write a book—perhaps even a novel—on the moon shot.

Before long, Rog switched from editorial to marketing—a catch-all department that included publicity and advertising, a term which was barely in his father's vocabulary. It was Rog's idea. "We had great editors," he says, "but the thing we were less good at was selling things." He crafted some winning ad campaigns—for Wolfe and for Gaia Servadio's novel *Melinda*—but mostly he left the review wrangling and the buzz building to Roger and his publicity girls. "My father's genius as a marketer, and it really was genius, was publicity," says Rog. "My interest was much more technical, it was much more in the distribution." Nor was his interest trivial, even in his father's eyes. Straus well knew that the firm still wasn't diversified enough. He let his son pursue the purchase of smaller houses dealing in niche markets, while figuring out how to make more out of Noonday.

This did not mean suddenly going into the cookbook business. Lyndon Johnson's Great Society programs, especially Title I, had boosted library and university funding, making scholarly work—not just textbooks but specialized journals that libraries had to stock—a growth industry. Rog knew FSG was well positioned to snap up a piece of the field. In 1968, he made a deal to acquire Octagon, a press specializing in scholarly reprints. Then, at a meeting of the anti–Vietnam War group Publishers for Peace, he met an editor named Arthur Wang. Wang was struggling with a quasi-academic imprint known as Hill & Wang, which focused on current affairs but also had big properties like Elie Wiesel's *Night*. FSG bought Hill & Wang in 1971, and Wang came over as the editor in charge of the program.

These were fairly canny moves; at the very least they were more successful than Rog's father's recent pursuits—first Grove Press, then Oxford University Press, then Everyman's Library with its giant backlist—all of which fizzled for one reason or another. Hill & Wang eventually stagnated, and Wang proved surprisingly unproductive. Rog was left to wonder if maybe they'd picked up the wrong editor and should have gone with Lawrence Hill. But it was a step in the direction of sustainability—something Rog believes he spent more time thinking about than his bold, impulsive father. "For all my long hair and facial hair and antiwar stuff, I think I was fundamentally more conservative than he was," says Rog. "I was always looking for stability someplace."

Indeed, it was Rog's business savvy, not his hippie streak, that led to a lucrative revival of the books of Hermann Hesse, the long-dead Nobelist. Working to beef up Noonday, Rog kept a close eye on the orders for its backlist titles. Generally they could move perhaps one thousand copies per year of a Hesse novel. *"Journey to the East,"* Rog says, a note of reminiscence in his voice as he rattles off the catalog identification number from memory: "N109." It had been barely selling well enough to stay in print, but suddenly was doing ten times its usual business. "We knew it was some kind of youth counterculture thing." Evidence of the trend was in FSG's own catalogs: Kerouac on his Buddhist kick; Wolfe on the conflation of drugs and spirituality. Even Trappist monk Tom Merton was writing a book about Zen. Mysticism and the East were hot. Yet it was the numbers that tipped off Rog.

In 1967, Straus quickly made a deal for nine more Hesse titles, which FSG rolled out one after the other, a mystical caravan of riches. It was a good fit for FSG and for Straus, who was just then deciding to cast aside his wariness of "the Krauts" and attend the largest international publishing rights bazaar in the world. In the wake of his first arrival at the Frankfurt Book Fair in 1966, FSG became arguably the most important publisher of foreign works in the United States.

It was that beautiful Mercedes convertible that thawed Roger's relations with the Germans. "When I came to work there," says Peggy Miller, "he had a Chrysler like a boat." But not long after she arrived, Roger fell in love with a Benz 250SE. The open-top became as much a signature accessory as the ascots, the house in Purchase, and the succession of black standard poodles (Maximilian and later Schwartz) that roamed his parties. Twenty years after the war, it was still a bold move for a Jewish-American to patronize a carmaker with a Nazi past. Even having crossed that Danube, Roger had a hard time deciding whether to set foot in Germany.

He already knew many of the most prestigious European publishers, and took them out whenever they were in town. Inge Feltrinelli, who still presides over her late husband Giangiacomo Feltrinelli's Italian publishing house, remembers elaborate lunches with Straus and Sontag and others at La Côte Basque, "with Truman Capote and all his swans. He took us to all the 'in' places." He showed them, in other words, that his New York was just as glamorous and cultured as the great European capitals. In his scarves and cuff links and almost feminine brooches, they recognized a fellow aristocrat. And in the thriving American scene, they recognized a gusto and vitality of which postwar Europe was still somewhat sapped.

"You are the man for Frankfurt," the Feltrinellis told Roger over one of those fabulous lunches. "But half my family was killed by the Nazis," he replied, though most of his relatives had been in the United States for a century. Still, they kept up the pressure. FSG's only presence at the fair was Herbert Lottman, another of Straus's scouts, sitting alone in a bare booth managed by a large distributor. Though Straus was now making regular business trips to Paris, Rome, and London, tending personally to everyone from Carlo Levi to Colette's daughter, here he was just another American doing business by proxy. Many American houses at least had a subsidiary rights specialist at the fair, and they published less work in translation than FSG did. Every important publisher in the world congregated there to do business. FSG was being left out.

"If you can buy a Mercedes, you can go to Germany," clear-eyed Peggy told her boss. Sontag prodded from a literary angle, raving about Theodor Adorno and other Teutonic geniuses. Roger began to listen. "We have been singularly unsuccessful in keeping au courant with the German market," he wrote a British publisher in 1966, "and we have reason to believe that there is a good deal bubbling there."

It wasn't just Susan's idea. The nine-book Hesse deal had been brokered by Michael Roloff, a German-American scout who worked for Siegfried Unseld, the charismatic head of the prestigious Suhrkamp Verlag publishing house. Roloff was Straus's kind of German—a leftist who spent his childhood "secure in castles while my parents were off in the resistance"—and Unseld was his kind of publisher. Since taking over the firm in 1959 from its founder, concentration-camp survivor Peter Suhrkamp, Unseld was building up a stable of writers so influential that critic George Steiner would refer to West Germany's "Suhrkamp Kultur." Straus put Roloff on FSG's payroll, securing a direct pipeline to Suhrkamp's young, dynamic authors, all loosely affiliated with the postwar German intellectual society known as Gruppe 47. Roloff brought FSG—mostly via Suhrkamp—not just Hesse but Adorno, Austrian playwright Peter Handke, Hans Erich Nossack, and Nelly Sachs, a Jewish refugee to Sweden who won the 1966 Nobel Prize (just as Roger made his first Frankfurt jaunt).

"Suhrkamp Kultur" represented the kind of intellectual dominance to which Straus aspired. Other Guggenheims could have their museums and scholarships; what he dreamed of was to spawn cultural movements, to grow "FSG Culture" in the petri dish of 19 Union Square West. That culture was high-minded and scrappy, aggressive and refined, quintessentially American but thoroughly international, like Roger Straus himself. And it was highly appealing to European publishers, who valued cultural capital far more than most of their American counterparts.

Even today, with deals being done in a few keystrokes, no serious publisher with global ambitions can afford to miss a rainy October in Frankfurt. What is now Europe's banking center has hosted book fairs as far back as the thirteenth century; it's only twenty-five miles from Mainz, birthplace of Gutenberg. The modern incarnation was founded in 1948, partly in order to overcome the ravages of Hitler but also to bring Europe together and to revive Germany's true cultural heritage. It was held in the grand neo-Baroque Festhalle, built in 1909, which has since become merely the gateway to an exhibition complex as sprawling and brutally modern as a major airport. A plaque under the Festhalle's immense dome reads, roughly translated: ON THE NIGHT OF NOVEMBER 8TH, 1938, HUNDREDS OF FRANKFURT'S JEWS WERE ROUNDED UP IN THIS HALL AND SEVERELY BEATEN. THE FIRST MASS TRANSPORT TO THE CONCENTRATION CAMPS DEPARTED FROM HERE.

Roger came to his first Frankfurt solo, planning on something "fast and furious and very business," but when he got there he was seldom alone. His old Italian friend Silvio Senigallia was staying in the same hotel, the InterContinental. A convivial morning nosh was followed by lunch at the stately Hessischer Hof just across the avenue from the fair, organized by Inge Feltrinelli to roll out the red carpet for the American newcomer. There were about ten other Europeans, including Claude Gallimard (French publisher of Gide, Proust, and Sartre) and the Brit George Weidenfeld (Isaiah Berlin, *Lolita*).

Roger knew some of these publishers already, but at Frankfurt, Feltrinelli's circle was a durable clique. Straus was quickly adopted into this exclusive crowd, which comprised not the biggest European publishers but the most literary and the most fascinating. Giangiacomo Feltrinelli was a militant leftist reputed to be involved in anti-government terrorism (a few years later he would be killed, officially by accidental detonation of his own explosives, beside a pylon near Milan). Heinrich Maria Ledig-Rowohlt had been recruited to work for a major publisher only to learn later, in a Dickensian twist, that the publisher was his long-lost father, who wanted to pass the firm on to him. Siegfried Unseld, while in the German navy, had escaped the Russians by diving into the sea and fleeing; he became a publisher on the recommendation of Hermann Hesse, who was impressed by his graduate dissertation.

Even the Brits were interesting. George Weidenfeld had fled Austria just before the *Anschluss*, worked in the BBC, and within ten years had befriended nearly every leader in Europe. Later he would become a lord, as would a closer friend of Straus, Faber and Faber head Matthew Evans. Frankfurt was paradise for a man whose dinner-party opener was "Tell me the story of your life"; everyone seemed to have a fascinating answer.

And what did Roger have to offer as the American delegate to this coterie? Unlike most American publishers, he bought foreign books rather than just selling American ones. Then there was his style. Roger's admirers in Frankfurt liked to think of him as the most European of American publishers, but what singled him out was a meld of Guggenheim-heir hauteur and John Wayne brashness. The ascots paired with gangster-striped suits, the mid-Atlantic drawl spiked with a New York tang, the low-toned gossip about high-toned intellectuals—it was a beautiful contrast to observe, playing to American stereotypes while siding with the elitists. It was perfectly encapsulated in one of his favorite toasts: "Fuck the peasants!"

Like building a publishing house, conquering Frankfurt would take years. But Straus made a great first impression, especially on younger people like Michael Krüger at Hanser Verlag and Matthew Evans at Faber. "Publishing in the sixties, when I started, was incredibly pompous," says Evans. "And here was this showman who I was absolutely attracted to—a sort of guru figure." Roger took cabs to and from parties the first few years, but after arriving at one meeting late and soaking wet, he decided "never again." He hired a driver with a Mercedes, Herr Roth, and used him ever after. In lean years, he paid for it out of his own pocket. It was more than just a luxury. Peggy remembers Roger's habit of picking up passing acquaintances and giving them rides to the fair—"if it was somebody you wanted to know. It was contact for him, that's what he wanted the most. And he met a lot of people that way." Eventually, in Feltrinelli's estimation, "he became the king of the book fair."

Before his second tour of Frankfurt, Roger was already referring to "my usual suite at the InterContinental." He invited his scout Michael Roloff along, figuring "I owe him one" for his role in the Hesse deal. Roloff says he played "introductory beagle for Roger among German publishers," among whom Straus was still standoffish. Roloff also took him to sketchier gatherings; they waited for pot once, but it failed to materialize. Not that Roger didn't have fun. Roloff saw him at the hotel with more than one woman whom the scout had never seen before and would never see again.

Straus made one more solo tour in 1968, but the following year he came down with a serious case of pneumonia. It kept him in the hospital for six weeks and away from Frankfurt in 1969. Lila Karpf went in his place, reluctantly. She preferred to leave the schmoozing to Roger, so in 1970 they went back to the old routine. Yet Frankfurt was becoming unmanageable for one person—especially the owner of the whole firm—and so in the seventies Roger began bringing Peggy Miller. The keeper of his schedule and his secrets was more useful to

Roger at Frankfurt meetings and dinners than she was answering his mail back at the office. In Germany she was his gatekeeper and constant companion.

The pair would always go to London afterward, seeing British publishers and attending plays that Peggy, a theater buff, also chose for Roger. They often left just after intermission. ("I don't like plays with old men in dirty underwear," Roger liked to say.) Soon they were taking a weekend before Frankfurt to stay near Munich, visiting a few publishers there but mostly staying in spas on the Tegernsee, a pristine Bavarian lake. They usually stayed in an old timbered hotel with a broad porch, where Peggy indulged in her favorite dessert, a delicate seasonal plum cake. The annual Frankfurt trip, lasting as long as a month, was the part of Roger's compartmentalized life that was devoted to European publishers and to Peggy. Some of those who didn't know him well thought she was his wife. Some of those who knew her better, in the halls of 19 Union Square West, speculated on the extra spring in Miller's step come September, trilling: "Peggy's gonna get laid in Frankfurt!"

In truth there was little time for anything but business. Meetings and meals were scheduled tightly. But deals were best done elsewhere. Straus learned this the hard way, after he was talked into buying a "hot" Hungarian book one year before having anyone read it. "When it was translated back in America," says Peggy, "everybody thought it was shit." Frankfurt was more about building relationships, generating buzz, or celebrating deals already done. Yet the fruits of the festival are easy to see just by looking at the catalogs; they tell the story of a house increasingly dominating the foreign market, snapping up buzz books the growing conglomerates couldn't be bothered to gamble on.

Take 1968, the year of Didion's *Slouching Towards Bethlehem,* Wolfe's *The Electric Kool-Aid Acid Test,* and upheaval all over the world. FSG also published *Lovers,* a play by Brian Friel; Carlos Fuentes's surrealist novel *A Change of Skin;* Gustavo Sainz's pop-obsessed Mexican debut, *Gazapo;* the comic picaresque *Melinda,* by the Italian-English bon vivant Gaia Servadio; two reissued Hesse titles; a new Knut Hamsun translation; Lowell's loose translations of Baudelaire; Aleksandr

Solzhenitsyn's *Cancer Ward;* and a collection of Isaac Babel stories edited by his daughter, Nathalie.

Leaving Solzhenitsyn aside, there were two other works by living dissidents on the list. Vassilis Vassilikos had been exiled to Paris during the Greek junta by the time FSG published the English translation of *Z*, a thinly fictionalized account of the assassination of a leftist politician. The novel, a Sontag favorite, was banned in Greece, lending the book some outré glamour. Nonetheless, the adaptation by leftist Greek filmmaker Costa-Gavras was far more successful. Straus was more closely involved in the case of Mihajlo Mihajlov, a Yugoslavian author whose anti-Soviet *Moscow Summer,* published by FSG, earned him several stints in Tito's prisons. Roger had managed to snag it ahead of better-heeled firms, including Viking and McGraw-Hill. He pleaded repeatedly with his friends in the State Department to influence Tito, and even became personally entangled a few years later, when the Yugoslavian government confiscated two letters Mihajlov had written Straus about his prison memoirs.

Tito probably didn't know that Straus had a history of Cold War associations, even beyond that black phone in his office. He ran the books committee of Eisenhower's People to People Program, which fought communist propaganda across the globe. The United States Information Agency, also involved in the program, pitched him books that they funded. He wouldn't say how many such books he published, but Roger certainly was not averse to vanity publishing (or what he liked to call a "whorehouse" book). He put out a puff guide to his family's own company, ASARCO, and in 1968—the year of all those brilliant FSG books—he also published a book on antique French paperweights by his banker friend and FSG shareholder Frank Manheim.

The USIA business, however, mattered to many more people—a fact that became abundantly clear with the minor furor over Jeane Kirkpatrick's *The Strategy of Deception: A Study in World-Wide Communist Tactics.* The book, which even a USIA committee member admitted was a "simplified statement," was published by Farrar, Straus in 1963, and its introduction noted the government's support, though not its extent: around $15,000, along with a bulk order of two thousand books to distribute across various agencies. The problem, as noted in a vehement *Washington Post* editorial, was that it was being sold in the United States, making it government propaganda distributed to its own citizens.

According to Straus, this was his final piece of government work. But he did have one last call from his CIA contact in the early seventies. Reluctantly, Roger agreed to a personal visit from a younger agent. The agent wanted a look at an early English-language typescript of a Solzhenitsyn novel. "Obviously, they wanted to cover the book fast," Roger surmised. He refused. "I said to this young man . . . 'Doesn't anybody read Russian at Disneyland East anymore?'" If they did, he said, they should go up to Brentano's, where they were selling the Russian edition. "That was my last intercourse with them." Roger III wonders exactly where his father's motivations had lain. "I have such an inexact sense of my father's political conscience," he says, "where the line was drawn between what he felt he was doing for his country and what he was doing for his business."

It was likely a combination of both. He opposed the Vietnam War and Goldwater's 1964 campaign. He was also staunchly against red-baiting when it interfered with the culture business, and didn't mind using his inside track to fight it. In a letter soliciting Arthur Schlesinger's help in allowing the novelist Carlos Fuentes into the country, Straus invoked his past work: "Lord knows I am sympathetic, to say the very least, to 'our position.' On the other hand, the problem of the 'artist-writer' is a rather special one." Fuentes was let in. Five years later, under Nixon, Fuentes was refused again, and again Straus worked tirelessly on his behalf. In letters and cables to various consuls and ambassadors, all the way up to Henry Kissinger, Straus pointed out the absurdity of a writer who was condemned by Mexico's Communist Party being denied a U.S. visa on the grounds that he was a communist.

During those five years between the U.S. bans on Fuentes, Straus had grown to love the Mexican novelist. Imposing and handsome, a diplomat's son who lived in more countries before puberty than most people see in a lifetime, Carlos Fuentes cut an impressive and very modish figure. Tales of his activism run alongside rumors of love affairs with Jean Seberg and Jeanne Moreau. Before he died in 2012, Fuentes said that at his first meeting with Roger, brokered by Carl Brandt, the two "discovered we had a common taste for dry martinis," and much else besides. Fuentes's *The Death of Artemio Cruz* had been the topic under discussion. This surreal saga, built around the final thoughts of a powerful and corrupt tycoon, was an exemplar of what was already known as El Boom, a new wave of Latin American literature that was just beginning to crest. Roger couldn't help admiring writers, such as Fuentes, Octavio Paz, and Pablo Neruda, who wielded such outsize influence at home that they were alternately persecuted and appointed ambassadors. Fuentes and Straus cemented their friendship on a visit to Paris, where Fuentes was serving as Mexico's ambassador, in October 1963. Fuentes followed up with a long, amusing letter about his boat trip back to Mexico, which Roger circulated around the office—to a chorus of marginalia: "Captivating!" said John Farrar. "Marvelous letter," raved Giroux.

Like Edmund Wilson and Susan Sontag, Fuentes quickly became a writer-consultant. But for a few twists, he could have helped Farrar, Straus sew up all the members of El Boom. Alas, Mario Vargas Llosa was under contract to Grove (Straus would pick him up years later). Fuentes also tipped them off to Gabriel García Márquez, and FSG had options on two of his books. They decided to pass, however, on the recommendation of a negative reader's report on the novel *La Mala Hora*, which read in part: "There is no ray of hope to light for the reader a way out of this rotten little world. Although I appreciate the literary quality that earned a prize for this book, I do not see a high sales potential for it in the U.S. market." A contract for *La Mala Hora* would probably have given FSG an option on the next novel, *One Hundred Years of Solitude*—to date the most acclaimed and popular work of El Boom. Maybe, in hindsight, the rejection was not such a smart decision. But Straus did pick up a bad-boy Spanish writer by the name of Camilo José Cela—who would win a Nobel Prize in the eighties—and he managed to get his foot in the door with Pablo Neruda.

Farrar, Straus was only one of the American firms publishing Neruda—just a single strand in a tangle of translators and editors who made a cottage industry out of the great communist Chilean poet. Neruda wanted information to be open and free, so he never bothered to discriminate among those making money off his name. Straus, who had published *The Heights of Macchu Picchu* in 1967, believed FSG could put his career in order. Roger asked Fuentes to make FSG's case to Neruda, a good friend of his. FSG was after the whole body of work, past, present, and future. "It ain't exactly the way to get rich," Roger wrote Carl Brandt, "but Neruda is a great poet." Fuentes was happy to oblige. He spoke to Neruda and wrote Roger: "I told him that being published by you means an amount of generosity, quality, exactitude, courage and friendship that go well beyond the usual bounds of the writer-publisher relationship."

Straus then enlisted Lila Karpf, who spoke and read fluent Spanish, in wooing the poet. She just missed meeting with him on a trip to Chile in 1967, but they later struck up a professional correspondence in Spanish. "I'm a meddler," Karpf once told Isaac Singer's biographer, "because I believe everything concerning an author's career—the look of a volume and the advertising promotion and rights and all—should mesh." Roger, never a stickler for exact titles, gave her a key role in the negotiations.

When Neruda won the Nobel Prize, in 1971, he realized he needed an agent in order to sort out his career. He was aging and had a day job, as the socialist president Salvador Allende's ambassador to France. Fuentes tried to sell him on his own agent, Carl Brandt, but Neruda opted for Carmen Balcells, who was also FSG's subagent in Spain. She traveled to New York in February 1972, in advance of Neruda's trip to the United States in April, with an eye to choosing the American publisher that would control his legacy. Unlike their more threadbare competitor New Directions, FSG could make a decent cash outlay despite the risks: $25,000 for five books, including an incomplete memoir. Balcells felt lucky to make the deal, considering the messy state of Neruda's rights.

The poet made 19 Union Square West a whistle stop on a highly publicized American visit in April 1972. The staff lined up for auto-graphs. Neruda, resembling a stately bloodhound, gazed down from Roger's office into Union Square, noting its history as a site of radical agitation during the twenties. The grubby headquarters that struck so many as a Dickensian sweatshop were, in the eyes of the famous Marxist, a workers' paradise. "This is the way a publishing office should look," Roger remembered Neruda saying. "Nothing but books, nothing but a view of the Square . . . All those uptown publishing houses I've seen are not for me." He then sat down to a long and com-plicated meeting. Aside from certain new ideas hatched by Neruda, Giroux, and Karpf—for example, a children's book—there was the new information that two of the contracted books had been published elsewhere while Neruda wasn't paying attention.

Two more works were thrown in as consolation, but Straus and Balcells went back and forth for eighteen months over amendments. In the meantime, Roger heard rumors that Neruda had terminal can-cer—which obviously didn't bode well for a finished memoir—but Balcells denied it. In April, FSG sent its check for $15,000, but over the summer of 1973, Straus almost reneged on the deal. Balcells insisted that Neruda's nearly complete memoirs were not part of the origi-nal contract. If they weren't, Straus retorted, there *was* no deal, and he'd like his $15,000 back. Eventually, Roger threw in another $5,000. Neruda relented—he was in fact dying of cancer—and signed the final contract amendment for seven books, plus options on all other En-glish translations of his work, on September 7, 1973.

Straus wrote Neruda to thank him personally on September 11. That day, forces led by Chilean general Augusto Pinochet deposed Neruda's friend Salvador Allende in a coup. At his home on Isla Negra, Neruda hastily sketched the conclusion of his memoir, writing that Allende had died not by his own hand, as Pinochet claimed, but under machine-gun fire. "The North Americans," he added, "instigated and financed the military action." (Documents released under President Bill Clinton finally confirmed that even if Nixon and the CIA didn't plan the coup, they generously funded people who did.) As Neruda was writing those words, his home was raided and ransacked. Questioned about incriminating documents, he told the unit commander, "Look here: There's only one thing of danger for you here—poetry."

A week later, Carlos Fuentes persuaded Mexico's President Luis Echeverría to send an ambassador to the hospital where Neruda lay, offering the poet and his wife passage on a plane out of Chile. According to Neruda's biographer, the couple would have left on September 24. But Neruda died on the 23rd. Over the next three weeks, neither Straus nor Balcells knew what had become of the memoirs. As it turned out, the Mexican ambassador had flown out with the manuscript. Neruda's widow, Matilde, had also managed to save a copy. She wound up completing and editing the final version, which Farrar, Straus published, as *Memoirs,* in 1977.

Neruda was big game but not the most thrilling, or even the most difficult. While in New York, Neruda was asked repeatedly what he thought of the dissident of dissidents, Aleksandr Solzhenitsyn. Privately he made fun of the persecuted writer's notorious irascibility, and publicly he said only that he had "no intention of becoming an instrument for anti-Soviet propaganda." Roger could only laugh. Even while showing off Union Square to the Chilean Marxist, the publisher was eagerly anticipating the final translation of what many considered the Soviet dissident's masterpiece. "The big fish," as he put it, "was *August 1914.*"

FSG had a short but fraught history with Solzhenitsyn. The author had published his slim novel *One Day in the Life of Ivan Denisovich* during the rule of Nikita Khrushchev, when Stalin's horrors were openly condemned and the fictionalized exposé of a Gulag prisoner openly published. But after Khrushchev's fall, the censors reasserted themselves, and Solzhenitsyn's work was banned. The Soviet Union was not a signatory to international copyright law, which meant that when Solzhenitsyn's work leaked out—his novels *The First Circle* and *Cancer Ward* preceded *August 1914*—publishers around the world considered it public domain, printing editions without even contacting the writer. Harper & Row made a legitimate deal for *The First Circle,* while FSG bought *Cancer Ward,* an allegory on Stalin's crimes set in a bleak

Soviet hospital. Straus got it through the Bodley Head, the British press run by his friend Max Reinhardt.

Solzhenitsyn received royalties via a Czech dissident who smuggled some of the work out, but unauthorized copies made their way to three other publishers. Two backed off in the face of FSG–Bodley Head lawyers, but not Dial Press in the United States. They managed to put out *Cancer Ward* before FSG did, without paying royalties to the author. This meant that FSG was putting out a book, for which they'd paid roughly $20,000, in direct competition with an edition that had already been out for several months. Straus could have balked and at least saved the cost of printing. But he was committed to publishing Solzhenitsyn. The FSG edition, published in the spring of 1969, sold fine, around fifty thousand copies, with paperback rights sold to Bantam.

FSG followed *Cancer Ward* with *The Love-Girl and the Innocent* (a play), *Stories and Prose Poems* (pieces in the public domain), and a new translation of *Denisovich*. All were acquired through Bodley Head, which owned English-language rights. Every book required a serious copyright battle, and a ream or two of FSG's Solzhenitsyn papers are devoted to the intricacies of such laws. Solzhenitsyn would publicly denounce and disavow foreign publication as anti-Soviet agitation—he had to, in order to remain a free Soviet citizen—but privately he was a devoted capitalist. He finally hired a Swiss lawyer, Fritz Heeb, to organize his affairs, and Heeb promptly threatened to tear up the FSG contracts.

At least Heeb was a reliable intermediary, rather than a number of loose associates—smugglers, after all—whose claims had to be taken on faith. The complications certainly added some drama to the annual Frankfurt jaunts. "We were running around like crazy people," says Peggy Miller. "Who had the rights? Who could get the rights? I always said that my gray hair started when we started publishing Russians." It seems from letters that Giroux, who'd gone white-haired long ago, did much of the worrying back home. Roger called him "sort of an expert in the matter" of the copyright details. For all of Roger's crowing about Solzhenitsyn, staffers say it was Giroux who persuaded him this particular Russian was worth the trouble.

After Solzhenitsyn was expelled from Russia and could finally meet his publishers, he proved just as difficult to deal with in person. When the Bodley Head's Max Reinhardt finally saw him in Switzerland, Solzhenitsyn began to read off a list of thirty specific publishing questions. His first question, which took a half hour to read, contained quite a few subquestions of its own. Reinhardt forced him to stop for a moment, and replied, "You are wrong on every point. What about the next one?" They went on like that for five hours, he recalled to Roger, before Solzhenitsyn agreed they could continue to publish him.

Once the rest of the world really got to know Solzhenitsyn—not just his didactic personality but also his illiberal views—his reputation began to decline. So it might be difficult to imagine how widely the dissident was read back then—certainly in the millions worldwide, though exact numbers among all the pirate editions would be impossible to pin down. Only a decade after Stalin's death, Solzhenitsyn's eyewitness account of the Gulags was a moral shock to the Left, another nail in the coffin of chic intellectual Stalinism. Even critics of his lesser work deferred to his powerful voice. A negative *New York Times* review of *Cancer Ward* called *Denisovich* "one of the masterworks of 20th-century fiction."

Putting up with the pirates, Soviet censors, Swiss lawyers, and the ornery author himself was worth it for both the esteem and the book sales. Roger said it best: "We were dealing with a great author, not with some schmuck who wrote a book or two." Almost as important, for Roger, he seemed a shoo-in for the Nobel Prize.

By chance—or rather on the strength of his many connections—Roger had already met the publisher who would soon control worldwide rights to *August 1914*, Otto Walter of the German press Luchterhand Verlag. The man who introduced them was a young *New York Times* journalist named Henry Raymont. Roger didn't consider Raymont the world's most careful reporter, but the two men found each other useful. Raymont gave little FSG great press. By his own admission, he'd give more coverage to a $150,000 FSG deal than an $80 million acquisition by William Jovanovich. In return, Raymont got all the choice gossip and contacts Roger could spare.

FSG's next Solzhenitsyn book, a collection called *Stories and Prose*

Poems, consisted of work that—being in the public domain—was essentially free. But Roger endeared himself to Otto Walter by paying royalties and a token advance anyway. He drove a hard bargain for *Stories*, but he knew the value of playing it straight with writers and publishers, especially when they were rumored to be front-runners for the Nobel. Just after another cordial lunch between Straus and Walter at the 1970 Frankfurt fair, the news came down from Stockholm that Solzhenitsyn had won the big prize. Two months later, he accepted in absentia—afraid that if he left the U.S.S.R. he could never return. It was the most dramatic Nobel moment in years, reinforcing the dissident's legend and the prize's geopolitical relevance. A short time later, word leaked out about *August 1914*. It would be the first novel in a great cycle, ultimately called *The Red Wheel*, carrying Russia from the first shot of World War I to the final purges of the Revolution. Who knew if Solzhenitsyn could broaden his scope from Gulag allegories to the grit and fog and snow of war? If he succeeded, it could be the *War and Peace* of the twentieth century. Either way, plenty of readers would be curious enough to buy a copy.

In May, Otto Walter let interested publishers know that he was the man to talk to; Fritz Heeb had given him world rights, breaking Heeb's earlier guarantee to Max Reinhardt at the Bodley Head. Straus had to assume Harper & Row was going to bid, since they had published *The First Circle*, and they were certain to bid more than FSG. Learning that *August* was available in Russian in Paris, he had it sent over. He later wrote Reinhardt that his "ESP" told him to call Otto, rather than make a bid by cable. He made a preemptive offer of $200,000 for the U.S. rights. A week later, Straus wrote Walter that the book was "a masterpiece." If it would help, he said, he could "come over and actually firm the terms and sign the contract in your office . . . I am completely available for such a quick trip at a moment's notice."

The following Sunday, the Raymonts came up to visit the Purchase house. All through lunch, and as they lounged at the pool, Henry pestered Roger about Solzhenitsyn. He said he knew nothing. Raymont wanted to discuss it over lunch on Tuesday, but Straus demurred. "As soon as I know anything, I'll let you know," he said.

Roger couldn't have lunch on Tuesday because he was going to be meeting with Otto Walter that day, alone, at the Frankfurter Hof. Walter was taking meeting after meeting with publishers all over the world in Frankfurt's grandest old hotel. Straus didn't know if any other American publishers were bothering to fly over. He met Walter and his staff at three in the afternoon. Roger recalled playing it very straight with Walter: "I was clean as a hound's tooth." He even said that should his friend at the Bodley Head get British rights (and they were by no means favored), he would cede Canadian rights to them. The subtext was that he stood by his friends. He offered $250,000. It was way too low. He got the sense that Walter wanted him to double it, so he made a compromise offer of $400,000. It didn't feel lowball to Roger; it was the highest offer he'd ever made. "I had had no conversation with paperback houses and no conversations with book clubs," he said. "I just assumed that I could cover myself when I got home, and whether the bank was going to cover me or not was another question."

Over two hours of negotiations, Roger was extremely generous with every other term: 16 percent straight royalties where 15 percent was the highest even for most-favored authors; 65 percent to the author of subrights that usually went 50-50. Otto Walter, finally, went for it. He and Roger shook hands, had an early dinner, and said goodbye. It was all over but the publicity. Roger flew home the next day, firmed up the deal in writing, and called Henry Raymont. It later came out that Little, Brown had offered more than $600,000, making FSG the underbidder by at least a third.

The story in the *Times,* a week after the meeting, was another Raymont air-kiss to FSG: "In the fiercest international contest for a work in fiction in years, Farrar, Straus and Giroux, a small but prestigious New York publisher, has obtained the American rights to Aleksandr I. Solzhenitsyn's latest novel, 'August 1914.'" Otto Walter was quoted as saying, "More important than money was their dedication to literary quality and their past regard for the works of Solzhenitsyn." FSG's bold publication of *Cancer Ward* was cited, and Roger was quoted spinning the coup—and Raymont's story—into the perfect advertisement for FSG: "I am glad to say that personal relations still cut more ice in publishing than cabled bids of huge sums of money."

8

Egg-Bound

Just before Christmas in 1970, Straus wrote Henry Raymont with unconcealed Schadenfreude about attending a holiday dinner at the Players Club for the editor of the *New York Times Book Review*. It was a "great success," he reported. "About half the people looked happy." As for the other half: "Viking had purged 36 people. McCall's have fired another 30 or so, jettisoned their juvenile department, and raped the editorial department . . . There is publishing blood all over the streets. Me, I am having fun and we declared a Christmas bonus for our staff!" Even as 1971 rolled around and the blood continued to flow, Roger felt removed from the horror show. In February he reported to Raymont, who'd left the books beat for Israel, that Simon & Schuster had cut their payroll by $300,000. "I didn't know there was anybody there anyway."

Roger was right about FSG's bucking the trend, but only for about another year. Solzhenitsyn and a few other successes generated over $1 million in trade sales during the first eight months of 1972, but over the comparable period the following year that number was cut in half—to less than the 1965 total.

The company banked increasingly on the scholarly presses Rog had just acquired. Some mornings, the elder Straus would visit his sales department, open the envelopes, and add up all the Octagon and Hill & Wang money that came in that day, ten dollars or twenty dollars at a time. It would have taken a lot of those tiny checks to pay off the money borrowed to acquire those imprints. As of late 1973, FSG still owed more than $600,000 to the shareholders of those companies, on top of unpaid debts to U.S. Trust and a wealthy investor (and distant cousin of Bob's), French film producer Claude Giroux.

Contributing to the sales decline, some core FSG writers were either "egg-bound" or drifting in mid-career, threatening not just the firm's bottom line but also its cachet as the house of the moment. *August 1914* proved easier to acquire than to publish. The ideal translator, Max Hayward, was contractually tied to a fierce rival of the Bodley Head in England, so FSG and the Bodley Head went with Michael Glenny, a British Sovietologist–turned–Russian professor. During a cocktail toast to Solzhenitsyn held by his worldwide publishers at the 1971 Frankfurt fair, everyone agreed to bring out his book simultaneously in August 1972. This promise turned into a nightmare, as Glenny begged repeatedly for patience and money. He fought off a near-breakdown just in time for September publication. Yet after the *New York Times Book Review* mocked Glenny's translation mercilessly, he was quoted in the same paper trashing FSG and the Bodley Head for rushing him, and added for good measure, "No one has dared to say how badly written the book is." It was a major embarrassment. The translator claimed he was misquoted. Straus canceled part of Glenny's American tour and demanded he write a rebuttal, which the *Times* never ran. ·

Though *1914* sold well into the hundreds of thousands in hardcover, *The Gulag Archipelago*—Solzhenitsyn's great nonfiction cycle, the works that would dominate his obituaries—had already been guaranteed to Harper & Row. FSG's sequels to *August 1914* were commercially disappointing. The immediate follow-up, *Lenin in Zurich*, disappeared just as the second *Gulag* book took off. Roger gave up on it after seeing it on page seven of the *Book Review.*

After her second essay collection, *Styles of Radical Will,* Susan Sontag entered what she called her "blocked period," failing to finish another novel and delaying projects Straus thought were in the can. After a contracted work on China failed to materialize, he had to redirect the advance to a later series of essays on photography. Sontag spent most of her time either in Paris or in Sweden making art films whose screenplays FSG dutifully published at a loss. While there, she got an advance from a wealthy backer, Henry Carter Carnegie, to make a movie—which she never did. After dunning her repeatedly for the five thousand dollars she owed, Carnegie turned to Straus. Knowing the type, Roger handled the wealthy scion's legal threats with a deft mixture of dismissal and appeasement, repaying Carnegie interest-free with the help of a short story here and a lecture fee there. It was time-consuming business, considering the returns.

Tom Wolfe, so fast out of the gate with his double-barreled 1968 release, had promised a novel about the 1969 moon landing by the end of 1970. Instead he wrote a series of nonfiction pieces about NASA for *Rolling Stone,* and the old $21,000 fiction advance was repaid out of royalties for pasted-together collections of the sort he'd so passionately deplored in his defensive letter to Henry Robbins. (*The Painted Word* was literally pasted together. The twenty-thousand-word *Harper's* essay, padded with art photos, was mocked up with rubber cement on Roger's conference table on a Saturday afternoon and rushed to press for emergency royalties.)

None of these, not even the game-changing *Radical Chic & Mau-Mauing the Flak Catchers,* was blockbuster material. In March 1973, Wolfe contracted for a book called *The Right Stuff* based on his *Rolling Stone* astronaut essays, promising delivery two months later. Robbins reported in a June editorial meeting that it would finally arrive in a couple of weeks. After that, it was expected in October, then May, September, and so forth and so on, as Roger would say. Carrying over from season to season, it was listed in nine of FSG's thirteen semiannual catalogs between 1973 and 1979. Only in 1978 was the copy rewritten to the effect that Wolfe was writing about the birth of the space program, rather than the moon landings. Julian Scheer, the NASA publicity director who had invited Wolfe to the moon launch, wrote the author cheekily in 1978, when Farrar, Straus ran an ad in *Publishers Weekly:* "I stopped believing in miracles when some people claimed to have put men on the moon (when we know they didn't), so I do not believe that FS&G ad in PW that 'reveals' The Right Stuff to appear in November!"

Scheer was right to be skeptical. (The book wouldn't come out for another year.) FSG paid Scheer, a Washington insider, a retainer to bring in political projects, and he'd seen a number of them come to naught. Scheer brought FSG very close to acquiring a memoir by John Dean, Watergate's key cooperating witness. They were set to make a deal, with FSG providing $50,000 and a paperback house throwing in $100,000. At the last minute, FSG's lawyers advised that publication would have to wait until Watergate was over, lest material be subpoenaed and become public domain. Faced with the prospect of paying Dean essentially a salary until the book was published, Roger balked. The book went to Simon & Schuster, which had the resources to handle it.

Scheer also arranged for Richard Nixon to offer his memoirs to FSG through Irving "Swifty" Lazar, the famed Hollywood agent who'd brokered FSG's second bestseller, *Courtroom.* But this was not 1949; connections weren't always enough anymore, not when conglomerates had millions to spare. Straus laughed off Nixon's request for $2 million over ten years. "We were not interested in publishing Mr. Nixon for two million dollars or any other price," he said. Lazar had another take on the deal: "Roger is a very good publisher," he said, according to Straus. "But he is not the kind of a man you take a million-dollar deal to."

Contracts with "egg-bound" writers would never approach Nixonian sums, but they did bleed money in a sort of vicious cycle: As unpublished manuscripts grew to Thomas Wolfe proportions, advances grew in order to sustain their starving authors. Farrar, Straus's "care and feeding" philosophy only encouraged such situations.

Michael di Capua is remembered, with a mix of fondness and exasperation, as the most fastidious of FSG's obsessive editors. "Michael, who's a very bright man, a brilliant editor—could drive you to drink," says a former longtime staff member. "If a dust jacket came in for a juvenile book one 89th of an inch off, he wouldn't release it. He was a perfectionist, so on the one hand he made perfect books. On the other hand, people were ready to cut their throats." Andrée Conrad, who was his assistant, remembers the hours he put into his elegant handwritten letters. "A thank-you note, a brief request, would cause him to sit there pensively, while I would be thinking, 'How about "Thanks for sending me the train schedule, Love, Mikey"?'"

Naturally, di Capua gravitated toward perfectionist writers. The results were mixed. Larry Woiwode came to Bob Giroux in 1968 courtesy of *New Yorker* editor William Maxwell. His novel, *What I'm Going to Do, I Think,* was a realistic chronicle of troubled newlyweds—the husband being compulsively indecisive. Giroux wrote Maxwell to thank him: "I read the manuscript at one sitting, marveling at his sense of form and the intensity of his writing." He made a few key decisions, plugging structural holes, and assigned him to di Capua (but not before Roger asked Woiwode, "Can you work with a faggot?").

What I'm Going to Do won Woiwode the William Faulkner Award and, thanks to the advocacy of Edmund Wilson, a Guggenheim grant. With the proceeds, he began his saga *Beyond the Bedroom Wall.* But Woiwode vacillated; first it was a novel, then stories, then a novel again. Giroux and di Capua were easygoing. "I thought you at least knew I'm not your stickler for totalitarian deadlines," di Capua wrote him in late 1970.

Woiwode's money began running out, and he lived off short-story sales and loans from his agent, Candida Donadio. He and his wife spent some time in a trailer in Wisconsin, where he taught. Once, they ran out of propane. Di Capua would wire money, sometimes bypassing Donadio for the sake of speed. The novel-to-come became a publishing inside joke, leading Wilfrid Sheed to quip, "No Farrar, Straus & Giroux catalogue would be complete without its impending announcement."

Straus, who was becoming close to Woiwode, soon loosened the purse strings. During the six years leading up to his final delivery of the book, the advance swelled from $3,000 to $16,200. Woiwode struggled with drugs, alcohol, the loss of part of a finger to an ax, and the departure of his wife. Roger insisted she'd be back once the book was done, and she was. "Since 1969 I've been grateful to you, almost speechlessly, sometimes, for what you did for my first book," Woiwode wrote Straus in December 1972. "During the last year or so what you've been trying to do for me personally has begun to get through my frontal bone. Dear, dear Roger, I'm not a person who ever forgets. God bless you and Dorothea and your son and his family."

Woiwode may have been a "Roger author," but it was di Capua who forced him to cut his thousand-page-plus manuscript sentence by sentence. Di Capua and Candida Donadio happened to live in the same building. While Donadio was away, Woiwode spent two weeks in her apartment so that he could work with di Capua every day. Woiwode would get a wake-up call and then come upstairs. "He would read each sentence and say, 'Is that all right? Are you satisfied with it?'" Woiwode remembers. "His view was if we can cut ten words in a page, we've cut ten thousand words. And we did." Woiwode was not allowed to drink during their time together. They met the deadline. Published in September 1975, *Beyond the Bedroom Wall* was considered a major novel, "sentimental in the best sense of the word," as Christopher Lehmann-Haupt put it in his otherwise mixed review. It sold almost one hundred thousand copies in hardcover alone.

Harold Brodkey's great, unfinished opus was a considerably less successful di Capua collaboration. The writer of one acclaimed book of short stories, Brodkey signed a three-book contract with di Capua in 1970, planning to deliver his novel "Party of Animals" later that year. Both lurid and beautifully wrought, the book had obvious appeal; excerpts published in assorted magazines included one about a woman's first orgasm. It was *Hecate County* updated for the seventies, complete with gay encounters. Bantam offered a guarantee of no less than $100,000 for paperback rights (a "floor"). But Brodkey's writing stalled. Straus blamed it on a "sado-masochistic" writer-editor relationship: Brodkey "worked extremely well with Michael di Capua, and this was probably the trouble—he became almost too dependent on di Capua as his editor." Brodkey changed editors, but the problems continued. Terry Adams, an assistant at the time, called himself Brodkey's "word processor," retyping version after version; the book came to be known in-house as "Party of Typing." Brodkey later justified the whole process by saying that publishing the book "would interfere with working on it." Eventually he switched to Knopf, which repaid FSG $75,000. Brodkey said that included "interest and paper clips." (It would finally be published—back at FSG—in 1991 under the title *The Runaway Soul*.)

The egg-bound condition seemed to spread like a virus. Even old Gaylord Hauser wasn't producing. A long cookbook had been in the works since 1968, and every year it seemed to be on the verge of completion. Peggy Miller would travel to Sicily regularly, visit Hauser and Frey Brown, and demand the copy they needed to publish the book. "All we needed was the connective material," Peggy says, "and every year I said, 'Gaylord, Roger's going crazy, just put these things together.' And every year it was another excuse. He was lazy was what it was." Then Frey Brown died, and Hauser wrote to Roger, "I am not in the mood. However, when times and life are easier again I intend to finish the book." He never did.

There was also the "care and feeding" of the legacies of the dead. Straus and Giroux were burdened with the baggage of the beloved writers they outlived. Flannery O'Connor had died back in 1964, T. S. Eliot a few months later. At Eliot's memorial service in Westminster Abbey, Giroux again met Ezra Pound, who, "looking like the ghost of Lear," gave him a deep, wordless bow. It almost made Giroux nostalgic for the raving Pound he'd encountered back at St. Elizabeths asylum. "The silence, after all the years of over-talk, was crushing," he wrote John Berryman. Eliot's reputation was secure, but O'Connor's needed nurturing. The beautifully presented *Complete Stories* won her a posthumous National Book Award in 1972.

Many more untimely deaths followed. Thomas Merton, whose courage and wisdom Giroux so admired, finally left the monastery in 1968 for a tour of Southeast Asia, his first long trip outside his Kentucky abbey in more than a quarter century. In Bangkok that December, he was killed—electrocuted by a standing fan—at the age of fifty-three. Jack Kerouac, Giroux's old on-and-off friend, died a year later, at forty-seven, from internal bleeding caused by cirrhosis. It was Berryman, though, whose leap off a Minneapolis bridge on January 7, 1972, really broke the surface of Giroux's reticence, leading him to break down in front of his new assistant, Pat Strachan.

In the years before he died, Berryman had been more productive than ever. After those 77 dream songs came many more—there are 385 in all—and Giroux published four more of his verse collections. But the poet had found fame as "intolerable" as he'd predicted he would. He grew a long, unruly beard, blundered through readings almost too drunk to stand, and became a caricature of the hobo bard. Yet by 1971 he was dry for about a year and working on a novel called *Recovery.* When Giroux visited him in Minneapolis for the christening of Berryman's daughter, he even found the poet and his teetotaler friends a bit boring. "Having suffered so much and achieved so much, he had I thought finally reached some kind of balance and acceptance," Giroux wrote to a friend after the suicide. He knew that Berryman had been hurt by the reception of his latest book, *Love & Fame,* which even some friends hated, and that he had been depressed around Christmas and gone on a final bender, to no avail. Giroux theorized that Berryman could live neither with nor without alcohol. "What a waste," he wrote. "What a terrible, terrible waste."

Giroux, the caretaker of so many of his writers—O'Connor, Berryman, Bishop, Stafford, Lowell—bore almost familial responsibilities following their deaths. There were a thousand things to do: secure copyrights and permissions for work published and unpublished; amend contracts for the benefit of heirs; work out editing and publishing schedules for manuscripts in various stages of completion.

Roger found himself in much the same position later in 1972, when both Edmund Wilson and Abraham Joshua Heschel died.

Wilson's journals, for which Roger had reluctantly doubled the advances, to $10,000 per volume, were still unpublished and would have to be edited posthumously. It was only the beginning of FSG's long and serious sideline in legacy management.

The company was also becoming self-conscious about its own legacy. Even its twenty-first anniversary in 1967 was enough of an occasion for Straus and Giroux to consider compiling their authors' work—under the pretense that they had reached their "majority," like a young gentleman coming into his trust fund. (Giroux used it as a chance to prod another of his flailing depressives, Jean Stafford, to finish her autobiographical novel "A Parliament of Women," only to receive the reply: "There is no book and I don't know if there ever will be." There never was.) As the more natural milestone of twenty-five years approached, Giroux began organizing a massive anthology of the house's best work thus far.

"Twenty-Five Years: A Retrospective" got much further along than even some of FSG's staff members knew. Meant to come out in the fall of 1971, it was held over for several seasons, always with the same catalog copy listing the same forty-two writers, before vanishing in 1974. There was a complete table of contents, a glossy full-cover mock-up of the gold-and-blue book jacket, and a more-than-halfway-finished introduction by Giroux. But instead of speaking in the collective voice of a mature publishing house, the book sparked an adolescent clash of egos. Its only legacy, over the long term, was a too-prominent place in Giroux's *Times* obituary—shorthand for his fights with Straus.

According to the writer of the obit, Christopher Lehmann-Haupt, the problem was in Giroux's introduction to the anthology, which described his first encounter with Straus in his navy office. Roger objected to a scene that depicted him with his feet up on his desk. "Dorothea doesn't like it," Straus said, and told Giroux to take it out. Convinced this was really Roger's vain objection, Giroux stormed out and canceled the project. Yet surviving drafts of the introduction complicate Giroux's version of the argument. In the first place, Giroux really was poking fun at his partner:

When we met he was Ensign Straus, about whose fabulous Navy assignment scuttlebutt had reached me even in the Pacific. The story went that Ensign Straus had an office of his own on Fifth Avenue where he pursued the interests of the book and magazine section of the Navy's office of public relations; that he was the only sailor in the Third Naval District not required to report each morning at 0800 to Navy headquarters at 90 Church Street to salute the quarterdeck; and that he was one of the few junior officers who had a direct line to the Navy Department in Washington.

It was all true. After being greeted by his attractive Wave secretary in the outer office, I found Roger with his feet on the desk, from which he arose with careless grace to receive me (a mere lieutenant, junior grade) like an admiral.

The feet on the desk were the culmination of two paragraphs sketching Roger's puzzling privileges. While Giroux had spent the war risking his life, Straus lapped up the plum connections and pretty secretaries. At any rate, that section was struck from future drafts, presumably at the request of Straus, who approved a later version in October 1972: "It does the trick and says it nicely." Evidently, he also dropped earlier objections to its self-aggrandizing conclusion. There, Giroux recounted Edmund Wilson imploring him, "Inspire Roger."

Henry Robbins, enlisted to help with the anthology selections and introduction, wrote a marginal note beside that paragraph: "Bob—I must admit I feel a bit dubious about this, + can see why it upset Roger. Let's discuss." In the Straus-approved draft, Giroux expands on how much he's benefited from Roger's editorial support. Like the real story behind Giroux's losing Kerouac, the tale of the doomed anniversary edition seems to have ended not with a stormy slamming of doors but with a slow fizzle. Even as 1973 came along and the press reported on the imminent anthology, neither of the partners was fully satisfied with its tone. (Farrar was by then fully retired, and would die a year later.)

Further stoking the flames, Robbins objected to Giroux's early selection of twenty-five excerpts. "The list still bothers me," he wrote, mostly due to "its very ultra-distinguished, established, (one might even say Knopfian) quality, partly conveyed by the fact that 10 out of the 25 are dead," and many of the others at retirement age. He would have preferred a list "leavened by the inclusion of some of our notable younger writers: Sontag, Wolfe, Barthelme, [James] Purdy, Didion." Most of Giroux's selections were his own authors, while most of Robbins's suggested additions belonged to him. Another, presumably later, table of contents in the FSG archives is longer, at forty-eight selections—looking like the overseasoned broth of too many credit-hungry cooks.

Maybe the anthology just wasn't worth the resources. Andrée Conrad notes that they had just finished a grueling collection called *The American Literary Anthology*. Publishing an anniversary collection would require months of permissions, copyright, and editing work by a bare-bones staff—another "hornet's nest," as Conrad puts it. "I don't think there was a willing candidate around" to do the grunt work, she surmises. But Conrad remembers no public arguments over it. "Fights were something that really didn't happen at FSG," she says. "We didn't have the prima donna situation—but you could imagine it building and building."

In the spring of 1973, Giroux succeeded the ailing John Farrar to the semiemeritus position of chairman of the board, and Henry Robbins became editor in chief. FSG's editorial succession seemed secure. But the notion that Robbins could be Giroux redux—patiently enduring the small indignities of Roger and FSG in return for the freedom and prestige—was wishful thinking. To begin with, he was part of a generation of editors no longer content to passively serve the whims of aristocrat-publishers. He also had a stormier temperament and a stormier life. Robbins had recently begun an affair with an FSG publicist, and before long, he'd separated from his wife and moved in with her. His children were in private school, and his wife barely worked (she was later diagnosed with schizophrenia). He needed to support two households, and his cost of living was rising every day. Doctors had also warned him that, at forty-six, he was already headed for heart trouble. "When I look back," remembers his son, Philip Robbins, "I think the amount of stress he had was just gigantic."

To make matters worse, he was picked that spring for a nightmare tour of jury duty. He became the foreman of a jury on the months-long, politically explosive trial of suspects known in the papers as "The Harlem Four." The prosecution for the murder of Margit Sugar in a Harlem robbery had resulted in four trials over eight years—a process snarled by overturned convictions, recanted and reinstated evidence, and hung juries. In this latest chapter, Robbins and the jury spent most of their time playing bridge while four separate lawyers aired their individual grievances before the judge.

The jury was hung yet again, but FSG got at least one thing out of it. Robbins met copy editor Lynn Warshow on the jury, and she became one of the house's longest-serving employees. She showed up on her first day at Union Square to find a warning scrawled in chalk on the sidewalk out front: HENRY ROBBINS IS A FASCIST PIG. Word had spread of not only the deliberations but the individual jurors' names, leading to acts of protest bordering on personal threats. Feisty Union Square may have delighted Pablo Neruda a couple of months earlier, but Warshow's first thought was, "Oh, I'm going to be killed the first day."

Then, on July 3, while packing for the holiday weekend, Robbins had a heart attack. He spent Independence Day in the hospital, with doctors telling his FSG girlfriend his condition was "touch and go." His recovery was slow, and he was essentially part-time into the fall. Robbins later told Wilfrid Sheed that it "frightened the whiskers" off him, making him realize he "had to try a new life."

This would mean not just easing up on the work but easing his financial burdens as well. He simply couldn't support two families on $25,000 a year, and he knew FSG was hardly in a position to offer more. In fact, Robbins had edited a report Roger III sent in September to U.S. Trust, the firm's main lending bank, addressing the company's shaky prospects. Its upshot was that the firm was bound in a Catch-22: It was undercapitalized and unstable as an independent, but if it rushed into the hands of a willing buyer (two firms were actively courting the house), it would have to settle for a valuation beneath its "real" cultural worth. So the plan was to expand independently and hope for the best.

On its surface the report sounded almost optimistic; nontrade sales were steady and growth was just around the corner. But the flip side of that was a promise to drop their more "marginal titles," focusing more on work like the forthcoming "Godfather type-book" *Number One with a Bullet* and the curious how-to "Rape: Prevention and Survival." Even if this was only misdirecting pablum meant to keep the bank happily lending, it wasn't the kind of double-talk that the painfully sincere Henry Robbins liked to participate in. It was hardly a goad to morale one way or the other.

Then insult flew in on the heels of injury. Robbins was still in the hospital when word came down that there would be a salary freeze, maybe even a pay cut for top officers. That fall, he began to think about what "a new life" might look like. He thought, mainly, of an offer made to him not long ago by Dick Snyder, the head of Simon & Schuster. He liked working at Farrar, Straus, knew it was ideal in many ways, but as he later said to Sheed, "I'm not a saint."

Richard E. Snyder, Robbins's courter, was both a catalyst and a beneficiary of recent tectonic shifts in the publishing landscape. Simon & Schuster, the most commercial trade house in New York, suffered an identity crisis in 1968 when its most talented editor defected. Robert Gottlieb, who'd discovered Joseph Heller and others, jumped ship to Knopf along with two important colleagues. Together they secured the future of Knopf—itself drifting in the wake of Alfred Knopf, Jr.'s departure—and left Simon & Schuster without even the pretense of a mission beyond simply making tons of money. Snyder was in many ways Straus's negative image: just as blunt, pugnacious, and fond of putting his feet up on his desk. But Snyder was a self-made populist, openly resentful of the gentlemanly code of publishing. His father had been a success in what Roger Straus would have called *shmattes*—the garment trade. "He positively glowed with ambition in a company— indeed an industry—in which it was crass to admit to personal ambition," writes Michael Korda, who had become his number two at S&S for many years.

Snyder and Korda, the Young Turks who were effectively running the place, failed to prevent literary writers from following Gottlieb to Knopf. Snyder fumed over the dismissive, snooty agents who strong-armed S&S into releasing Gottlieb's authors from their contracts. But as soon as he officially became publisher, he tried to do much the same thing. Snyder hired away several leading literary editors, offering doubled salaries and grand titles, in hopes of poaching their authors from the competition. He'd already moved on from his rejected offer to Robbins when he got a call from the editor, in late 1973, saying he'd changed his mind. Snyder was "taken aback," according to a friend of Robbins, but he "decided to go through with the offer, champagne was sent to the house, and Henry was leaving."

The *Times* story announcing his departure on Christmas Eve was headlined SIMON & SCHUSTER ELATED OVER EDITORIAL COUP. Robbins would be an executive editor and a vice president, earning more than $40,000 per year. "Financial considerations," he told the reporter, "are very important." Several years later, Robbins would say that FSG "was a fine place to work," but that Straus "believed that everyone in publishing had independent means. I didn't, and I had children in private schools and heading for college. I simply wasn't being paid enough . . . It was hard to resist the enticement."

Another editor, Nan Talese, was also coming to S&S—both of them just in time for the fiftieth anniversary of the house. Straus crafted a studiously quippy quote for the *Times:* "Henry Robbins has been a fine editor for us, and I certainly wish him well in his new association with a struggling young company."

Reading the story over his breakfast on Christmas Eve, Roger lost whatever magnanimous veneer he'd displayed for the paper. "No announcement has been made," it read, "as to which of the authors Mr. Robbins has already been editing at Farrar, Straus may follow him to S & S. The group includes Donald Barthelme, Joan Didion, Marjorie Kellogg, Grace Paley, Walker Percy, Wilfrid Sheed, and Tom Wolfe." It was a careful, hedging statement, not even in Henry's words, but to Roger it looked like a waving red cape, a great big "Fuck you very much." Roger would often use the term "brooding" hyperbolically, meaning simply that he'd thought over a decision for more than a couple of minutes. But Henry's Christmas surprise—not only was he throwing Roger over for the son of a *shmatte* salesman and a paltry $15,000, but he was promising to steal Roger's greatest assets and best friends—truly gave him something to brood over. Didn't loyalty count for anything anymore? Not among editors, and as for writers, he'd find out soon enough. "There was a series of people in whom Roger would place almost his entire trust and future," says the British agent Deborah Rogers. "Whatever happened with Henry, I think Roger must've felt quite betrayed."

Straus came to the office early, as usual, after picking Peggy up in his Mercedes. On the ride downtown, his mood continued to darken. "By the time we got to the office, Roger was absolutely boiling," says Peggy. She was to summon Robbins the moment he came in; the wait felt eternal. "And when Henry came in, there was blood on the floor." Shouts were heard, mostly Straus's. "He was crazed," Peggy says. A minute later Robbins came storming out, followed by Straus. Roger caught his breath, then turned to Peggy. "None of those authors are leaving Farrar, Straus," he said. "Over my dead body."

Robbins did everything he could to bring them over to Simon & Schuster, but he may have overplayed his hand. He flew down to New Orleans to see Walker Percy, to no avail. Yet he neglected to even tell Donald Barthelme he was leaving. Barthelme wrote a letter to *Harper's* objecting to an article about the fracas. The reporter, he wrote, had implied that "authors are large striped or spotted animals to be trundled bound and gagged . . . from one game preserve to the next." But Barthelme didn't sour on Robbins. Rather, as he explained to Straus in a kind and measured letter, he had enough to worry about without abandoning his editor. "I would have much preferred that Henry had stayed with you," he wrote, "but what's done is done. In sum, I would be deeply grateful, and much eased in the mind, if you could see your way clear to letting me go."

Roger explained why he would not. Henry, he wrote, "implied to a number of literary agents that we would welcome the return of advances because of our alleged financial condition. This is a serious and damaging allegation, and leaves us no recourse except that of counteracting it with a blanket decision." He also reminded Barthelme that, in addition to a nonfiction work already headed for publication, they had a contract for two more books and a long-standing option on a novel. Barthelme was shocked; Henry had never badmouthed FSG to him, nor did the agent Lynn Nesbit recall hearing any such rumors. He stopped short of doubting Straus's story, but made one last plea for his release: "You of all people understand the significance to this." Roger was unmoved: "The more I've thought about our decision . . . the more certain I am that it is right." In the end, Barthelme stayed.

Joan Didion was more insistent. Her agent, Lois Wallace, wrote to Straus a week after Robbins left that Joan regarded Henry "as a surrogate father," and offered to repay the $30,000 advance on a (delayed) nonfiction book that they'd signed the previous year. After Straus refused "as a matter of policy," Didion wrote him personally. Robbins happened to be her houseguest at that very moment, and it was ridiculous, "painful for me," to find that she was contractually forbidden to discuss her manuscript with him. Straus again stood firm because of "verbal stories of our dire financial situation (I'm afraid Henry panicked on this one)." He had to prove Robbins wrong the only way he could, by refusing to let go of a single author.

The situation was tabled pending the sale of Didion's next novel, *A Book of Common Prayer*. In advance of an auction for the book, Wallace came down to Straus's office in late July 1974 and, according to him, agreed to let FSG match the highest bid. This would, in Roger's mind, honor the old nonfiction contract, under which they had an option on the next novel. A week later, Wallace balked, and let him know she'd spoken to five other publishers. He wrote her the next day, furious, after hearing she was planning an auction. "Now I also find that your auction block is all over town," Roger wrote. "Frankly, we want no part in this . . . I must also now become legal as I feel you have violated the spirit of our meeting as well as the contract situation . . . If in fact you proceed with your auction on August 8th we shall take whatever legal steps are necessary to protect our rights." The auction went as planned, and, as expected, Wallace and Didion went with Henry at Simon & Schuster. Roger eventually backed off.

It was just as well: Straus would have been forced to argue against his own professed position on options. Ever since he'd waived Edmund Wilson's option clause (the right of first refusal on the next book) in 1949, Straus was never a big believer in that controversial bit of contract. Just three years after threatening Didion, he fought, and won, a lawsuit brought by Harcourt, Brace that accused FSG of interfering with one of its auctions. Still feeling little love for his former employers at Harcourt, Brace, Bob Giroux had decided to sign up William Golding's novel *Darkness Visible* in spite of Harcourt's option on it. Harcourt president William Jovanovich showed that the ill feelings were mutual by suing FSG for $1 million. The suit was dismissed and contract law rewritten to weaken the legal force of unpaid-for options.

A couple of days after Straus lost his first Robbins author (Didion's husband, John Gregory Dunne, would be the second), he played it cool. In a letter to Wallace's business partner, he said that Didion's imminent departure was "not that serious to me," but added, "She is not the kind of a writer that should be put on the block. Besides, there was no way she'd earn back her S & S advance: Not good agenting!" This time he wasn't so much defending his option as railing against the process of auctioning an author's work, which of course favored publishers with money to burn. It was a fine, high-minded position, which also happened to have nothing to do with the present situation. And it wasn't the last time Roger would blame an agent for something the writer had clearly chosen to do. He failed to mention Robbins at all.

In fact, Roger almost never mentioned Robbins again. When his oral historian listed those writers who were edited by Henry, Straus snapped at him. Some were only *assigned* to Robbins: John McPhee was inherited from a retiring Hal Vursell; Walker Percy was really a Giroux writer, who needed no editing anyway (this was demonstrably untrue). "That list of authors—I mean that's a ridiculous statement," Roger said. "Frankly, I suggested that Robbins leave for various reasons." Whenever he saw Robbins at industry functions, he kept walking.

Though Straus may have overreacted, the fact remains that Farrar, Straus was left in the lurch. "It was a terrible time," says Roger III. "Henry was the first editor who was everything to his authors." Rog was sure the Robbins authors were as good as gone. "I thought Wolfe was going to be out of the picture." Keeping Tom Wolfe on the FSG list, as much as reeling in *August 1914,* was "one of my father's signature achievements." Wolfe stuck around out of loyalty, but also out of necessity. He had finally contracted for *The Right Stuff* only a year earlier and was already delayed, and he was still $21,000 in the hole for a fiction advance. For better or worse, he was tangled up in FSG.

Straus turned out to be right about Robbins and Simon & Schuster and Joan Didion. Robbins never delivered on Dick Snyder's expectations—and vice versa. Even Michael Korda admitted that Snyder toyed with editors: "New ones were hailed briefly as 'stars,' given freshly redecorated offices and inflated titles, then subjected to what must have seemed to many of them a system of institutionalized hazing that few survived." Robbins got it worse than most at S&S. "I thought that their power could do a lot for my authors," he later said. Instead, he found "an adversary attitude toward writers. Writers were difficult, dreadful, demanding, egotistical—all of which many of them are without a doubt. Even so, at Knopf and Farrar, Straus we *liked* our authors." Many of his acquisitions were vetoed, and he grew embittered.

If Roger and Henry had still been on speaking terms, they might have commiserated over what happened next. In 1975, Simon & Schuster was acquired by Gulf+Western. It was one thing for RCA to buy Random House, quite another for a publisher to be acquired by a conglomerate that dealt in industrial valves, mattresses, and zinc. G+W also owned Paramount Pictures, and the head of the studio, Barry Diller, flew east one day for lunch with Simon & Schuster's editorial board. He gave a speech around the concept of synergy. According to Michael Korda, Robbins grew so enraged that he flung his full soup plate in Diller's direction. "I'm not going to sit here and listen to some goddamn movie person tell us how to publish books!" he shouted. Not much later, he resigned.

Snyder, meanwhile, would become Straus's favorite nemesis, the stand-in for all that was wrong with corporate publishing. Their disputes would metastasize into a full-on media war—joint appearances on talk shows as acrimonious (if not as erudite) as Norman Mailer vs. Gore Vidal. "It got to be sort of a joke," says Peggy Miller. "It started to be amusing and then it got to be stupid." These fights, albeit over substantive differences, were clearly rooted in personal animosity. Snyder had stolen Henry Robbins, a potential successor to Giroux, only to chew him up and spit him out.

Joan Didion, unfortunately, was stuck with Simon & Schuster, and they would not relent as Straus had. Using the same unfulfilled book contract that Roger had held over her, they kept her from leaving S&S for twenty years. She named her 1992 collection *After Henry* not only as a tribute, but as a rebuke to her jailers. It was all there in the dedication, which referenced S&S's famously shabby treatment of another writer. "This book," she wrote, "is dedicated to Henry Robbins and to Bret Easton Ellis, each of whom did time with its publisher." In the title essay, she declared herself "Henry's orphan sister."

Robbins fared better at his next and last station of the cross, Dutton, where he was given his own imprint. Imprints named for their editors ("a Henry Robbins Book") were a new phenomenon in the mid-seventies, an evolutionary adaptation to two interlocked trends. First, corporate-owned houses were becoming interchangeable: Harcourt Brace Jovanovich, Harper & Row, and Simon & Schuster were too diverse to *stand* for anything. Second, editors were increasingly interested in every aspect of a book's publication. This explains why Straus hated imprints; he preferred that editors edit and publishers publish. It also explains the long détente between him and Bob Giroux. "Giroux really felt that his involvement with the book ended when the book went off to copy edit," says Rog. "Whereas the people that my father tended to tangle with wanted to be involved with the book up through the remaindering of it." Roger may have hurt Bob by saying, years later, "You don't know the difference between an editor and a publisher," but their partnership worked because Giroux left the publishing to Straus.

In the aftermath of what Giroux called "the December-January crisis" (i.e., Robbins's departure), he wrote to Straus about amending his deferred-compensation contract—a sort of senior-level retirement plan—to make it more generous and ironclad. It would guarantee full income for a ten-year period of "semi-retirement," beginning in five years. It was meant to spell out their partnership during a period of uncertainty and simmering distrust. Giroux couched it in terms of mutual benefit: "I have not only devoted my life to the company in which I am a partner, but I have also invested my lifetime's savings . . . I wish to do everything in my power for the preservation and continuation of its present efforts . . . Finally, in view of the relatively small compensation (averaged over the eighteen years of my association) I and others have received, I consider my request to be minimal." Roger signed a revised contract within two weeks.

9

This Classy Little Yacht

"Having a wonderful time here," read the postcard up on the FSG bulletin board. "Tennis is to Scribner's as sex is to Farrar, Straus." The handwriting was Anne Sullivan's. She'd left the FSG contracts department for Scribner's and now reported from midtown as though writing home from a dull cruise vacation. (She would return to Farrar, Straus a few years later, among the many employees who obeyed Roger's favorite send-off toast: "You'll be back!") The note delighted Roger; nothing could please him more than seeing the rest of the world cast as a pale reflection of his realm. In fact, as she admitted to friends, she and Roger had a fling after she left (but before she was married). Rumor had it that Roger called her after getting the card and made a proposition: "How about a Farrar, Straus lunch?"

"Everybody was fucking everybody in that office," says Leslie Sharpe, a former FSG assistant who occasionally slept with Roger after she, too, left the firm. Sharpe had come in as Michael di Capua's assistant, following someone who'd made a less favorable impression on Roger. "Goddamn it," he'd half joked to di Capua, "can't you hire somebody who's pretty *and* smart?" At Sharpe's first outing with the editors, Roger proposed a toast: "Fuck our enemies!" Leslie looked at him and said, "Mr. Straus, shouldn't we be saying 'Fuck our allies'?" He was smitten, and so was she. "When I think of Roger," she says, "I think of the statue of the wonderful bronze Poseidon holding the trident." He wasn't, she insists, any kind of run-of-the-mill misogynistic lecher. "Roger loved women as people," she says. "He was the best lover anybody could ever have, and part of that was that he really understood women, and he understood that every woman was different."

It wasn't all about Straus. At least two editors—Robbins and a man named John Peck—left their wives for women they met at the office. A short-lived Robbins successor had a young male assistant in his office and the door was always closed. The next editor in chief, Aaron Asher, had a couple of affairs in the office. People were having sex in the mailroom after hours. Dorothea Straus was perfectly justified in calling it a "sexual sewer."

If Roger used sex to cement loyalty, he could also wield raunch as a weapon. He assumed the publicist who'd moved in with Henry Robbins would follow him out the door, but Giroux reassured her she could stay as long as she liked. When she finally did go, Roger expressed his regret: "You were a nice bauble to have around." It may have been a touch of revenge on Robbins; other times he had less discernible motives. Michael di Capua, who was not only openly gay but also took on important gay writers (Maurice Sendak, Chistopher Isherwood), often bore the brunt. Once, di Capua returned from his Hamptons house with his balding pate bright red. "Hey, Mikey, did someone suck your head off on the beach?" Roger asked at an editorial meeting. "Why must you be so crude?" Giroux snapped—a common refrain. Roger just laughed.

On the other hand, it was the seventies, and it was publishing. Straus got away with things he might have been arrested for today. One woman reports feeling left out of the action when, for months, he failed to comment on her breasts. After he finally made a crack about how she could make room for several manuscripts in her luggage by taking out a few of her oversize bras, she was relieved.

Authors, not a prudish bunch, often got a kick out of it, too. How many publishers were just dying to tell them a dubious story about Isaac Singer breaking a sink while performing cunnilingus? Sendak, for one, felt secure enough in their camaraderie to draw Straus two Christmas postcards that would surely have scandalized the school librarians. "Farout, Strut and Xerox presents the *true* version of Hansel & Gretel. $39.95," read one. Beneath that line was a drawing of the imprisoned Hansel being manually pleasured by his witch captor. The other featured "Snow White & the 7 buggers," with the dwarves lined up to ravish the fair damsel.

In the office, "Young Roger" inevitably followed Straus's example. Already on the verge of separating from his wife, Nina, with whom he had three daughters (including twin toddlers), Rog began seeing someone at work. It blossomed quickly into a much more serious romance than any of his father's. Eventually, Rog's lover decided she had to leave FSG, thinking to herself, "I don't want to become another Peggy." When she told Rog's father about it, he was bemused. "Why can't you kids be calm, cool, and collected about such things, like we were?"

The Strauses were distraught over the separation. Finally, Roger sat his son down for a rare event: a man-to-man talk unrelated to publishing. Marriage was about family, he told Rog. Sex—even love— could be sought outside of it. Rog disagreed. (He would get married and divorced twice more.) His father had defied his prim, wealthy family in important ways, but he'd never shaken the idea that duty trumps passion—or, at least, that the two could be placed in separate compartments. One could live adventurously, even somewhat carelessly, without violating fundamental principles. But Rog already lived on the other side of a yawning cultural divide, within the new sensibility espoused by young FSG writers like Sontag, Wolfe, and Didion, where the only mortal sin was hypocrisy. Rog believed in integrity and so did his father, but it meant something different to each of them.

Their divergent ideas about it had consequences beyond private behavior or family cohesion. For the elder Roger, structure and values were of paramount importance, even in the breach. Yes, FSG published Gayelord Hauser; yes, it paid its precious authors bupkes; yes, it factored the sales potential of a book into the decision about whether to publish it. But it was all, Roger believed, done for the grand purpose of preserving FSG's basic principles and culture. Editors and the publisher made all the key decisions, without marketing input; poets and foreign authors had to be published even if they sold next to nothing; the company's value lay in its reputation. The day-to-day reality didn't always reflect the self-image. But that didn't abrogate those values, any more than the presence of sin abrogated religious doctrine, or a lover nullified a suitable marriage.

Rog never trespassed onto his father's work domain: He kept his distance from Sontag and Wolfe, didn't ask about Peggy or the machinations of the Frankfurt Book Fair. But there were other parts of the business he did know about—maybe even thought he knew more about. He remembers walking into a meeting during which his father and two editors were deciding what to charge consumers for their upcoming books. "There were no numbers there," says Rog. "Nobody knew what the manufacturing costs were, the royalties, if there was any kind of a marketing budget attached. I said, 'How are you pricing these books?' 'Well, son, when you've been doing this as long as I do, you just kind of—heft them.' I said, 'Some people work on a five times multiple or a six times multiple—' and he just laughed at me."

Rog no longer assumed father knew best. "When I started," he says, "I was twenty-one, and it was easy and comfortable to do it his way. But by the time I was thirty-one, I started having ideas of my own, which were sometimes not his ideas. The people I think he had the hardest time working with were people who were too much like him. And I think I was too much like him."

Like his father, Rog was interested in the larger problems of publishing—even if father and son didn't always agree on what the problems were, never mind the solutions. Although Straus was on the board of the Association of American Publishers (he'd later resign in protest), he had little interest in his son's pet project there, a campaign to promote books as holiday gifts. "A ridiculously small percentage of the American public buys the product," says Rog—referring to books in a way his father never would. "The theory was that if you could increase the number of book buyers then all publishers and all authors would benefit." Rog and another publishing executive, Erwin Glikes, his former dean at Columbia, hired Grey Advertising to run TV ads in a few markets—celebrity endorsements of books in general—and then analyze the subsequent sales trends there. "It did boost sales in those test markets," Rog says.

The project soon died, owing to a lack of publisher interest, but Rog had other things to think about. Two years after Robbins left, Rog got a call from Glikes, who was about to take over the trade department of Harper & Row. He wanted Rog to join him. "It was a heady proposition," says Rog. "I wanted more oxygen. I wanted to flap my own wings, or whatever. And also, since marketing had become my thing, I wanted a place where I had more money to spend, a more diverse list to market." Harper & Row did four or five times as much business as FSG, and the gap was growing.

Rog spun it to Dad like a stifled boyfriend: He needed to play the field, see other publishers. "He said, 'Well, do what's best for you,'" Rog remembers. He thinks his father was privately in turmoil: "He couldn't imagine someone in his right mind, which I guess he thought I was, bailing out. I think he drank his own Kool-Aid. He really believed that Farrar, Straus was uniquely magnificent, and there was nothing comparable, and if you left you would be going into Purgatory." What he showed on the surface was the assurance of that going-away-party toastmaker: *You'll be back.*

To make matters worse, Roger acted as though his son would soon return to Nina as well. Even as she was filing for divorce, he encouraged her to stay in the Gwathmey house on his estate. With help from her father, she bought the house and five acres of land from the Strauses. Now Nina had a place to live just down the road from her teaching job at SUNY Purchase, and the kids would always be within shouting distance of their grandparents. On weekdays they could even ramble in the manor house while Roger and Dorothea were in town.

"These were dreams of Roger's," says Nina, "that the whole family would be together on the property until the end of time." They all got what they wanted, except for Rog.

Roger gradually became reconciled to his only son's divorce, but in business he could never let go of the conviction that Rog's Purgatory was temporary, that the prodigal son would return. Just as Rog was being considered for a promotion to the position of Harper's trade publisher, his father told *Publishers Weekly* that his son was still next in line to run the firm. Rog called his father up to yell at him. "This makes my life very difficult," he said. "They think I'm just here as a spy, and it's detrimental to my career!" Rog had left FSG, and he'd left his wife, and he wasn't coming back, no matter what his manipulative father did. His choices felt, at the moment, serious and permanent. "At that point," he says, "I didn't think I was ever going to come back."

It was difficult for Roger not to take personally both the defections to conglomerates and the growing assumption that FSG was about to join them. In that long *PW* interview in 1976, Roger insisted that the company's finances had vastly improved over the past three years. Evidently, his banker at U.S. Trust wasn't so sure, because he was just then threatening to cut FSG's line of credit. Straus responded by pointedly referring to "the rather involved situation with the United States Trust Company, both from the viewpoint of Farrar, Straus and Giroux, my personal accounts, and my association with other family accounts present . . . and future." Critics who believed FSG depended on Straus's personal wealth were definitely right in one sense: The bank's long-term note was guaranteed by other Straus accounts, which were always the final bulwark protecting FSG from ruin. So Roger threatened to take his business elsewhere, but he also made a personal appeal. "It may be that at some future time, Farrar, Straus and Giroux will have to become a division of X or Y or Z . . . However, when that day comes, I want to choose my own shots for the company and my associates, and at the best price, and for that I need support, both financial and moral."

Straus did entertain an offer a year later from his old friends at Thomas Tilling, the bus company that had been involved in the aborted McGraw-Hill and Heinemann deal. They almost settled on acquiring a 30 percent interest, with an option to buy the firm upon Straus's death. But then the company balked for two reasons: Profits were nothing to drool over, and, more important, Straus wasn't willing to relinquish enough of his personal share. "My problem, to be honest with you," Straus wrote to Tilling's managing director, "is that philosophically speaking, I think the plan in principle is probably a good one for both sides, but I do have slight psychological problems."

He had, too, a few causes for optimism. There were some surprise successes and, more important, a thriving new editor in chief. For almost every FSG staff member who fled to conglomerates, there was a disaffected corporate pawn, a modern-day Giroux, tacking in the opposite direction. Aaron Asher, the editor in chief of Macmillan's trade division, was a cultured Europhile, a Jew whose family had fled Lithuania in 1937. He was equally adept at playing Bach fugues, translating French fiction, editing great authors, and revitalizing troubled publishers. But a few months after Asher started at Macmillan, the conglomerate that owned it hit a slump and two hundred editorial employees were fired. A month later, he quit, and shortly after that he joined FSG. After laying off an assistant editor, Straus was able to offer Asher an almost-competitive $35,000.

Asher, whose widow remembers him today as "an absolutely passionate book man . . . full-hearted in a way that brings tears to the eyes," put into his change-of-business letters his unabashed relief. They always had a sentence along the lines of, "I've managed to get off the Titanic and have landed on this classy little yacht."

Asher was restless, quick, and ambitious; staff members could foretell his approach from the change bouncing loudly in his pocket as he sped down the hall. With Asher's arrival in late 1974, a year of editorial drift came to an end, and the yacht finally found a favorable wind. Asher brought in Philip Roth, bringing FSG, publishers of Singer and Malamud, one step closer to a lock on the great Jewish-American writers.

Roth was already part of Roger's social circle. He had been at the memorable Straus dinner during which, after the sexes were separated, Norman Podhoretz remarked, "Where the fuck did the dames go?" He must have appreciated Roger's rant against the 1970 National Book Awards, which cited their snub of Roth's groundbreaking *Portnoy's Complaint* as evidence of the judges' incompetence. But Roth was also a tough customer, another writer who had no agent but demanded real money and attention from his publisher. FSG couldn't even have paperback rights to his next book, the essay collection *Reading Myself and Others,* because Roth had sold them to Bantam.

The Professor of Desire, on the other hand, went straight to FSG for $25,000, and Roth went straight to the top of Roger's "care and feeding" list. Straus worked Frankfurt relentlessly to move his new writer to better foreign publishers. Roth requested his direct personal help in Germany, where Rowohlt had let several books go out of print. Roger extracted almost all of them with minimal fuss—"I too am sad but perhaps it is all for the best," he wrote consolingly to the publisher—and made a three-book deal with his friend Christoph Schlotterer at Hanser. At home, FSG sold fifty thousand hardcover copies of *Professor* and brought in $600,000 for the paperback rights. "We did a hell of a job for him," said Roger. Of course, he *would* say that, but years later, after Aaron Asher had left FSG, the only positive thing he'd say about Roger had to do with Roth. "There was personal hard work done to get people onto good lists abroad, comparable lists," said Asher. "Authors appreciated that." Roth would repay the effort with his next book, *The Ghost Writer,* which hit the bestseller list.

FSG's fortunes were also buoyed by several in-house writers, carefully and patiently cultivated, who finally dropped some golden eggs. Susan Sontag's resurrection was the hardest fought of all. In the fall of 1975, she was diagnosed with stage IV breast cancer and given a very poor prognosis. She had a radical mastectomy in the autumn, followed by more than a year of aggressive chemotherapy and immunotherapy. As she had no health insurance, Bob Silvers at *The New York Review of Books* headed a committee, which included Straus, to raise funds for Sontag's care. Carlos Fuentes donated a $2,000 prize he'd just won.

Straus brainstormed deals to repackage or reissue or renew her books abroad, and redoubled his efforts to sell her papers. After Sontag improbably recovered, she was put on FSG's health-insurance program.

Straus's storied closeness with Sontag led many to believe that the publisher personally funded her hospitalization. Asked about the rumor during an interview, her son, David Rieff, mumbles, "Quite the opposite." He should know, he says, his face tightening: "I spent six months of my one and only life going around to every rich person Bob Silvers could think of." Much of the money came from the de Menil family of art collector–philanthropists in Houston. "Roger was having none of it," Rieff says. He doesn't think Straus even contributed to the *NYRB* fund.

Roger's tightness, personal and professional, would have lasting consequences. He was not, after all, the only one who knew how to hold a grudge. But his relationship with Susan only grew more enmeshed after her recovery. Rieff, who had dropped out of Amherst College and spent a few years wandering the world, occasionally checked in with Roger at Union Square. After Rieff finally got his degree, at Princeton, Roger asked him to join FSG as a junior editor. Susan was against the idea; she thought he'd be better off living with her and writing full-time. Roger respected the bond between mother and son, but in subtle ways he encouraged David to mature. Sigrid Nunez, who was dating Rieff at the time, remembers a visit to the Purchase estate, during which Sontag showed off her and David's brand-new tennis rackets. They were taking lessons together. Nunez felt left out, but said nothing. Roger, picking up on it, went upstairs, dug out a racket, and gave it to Nunez as a gift. Soon after that, Nunez broke up with David because his mother had become too overbearing. He began working for Roger in the summer of 1978. One of the first writers he edited was his mother.

Sontag's illness had interrupted a comeback already in progress. In February 1975, *The New York Review of Books* had run "Fascinating Fascism," Sontag's attack on a collection of African photographs by the former Nazi filmmaker Leni Riefenstahl. The subject of photography was becoming a consuming passion. What began as a single assignment, a 1973 review of a Diane Arbus retrospective for the *New York Review*, had turned into six intricate essays critiquing the place of photography in contemporary culture. Interest grew as they were published in the *Review*, and as soon as Sontag recovered she readied the essays for publication under the title *On Photography*, which FSG put out in late 1977.

Reviews, Roger wrote an English publisher, were "'combative,' which is good." By the end of January there were more than 41,000 copies in print and another 5,000 on the way. In the meantime, Sontag had finished another series of articles, *Illness as Metaphor*, which in some ways paralleled her thoughts on photography (photos can debase our experience of the world; metaphors diminish our understanding of illness). They also had the added authority—and voyeuristic appeal—of being informed by Sontag's struggle with cancer. The issues of *The New York Review* containing the first two parts of *Illness* sold out so quickly that 10,000 extra copies were printed for Part Three. The book version was published that June. Three Sontag books released in succession—*On Photography*, *Illness as Metaphor*, and her short-story collection *I, etcetera*—sold 150,000 copies collectively.

Sontag had also read *Illness* as a lecture at New York University, where she was the linchpin of a burgeoning cross-disciplinary department known as the Institute for the Humanities. Sontag dominated the institute along with her new friend Joseph Brodsky, an exiled Soviet-Jewish poet who was soon published and befriended by Straus. Barthelme taught there, and so did the Caribbean-born poet Derek Walcott, an FSG mainstay since the late sixties. The institute functioned at times as an off-site delegation of Farrar, Straus and Giroux, a bonding agent and an advertisement for the firm among the intellectuals and student writers of New York. It was also the first real literary circle to coalesce around FSG since Lowell's heyday.

Sontag wasn't the only succès d'estime to surprise her publishers with actual success. Straus and John McPhee had, over fifteen years, developed a mutual fondness based on humor and a keen understanding of each other. McPhee had modest financial expectations, and Straus met them. When McPhee offered to forgo an advance on a new collection, Roger insisted he take one, but when he asked for an advance on *The John McPhee Reader* (all previously published pieces), Roger said, "Fuck you." After one of McPhee's books sold out of stores during Christmas and was not reprinted for more than a month, he threatened to steal Straus's beloved Mercedes, whereupon Roger told him to please leave the hubcaps. Straus played the stingy Semite, McPhee the tight Scot. "That was part of the conversation," McPhee remembers, "that we were both cheap." Each year, Roger would come down and speak before McPhee's writing class at Princeton, charming everyone. "He would start talking and he just didn't stop," says McPhee. "He had an amazingly low percentage of repetition."

The camaraderie thrived on a pleasing stasis: McPhee wrote with spare, understated beauty, Straus kept his books in print, and *The New Yorker* paid the bulk of the bills and did most of the editing. Then along came *Coming into the Country,* McPhee's typically rich but deadpan survey of Alaska, which proceeded to sell around 140,000 copies within a year. "That surprised him more than anybody else," McPhee says of Straus. McPhee's friend Peter Benchley had recently come out with the massive bestseller *Jaws.* Shortly after *Country* hit the bestseller list, McPhee called Roger and said, "I went to a dinner party last night. I was *Jaws* for a day."

Straus wasn't caught completely by surprise when Isaac Bashevis Singer won the Nobel Prize just a year later. He'd heard rumors, but those were rampant in Stockholm. Even more than publishing McPhee, working with Singer had become a fulfilling routine, a predictable source of joy and pride, with the added benefit of Singer's side business in children's books. *Shosha,* Singer's thirty-sixth book (his twenty-ninth with FSG), was released in the summer of 1978 to the usual good reviews and a sale of roughly 35,000 copies by October. That was when Roger got a call from a publisher friend in Stockholm tipping him off about the prize.

Though FSG could claim earlier Nobel recipients, Singer was the first winner they'd built from scratch. Years of careful tending—pleading with publishers all over Europe and especially Sweden—had gone into cultivating the first Yiddish Nobel Laureate. It was a banner moment for Jewish literature and for FSG, and it wasn't so bad financially, either. Farrar, Straus carted over a load of Singer titles to Frankfurt that year. Straus's tiny booth was swamped with publishers from far-flung corners of the world. He estimated they did $150,000 in Swedish contracts alone, to say nothing of Finland, Denmark, Norway, and Iceland. Then there was Yugoslavia, and so forth and so on. A grand Frankfurt cocktail party for Singer was attended by the small army involved in publishing him around the world. In the center of the swirl, in his broad lapels and ascots and silvery mane, Roger Straus held court.

It was all just a prelude to Stockholm. The Strauses accompanied Singer on the Scandinavian Airlines flight (Frankfurt was for Peggy, but Stockholm was Dorothea's turf). Also along for the ride was Singer's editor, Bob Giroux, finally headed to the ceremonies exactly thirty years after he watched his friend T. S. Eliot soar Sweden-bound out of LaGuardia. In fact, it was everyone's first Nobel week. They all enjoyed first-class travel across the Atlantic except Singer's wife, Alma, and her friends—"a couple of yentas from Miami," per Roger—who were relegated to coach. They were dead tired by the time they arrived, but the weather was unusually bright, the snow glinting in the brief midday December sun. While Isaac warmed to the attention, dropping one-liners to the press, Roger basked in the glow of an elegant, almost defiantly Old Europe affair. "The thing was handled with enormous style," he said. Frankfurt was elegant but frazzled, and so very . . . German. Stockholm was pure class.

Unlike the 1976 winner, Saul Bellow, who didn't want to be boxed in as a Jewish writer, Singer made a special appearance before Stockholm's Jewish community, which Roger happily attended. "They were hanging from the walls," he remembered. Later, giving his official Nobel address, Singer spoke the first few sentences in Yiddish, followed by a paean to both the language and the ghetto from which it emerged, "not only a place of refuge for a persecuted minority but a great experiment in peace, in self-discipline and in humanism." Someone told Giroux that it was not only the first time Yiddish had been spoken before the Swedish Academy, but also the first time the audience had laughed. At the end of the weekend, Roger, Dorothea, and Giroux made a brief visit to Leningrad. Straus put "business executive" down on his visa rather than "publisher," fearing officials would realize he was a major publisher of dissidents. It was his first time in Russia since his brother, Oscar, had left him stranded in Europe, that time Dorothea had bailed him out with a loan he'd never repaid.

"I don't want a yacht off the coast of Spain," Roger Straus said, answering the question of whether, at sixty-one, retirement had crossed his mind. Just before leaving for Stockholm, he gave another long interview in his office. He sat puffing on a cigar behind his mother's table, all but oblivious to the junkie jungle outside his window and the fire-trap squalor just beyond his office door. It was like a scene out of Giroux's discarded twenty-fifth-anniversary introduction—only instead of avoiding the war, Rajah was sitting out the rat race of corporate publishing. He gave his Cuban a healthy drag. "Many people have accused me of being an elitist." He tapped some ash off the end. "I'm guilty. I am an elitist. I like good books."

In the closing days of 1978, *New York Times* reporter N. R. Kleinfield was covering Roger's "success story," and soaking up some color to put in front of the numbers. (Sales up 15 percent, nearing $10 million a year; several bestsellers; eleven editors producing around one hundred books annually.) But, really, it wasn't about the numbers at all. "I think that a lot of publishing houses are being run by accountants, businessmen and lawyers with very little concern for books," said Roger, who certainly didn't look like a modern businessman. "They could just as well be selling spaghetti or rugs."

This last dig was meant for Simon & Schuster CEO Dick Snyder, by now a regular adversary. "I think his opinion is not only groundless, but opportunistic," Snyder fired back, saying Straus disparaged corporations in order to convince writers they were better off with an impoverished independent. Which was, of course, true. There were other small firms around, but few of them battled openly with the big boys. Roger, on the other hand, was still doing what he'd done best in the navy: fighting a PR war. Only this was asymmetrical warfare, and

FSG was a guerrilla movement making a last stand in the Olympian hills, sniping away from the moral high ground. Every success was a victory for the revolution, every opinion a manifesto.

By no means, however, was Roger being disingenuous. In the same *Times* story, someone anonymously called FSG "an object of great curiosity," something "very rare—like an antique spinning wheel or a nickelodeon." Straus would have retorted that he would prefer hand-spun clothes to off-the-rack Loehmann's. He'd never meant to become an anachronism, but like Dorothea with her form-fitting riding outfits and burgundy bowler hats, he was absolutely sure of his style, and he used it to his advantage. Roger III concedes that, in an alternate universe, his father might have used his talents to sell anything—even rugs or spaghetti. "But I don't think he would have been happy selling a kind of pasta that you could get anywhere else. I think he would have had to find a crazy shape or taste, or something that made his spaghetti different from anyone else's."

As if to underline Roger's uniqueness and panache, it was his stylish and eccentric friend Tom Wolfe who gave the firm its final and greatest success of the seventies. *The Right Stuff,* Wolfe's nonfiction opus on the manned space program, seemed to herald the more grandiose decade to come. Its brave, unapologetic American heroes and its flag-bedecked cover might as well have featured in Ronald Reagan's convention speech. *The Right Stuff* hit the bestseller list and stayed there for twenty-five weeks. Wolfe's feat occasioned another *Times* piece, in March 1980, running to three broadsheet pages, the longest mainstream media story yet about FSG. The history of the company was unfurled from beginning to end. There was also more room for Dick Snyder: "Roger almost thinks that if books sell, that's commercial and therefore bad. When he has a bestseller, it's more accidental. He uses the line, 'I cry for the trees when the conglomerates publish a commercial book.' I cry for the authors when they sign with Roger." Snyder also put Straus on notice. "I just used to giggle," he said. "I'm taking him more seriously."

As any student of assymetrical warfare knows, being taken seriously is at least half the battle, if not the war itself. Roger's anger at

S&S may have had deeper roots than most people knew, but it found a highly productive target and a very catchy message. In order to keep his authors, Roger had to keep the playing field tilted in his favor, so that Farrar, Straus could confer a cultural premium on its writers—pride of place, personal attention, snob appeal, and maybe a better shot at the Nobel. Life was never as black-and-white as a Snyder-Straus debate, but the more it looked that way, the more FSG stood to benefit. It didn't hurt Roger's ego, either.

Bob Giroux also had his moment in that *Times* piece. His life had been the subject, two months earlier, of a separate profile, which opened with Peter Taylor calling him "the best publisher there is." Now, Kleinfield depicted him fiddling with his papers at his desk, "short, stocky, amused-looking," and "generally modest almost to a fault." But Giroux wasn't modest in his opinions, which dovetailed with Straus's. He'd recently coined the term "ooks" to describe the "not quite books" that dominated the bestseller lists and gift sections of bookstores. Kleinfield conveyed the sense, maybe gleaned off the record, that Giroux thought Straus hogged too much credit. (He left out one argument between the two men: Giroux had asked Straus to stop attending the editorial meetings. Roger agreed amiably, then returned the following Tuesday, ready to emcee.) On the record, Giroux would only say, "'There's a line in George Orwell's *1984* about being dropped down the memory hole. That ain't about to happen to me.'"

Giroux was "semi-retired" and working on his first book, an investigation into the origins, intentions, and publication of Shakespeare's sonnets. And he managed the estates of his late authors, fighting the memory hole on behalf of others. After Hal Vursell died in 1977, Giroux helped Vursell's longtime partner, Frank Kissner, establish the Harold D. Vursell Memorial Award, given to a work each year "for the quality of its prose style." Giroux, drafting the award proposal, borrowed Jonathan Swift's definition of style: "Proper words in proper places." He continued, crankily, "This demands work and clear thinking, and may explain why—in an era of illiteracy—style is denigrated or ignored." Tom Wolfe earned the second award in 1980.

Giroux's writers were quickly becoming legacies, one after another.

Robert Lowell died of a heart attack, at age sixty, in September 1977. His funeral brought the core of FSG to an Episcopalian church in Boston's Beacon Hill (Lowell had given up Catholicism). The Strauses were there, and so were Sontag, Elizabeth Bishop, Derek Walcott, Joseph Brodsky, and Lowell's ex-wife Elizabeth Hardwick. Lowell had dropped dead in a cab on the way to Hardwick's New York apartment, possibly to reconcile—bequeathing one last lurid literary anecdote to posterity. Giroux had been with Lowell through every phase of his illness, the manic highs (standing up in Giroux's box to mock-conduct an opera) and the dangerous lows (passing out from excess lithium at the Dardanelles, FSG's go-to Armenian restaurant on University Place). He had also published all his triumphs. Now he was one of ten pallbearers who carried Lowell's plain coffin into the church.

Jean Stafford was, by then, a widow spending her final years in the house of her last husband, A. J. Liebling, on eastern Long Island. She had emphysema, and a stroke had robbed her of her speech. "For one of America's most expressive and articulate users of the language, this was hell," Giroux wrote. She'd never delivered on her promise to write another novel, but with Giroux's help she did finally publish a story about that awful summer with Lowell in Maine. Giroux wrote William Shawn at *The New Yorker* that "An Influx of Poets" was "a brilliant and disturbing story, one of the best Jean has ever written, and one that will be much talked about." It needed quite a bit of editing, which wasn't easy given Jean's aphasia. She could, however, say "yes" and "no," so Giroux worked on the story by asking her yes-or-no questions. (Occasionally she'd muster the energy for a "Damn it! No!" or a "Yes, yes, yes!") After the last round of edits, he left her quarters in a rehab center in White Plains. Giroux thought, while hugging her goodbye, of "how sad and arduous and triumphant her life and art had been, how frail the body and how strong the spirit." "An Influx of Poets" ran in *The New Yorker* in November 1978. Stafford died four months later. Elizabeth Bishop passed away the following autumn, and her reputation, too, came under Giroux's protection.

In 1979, Henry Robbins died at the age of fifty-one. Just a year earlier, he had edited John Irving's *The World According to Garp,* a book

Straus surely would have loved to publish. Robbins still lived near the Farrar, Straus offices and was headed up to work that summer when he suffered his final, fatal heart attack in the Union Square subway station. When Bob said he was going to the funeral, Roger, according to a friend, "threw a fit—it was so terrible of Roger." Straus happened to be wrapping up some business with Didion at the time. Willfully oblivious of her close attachment to Robbins, he took the opportunity, nine days after Henry's death, to ask if she wanted to "come home again" to Farrar, Straus.

Bob not only went to the funeral, held on a sweltering day at the Society for Ethical Culture, but he spoke at some length. He praised Robbins as "a real editor-in-chief . . . to whom other editors could go for advice, and from whom they could learn"—and thus a loss to FSG twice over. And he added a private memory: a scene of the Robbins family visiting his and Charlie's summer home in rural New Jersey (though he didn't mention Charlie), drinking and playing croquet in the April sun. "Just a day in the country," he said, "but so colored with Henry's love of his family and his love of life, that it was no ordinary day."

Then he read a passage he'd recited only two years earlier, at Hal Vursell's service. It was Giroux's own loose translation of that deathbed poem by the Emperor Hadrian. Robbins, attending his old friend Hal's funeral, had liked the fragment so much that he'd asked Bob for a copy. Giroux thought it only appropriate to send Henry off with it, too:

> Little soul, gentle and drifting, the guest and comrade of my body, where will you now find a dwelling place? Poor little, naked little, pale little soul, without your old power of joking.

Henry's death produced a different line around the FSG offices, courtesy of that fount of one-liners, Anne "Sex is to Farrar, Straus" Sullivan. "Can you believe it?" she told a friend. "He had to drop dead under Roger's gaze," out on Union Square. "What an irony. To the end, Roger was looking down on Henry."

10

A Fraught Summer

In June 1984, Roger Straus spent a long week at Memorial Sloan-Kettering Cancer Center, waiting for test results on a malignant tumor in his colon, wondering if he'd make it to seventy. And that wasn't even the worst of it. His son, deposed from his job as editorial director of Harper & Row, was licking his wounds at Times Books. His "illegitimate son," David Rieff, was recovering from a nervous breakdown. His editorial department was—he had to admit it—flailing. Even FSG's supposed "friends" abroad were selling T. S. Eliot's letters not to Bob Giroux but to "this Serb," William Jovanovich.

The vultures were beginning to circle over Union Square. "The Dwarf," S. I. Newhouse, Roger's onetime neighbor on 70th Street and now the proud owner of Random House, was calling Peggy at the office, ostensibly to ask after Roger's health. He'd already ruined *Gourmet*, cofounded by Roger's mother, Gladys Guggenheim, by "putting fucking tampon ads in it." Then he'd wreaked havoc at *Vanity Fair* (and would buy 17 percent of *The New Yorker*'s stock that fall). And now he was salivating over Roger's prostrate body. Straus knew what he had to do. He had to ask his son to put aside his independent notions and *come home*. At the hospital, Rog refused to commit. Mostly, they spoke about his father's prognosis. "I'm dying," said Roger. "You'll live forever," Rog replied with a laugh. "It turns out we were both wrong," Rog says now.

Just after Straus was diagnosed with cancer, the first installment of Tom Wolfe's decades-delayed novel-in-progress came out in *Rolling Stone* magazine. The eighties, the real subject of *The Bonfire of the Vanities*, were custom-made for Wolfe's candy-colored satire. His ambition was Dickensian both in its broad scope (justice, class, race) and in its form (a year's serialization in a splashy magazine). Also like Dickens, he relied on contrast and counterpoint—black vs. white, rich vs. poor, selfishness vs. the common good. He probably would have cribbed the opening of *A Tale of Two Cities* if it weren't so well-known. The eighties were the best of decades and the worst; it was Morning in America; it was the Age of Greed . . . and so forth and so on. Farrar, Straus, too, was conflicted. But where the eighties are said to have been materially rich but artistically impoverished, FSG had the opposite dilemma.

It was, on the one hand, the era of Nobel Prizes. From Isaac Bashevis Singer's Stockholm trip in 1978 to Seamus Heaney's in 1995, FSG published the work of ten out of the eighteen winners, an almost unthinkable market share for a house of any size. Two years after foreign publishers had mobbed Roger's Frankfurt booth in pursuit of Singer, they lined up to ask about Czesław Miłosz, the 1980 Nobelist, a Lithuanian-American poet writing in Polish. Ecco Press held the rights to his poetry, but FSG had managed to grab his fiction, beginning with his 1955 novel *The Issa Valley*.

Straus, Sontag, their European friends, and the deepest bench of in-house Slavic readers this side of Warsaw had led the house deeper into the Eastern Bloc, which was exactly where Stockholm was turning its gaze. Aaron Asher and Philip Roth had a lot to do with it. Roth's friend Tadeusz Konwicki was brought onto the list; *A Minor*

Apocalypse, the writer-director's second novel translated at FSG, is still considered a classic antitotalitarian satire.

Younger editors Jane Bobko, Tamara Glenny, and Nancy Meiselas all read Russian. Meiselas, who became close to Asher, was Joseph Brodsky's acquirer, editor, and good friend. Brodsky also became chummy with Straus's poets Seamus Heaney and Derek Walcott, and together they made up FSG's inner sanctum in the post-Lowell era. When Brodsky moved briefly to England, less than a year after meeting Straus, he wrote to ask, "Can I do anything for the house?" They made him an unofficial scout, and then scoured their Rolodexes to find him a berth at a university near FSG. He landed for a year at Columbia. Brodsky soon became a consultant almost as influential as Sontag, whom he'd briefly dated. Sometimes his suggestions were too scholarly, but he convinced Straus to sign poets Alexander Kushner and Adam Zagajewski.

Asher had avidly pursued Elias Canetti, but the Bulgarian-born Jewish novelist and critic ultimately came courtesy of Straus's German friends at Hanser Verlag. FSG contracted for his final project, a four-part autobiography examining the conflagrations of Europe through his peripatetic upbringing. Peggy Miller says Canetti was one of only two writers who intimidated Straus on their first meeting. (German philosopher Theodor Adorno was the other.) At an intimate dinner organized by Hanser, Roger asked the intellectual to name his favorite book in English. It was John McPhee's *Oranges.* Well, McPhee was a subject the publisher knew a thing or two about, and Roger's gossip won the day. Canetti won the Nobel Prize the year after Miłosz.

Alas, the following year's winner was Gabriel García Márquez, whose first novel FSG had so casually rejected. But then FSG's William Golding took the prize in 1983. Roger basked in the glory of the Nobel, whose coffers funded his writers so generously. In Frankfurt he began hosting elegant dinners in the Parkhotel, organized by Peggy with military precision and tact. As often as not, he used the occasion to toast his latest Nobel. (Roger had moved to the smaller hotel following a falling-out with the InterContinental; the Parkhotel had a much grander, older atmosphere anyway. He would also leave London's Connaught, after a valet dared to ask for a tip in advance.)

Closer to home, though, it was the era of insecurity and sclerosis. The dark flip side of that famous FSG culture—the careless squalor of the haughty intellectual—was beginning to overwhelm its advantages. The state of the place surprised newcomers like Kristin Kliemann. Hired to assist the subsidiary rights director in 1981, Kliemann was excited to come to FSG, but not quite prepared for what she found there. Across from the park—still a scary place for a Texan woman a couple of years out of school—Kliemann was met at the door by a girl even younger than she was. Her name was Karen Everett, and she was, as it happened, Kliemann's new boss. They went in and locked the vestibule door behind them, turned the key in a panel to call the elevator, rattled up to the fourth floor, and opened a rusty gate. Through a reception area, beyond another flimsy door, was a desolate, fluorescent-lit hallway.

Kliemann's first day was a Saturday—another unpleasant surprise—and FSG's offices were more forlorn than usual. The ceiling didn't thump constantly, as it normally did, from the folk-dance studio on the fifth floor. But most of the children's department was around, burning the weekend oil on some much-delayed project. Kliemann, too, was already behind. Her position had been empty for months, and there was a lot to catch up on before hitting the phone on Monday. "I'm put into an office with a slumpy pile of envelopes and paper that have not been touched by anybody," she said, "contracts and checks and letters and offers and correspondence from all over the world."

It looked as if a bomb had hit, and in a sense it had—in the form of a recession and a series of shake-ups that had nearly destroyed morale. In 1980, with financial forecasts dire, rumors had begun to spread that FSG was on the verge of going under, prompting editor in chief Aaron Asher to reassure his staff by saying, "If you're concerned about FSG, royalties are due on April 1. Call any of our authors on April 2." The writers would always be paid. The staff was, perhaps, another matter.

Much as Roger liked to rail at corporate raiders, there were certain parts of the office where he didn't mind wielding the ax. This was especially true in subsidiary rights, where a series of freak departures had eroded his faith in the department. First Lila Karpf—who'd helped snag Neruda and build up Singer—had left in protest over the poor treatment of Malachi Martin, of all people. Then her successor, Barbara Neilson, had been caught stealing books en masse and selling them to the Strand, the famous used-book emporium down the street. When Roger had called her in about it, she'd said, "I'll stop if you give me a raise." The answer became legendary, both for its audacity and for what it implied about the salaries at Farrar, Straus.

Then, just after Neilson's successor, young Mary Sonnichsen, was promoted, she was hit by a car in London and suffered a brain injury. FSG paid for her long and slow recovery and put her assistant, Faith Barbato, in temporary charge. But as 1980 wore on and the budget tightened—and the subrights department failed to bring in enough business—Roger suddenly fired Barbato. The heads of other departments, who thought she'd done an excellent job, were baffled. So were the heads of the paperback houses Barbato did business with, including Putnam CEO Phyllis Grann. She called to tell Roger he'd done something stupid. Aaron Asher told Roger the same thing.

The following Monday, Straus relented. He called Barbato at home and told her he'd made a big mistake. But then, a few months later, came terrible year-end numbers. Those rumors of FSG's imminent demise began to spread. Whatever the ultimate cause, Straus decided, in early January 1981, to lay off Barbato after all. But instead of Sonnichsen, he put young Karen Everett, roughly twenty-three years old, in charge of subsidiary rights. "I was pretty shocked," Barbato says now. "It didn't make sense except as a money-saving venture. Roger very much had an eye for young and pretty girls, and I was neither." The following day, Sonnichsen turned in her resignation. Roger also laid off one of the publicity assistants, leaving his head of publicity alone in the department. She also quit.

Roger confessed the scheme to the press, and insisted (as always) that it had *nothing* to do with financial difficulties: "Like everyone else, we're tightening a little, and we may even publish five fewer books this year, but that's not what this was all about. It's reorganization of certain departments." Barbato told the same reporter, "Things have been very tense around Farrar, Straus for a while."

"This is what you have to understand about Roger—he *likes* to be skating on the thin edge of nothing. He *likes* to feel he can pull himself out of anything." So Dorothea Straus explained to one writer while her servant, Wong, poured her tea. Sure, Straus fretted and scrambled, but his optimism was boundless, his sense of the downside never too finely honed. What did "the thin edge of nothing" really mean to a Guggenheim?

Roger had foreseen the squeeze on small publishers decades earlier, but his optimism had somewhat blinded him to the consequences. He'd opined in 1964 that the "medium-sized independent" would lure "the truly creative artist" away from conglomerates. But twenty years later, many writers were perfectly happy to share catalog space with bestsellers if it meant more money and more marketing muscle. Even Roger's charm and FSG's laurels couldn't make up the difference. It was around the turn of the eighties that the cracks in those relationships first began to show.

In 1973, FSG had managed to hold on to Donald Barthelme by assuring him stability and advances (however low) no matter what his sales were. Nine years later, he was tired of what his biographer Tracy Daugherty called "FSG's penny-pinching, its lack of commercial chutzpah." It's not that FSG hadn't tried to sell Barthelme, at least early on. Lila Karpf had pitched his story collection *City Life* as the second coming of Kurt Vonnegut. But, as happens with so many longtime authors at so many houses, the lack of breakout success had dampened the enthusiasm.

So intent was Barthelme on leaving FSG—for a three-book contract at Putnam—that he not only repaid a $30,000 advance for a not-yet-published story collection, but agreed to give up close to half of its royalties—should there be any—to Farrar, Straus. This was only three years after Alfred A. Knopf bought out Harold Brodkey's contract for $75,000 including "interest and paper clips." Straus had raged over Henry Robbins's supposed rumors about FSG's being so cash-desperate it would let writers go for a song. Ten years later, that scenario seemed plausible.

At least Roger didn't have to worry that Joseph Brodsky or Derek Walcott would come to him hats in hand. Each won $250,000, no strings attached, from the MacArthur Foundation in 1981, the inaugural year of the famously lucrative "genius" grants. But Susan Sontag didn't, and she began to wonder if her fame would ever translate into freedom—which is what financial security really was. "Between the fact that she'd had cancer, had been called a genius many times, she really felt of all people, why not her?" recalls Sigrid Nunez.

Even success was threatening to spoil Roger's writers. In May 1980, with *The Right Stuff* still selling briskly, agent Lynn Nesbit wrote Straus asking for a $500,000 advance on a sequel to Tom Wolfe's modern-art book *The Painted Word* and an unfinished novel to be delivered in 1983. Roger, defying protocol, wrote to Nesbit and Wolfe together. "I am deeply disturbed by Lynn's proposal for a new two-book contract," he wrote—implying the agent had started the trouble. "It seems to me that this request is both unfair and unreasonable unless it has been thought out as a way to move Tom from Farrar, Straus and Giroux." He noted that there was still at least $270,000 due to Wolfe from sales of *The Right Stuff. The Painted Word* had made only $35,000 and Nesbit was asking more than twice that for its sequel alone—not to mention more than $400,000 for what was, despite Wolfe's fame, still a long-delayed first novel. Roger went on:

> I do not understand why you both are unhappy with Farrar, Straus and Giroux. I have heard nothing but praise from both of you about the way in which we have published THE RIGHT STUFF . . . I want Tom to be comfortable on money not only now but in the future; and I want Tom to want to be published by me. I should like the three of us . . . to sit down and talk together, for there seems to me more here than meets the eye, and I am prepared to fight to hold Tom on the FSG list until he tells me he no longer wants to be published by me.

Instead, Nesbit and Straus hashed it out between them, agreeing on $300,000 for three books, including an omnibus collection and $25,000 already paid for a canceled sequel to *The Right Stuff*. The relationship was salvaged, though at great cost to the company in a rough year.

Another threat to Roger's stable of writers stemmed from his persistent inability to retain top editors who weren't named Bob Giroux. A month after Roger's whirlwind "reorganization" of publicity and subrights, Aaron Asher left. He'd been angry about Roger's first firing of Barbato, but then Roger had backed off—only to fire her again and promote a child in her place. Asher knew plenty about working for bosses who made boneheaded decisions. He later told Sontag's biographers that Roger "doesn't know about design, about production, about what copy-editing involved . . . He knew about the financial side." As for everything else, "he had no feel for it."

Asher insisted that "the breakup was not a matter of a long-festering thing," but others felt differently. "Maybe [the Barbato firing] was the proximate cause," says David Rieff, "but more on the straw-that-broke-the-camel's-back principle. Aaron was very unhappy for quite a long time for a very understandable reason. You weren't a real editor in chief at Farrar, Straus. You just weren't. Roger wanted to have all the real power. That's why you see this idea"—which Rieff disagrees with—"that Roger didn't know what he was doing."

A month after the "reorganization," Roger III asked his father's blessing to hire Aaron Asher away, for Harper & Row. "I thought he was a terrific editor," says Rog. "I remember going to my father as his relationship with Aaron was deteriorating, and asking how he felt about taking Aaron over to Harper, and he said, 'I'd be delighted, help yourself.'" Asher noted the irony publicly, while settling in at Harper. "It's probably amusing that there's a Roger Straus here, also," he said, "but there's nothing to be made of that. He, too, left his father's company."

Whether Asher left because of Straus's outsize ego or his own is a matter of debate (which probably means it was both). "Aaron was a big-company guy," says Peggy Miller. "He started making cliques, playing politics, and we don't do that." To hear her tell it, Asher had begged Straus to hire him in the seventies, which he did reluctantly and to his later regret. That narrative smacks of Roger's tendency to inflict revisionist history on the victims of every "divorce." Like Robbins, Asher was never spoken of again—except when Roger would refer to him as "the late Aaron Asher."

As always, it really came down to the authors. Immediately after his fight with Asher, Roger had lunch with Philip Roth. Roth was contracted to FSG for his latest novel, *Zuckerman Unbound*, which was ready to go for the following year. But Roger wanted to let Roth know he would receive personal attention without his longtime editor. (He had, after all, followed Asher to FSG.) Though Roth won't discuss his relationship with Straus, Roger likely hammered home what FSG had done for him as both publisher and agent. Roth earned 70 percent of paperback deals through FSG, as opposed to the usual 50 percent. FSG sold most of his foreign rights for a small 10 percent cut. Straus nailed down Roth's commitment to stay at least through the end of his contract. In April, Roth simply told the *Times,* for a piece on Asher, "My plan is to stay where I am. My book is coming out soon, and I haven't even begun another."

Two years later, Straus felt compelled to pay $100,000 for *The Anatomy Lesson,* the next book in Roth's Zuckerman series—doubling FSG's previous advance. For *The Counterlife,* a larger novel, it was doubled again, to $200,000—plus a guarantee of another $250,000, to come out of FSG's subrights sales. *Zuckerman Unbound* sold fewer copies than previous Roth novels, *The Counterlife* only about ten thousand more. Roth may have been grateful, but he noticed the low sales. What he probably didn't realize was that, in order to secure such a lucrative deal, Straus had to give up *The Counterlife*'s paperback rights for the full term of Roth's copyright, rather than the usual five to ten years. This and other jerry-rigged Roth deals would come back to bite Straus in a few short years.

David Rieff took over editing Philip Roth. He says they worked well together, but insists he served merely as an intelligent "sounding board." "One of Roger's most brilliant coups," says Rieff, "was to make authors want to be published by the house, because there was this critical mass of writers that you wanted to be associated with." Roth, in spite of his outlaw reputation, "was interested in the prestige," says Rieff. "He's a very cultivated guy of the Chicago school, like my mother and like Robert Silvers." Roth eventually adopted the persona of a reclusive workaholic, forsaking social obligations to pursue the hard, brilliant truth. But at the time, still married to the actress Claire Bloom, Roth thrived in society. He, Bloom, the Strauses, and the Fuenteses took a memorable trip to Spain in 1986, with Fuentes playing tour guide. Roth was cranky on that trip, but he enjoyed Roger's company, and joked in letters about casting him in movies based on his books. But Roth was also a cold realist and a tough negotiator. His career was in its soft middle period, and Straus indulged him with increasing advances despite disappointing sales. The loyalty went both ways—for the moment.

The post-Asher transition was supremely orderly—maybe too orderly. Michael di Capua was made editor in chief, and Patricia Strachan, Giroux's former assistant, was promoted to executive editor. Di Capua, the perfectionist equally at home with adult and juvenile titles, was a reasonable successor. He was the most senior editor after Giroux, and cheaper to promote than a newcomer would be to hire. What di Capua cared about most, however, was his own books. For these he was much admired—one reason so few editors will go on the record saying he was not a good choice to step into the shoes of Giroux, Robbins, and Asher.

"It wasn't that he was incompetent in that position," says one alumnus. "It's just that an editor in chief's main function, as much as their ability to edit, was hunter-gatherer, was bringing in new blood"—meaning new writers. "And this wasn't one of Michael's strengths." Another function is management, and this is where the litany of complaints really clusters. "He was the last person to turn anything in," says another former staffer. "For him to be in charge of overlooking other people's books, it just didn't make any sense." Still another says, "I don't think he wanted to manage anyone. It was in

effect appointing someone editor in chief who would never actually
take that role."

Di Capua knew where he stood. "Michael was a grown-up in a
way that Aaron was not," says Rieff, "and understood the terms of
reference in a way that Aaron didn't want to. I think Aaron just kept
pushing to be the real editor in chief and that was never on offer,
which is what everyone else knew."

Di Capua handled many children's authors, about which neither
Straus nor Giroux trusted his own judgment. Yet they were a lucra-
tive part of the business, far out of proportion to the resources they
required, and they included luminaries such as Roald Dahl, Maurice
Sendak, William Steig, and Margot Zemach. On the adult side, it was
Pat Strachan who set the tone. Though not an aggressive acquirer like
Robbins or Asher, she had both a keen eye for detail and a classic sense
of style. Having taken over Giroux's most important poets—Philip
Larkin, Derek Walcott, Thom Gunn—she added to the list Gjertrud
Schnackenberg, Seamus Heaney, and Czesław Miłosz; already assigned
McPhee, she recruited young *New Yorker*–affiliated writers like Jamaica
Kincaid and Ian Frazier. She discovered Marilynne Robinson and
Padgett Powell. None of these were flashy titles or blockbusters, just
excellent work at a time when cash-strapped FSG had to be as selective
as possible. (The correspondence is full of rejections pleading a surfeit
of superb books with modest sales.) Like Giroux, Strachan was determined to ignore the office politics. "I barely noticed who was editor in
chief the whole time I was there," she says.

In the absence of overbearing personalities, Roger ruled unop-
posed. His two women, Peggy Miller and Susan Sontag, saw their influence increase. Years earlier, Peggy had had a fight with Roger about
having given her life over to him for not very much in return. He'd felt
guilty enough about it to sound out another confidante on the subject;
she consoled him by saying it was ultimately Peggy's choice. By now,
it was paying off—at least in line with her midcentury expectations.
She was put in charge of the intern program, which teemed with European publishing scions like young Karl Otto Bonnier and Antoine
Gallimard. She had the power not only to police dress codes ("Try a

little lipstick, maybe?" "It doesn't cost anything to iron!") but also to provide a shortcut to the boss for favored strivers. Once, she sulked in front of Giroux that her name had been excluded from an FSG staff list. "But, Peggy," he said, "you're special."

Susan Sontag had, of course, a very different role. "I really felt that in some ways Susan was editor in chief," says Rog, echoing something Giroux was known to grumble about. Sontag was the first reader, in English or French, on many of the manuscripts that came Straus's way, even by old-time authors like Marguerite Yourcenar.

Sontag's tastes, like her fiction, favored ideas and atmosphere over narrative—a preference that cost FSG at least one massive opportunity. Straus knew of the author, editor, and professor Umberto Eco from way back, but he deferred to Susan's judgment on Eco's new book, *Il Nome della Rosa*. Roger told her that, in these strapped times of too much literature and not enough sales, he could only take either Eco's novel or Salvatore Satta's *The Day of Judgment*. She urged him to buy both. "Come on, how many Wops can I publish?" replied the American publisher who'd had a lock on postwar Italian fiction. Then it must be Satta: Sontag not only preferred it, she thought it would sell better. Eco had entire passages in Latin, after all.

FSG wound up selling about two thousand copies of *The Day of Judgment*, while *The Name of the Rose*, eventually picked up by Harcourt Brace Jovanovich, became one of the bestselling books of the century (at least fifty million worldwide). In 1982, while considering Eco, the company barely broke even, and then only with a little cash from the Strauses' personal coffers. Had Farrar, Straus published Eco, the following year would have begun with a bonanza, instead of six months of frozen salaries.

Roger loved to tell the story of Eco vs. Satta, partly to show deference to Susan's taste and partly to illustrate how arbitrary publishing can be. But Sontag's choice wasn't arbitrary. *The Day of Judgment*, a Chekhovian meditation on life and family in a Sardinian town at the turn of the twentieth century, was an FSG book—and a Sontag book—while *The Name of the Rose*, a historical thriller and highbrow progenitor of *The Da Vinci Code*, was not. In fact, though Roger loved

Memoirs of Hadrian, he generally disdained historical novels, especially medieval ones. "Knights are for sleeping in," he once told the British publisher Christopher MacLehose.

As Julian Barnes wrote in his *Times* review, "Satta often seems to be 'doing' subjects—beggars, the election—rather than advancing a narrative." Sontag sometimes preferred this sort of thing. When she met FSG author Larry Woiwode at a party, she told him, "I'd like to comment on your book"—his National Book Award–nominated family saga *Beyond the Bedroom Wall*—"but of course, I don't read those kinds of books."

Sontag's proxy at FSG was her son, David Rieff. Brought on as a senior editor just out of college (albeit four years older than most grads), he worked mostly on inherited writers. Very much his mother's son, Rieff tended to make flamboyant pronouncements. Sensitive to being written off as a legacy kid, he overcompensated by playing up his erudition and his fabulous friends. Journalist Michael D'Antonio, whom he edited, later profiled him for *Esquire.* "I found him at once charming, tormenting, and brilliant," D'Antonio recalled in the piece. "His co-workers at Farrar, Straus kept telling me, 'There's only one David Rieff. We're not like that.'"

"He was very bright and very competent," remembered Aaron Asher. "When he was able and willing to work on something he was good." But when he wasn't, he could be a terror. He was careless with manuscripts by less important writers. He lost the only marked-up draft of a Brodsky essay collection, according to a former staffer. Karlo Stajner's *Seven Thousand Days in Siberia* was nicknamed "Seven Thousand Days on David's Desk."

As he later admitted, Rieff was using cocaine very heavily. After the end of an affair with an FSG employee, he suffered a nervous breakdown. "During that period I fucked up a lot of things," he now says. "I was barely holding it together and it was very kind of Roger not to fire me." He gave a more general apology in D'Antonio's profile: "I had been inhumane up until [the breakdown]. I didn't understand feelings."

Finally, Rieff says, "One day I woke and I couldn't get up." He checked himself in at Payne Whitney, the clinic where Robert Giroux had visited Jean Stafford in the late forties. Giroux had been the placid editor in the eye of many a storm, nurturing writers in ways even their friends and lovers could not. Rieff, Roger's "illegitimate son," was a storm unto himself. Eventually, after recovering and writing a well-received book, Rieff would leave "the only home I'd ever had" to become a full-time writer. Perhaps his mother had been right all along about not wanting him to work there. "I remember thinking it was a terrible idea," says Rog. "David could do damn near anything he put his mind to, but I don't think he fully had his heart in it." There was even more to it: By the time he left, in 1989, he was disillusioned not just with editing but with Roger Straus.

Roger's cancer turned out to be in his rectum, not in his colon, and thus embarrassing but easily removed. The whole thing was quite literally a "pain in the ass," he liked to say as he waved around the medical "whoopee cushion" he was forced to sit on. Roger seemed to have cheated fate, but as the summer of 1984 wore on, fate pulled a few trick moves of its own. He was looking forward to a summer of slow recuperation on the Purchase estate: lounging and gardening, more and more sets of tennis, more and more visits to the office, followed by the spirit-lifting annual jaunt to Frankfurt.

Then, a couple of days before his release from Sloan-Kettering, Dorothea called Roger at the hospital. Most of the old manor house on Sarosca Farm, his pride and joy, was gone. No one had been there when the electrical fire began, but someone at the country club next door had noticed the smoke just soon enough to salvage a room or two. Nina Straus walked through it with her daughter Tamara soon after it stopped smoldering. The entire frame was still intact, so you could see exactly where the walls, rugs, and furniture had been. Tamara, sixteen at the time, compared it to "walking inside a burnt skull, where the brains have been hollowed out." Only a couple of grandfather Oscar's artifacts survived: a Turkish sedan chair and a large engraving of the European counsel of Jews receiving their civil rights from Napoleon.

Eventually, Roger would have the house restored to look exactly as it had before: same moldings, same sleeping porch, same banisters, same spine-jarring gravel driveway. Peggy's sister-in-law did the interior work. Only the heirlooms were missing. But in the aftermath of that terrible June, Roger needed a country place where he could recover from his cancer, so the Strauses rented a house in Connecticut. There was another tenant in the pool house out back, and while they were staying there, he committed suicide. In August Roger was well enough to head into the office, but not to drive. A chauffeur was taking him into the city one day when the hood began to smoke. They pulled over, got out, and watched his glorious tan Mercedes burn. They wound up selling the remnants to a gentleman whose name was actually Mr. Blood. "Shall we say it was a fraught summer?" says Peggy, almost tearing up at the memory.

It seemed that every major piece of Roger's domain—his health, his estate, his marvelous car—was being systematically demolished. Even his publishing house, the core of his identity, was becoming a little less independent. S. I. Newhouse's phone calls that summer, which Roger later portrayed as predatory, weren't completely unsolicited. Newhouse was, in fact, looking to handle a piece of FSG's business that Roger was already resigned to giving up. The lease on the old warehouse deep in Bushwick, Brooklyn, had come up for renewal, and the new rent was steep, but that wasn't the only problem. Deliveries and inventory were still recorded by hand, while other publishers were already on their second generation of automation. The antiquated facility wasn't cutting it anymore. Nor was a vintage Honeywell mainframe that still tallied up sales on FSG's tenth floor. Newhouse was proposing to take over shipping, warehousing, and sales.

In a letter to Newhouse that September, Roger seemed to take his offer seriously. But after he returned from Frankfurt, he changed his mind, claiming that, "with your takeover of the New York Times Company, this may not be the moment to explore the situation with us further." There was no such takeover, but Newhouse's Random House *had* just acquired Times Books—a move that resulted in Rog's firing as its director of marketing. Perhaps his son's dismissal led to

Roger's change of heart, or maybe he had been teasing all along. He was fond of letting a suitor buy him lunch before returning to the office, calling in a few editors, and gossiping viciously about the bastard. "I had a marvelous lunch," he'd say. "I lied to him and he lied to me."

The warehousing went to Harper & Row. Straus took pains to deny that he was losing even a shred of his autonomy, but in fact, Harper did take over a few more operations over the years. There were clear advantages to outsourcing, even if, to a descendant of robber barons, it felt a little like losing one's grip on the world. "Roger was very proud of the fact that we stood completely on our own, from soup to nuts," says Joy Isenberg, who handled some of the changes. "But he was a businessman, too, and it was very sad for him but he saw that we had to do it."

Roger's other concession to time was a soft green velvet chaise longue that he brought into the office on his doctor's advice for afternoon naps. Johnny Farrar had used a similar couch, but the aging Roger wasn't about "the Century and home." Giroux was a little happier to sit back, filling his semiretirement with lectures, travels, and book projects, and letting Straus worry about the company's future. Giroux spent the eighties collecting lifetime achievement awards, advancing his late writers' reputations, and trying to shake the secret suspicion he'd shared with Eliot: that he was a failed writer.

In 1981, Giroux finally put between hard covers one of his enduring obsessions, the story behind Shakespeare's sonnets, under the title *The Book Known as Q*. Among the subjects he explored was Shakespeare's possible homosexual inclination. It was really a gloss on established debates, but some of his most original observations centered on the publishing history of the eponymous book, the 1609 quarto edition of 154 sonnets. Fittingly, Giroux was as interested in the mysterious challenges of editing and printing Shakespeare as he was in his metaphors and meter. In the process, he finally learned firsthand what it was like to have one's own book put through the publishing wringer.

Giroux pitched the book mercilessly to friends, including the critic Robert Fitzgerald and the publisher Matthew Evans of his beloved Faber and Faber, T. S. Eliot's old house in Britain. Atheneum was putting it out in the United States, but England was, as always, vital to Giroux. "If I'm not careful, I'll soon qualify as one of Sheila Cudahy's 'wretched authors,'" he joked to Evans. A couple of months later, Evans broke the news that an outside reader, a don no less, had rejected it harshly. "As you are a pro, I don't mind sending you the report," Evans wrote. "I'm sorry our decision came as a blow to you." Weidenfeld & Nicolson, a less prestigious English house, finally published it. Giroux dedicated it to his two late friends Mark Van Doren and John Berryman.

Giroux took Faber's rejection reasonably well. After all, how often had he been the one letting friends down easy by saying their books were "too special"? Far more damaging, in his opinion, was Faber's sale of T. S. Eliot's letters to a rival American publisher. It was one thing to reject his book, entirely another to come between him and the legacy of *his* most famous author. Never mind that it was Eliot's widow who betrayed Giroux, assigning the letters to William Jovanovich at Harcourt, the very firm from which Eliot had fled to continue working with Giroux. Jovanovich had apparently offered Valerie Eliot half a million dollars. Straus and Faber's Matthew Evans agreed that Jovanovich had done this out of revenge over Giroux's poaching William Golding in the seventies.

Giroux wrote personally to Valerie that August, saying he was "still deeply hurt." He reminded her that he'd helped ensure her financial stability toward the end of Tom's life. "It must be wonderfully convenient to have a private company-owned jet, like Jovanovich," he couldn't help adding. She responded that she thought he was retired and shouldn't be bothered with such things. "Far from having withdrawn from the publishing scene," he bristled, "I had six books on our last list. Roger and I both agreed years ago never to retire. I've been coming into the office the first three days of the week for over five years, but I find I do more and better editorial work (like the Elizabeth Bishop prose) when I work out of the office. Alfred Harcourt used to say, 'An editor's desk is wherever he is.'" Insisting that he still "felt the wound," he signed off, "I shall say no more lest I turn into a Lear."

•   •   •

The legendary Giroux had grown wistful, the indomitable Straus resigned to a chaise longue and the prospect of a diminished house. Torpor seemed to be setting in—and then, just in time, the prodigal son returned.

In the autumn of 1984, just after his father's recovery from cancer, Roger III had taken a new job, as the executive editor of Avon Books. But he'd barely settled in before its owner, Hearst, reshuffled the corporate deck, and Rog was fired once again. He was growing weary of "chess games where I was swept out with the other pawns." It was time to come home.

But before he could, Rog had some questions for his father. What would his position and his responsibilities be? How much stock would he have? How and when would he take over? And how would things be different this time? Underlying the ensuing negotiation was the plain fact that succession was now visible on the horizon. Father and son agreed that Rog would run business and marketing, while Roger remained firmly at the editorial helm. Rog got 10 percent of the stock, with more to be passed on later. "That never happened," says Rog.

PUBLISHER NAMES AIDE, read a slightly undermining announcement in the *Times* in August 1985. Almost from the moment Rog arrived, there was a major difference of opinion about both the scope of his job and the problems that needed fixing. Roger thought that the company's business structure was shaky but its editorial department was splendid as always. One of Rog's first pieces of advice was that his father had it all wrong. "The marketing and business departments are better than ever," he told his father, "but we're really missing a strong editorial presence." Today he says it more plainly. "A Giroux in his prime, a Henry Robbins, was missed." There was a hole in the house, all right, but it had nothing to do with sales.

For years, his father had insisted that marketing didn't make books. Now Rog was making the same point: Developing writers aggressively and robustly had to be *the* top priority. Roger conceded that his son was right. Now all they had to do was find someone up to the job.

11

A Little Less Hothouse Literary

I f Jonathan Galassi didn't exist, FSG would have had to invent him.
Roger first learned about the young editor through the agent
Harriet Wasserman, who passed on the news that he was being
treated abysmally by Si Newhouse's underlings at Random House.
When he met Galassi in the spring of 1986, Straus knew right away
that the editor would fit FSG like a glove. Galassi was tapped into
"class-mass," as Roger called it—respectable work with commercial
potential. "You got a guy who was both a translator of [Italian modernist poet Eugenio] Montale and also published Pat Conroy successfully," says David Rieff. (Conroy's *The Prince of Tides* would soon tear
up the bestseller list.) Galassi also turned out to have just the right
temperament—passion leavened with calculation—to tolerate Roger
Straus.

By no means, however, was he *like* Roger. That would never have
worked. Straus was a born jock who ingratiated himself with book-
worms by dint of his quick wit, hauteur, and magnetic personality.

Galassi, on the other hand, is patrician only by training, a bon vivant only by necessity, but a nerd through and through. He invited his fourth-grade teacher to his ninth birthday party. He seems to have learned the bold body language of an alpha male, but never quite vanquished his low, slightly nasal voice or downcast expression. Galassi's grandfather, an Italian immigrant, launched a successful terrazzo business, married a WASP, and worked tirelessly to send his children to Harvard. Galassi's father, a Boston lawyer, sent him to Phillips Exeter Academy in New Hampshire, then to Harvard.

Galassi developed the creative ambitions prototypical of the third generation. He studied classical languages at Exeter and poetry at Harvard, the latter at the feet of one of his idols, Elizabeth Bishop. He also took a class with Robert Lowell. After winning a Marshall Scholarship to the University of Cambridge, he mastered his ancestral language in Italy, the better to read Dante and translate Montale (one of the few Italian luminaries not published by FSG). Already a translator and a poet, he went the editorial route because he "got a real thrill out of being present at the creation of somebody else's work." To put it less charitably, he may also have craved security and influence. (A journalist later wrote, "It's hard to say whether Galassi is a yuppie with the soul of a poet or vice versa.") In 1973 he wrote to Robert Giroux requesting a job interview and touting a letter from Bishop. But before they could meet, he took an internship at Boston-based Houghton Mifflin.

Galassi made a reputation for himself in an important niche that might be called the upper-midlist: intelligent but accessible novelists with breakout potential, like Pat Conroy and the more literary Alice McDermott (along with a stable of distinguished poets). But genteel Boston didn't hold much appeal. Galassi got himself transferred to the New York office and waited until he could trade up. "I was very interested in publishing young writers," he has said, "and I felt that Houghton was kind of stick-in-the-mud-ish and that a place like Knopf or Random House would do that better."

Jason Epstein soon hired him at Random House, and he had five years to learn how wrong he was. "It turned out that Houghton Mifflin was actually more willing to take chances on the kinds of authors I liked than Random House was," he later said. Galassi arrived just as Random was sold to the Newhouse family. Four years later, Newhouse brought in Howard Kaminsky, formerly of commercial paperback house Warner Books, as Random's new publisher. Kaminsky decided that Galassi "didn't have any books with commercial potential." Yet when Galassi had wanted to bring the bestselling Pat Conroy over from Houghton Mifflin, Epstein and others had blocked the move. In the spring of 1986, Kaminsky told him to look for a new job. "I almost left the business," Galassi remembers. "I didn't really have a lot of options. I tried to go back to Houghton Mifflin. They didn't want me." That was when he came in for an interview with Roger Straus.

Soon after their first meeting, Straus took Galassi to the Lotos Club and offered him the job. The publisher had sniffed out a familiar type. He'd always had a knack for finding editors lost at sea and reeling them into his classy little yacht. Like John Farrar, Galassi had been cast aside without so much as an apology; like Bob Giroux, he'd found his literary taste marginalized; and like Roger III, he was tired of being a corporate pawn.

At FSG, Random House's money-losing elitist looked refreshingly commercial. On that, father and son agreed. "I think Rog was looking for an attitude that was a little less raffiné," says Galassi. "There was a group mentality at FSG that he thought was out of touch with reality in some way. He wanted some realism, some commercial sensibility— a little less hothouse literary." Rog and Galassi quickly became simpatico. Beneath Galassi's tweed sport coat beat the heart of a competitor, one who admired Knopf's longtime editor Bob Gottlieb not only for his great taste but also for his fierce survival instinct. He was more like a younger Gottlieb—an avid fan of both art and commerce—than the second coming of Aaron Asher. "It's a business," Galassi said later, "and I love the fact that it's a business. I really think it's much better for publishing to be a commercial enterprise."

As if to underscore how badly FSG needed a turnaround, Galassi was hired in May 1986 but couldn't start for several months because there was no money to pay him. During that grace period, FSG signed up several fresh new Galassi titles from authors whom Random House was happy to let go. Works by the poet C. K. Williams, the scholar and memoirist Vivian Gornick, and the novelists Lionel Shriver and McDermott were added to the list.

Some of them landed in the Fall 1986 catalog, which bore all the hallmarks of a Rog redesign. For decades FSG's books were listed in black-and-white four- by eight-inch pamphlets full of running text seldom interrupted by anything so vulgar as an illustration. The fortieth-anniversary catalog, by contrast, sported a textured pearl-gray cover, a wider format, thick case binding instead of staples, and cover images or author photos for almost every book. The lead title: *The Bonfire of the Vanities,* Tom Wolfe's novel at long last. Wearing a cream sport jacket over his pristine many-buttoned vest, the Man in White was featured in a full-page, full-body glamour shot, leaning insouciantly on a glass door. On the next page was *Quiet Rage: Bernie Goetz in a Time of Madness,* a book of pop psychology on the subway vigilante case dominating the news. Unsurprisingly, it was Rog's acquisition (and a commercial disappointment).

"I have just hired Jonathan Galassi of Random House, living proof that I intend to go on," Straus told *Publishers Weekly* that fall, for a profile titled "Outliving the Bastards." The first person was not an accident: On the verge of seventy, Roger felt as secure as ever in his own Sun King supremacy. In fact, he took Galassi's hiring as an opportunity to remove Michael di Capua as editor in chief, giving the editor his own eponymous imprint and taking the editor in chief title for himself. Galassi would share the title of executive editor with Pat Strachan.

That October, as the editor in chief and his secretary took their annual Frankfurt trip, his son and his new hire decided to pursue a courtroom thriller. Galassi already knew the lawyer and aspiring novelist Scott Turow; they'd discussed a short novel a few years back. Turow's new manuscript, which would become *Presumed Innocent,* was definitely a genre work, but there was craft and intelligence in it. The writing was considerably better than it had to be, and the haunted main character was psychologically compelling. Clearly something was going on in prosecutor Rusty Sabich's subconscious, whether or not he was actually the killer.

"Rog and I kind of plotted this while Roger was at Frankfurt," says Galassi. Like Straus and Farrar going after *Courtroom* so many decades earlier, Rog and Jonathan worked as a team to bag Turow's book. Rog was the glad-hander, Galassi the attentive caretaker. Viking and a few other publishers were in the bidding, and the highest offer was $350,000. Rog and Jonathan wouldn't go over $200,000. Turow, who'd earned a fiction MFA at Stanford before going to law school, had a literary mind-set. He asked each editor to submit detailed comments about how to improve his work. "Jonathan gave me the straightest answer," Turow says. "He was willing to chance being direct, and I found that appealing." Where Galassi pushed, it was usually in a *less* literary direction, away from abstract musings. He wanted to accelerate the beginning, break up the flashbacks, and cut down on "philosophical speculations."

Turow's decision to take the $200,000 underbid—a 43 percent pay cut in return for the pride and cachet of being at FSG—wasn't just driven by Galassi's forthrightness or Rog's enthusiasm. Like them, he had grown up in awe of the hottest literary publisher in the country. During the late sixties, when Rog was working under his father's shadow and Galassi was studying under Bishop and Lowell, Turow devoured the acquisitions of Giroux and Robbins, including Walker Percy, Leonard Gardner, and Grace Paley. "There were lots and lots of places where those fish turned up," he says. Of all the rejection letters he'd received over the years, the two most thoughtful, the ones he saved, were from Michael di Capua in 1967 and Jonathan Galassi (then at Houghton) in 1974.

FSG's hard-earned reputation was a factor in many writers' decisions to sign on in the eighties, often in spite of a pay cut. Jamaica Kincaid says that once Pat Strachan came calling, FSG offered her "the least money," but she had already turned down higher offers "because I hoped, hoped, hoped that somebody at Farrar, Straus would notice . . . All the writers that I admired were published there." Long before Ian Frazier began writing for *The New Yorker* and Farrar, Straus, he had looked to both institutions to "let you know what's first rate."

John Farrar (*left*) and Roger W. Straus, Jr., in 1946, not long after Farrar, Straus & Co. was incorporated. Their inaugural catalog read: "The first list of a new publishing house is always an adventure."

Straus and Robert Giroux in the early 1970s, around the time Giroux advanced from editor in chief to chairman. Straus called Giroux's arrival "the single most important thing to happen to this company."

The Strauses, circa 1925. *Front row from left:* Roger W. Straus, Jr., Sara L. Straus, Oscar S. Straus. *Back row from left:* Roger W. Straus, Sr., Gladys Guggenheim Straus, Oscar Straus II.

Left: Straus in U.S. Navy uniform during World War II; he handled book and magazine PR—excellent training for civilian life. *Right:* Dorothea Straus: Heiress, memoirist, flamboyant and cerebral hostess and, occasionally, FSG's first reader.

Left: Robert Giroux's yearbook photo from Regis High School, where he excelled—but dropped out in his senior year to earn money during the Depression. *Right:* Giroux, when he was FSG's chairman and elder statesman. He and Straus made a pact early on in their partnership: Never retire.

Young Giroux, on floor left, with his lifelong companion, Charles Reilly (standing behind chair), and Reilly's family and friends.

Giroux with his author and friend T. S. Eliot at La Guardia airport, 1948; Eliot is bound for Stockholm and the Nobel Prize.

Robert Lowell, Jean Stafford, and Robert Giroux in Maine in 1946, during what Stafford would later call "that awful summer."

Jack Kerouac in 1950, not long before he threw the scroll of *On the Road* onto the desk of his good friend and editor, Robert Giroux— who, in the end, rejected it.

John Berryman, Giroux's best friend from college, whose suicide devastated the editor.

Flannery O'Connor: Early on, Giroux "had a hunch" about her. "She had electric eyes," he remembered. "Her integrity impressed me."

Farrar, Straus's splashy ad for *Be Happier, Be Healthier* by Gayelord Hauser, whose fad diets kept the fledgling company afloat in the early fifties.

Tom Wolfe, who, despite a few testy letters over the years, was always one of Straus's biggest fans. "God bless the fact that he was among us," Wolfe concluded, giving the final eulogy at Roger's 2004 memorial.

Joan Didion in the late sixties. When her beloved editor, Henry Robbins, left FSG, Didion followed. Years later Roger implored her to "come home," to no avail. She titled a later essay collection *After Henry*.

For all his prickly rivalries, Roger was an expert at building camaraderie with authors, building the kind of relationships his son glosses as "two towering egos beating as one." Straus with, clockwise: Sammy Davis, Jr., Edmund Wilson, Susan Sontag, Josef Brodsky.

FSG's classic covers were almost as distinctive as its three-fish colophon.

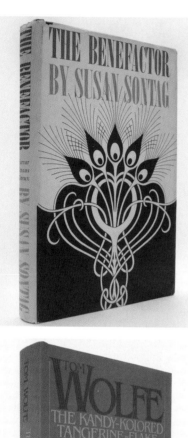

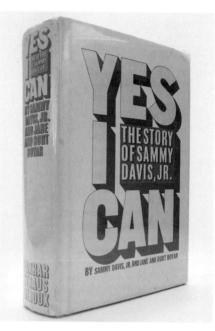

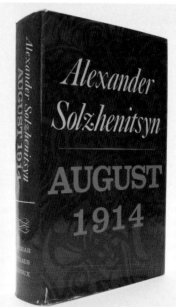

Some later covers were just as striking:

The main house at Sarosca Farm in Purchase, New York, where Roger played the country squire to Nobel laureates.

Roger Straus III's house on the same estate, designed by Charles Gwathmey, speaks volumes about the generational differences between father and son.

Roger Straus and his son, Roger Strauss III. Once his father's presumed successor, "Young Roger" eventually left FSG due to "philosophical differences," according to father and son's joint press release.

Roger and Jonathan Galassi, his actual successor, at the National Book Awards in 2000, the year Susan Sontag won for her novel *In America*.

An original James Thurber drawing, which Giroux framed and mounted behind his desk and nicknamed "Author and Publisher."

At lunchtime, FSG's authors could often be found at table 38 of the Union Square Cafe, which was owned by Straus's friend Danny Meyer. *Clockwise from bottom left*: Derek Walcott, Jonathan Galassi, Marie Heaney, Roger Straus, Sigrid Nama, Seamus Heaney.

Roger revels in a standing ovation after the closing speech of FSG's fiftieth-anniversary celebration, September 19, 1996. To his right, FSG authors Jamaica Kincaid and Ian Frazier.

Galassi chats with Philip Roth at the Lotos Club at a reception following Straus's memorial service, September 24, 2004. Andrew Wylie—who took Roth away from FSG—hangs back between them.

Top to bottom, FSG's photogenic new guard: Jonathan Franzen, posing for the jacket of his 2001 literary blockbuster, *The Corrections*; Jeffrey Eugenides, in the photo used on a billboard promoting *The Marriage Plot* in Times Square under the headline SWOONWORTHY; and Roberto Bolaño, whom FSG turned into a posthumous bestseller.

Farrar, Straus in 1956. *Front row, left to right:* Claire Costello, Sheila Cudahy, Kuna Dolch, Roger Straus, Patsy Van Doren, Lynn Caine, Dorris Janowitz. *Back row, left to right:* Robert Wohlforth, Robert Giroux, John Farrar, H.D. Vursell.

FSG, circa 1973. *Front row, left to right:* Julie Coryn, Henry Robbins, Elizabeth Nichols, Henry Schlanger. *Middle row, left to right:* Rhoda Gamson, Robert Giroux, Arthur Wang, Roger Straus, Dorris Janowitz, Sam Kam. *Back row, left to right:* H.D. Vursell, Lila Karpf, Roger Straus III, Michael Di Capua.

One third of the firm, 1999.

The senior staff in 2013, in Galassi's bright new office. *Back row, left to right:* Creative Director Rodrigo Corral; President and Publisher Jonathan Galassi; Sarah Crichton, Publisher of Sarah Crichton Books; Faber and Faber Publisher Mitzi Angel; Executive Editor Sean McDonald; Jeff Seroy, Senior Vice President, Publicity and Marketing. *Middle row:* Publicity Director Sarita Varma; Erika Seidman, Director of Contracts, Copyrights & Permissions; Executive Vice President and Deputy Publisher Andrew Mandel; Editor in Chief Eric Chinski. *Bottom row:* Executive Managing Editor Debra Helfand; Art Director Charlotte Strick; Subsidiary Rights Director Devon Mazzone.

Writers gravitated to such places, he believed, "in the same way that people gravitated to George Balanchine."

It's astonishing to note that both of these writers—and John McPhee besides—put *The New Yorker* and FSG side by side as cultural institutions. Consider that FSG was just a twinkle in the eye of a callow navy lieutenant a full fifteen years after the demise of the original Algonquin group, and that *The New Yorker* lavished money on writers who barely wrote while FSG staffers complained of malnutrition. And yet, just in time for the seventies downturn, Farrar, Straus had joined the rarefied ranks of companies whose cultural value deserves its own column on the balance sheet. Not only was it greater than the sum of its sales, it punched higher above its weight than any other publisher. For cultural climbers like Kincaid, a poor Antiguan immigrant who'd grown up to marry William Shawn's son, its appeal was almost religious. As a writer, "you're engaged in a truth," she says, "in something grand, something bigger than your cup of coffee or whether you can take a cab or whether you have a nice chair. You're engaged in something that really has no value that you can put in your hands . . . I would sell my soul to the devil to write a great book but I wouldn't sell my book to the highest bidder."

Yet Turow's sacrifice was greater than the others' by a solid six figures. As soon as he was signed, Rog called him up and asked, "Where have you been all these years?" "The answer to that," Turow says now, "was *in your fucking slush pile*—not that I had the temerity to say that." Instead, he graciously accepted Rog's offer to fly to Chicago and take him out, anywhere he'd like. Turow chose pricey Ciel Bleu, with its sweeping view of Lake Michigan. It was hardly Jovanovich in his private jet, but for FSG it was a grand gesture. On the publication of Turow's second thriller, Rog would send a case of wine. "Dear God, you must think you're Simon & Schuster," Turow would write in gratitude. "You could have made an advance against two books of poetry."

While Rog wined and dined, Galassi stoked Turow's literary aspirations. On the occasion of a Turow book publication, Galassi would regularly compose doggerel to read for a toast, some of it running over a dozen long stanzas. It may have been the first and last time in history that a writer of legal thrillers was serenaded in the same manner, and by the same editor, as a klatch of Nobel Prize–winning poets. Galassi would celebrate Turow's trouncing of Stephen King and Danielle Steel on the charts ("Then just for kicks along the way, / you killed the King and proved you have / more tensile strength than Steel"). Reinforcing the clubbiness of the house, he made parallels between Turow's characters and his publishers. Celebrating *The Burden of Proof*, in Chicago, Galassi read:

> *I combed the book and couldn't find*
> *a single Jewish lout*
> *(except of course the rabbi,*
> *but the rabbi doesn't count):*
> *no swindler in commodities,*
> *no fiscal mole or mouse,*
> *no codger you call Roger,*
> *no sharpie known as Straus.*
> *Well, I may be a shaygitz,*
> *But I can tell an artful dodge,*
> *For Nate the randy cameraman*
> *I know is based on Rog.*

Returning from Europe at the height of the Turow auction, Straus gave his approval to the acquisition, but he could never quite make peace with *Presumed Innocent* or its successors. "What would Susan say about this?" a few people recalled him saying. "Okay, let's get back to real books," he told Galassi once. The snobbery was a little disingenuous coming from a publisher who not only had survived off *Yes I Can*, the Sammy Davis, Jr., biography, but was just then preparing to publish the sequel, the racier and more candid *Why Me?* No, there was something else behind Roger's high-handed coolness toward Turow. Many people on staff thought it was simply that the Sun King felt, for a moment, eclipsed.

Turow's pay cut notwithstanding, $200,000 was still a rare sum for FSG—the same amount Roger had paid to hang on to Philip Roth.

But Roth was famous, and his coming novel, *The Counterlife*, was one of FSG's best shots for a bestseller in 1987 (following a year with exactly zero books on the *Times* list). Turow, on the other hand, was the kind of gamble FSG didn't usually make. "You just spent the whole acquisitions budget," di Capua remarked sardonically to Galassi. Then they had a paperback auction and got a $670,000 guarantee. They had made money before even publishing the book. "Everyone shut up after that," says Galassi.

Until 1987, Roger's boastful memos to the staff generally listed all the awards and year-end best-of mentions FSG books had earned. There was no shortage of those in the year Wolfe's and Turow's books would be published. The company won two National Book Critics Circle Award categories—*The Counterlife* for fiction and a C. K. Williams poetry collection. *Paco's Story*, by Larry Heinemann, a Pat Strachan author, won the National Book Award for fiction. Joseph Brodsky would take the Nobel Prize—and put Straus down on the forms as his next of kin, a designation that allowed Roger, as "immediately family," to meet the king of Sweden.

But it was also the first year in a long, long time that the firm paid serious attention to the *Times* bestseller list. Roth's *Counterlife* crept in for a month but never broke the top ten. Walker Percy's last novel, *The Thanatos Syndrome*, was also one of his most accessible—a dystopian thriller with shadings of *The Body Snatchers*—and it spent nine weeks on the list, reaching number six.

Then in June came *Presumed Innocent*. Within two weeks it was on the list; within a month it dinged number one. Then it stayed at number one or two through the fall, before being joined by *The Bonfire of the Vanities* just as it was easing into the number-three slot. Some weeks only Danielle Steel or Stephen King or Tom Clancy kept it off the top—strange company for a Farrar, Straus book. For three glorious winter weeks in 1988, *Bonfire* was number one and *Presumed Innocent* number two.

Each book was a different kind of vindication for FSG. Tom Wolfe was the old stalwart. His careful, modest editor, Pat Strachan, was a good caretaker and a check on Wolfe's exuberance. As he had been predicting boldly, cockily, for decades, fiction was his proper milieu.

The plot catalyst in *Bonfire*, a fatal clash of classes in a derelict Bronx neighborhood, seemed to mainline the zeitgeist. Wolfe's success was of a piece with Sontag's, though the numbers were much greater. Both were a triumph of the Straus brand of publishing: Let the writers steep, develop, delay. Feed them steadily but never beyond your means. Eventually they will deliver. Fittingly, though Turow and Wolfe sold almost the same number of copies (three-quarters of a million each), *Bonfire* was the one that built more slowly but spent more time on the list—fifty-six weeks to *Innocent's* forty-five.

Turow's sweeping success, on the other hand, vindicated Rog's prescription for the future of FSG. While the company's growth would have been impossible without these two novels, which helped drive sales up 50 percent over two years, the fact is that plans for expansion were already in place. Before either book came out, Rog and Galassi were busy meeting with agents to inform them that FSG would be participating in more auctions. The list of adult titles was meant to increase from sixty to more than eighty per year.

Before long, Rog began fretting that some rival publisher would whisk Galassi away. At his urging, in January 1988, Roger relinquished one of his titles and promoted Galassi to editor in chief. Pat Strachan was promoted to associate publisher, but she was far from pleased. "I was hurt when they just told me that Jonathan had been promoted," she said. "It didn't feel courteous" not to consult her. "When you're forty and your entire adult life has been at this place—not just a job—you feel somehow slighted."

A month or so later, Charles McGrath at *The New Yorker* called and asked if she wanted to become a fiction editor there. She took the job and announced her resignation, surprising herself as much as anyone. Someone who insists that what made FSG special was its team-of-equals quality, its indifference to titles, left precisely over a title. Many of Strachan's writers were baffled, even angry, at her departure, but they all stayed at FSG (there was nowhere for them to follow her). Galassi isn't alone in lamenting her decision to leave, which he calls "a great loss to FSG," unnecessary collateral damage on the road to succession.

12

The Day of the Jackal

Susan Sontag woke up one morning in March 1987 to find her bedroom on fire. Roger Straus came home one evening not long before that to find his stately brick town house ransacked and robbed. The fire was put out quickly, and the town house doors fixed; neither writer nor publisher suffered serious injury. But something inside both the writer and the publisher was broken, some sense of untouchability that had helped them endure every bout of illness or crisis in their lives. Now, neither felt safe in his or her own home. Something broke in their relationship, too, and as their dealings became strained, a young, ambitious agent named Andrew Wylie was only too happy to step into the breach. Whether he was a catalyst of the eventual rift or just a scapegoat depends on whom you ask.

In other circumstances or other decades, Straus and Wylie might have been friendly rivals, even kindred spirits. In some alternate universe, one can almost imagine them in group therapy, commiserating tearfully over their cold, domineering fathers. Roger might have taken him under his wing instead of cursing him under his breath. Andrew might have expressed his avowed love of Roger by dealing favorably with him, instead of setting his most beloved authors against him. Then again, maybe many of Roger's colleagues were right, and it was simply impossible to like the agent at all.

Wylie is probably the only one of Straus's antagonists to be known in publishing by a vicious nickname Roger didn't invent. No one knows who coined the epithet "the Jackal," but the name has stuck to this day. Maybe it had to do with Wylie's habit of scavenging—poaching established authors from other agents, or from paternalistic publishers like Straus—rather than building up authors of his own. It doesn't help that his face tapers from a broad bald pate to a V-shaped brow, icy eyes, and a chiseled, lupine chin, or that his laugh sounds like that of the world's most cultured hyena. The label offends Wylie, but he takes an obvious pleasure in stoking his reputation as a cold operator whose cunning places him just slightly beyond good and evil. One journalist was inspired to call him "a moisturized fist of virile elegance"—only the most memorable of a trail of contrapuntal adjectives piled on whenever Wylie commits another one of his outrageous acts. (THE NAUGHTY SCHOOLBOY, read the headline in *Time.*)

"I had a great love of Roger and a considerable appreciation of what he stood for," Wylie says, over sixty but still trim and moisturized, hands steepled over a monolithic desk in his obsessively neat office at the Wylie Agency, seven hundred clients strong. He's often spoken derisively of the dowdy agents from whom he poached many of his clients, with their dusty windows and "dying spider plants." But on the subject of the late head of Farrar, Straus, Wylie waxes nostalgic. "He had flair. He was tempestuous in a kind of theatrical way. But the drama that followed him around was good for publishing," he says. "Publishing needs a little drama." On the other hand, he's not completely nostalgic: "You could anticipate how much Roger would surrender. He was volcanic but predictable—like volcanoes . . . His strategic weakness was that he was prey to his emotions."

Wylie had some trouble with his own emotions as a young man. His personal drama seems, like Roger's, to stem from that primal family tension between assimilation and rebellion, tradition and ambition, patrician expectations and barbarian appetites. In other words, Wylie didn't much like his father, either. Craig Wylie served two terms in the New Hampshire legislature, followed by a long editorial career at Houghton Mifflin. He had also been a master at St. Paul's, the Episcopal boarding school that had rejected the ne'er-do-well Roger Straus, Jr. Andrew Wylie got in, of course; he was a legacy. But he soon made his masters regret the admission. Favoring black over the Oxford shirts and loafers of his classmates, Andrew would occasionally introduce himself as an alter ego, Mario Black. He would take the train down to New York in search of what he has called "the intimacy of underprivilege," and return with anecdotes involving transvestites and drug dens—an edgier sixties update of Roger's scurrilous stories. He was dismissed in 1965, he's said, for running alcohol from Boston for profit. Nonetheless, he was admitted to Harvard. He and Jonathan Galassi overlapped there, but they didn't know each other well.

Wylie learned less in prep school than he did by perusing his father's vast library in Sudbury, Massachusetts—including three complete sets of Voltaire—becoming as zealous and showy as an autodidact with something to prove. As a Harvard freshman, he got himself into an advanced literature seminar by reciting a long passage from James Joyce's *Finnegans Wake*. He later used the same tactic to bag his first big client, the journalist and classicist I. F. Stone, singing stretches of Homer in Greek. But that was years later, after kicking a raging amphetamine habit. For all of Wylie's promise, the seventies were a lost decade: devouring drugs, driving a New York City cab, hanging with Andy Warhol in Max's Kansas City, writing poetry that would have made Joyce blush ("I Fuck Your Ass, You Suck My Cock"). But in the end, you couldn't take the Boston out of the Brahmin. Wylie's path, unlike Straus's, led back to his father's profession.

Instead of becoming a publisher, though, Wylie set himself up as a literary agent—and not just any literary agent. He would become the scourge of his father's people, armed with a very simple philosophy: "When an author earns out his or her advance, that is the point at which the publisher's profits exceed the author's, and we are not hired by authors to do that." Publishing, in other words, is a zero-sum game, and a good agent makes sure the author wins and the publisher loses.

One former Farrar, Straus editor speaks of Wylie's "patricidal desire to kill publishers," a common refrain that Wylie dismisses as dime-store psychoanalysis. It does sound silly, but some of his oldest former colleagues insist that it's true. "That's where it all comes from," says someone who worked with Wylie for years. "A lot of his behavior is vengeful about his father." Aram Saroyan, the son of William Saroyan, was a close friend of his in the seventies. Saroyan visited Andrew shortly after Craig Wylie's death, which was (perhaps not coincidentally) around the time Andrew traded in drug addiction for workaholism. Wylie showed Saroyan photos of his father's body. He said he'd smuggled a small camera into the morgue because "I needed documentary evidence. I had to make absolutely certain he was actually dead."

Wylie blames his decision to become an agent on the sorry state of corporate publishing. He remembers interviewing for editing jobs with potential employers who were interested purely in middlebrow drivel like James Michener—at best. (Never mind the Kings and Steels and Clancys and even Turows who would soon dominate the bestseller list.) Of course, Giroux had fought the pressure to focus on commercial work as far back as the 1940s. But things did seem to have gotten worse. Fewer independent publishers and fewer literary authors meant fewer literary editors.

Yet Wylie's career move was never entirely about art, nor was it purely some kind of symbolic patricide. It was strategy. A seventies casualty already past thirty, Wylie could have gone the publishing route—could have drawn a salary in the very low five figures from a Roger Straus type, fixing typos for an Aaron Asher type, while his fellow Harvard alumni were halfway to becoming Masters of the Universe (in Tom Wolfe's immortal shorthand). As Wylie has pointed out, he was descended from bankers as well as literati. The eighties, the age of the book auction, could be a very lucrative time for an agent, even if your tastes were inconveniently highbrow. Authors such as

Roth, Wolfe, and Sontag were restless in their paternalistic relationships, eager to get a cut of the action. Wylie, too, was undergoing a yuppie conversion, and the luxury literary niche, like the Savile Row suits he substituted for his old berets and turtlenecks, was tailor-made.

Until now, literary writers had been underpaid relative to their status (if not their sales). That's why Straus had been so savvy to seek discounted quality authors abroad in the late forties. The less he paid them up front, the smaller the risk. But as his writers began asking for more, they needed someone like Wylie as a counterweight. An agent, unlike a publisher, makes money in direct proportion to his clients. Straus had profited by paying writers less than they were worth. Wylie could profit by convincing them they were worth even more than they could earn—and then going out and finding them more, while taking 15 percent for himself.

Union Square may have been a little less scary in the late eighties, but urban crime was still spiraling toward its early-nineties peak. Not even the stately homes of the Upper East Side were safe. In fact, they made enticing targets. The Strauses installed an alarm system but found it confusing. They still had a waitstaff of two, but a cook and his wife were hardly the security they needed. Roger's granddaughters sometimes spent the evenings there alone. Eventually there was a break-in.

Dorothea had already been agitating for a move. "Neither of them was up there repointing the bricks," says Rog, "but most of the maintenance fell on her and she was sort of sick of it. I think she liked the idea of living in an apartment." But Straus had resisted. It was a landmark of literary and social history, a monument to his accomplishments. Yet the costs of maintaining homes in both town and country were becoming harder to bear, especially with Straus's occasional cash outlays for FSG. After the break-in, they both realized it was over. In April, they traded in the house for a co-op in a postwar high-rise on East 65th Street. The midcentury furniture, the slip-covered white couches, and the first editions were all squeezed into a 1,500-square-foot three-bedroom. (One of the bedrooms was for the servants, whom they kept.)

After the devastating fire at Sarosca Farm, Straus might have been expected to sympathize with his friend Susan Sontag when her own place nearly burned down. Sontag was living in a duplex on King Street, in far west SoHo, when a neighbor's fireplace caught fire. "I'm lucky to be alive," she said at the time. The blaze was soon controlled and she lost very few possessions, but it drove home to her how vulnerable she was financially. Her son says it was this incident, and not her first cancer battle or her failure to win a MacArthur grant, that caused her to really think about money for the first time in her life, at the age of fifty-four. "She was underinsured," David Rieff says. "She realized she didn't have any reserves." This time, according to Rieff, Sontag explicitly asked for Straus's help. "Roger was simply unresponsive," he says. "He could have given her some money. He never gave her a dime, and he underpaid her for her work."

A year earlier, Andrew Wylie had teamed up with Straus's old friend and colleague, the British agent Gillon Aitken, to launch the agency Wylie, Aitken & Stone. He heard from Aitken and others about Roger Straus's legendary combativeness. He asked Aitken for an introduction. Soon he became friendly with one of Roger's senior editors—David Rieff. Over lunch, Wylie would ask about Rieff's writers, his mother, and his own writing. He lavished praise on Rieff's first book, *Going to Miami,* an essayistic journal about that city, which was published early in 1987. Three months later, several days after Sontag's apartment caught fire, Rieff's agent, Luis Sanjurjo, died. Lynn Nesbit worked with Sanjurjo at the time, at the mega-agency International Creative Management, and she took over Rieff as a client.

Wylie was soon telling Rieff how much better off he'd be with him, but Rieff stayed with Nesbit. Eighteen months later, Nesbit jumped ship to start her own firm with Morton Janklow, a pioneering big-money agent (representing Judith Krantz, Danielle Steel, and Sidney Sheldon) whom Straus loathed. She told the press she'd informed all her clients of the move, but she never called Rieff. His pride damaged, Rieff went to Wylie.

Wylie admits he's worked with certain people just to get closer to their more important author-friends. He hired a cousin of Martin

Amis's before poaching Amis from Pat Kavanagh, his agent of twenty-two years and the wife of his good friend Julian Barnes (destroying that friendship in the process). He signed Pakistani prime minister Benazir Bhutto specifically to impress Salman Rushdie, whom he later acquired. Did he butter up David Rieff in order to get to Sontag? "I was actually not thinking about that," he says, before conceding, "He knew a lot of people, yes." But he had something to offer Rieff. "What I persuaded David to do was to stop editing and start writing, that's what came out of my relationship with him. Lynn didn't do that." Rieff agrees: "It is because of his belief in me—stronger than my own at the time—that I became a writer." And so, even before Wylie touched a single FSG writer, he convinced Roger's "son" that he should quit.

Rieff advised his mother to meet with Wylie. She came to him with a list of requests. The first thing she said was, "You have to help me stop being Susan Sontag." In other words, he had to take off her hands the many burdens of a being a Famous Intellectual: lecture offers, interview requests, unsolicited assignments. Straus handled some of this, but not enough. Sontag also had a novel almost fully formed in her head—what would become *The Volcano Lover.* (Ironically, it was a literary-historical hybrid like the blockbuster *The Name of the Rose,* which she'd told Roger to decline.) "I'm bursting to write it," she told Wylie, "but I can't because of this 'Susan Sontag' thing." She also needed a financial cushion, money in the bank, real assets. Before signing with Wylie, she said publicly, "The economy got way ahead of me. I'm not making any more money than I was making ten years ago, so I'm a lot poorer." After Wylie took her on, she said, "I don't want to be this totally undefended person who just says, 'Oh, just give me a contract; I'll sign it and not read it.'"

"Every writer has that feeling of gratitude declining into resentment, just by virtue of the way the relationship is structured," Wylie says of the paternalistic-publisher model. By contrast, "Our relationship with them is structured as that of the gardener. If the gardener does what you tell the gardener to do, and is attentive and careful, and does the job thoroughly, why are you going to fire the gardener?"

Shortly after signing with Wylie, Sontag wrote a letter to Straus—one of those indiscreet scraps of paper that Peggy Miller threw away, consigning it to oblivion. Rieff read it, and he says it rehashed (and recast) Sontag and Straus's personal history. Susan mentioned the fire as the precipitating incident and essentially concluded, as Rieff remembers it, "You're a rich man. I'm not a rich woman. I don't have any money. I don't think you quite get it." Wylie, meanwhile, wrote Straus a letter that was all business. Susan was ready to put four books under contract, but she wouldn't sign one unless he was ready to put real money—not just Roger money—on the table.

Whatever recriminations and vulgarities Straus threw around in the intervening weeks (some remember the word "cunt" echoing down the dingy hallways), he made his final offer to Wylie—an unprecedented $800,000 for the four books—with sangfroid. "As you have gathered," he wrote in February 1989, "we have been working very, very hard to come up with a proper offer for Susan Sontag's books as described in your letter of the 30th. We want, as you can imagine, to continue to publish Susan and have evolved an offer that I hope you will agree is not only generous but meets her needs."

Rieff, who was closely involved in the negotiations, scoffs at Straus's choice of words. "I don't think it was 'generous' at all. *He* thought it was generous. It is a very Roger word. What he was doing was paying market price for something, not getting a discount because he was Roger Straus. And he thought he was entitled to a discount for being Roger Straus and for FSG being FSG."

Rather than healing the rift, Straus's "generosity" deepened the distrust. Now that she was being amply rewarded, Sontag felt as though she had been underpaid for years, and for no good reason. "That didn't leave a very good taste in her mouth about the past," says Rieff. Nonetheless, she stayed at FSG for the rest of her life. "Did she fall out of love with Roger and, realizing this, turn her back on him? Nothing could be further from the truth," Rieff says. "But she could have two feelings in her head at the same time, and it wasn't the same."

Jonathan Galassi pushes back a little on Sontag's indignation: "Is a publisher's job to support a writer? I don't think so. A publisher's job is to publish a writer's books as well as possible, and make as much money as possible." He does concede, though, that Sontag and Straus had something a little different, a "symbiotic" relationship. "It was much different from a strictly professional relationship. It was paternalistic. I remember Susan saying once to me, 'I was happy to be a poor intellectual in New York when everyone else was, but then when money came along in the eighties, everything changed.'"

Sontag may have been a special case, but she wasn't the only writer who saw Roger differently after Andrew Wylie showed up. Ian Frazier had a lesser epiphany. After Pat Strachan angrily decamped to *The New Yorker,* both Frazier and his *New Yorker* friend Jamaica Kincaid were left without an editor. Seeking stability, they both ran into Andrew Wylie's open arms. "Andrew would say, 'FSG's fucking you, and you should be getting more money,'" says Frazier. "He suggested that I get bigger advances." And just like that, Frazier did. He was pleasantly surprised, and then dismayed.

"I realized that he probably could have paid that all along," says Frazier, who got $450,000 for two books in 1995, far more than he'd ever gotten before. "I felt retroactively some resentment that I hadn't had more money when I could have used it. Through Andrew, I got much more a sense that this was a business . . . that it was not in fact a family."

There's an easy counterargument to this resentment, with its underlying assumption that buckets of unpaid advance money had been sitting for decades in miserly Roger Straus's vault. The fact is that 1988-vintage FSG could have eaten 1982 FSG for lunch. In the old days, the cash simply hadn't been there. Roger's cheapness may have been inborn, but it was refined by forty years of hard, break-even experience. Asked about FSG's new willingness to play in auctions—they'd just bought Thomas Friedman's first book for six figures, but lost their bid for Salman Rushdie—he conceded that they were "nouveau riche"—but this meant they needed to be cautious. He'd had two bestsellers in a year once before, *Look Younger, Live Longer* and *Courtroom,* in 1950. "Flushed with that success, I bought another publishing company and a lot of new books," he said. "But pretty soon we found we had over-expanded and the money stopped rolling in, and we had to cut back."

Still, Roger knew his two tent-pole writers wouldn't settle for the Roger Straus discount. Turow he considered a straight commercial proposition, which he left in the hands of Rog and Galassi. The 1990 follow-up, *Burden of Proof,* would sell even better than his first thriller. But the Tom Wolfe negotiation, which just preceded Andrew Wylie's dramatic entrance, was both riskier and more personal. Flush from *The Bonfire of the Vanities,* Wolfe had received via Lynn Nesbit, his longtime agent, a blind offer from a publisher of more than $7 million for his next novel. So Tom wrote Lynn a letter and allowed her to pass it on to Roger.

Tom reminded Lynn (and Roger) of how easy they'd been on FSG in 1980: "Farrar Straus's special position in the literary world and its difficult position in the publishing business were on both our minds at that time." As a result, he'd been forced to earn extra cash by publishing *Bonfire* serially in *Rolling Stone,* exposing his raw first draft to critics and readers. By the time *Bonfire* was published, Wolfe was deeply in debt and had sold off securities that were meant to serve as "long-term principal." But he was done with all that. "In 1980 I leaned over backward to avoid negotiating in terms of the actual market value of my work. This time I think Farrar Straus should stretch in my behalf."

"Tom's got a tremendous habit now," Roger complained to editors, as though his old friend had picked up a nasty addiction. Straus put together a joint offer with Alberto Vitale, the head of paperback publisher Bantam, for around $6 million. Scott Turow may have taken 43 percent less to go with Roger for *Presumed Innocent,* but the spread between offers in Wolfe's case was seven figures long. Few and saintly are the authors who would turn down a million extra dollars for any friend, let alone one whom they believed to be holding out on them.

"He couldn't decide what to do," Nesbit remembers. "He just sat in my office and went back and forth, back and forth. Then one day he just said, 'Okay, I'm taking Roger and Alberto's offer.'" Nesbit called both of them with the good news. Then Wolfe got home, called Nesbit, and told her he'd changed his mind; he would leave

FSG. When Nesbit called to break the news, Roger, still reeling from Sontag's emotional purging, was devastated. But then Wolfe changed his mind one last time, accepting the FSG-Bantam offer. The elegant author's old-fashioned code of loyalty had trumped his "habit," and Roger found his way toward making up with Wolfe. "But from that day forward," says Nesbit, "I was anathema to Roger. Alberto [Vitale] understood, these things happen, but Roger blamed me. 'Oh, it's the agent, pushing for the big dollar, he'd never leave,' blah blah blah."

So intent was Straus on revising history to discredit agents that he often contradicted himself: Either they were pure evil or they were puppets on his string. It was the old demonization trick politicians know so well: My opponent is an evil mastermind—and incompetent, too. Roger claimed (and Peggy would repeat) that *he* had come up with the idea of getting Sontag an agent. FSG was simply overwhelmed by her needs, and he didn't want to "ruin our relationship." Then, the story goes, she asked him whom she should sign up with. He unwrapped this chestnut for *W* magazine years later. "It was between Andrew Wylie and the bimbo," he said, meaning Lynn Nesbit. Roger, sage that he was, had advised Susan to go with Wylie: "If she started talking about Plato's Cave, Miss Nesbit wouldn't know what she was talking about . . . she's not exactly, shall we say, a deep thinker." It was a masterstroke of gratuitous insult: In one fell swoop, he could take credit for Wylie's maneuvers and get revenge on Nesbit for trying to take Tom Wolfe away. Nesbit broke off their friendship.

In the same interview, headlined THE LITERARY LION, Straus told another dastardly tale of the Jackal. He claimed that Wylie seduced Philip Roth "in my own living room," during one of his cocktail parties. "He went up to Philip" and said, "'Of all the authors in the world, you're the one I'd want most,'" and proceeded to quote scenes and dialogue from the Roth oeuvre. David Rieff calls this scenario, which has passed into Wylie legend, "total bullshit." Or, if it happened—Wylie says he doesn't remember—that wasn't the moment when Andrew made his pitch. The reality is simpler but just as dramatically ironic: Wylie asked Rieff, the surrogate son, to arrange an introduction. Over lunch with Roth, the agent explained what he could do for him.

"His finances were not in particularly great shape," Wylie says, "and he didn't have a sense of independence, which is really what he thrives on." Roth was well advanced toward his next novel, *Deception*, a series of bedroom dialogues between an adulterous couple, and he was already contemplating a book about his terminally ill father (*Patrimony*). Wylie told Roth that having Farrar, Straus as his agent was costing him lots of money. FSG's paperback deal for *The Counterlife*, for example, had earned Roth a quick $200,000—which sounds great, except he gave up the copyright, which would have generated income decades into the future.

Wylie came to Straus with a proposition: He thought he could get $2 million for three Roth books, and that was what he expected from FSG. The house had just ponied up millions to keep Wolfe; surely a publisher of such stature would pay less than half that for three books by someone who, in Wylie's opinion, was a thousand times better. "It all had to do with Tom Wolfe," says someone who was at FSG at the time. After hearing about Wolfe's contract, "Roth said, 'My penis is as big as his.'"

Straus argued that the Tom Wolfe deal was a ridiculous point of reference. Wolfe had written five bestsellers, while Roth was lucky to sell more than thirty thousand copies. He didn't even always earn out those FSG advances Wylie scoffed at, and Wylie wanted to keep foreign rights (which he believes he can sell better than publishers can). Roger later said he'd offered $700,000; Wylie says it was less. Roger also said he bet Wylie one hundred dollars he'd never get his $2 million, and the agent paid up when he lost. "I never, ever, ever make bets with anyone," Wylie says. Elsewhere he said, "I think one of the reasons Roger is such a skilled publisher is that he's such a marvelous inventor of stories."

"Neither Philip nor I was of a mind to leave," Wylie says now, "but Roger pushed." According to him, Straus called Roth and told him, in exactly so many words, to fuck off. "That was Roger's both strength and weakness: He was a tempestuous man. He was not cool; he was hot. That was a crazy fucking thing to do, really crazy."

Even if this is true, Straus fired Roth because he was about to quit. "Roth liked Roger well enough," says David Rieff. "He didn't love him the way my mother did, or Brodsky or Walcott. If Roger met the price, he would have stayed. I know that. But there was no way. I don't think Philip would have taken a penny less." That summer, Roth had also had a quintuple heart bypass operation, just barely staving off a heart attack. His father was also seriously ill—another reason to chase the freedom of money.

Dick Snyder, roaring back into Roger's life, put down $1.8 million for three Roth books, and Simon & Schuster had itself another FSG refugee. Naturally, Straus was apoplectic. He had spent the past two decades of his precarious life in publishing having public fits of pique. Yet they usually had a whiff of theater, seeming at least a little calculated (as Snyder claimed) to attract writers who disdained commercial publishing. Whenever he took umbrage at an agent or publisher who'd acted dishonorably, Straus would circulate the indignant letter proudly around the office. His reaction to Philip Roth's departure, though, seemed more visceral.

A note from Andrew Wylie, sent only a day before the *Times* announced Roth's deal with Simon & Schuster, indicates the types of things Straus had been spreading around:

Dear Roger:

You should know:

(a) *Philip has not had a "massive heart attack"; he has had a bypass operation, and is sitting up in bed;*

(b) *Philip's father, who is terminally ill, does not know about this—and should not learn of it from anyone other than his son;*

(c) *Your widely quoted estimate of Simon & Schuster's advance [$1.2 million] is thoroughly inaccurate.*

Can't you (we?) talk about something else?

Wylie was all business after that, but Roger kept needling him. He gladly provided Wylie with sales figures for all the Roth books FSG had published, revealing that none broke forty thousand copies in sales. "You were so wise not to ask for this information until after you had closed with S & S," Roger added in a P.S. While on his annual Frankfurt-London jaunt that fall, Roger was asked by an agent in Wylie's office if maybe it was time to cancel all contracts between Roth and FSG. He sent back a note on Connaught hotel letterhead, handwritten in block capitals: "EITHER YOU ARE CRAZY OR YOU MUST THINK I AM CRAZY. FOR I HAVE NO INTENTION OF ABROGATING ANY EXISTING AGREEMENTS BETWEEN FSG AND ROTH. WE LOOK FORWARD TO RECOUPING SOME OF OUR LOSSES." The agent, Deborah Karl, responded: "Let's just say I am crazy. I hope you had a productive Frankfurt and a good visit to London."

Straus tried to play it cool when the deal was announced. "I could have bought this contract a good deal cheaper than S&S," he told the *Washington Post*, "but I didn't think we were going anywhere. I didn't think either of the books were breakthrough books . . . Simon and Schuster needs a name more than I do." It was a snide though even response, but he couldn't leave well enough alone. When Simon & Schuster published Roth's *Deception* the following April, heralded by splashy, very un-FSG posters (a man's hand on a woman's bare flank), Roger refused to let Dick Snyder hog all the attention. He told the *New York Times,* "Mr. Snyder is trying to class up his act by acquiring Roth, because Simon & Schuster does not exactly have a plethora of works of fiction of literary merit. But I am afraid he is going to lose $1 million on the Roth deal, despite these posters trying to show how hip they are." He predicted Simon & Schuster wouldn't sell out its first printing of a hundred thousand copies. He concluded, "'Deception' is a bad book, by no means Roth's finest hour."

And yet again, Roger Straus was mostly right. He had predicted both the sales and the critical reception fairly accurately. *Deception* did even worse on the extended bestseller list than *The Counterlife,* which had sold 36,000 hardcover copies. Christopher Lehmann-Haupt wrote that it was time for Roth to "stop analyzing his imagination and start exercising it." Of course, Roger would have gladly published any number of Roth's books. He must have felt considerably worse when Roth went through a phase of brilliant, blockbuster novels—*Sabbath's Theater, American Pastoral, The Human Stain*—that probably excelled anything he'd ever written.

Like the FSG refugees of the seventies, Roth didn't last long at Simon & Schuster. After running out his contract, he went to Houghton Mifflin with *Sabbath's Theater,* the novel that launched his literary comeback and won him his second National Book Award. Houghton, where Roth had published his first book, *Goodbye, Columbus,* has been his home ever since. The payout for *Sabbath* was around $300,000, well within Straus's price range. Over the years, Galassi repeatedly asked Wylie if Roth would be willing to return, but he never was. "Roger said publicly that Philip Roth needed FSG more than we needed him, and that's just wrong," says Galassi. "That was one of his worst moments as a publisher. It should have never happened, and if he had been a different person, maybe Roth would have come back."

If Roger had been a different person, would his son have stayed?

13

Profit and Loss

As FSG's dissident artists marveled at the collapse of European communism, their publisher seemed to be in the midst of its own Velvet Revolution. Brought in to do some light restructuring, the boss's son was making irreversible changes, cleaning out the mold of paternalistic oppression and letting in the air of capitalism. Or so it seemed, at least to some, in those heady days at the close of the eighties.

As Scott Turow poured in the profits—his follow-up thriller, *Burden of Proof,* sold well over a million copies and made 1990 FSG's best sales year ever—the heir apparent moved swiftly. The staff grew by double digits and expanded into the ninth floor. Roger III reigned on the tenth with his loyal team: Bridget Marmion in marketing, Helene Atwan in publicity, and a new chief financial officer, Ellen Faran—who, unlike her predecessor Sam Kam, didn't record the accounts in pencil on graph paper. Before long there were (a few) computers, pension plans, real budgets, and even, on the bigger books, profit-and-loss statements. Rog reached a warehousing agreement with his friend

Phyllis Grann at Putnam, tapping into that company's vast distribution system, and FSG's print runs grew, often exceeding fifty thousand. Turow's third book, *Pleading Guilty,* had a run of eight hundred thousand copies, more than *Presumed Innocent* had even sold.

Accompanying such substantial changes were developments that the editorial team on the fourth floor, Roger included, found more alarming. After Michael di Capua left—tensions between him and Straus had been building for years—consultants were brought in to "re-brand" the children's division into "FSG Jr." One of several "focus groups" suggested changing the depressing ending of a beautiful Sendak-illustrated Grimm fairy tale, *Dear Mili.* These were just extreme (and failed) examples of a broader phenomenon that bothered Roger almost as deeply: the sudden ubiquity of meetings.

Roger's routine was almost purposely designed to obviate the need for meetings (except for editorial meetings, which were his show). Circulating correspondence informed staff of key decisions and allowed them to weigh in with comments. Lunch, which he was now having almost daily at the elegantly cozy Union Square Cafe, was an opportunity to educate invited underlings about the books he considered most important. Roger's daily morning walks through the office, following the opening of the mail and the depositing of the checks, served a similar function: business under the guise of schmoozing. He'd pick up the latest news from sales, marketing, and publicity, hit the bathroom, and, on the return trip, pass that news along to others and resolve nagging issues.

Rog, on the other hand, had picked up the habit of brainstorming and group analysis. He made his father sit in on postmortems, sorting out what went right and wrong in publishing a book. Straus, who hated looking back, wouldn't sit still for it. At one such meeting, he just got up and walked out, yelling over his shoulder, "If you guys want to sit around in a circle jerk, that's your business, but I don't want to have any part of it." Rog has a different spin on why his father loathed his meetings: "He either drove the bus or he got off the bus. He was never a passenger."

Still, he went along for the ride—but not happily, and not for long. Bold ventures were all well and good in the boom years, when a few thousand spent on consultants or assistants could almost pass unnoticed. But the Turow boom was unsustainable. FSG's revenue chart for those years looks like an EKG, with one in three years a Turow-led spike and deep Turow-less troughs in between. When the economy finally turned south, Roger's short-lived indulgence followed suit.

The early-nineties recession led to a sales crash at FSG. Roger deferred salaries for a pay period—a familiar move—and promised to prevent layoffs, but then was forced to make job cuts anyway, only breeding further resentment. More than a dozen people were let go, including editors. The Rog expansion was scaled back to pregrowth levels. It was hard to pin the blame on a single cause. It wasn't just that FSG had gambled on big print runs, or that they were forced by a new breed of agents to pay more even while ceding subsidiary rights to them, or that they had hired too many people. Really, it was the fatal cocktail of a deflated economy and inflated expectations.

Straus had been facing such dips at least once a decade for nearly half a century. But this one was more severe. For decades he'd fought off buyers, even in the face of seemingly existential threats. For a mix of reasons—narcissism but also loyalty and conviction—he could never trust another company to preserve the things that he felt made FSG exceptional. Now he was beginning to worry that the threat to Farrar, Straus—its priorities, its integrity, its resilience, and even its independence—was coming from within his own family.

"He probably thought I was profligate," says Rog. "His criticisms tended to be implied rather than specific. You just had a sense that he wasn't happy with the way things were." But as the recession dragged on, the arguments became more direct. In public, Roger undermined his son's orders. Behind closed doors, it was even worse.

One terrible fight was over *Smilla's Sense of Snow*, a smart, moody thriller by the Danish author Peter Høeg. It was, everyone agreed, FSG's next contender for bestseller success. It was also the first big find of the young editor Elisabeth Dyssegaard (whom Roger dismissed with a favorite saying: "Even a blind pig finds a truffle once in a while"). Both Rog and Helene Atwan were excited by the chance to sell another FSG thriller, but concerned about how a book in translation would go over with a mass readership. There was the original title, *Miss Smilla's Feeling for Snow*, which even a *New York Times Book Review* editor thought sounded too effete when Atwan brought it up. And then there was the last name, with that fatal slash through the "o." (This was a full fifteen years before the phrase "Scandinavian thriller" went from oxymoron to publishers' catnip, thanks to Stieg Larsson's *The Girl with the Dragon Tattoo*.) FSG was arguably the best American publisher of European literature, but a mass-market foreigner was a different beast. No one was trying to get Jarosław Rymkiewicz's book *The Final Station: Umschlagplatz* sold in airports.

In the spirit of Rog's new brainstorming sessions, FSG's marketers threw around all sorts of ideas. One of them was to think about changing Høeg's last name to "Hawk." Rog now denies it was ever brought up. "I swear that's not true," he says. "It doesn't make sense! You can't change the author's name." But Atwan says she brought it up at least once, and Rog didn't object vociferously. "No one thought it would actually happen," she says, "but we toyed with that."

One thing he and Atwan were dead serious about was changing the title—an idea that did originate from Rog. He had managed to extract, from Phyllis Grann at Putnam, a guaranteed minimum (a "floor") of $300,000 for paperback rights. But there was one condition: "She said—and I agreed with her—that no one in America knew what a Smilla was, that it wasn't recognized as a proper name." She wanted to take that out of the title. Grann confirms the story.

What happened next is a *Rashomon*-like tangle of scenarios, almost as irreconcilable as the differences between father and son. Unquestionably, Roger was offended by the suggestion that they change it to *A Sense of Snow*. (He also couldn't stand Phyllis Grann.) Atwan says Høeg himself objected, but all parties compromised by taking the "Miss" out of the title. Someone else says Rog then pressed Høeg even after he refused. But Rog insists that his father refused to check with Høeg at all—and that this is what angered him most. "If the author said no, then I would have agreed. But not without at least asking the author, 'Would you mind, and by the way, there's at least three hundred thousand dollars, which you get half of, sitting here on the table? What do you think?' But he wouldn't do it, and it pissed me off." Putnam withdrew the offer. In any event, the book sold very well with *Smilla* in the title, and Dell eventually paid $650,000 for the paperback. "As usual," says Rog, "he was right."

The final falling-out between father and son was, fittingly, over the budget. The year 1993 saw another Turow spike, nearly matching the sales heights of 1990. With the recession nearing its end, an optimist like Roger might believe FSG was finally hitting some open road. Then Rog came in with a dire forecast: 1994 would be another bad one, maybe as bad as 1991. Too many copies of *Pleading Guilty* had been printed, and returns would hit the following year hard. Roger put the blame solidly on his son; before his time, they wouldn't have gambled on such a large run. "It was a huge blowup," says Rog.

Among other charges and recriminations, his father accused him of intentionally sabotaging the budget, or lowballing it, in order to persuade Roger to sell the company. The rumor was that Putnam's takeover of Farrar, Straus warehousing was part of Phyllis Grann's master plan to buy the firm, with Rog playing the role of traitorous collaborator. It felt like a low blow. Rog says the thought of selling had never crossed his mind, "partly for selfish reasons. I wanted to drive the bus, and that meant the bus had to be there." The only thing that stood in his way was, frankly, a seventy-six-year-old father for whom any loss of control was tantamount to retirement, and retirement equivalent to death. "He said a bunch of things and I said a bunch of things and I said, 'If that's the way you feel I'm gonna quit,' and he didn't say anything, and I quit."

Rog left the company due to "philosophical differences," according to a joint press release issued in late September 1993. The *Times* called the departure a "genteel family tiff." "Genteel" isn't the word many people would use to describe an argument involving Roger Straus, but no matter. Rog has since concluded that what came between him and what his father deemed to be his destiny was more than just a cantankerous old narcissist. It came down to what FSG was and what it wasn't.

"I was probably interested in commercializing the list more than he was comfortable with," Rog says now, "in diversifying the kinds of books we were publishing . . . to be less dependent on the inevitable ups and downs of publishing, and that would increase our security. With hindsight, the only time the company ever successfully did that was with Turow. He felt, and I think he was more right than I was, that the focus had to be on what made FSG unique, and anything that diverted that was a step in the wrong direction."

Importantly, Rog *doesn't* say that the choice was between uniqueness and survival. His last stint at Farrar, Straus made him realize that the two were inseparable. Rog had made many changes for the greater good of FSG, and his father preserved most of them. There would, in the future, be a greater emphasis on nonfiction, greater participation in auctions, more benefits for the staff, and a bigger role for the sales department. Such adaptations arguably helped carry FSG over the bridge to the era of auctions and agents. It was only when Roger saw that things were moving too quickly and too far—that FSG really *was* becoming the "Knopf de nos jours"—that he applied the brakes. Because FSG wasn't Knopf. For one thing, it didn't have the corporate backing, and Roger didn't want it to. It's probably true that he never meant for Rog to leave, that, as with Philip Roth, he drove him away in spite of himself. But in his gut—which was where his decisions came from—he knew exactly what he was doing.

"I think Roger was totally right and Rog was dead wrong," says David Rieff. "As a business proposition, what Roger saw and Rog did not is that the house had neither a staff nor the public-relations machine, nor frankly the financial resources, to bid for the nonfiction that would have worked. It was always going to be the bidder of last resort. Look, I thought that on a human basis, there was a lot to criticize about Roger's treatment of his son—a lot. Roger was a ruthless man. But I think that as a publisher, Roger was completely right."

Nevertheless, the split was emotional, tied up with buried

resentments and longings that would never be resolved. "Rog was always looking for a certain kind of approval from his father that he never got," says one former FSG editor. But how could this editor, or several others who said similar things, know just how desperately the elder Roger had once wanted his own father's approval—only to be told, in one of the last conversations he had with Roger Sr., that he should sell his fledgling company to *Reader's Digest*?

Straus was self-aware enough to see the parallel. In only the second personal talk he had with his son—the other being his lecture on finding sex outside of marriage—Roger described fully his awful relationship with his own father. Rog guesses the talk must have happened "after an argument or something"—the kind of conversation "you have to have if you're not going to repeat those mistakes."

Straus told the press that he was "sad that my son has decided to resign from the firm." He praised Rog's "enormous contributions" and called the split "friendly, amicable, and loving." He said Rog would still one day inherit a majority stake in the company. And he claimed to be taken aback by his son's decision. "He wants to try something else, I think, but I'm not sure what it is."

Still, like any publisher recently rid of a senior employee, Roger proceeded to clean house. When Helene Atwan resigned, just a month after Rog left, Roger cited her "honorific title of associate publisher" as proof of her overweening ambition—and her desire to impose mercenary values on FSG. "We're too small for that. Is she going to be telling my marketing and sales director what to do or is she going to be telling [senior editor] Elisabeth Sifton how to run Hill and Wang?" Straus eased Atwan out by forcing her to fire her assistant, pleading cutbacks she knew to be unnecessary—a neat old trick.

Straus made another, very interesting power move around this time: He hired Tamara Straus, his granddaughter and, of course, the daughter of his departed son. Tamara had studied Russian in college and was the most ambitious of Roger's three granddaughters. She proved an able editor with good instincts. "Everyone loved her," says her sister Laura, "and there wasn't that intensity with my grandfather, because it was a skipped generation." Everyone was pleasantly surprised. Joseph Brodsky told Roger that he should just pass the firm on to his granddaughters instead of Rog. But Tamara had seen what her father went through. It didn't help that she was shunted into the very same tiny, shoddy office where Rog had gotten his start. "I thought, 'Oh my gosh, there are so many ghosts here; this is not a good place for me,'" Tamara remembers. "I got a taste of it," less than two years' worth, "and then I thought, 'I've got to get out of here.'"

Jonathan Galassi, meanwhile, became executive vice president, Roger's new second-in-command. Rog had always been Galassi's champion and confidant. When the editor got offers from deeper-pocketed publishers, Rog was the one who engineered a Rube Goldberg–like scheme to award Galassi "phantom stock"—which would turn into very real money, well over $1 million, at his retirement or in the event of the company's sale.

Yet it was Galassi whom Roger, in the end, chose over his own son. On the one hand, it made perfect sense. Roger may have wanted to "get back to real books" after *Presumed Innocent,* but he knew that Galassi had made it rain. He was also pleased with the editor's taste in the kind of books of which Sontag *would* approve. Galassi knew European literature as intimately as Aaron Asher, had learned verse from Giroux's poets, and had Henry Robbins's feel for inimitable pop prose. And his nose for potential was as good as any of theirs. Among his early acquisitions were Jonathan Franzen's *The Twenty-Seventh City;* Jeffrey Eugenides's *The Virgin Suicides;* Thomas Friedman's first collection of reporting; David Grossman's Israeli fiction; and Oscar Hijuelos's Pulitzer-winning bestseller *The Mambo Kings Play Songs of Love.* He also edited Michael Cunningham's 1990 novel, *A Home at the End of the World*—though that promising young novelist came to FSG via Dorothea Straus, who'd fallen in love with a Cunningham story in *The New Yorker.*

But why did Galassi get along with Straus where so many editors had failed? And how did he manage to navigate between father and son? That's the slightly mysterious part. Roger's best pals at the time were poets almost his age, Walcott and Heaney and Brodsky, and their friendships were all gruff effusions, macho sentimentalism,

Jesus-on-the-Cross jokes at the Russian Samovar or the Union Square Cafe. Galassi was a generation younger than those old boys. Elisabeth Sifton remembers asking Roberto Calasso, the author and Italian publisher, why he thought Roger had finally found a top man he could get along with. "You do not think this is subject to rational investigation, do you?" Calasso asked. "Don't be ridiculous."

Galassi says that FSG was a respite from office politics, and that thriving at a place like Random House "would have taken being more of a politician inside." But Rog considers him "the most deft person, politically, I've ever met in my life." Turow has another word for it: "Ductile. He's supple in his dealings with very strong personalities, and knows how to get around them. Rog is very much his father's son—one with his cravat and the other in his corduroy sport coat—but a lot of that beguiling personality of the father was planted in the son. When you punch Roger III in the nose, he is not the kind of person who is likely to step back."

Perhaps Galassi's political masterstroke was realizing that, as Peggy Miller liked to say, "There are no politics at FSG. There is only one king." He also noticed that previous editors had been more or less Straus's contemporaries. "When you're a son," Galassi says, casting himself in that role, "it's much easier to let the father be the Sun King and you can do the work. There's Oedipal issues but there's not Cain and Abel issues." And where Oedipal issues were concerned, Straus already had his target, his foil. "Roger always needed enemies in a certain way, probably inside as well as outside," says Galassi. "Rog sort of fulfilled that role. So I was the good son, he was the bad son."

Still, Galassi wasn't a real son. He could easily take over editorial operations, but he wasn't going to inherit the company. When it came to FSG's financial future, Roger's options were running out. "First he thought about it and he said, *après moi, le deluge*, the hell with it," Peggy Miller says. "That didn't last too long, because he said to himself, 'I've built up a wonderful company, why would I let it go down the tubes?'"

By this point, Rog had found another job, as publisher of the photo-book press Aperture. He was still there when his father asked him to lunch at the Union Square Cafe the spring after he'd left. "He said, 'Are you happy?'" Rog remembers. "And I said yes. He said, 'You're not coming back, are you?' I said no." His father, "taking my temperature," told him he was thinking about selling the company. "I said, 'That must be tough.' And that was the only discussion."

Right after that, in March 1994, Roger made a phone call—one rich man to another. The publisher who picked up wasn't Si Newhouse, or any other American. On the other end was Dieter von Holtzbrinck, billionaire chairman and co-owner of Verlagsgruppe Georg von Holtzbrinck. Straus had palled around with Georg, and later his son Dieter, all over Frankfurt. In the United States the Holtzbrincks owned only Henry Holt and *Scientific American*, but they were well-known for a uniquely decentralized approach to ownership. They were also privately held and had a chairman who could essentially make a multimillion-dollar deal over the phone.

"Would you like to buy the company?" Roger asked Dieter. "Yes! How much?" Dieter asked. Roughly thirty million, said Roger. That was about twice FSG's annual revenue—well over its presumptive value on the open market. "Fine," said Dieter.

14

Chairman

"There have been a lot of sweaty palms on my thigh over the years," Roger said, projecting to the back of the largest room at Farrar, Straus. It was in the children's department, up on the ninth floor, the only space big enough for the entire staff. Explaining why, after decades of public defiance, the quintessential independent American publisher was selling his company, Roger hit one of his favorite lines: "My priorities, in order of whom I want to protect, are: a) my authors, b) my staff, and c) my lousy shareholders." The best thing he could do, he told them, was to sell the firm while he was still strong enough to have a say in its direction. And the most important thing, he assured them, was that nothing would change. "He didn't look like a worried man," remembers Ethan Nosowsky, a former FSG editor. "He looked assured of what he was saying. Whatever fears he had he kept from the rest of us."

Roger's staff had to take on faith von Holtzbrinck's assurances of FSG's continued autonomy, and so did Roger. He had a contract to remain publisher through 2000, which could be renewed annually after that. He and his lousy shareholders were getting more than $30 million, with Straus retaining a minority share of the stock. What he emphasized to the assembled crowd in the children's department was the track record of their new German owners. Verlagsgruppe Georg von Holtzbrinck was the antithesis of Si Newhouse's Advance Publications. Newhouse, whose sweaty palm had dampened Roger's thigh for a decade, was the kind of bull who bought a china shop, shattered everything in sight, and replaced it with his own flashy toys. As night followed day, a Newhouse acquisition brought a change of management and character. It was Si who put tampon ads in Gladys Guggenheim's *Gourmet*, Si who'd left Roger's son out in the cold at Times Books, Si whose casual firing of *The New Yorker*'s legendary editor William Shawn had so incensed Roger that he briefly hired Shawn as a consulting editor. (Shawn worked desultorily on a couple of books, but hardly ever showed up and soon drifted away.)

When Roger raged over business-minded louts, his scorn most often fell not on dull number crunchers but on egotistical tycoons and their entitled viceroys. Rupert Murdoch, Si Newhouse, and Dick Snyder didn't suffer from a lack of personality. In fact they had too much for Straus's taste. They never met a company they didn't want to put their own enormous stamp on, the editorial equivalent of a Trump sign in the sky.

Dieter von Holtzbrinck was different. To the extent that he even had a reputation, it was for leaving people alone. The company his father founded in 1948 had grown rapidly over the ensuing half century. In 1963, the year RCA bought Random House, Holtzbrinck acquired S. Fischer Verlag. That company's Jewish founders had fled the Reich for New York and published Thomas Mann at Harcourt, Brace, where a young Robert Giroux had reverently handled the first edition of *Lotte in Weimar*. Fischer was now in the hands of Monika Schoeller, Dieter von Holtzbrinck's sister. She was even more private than the other von Holtzbrincks—Dieter and their much younger half brother, Stefan—but she and FSG did a lot of business. More recently, Holtzbrinck had bought Rowohlt from Roger's friend Heinrich Maria Ledig-Rowohlt, who'd personally translated Nabokov, Baldwin, and Henry Miller. Old Georg had tried to buy Farrar, Straus in the seventies but had been rebuffed; his son Dieter had always told Roger the family was there if and when he was ready.

By the eighties, Holtzbrinck was right behind Bertelsmann, another family-owned conglomerate, as the second-largest media corporation in Germany. Both companies had designs on the English-language market. Bertelsmann had acquired Bantam and Doubleday in the eighties and would eventually buy Random House, becoming the world's largest trade publisher. Holtzbrinck, more modestly, had bought the small trade arm of the CBS-owned, textbook-focused Holt, Rinehart and Winston (yes, the same Rineharts who'd axed John Farrar). The new company was renamed Henry Holt, reviving a name that went back to 1866. Not long before Roger gave Dieter that call in March 1994, a dour *Times* story about the evaporation of medium-size imprints announced that, "amid all the grimness," Henry Holt was "bucking the trend" by acting autonomously, avoiding huge auctions, and trying, in the words of its president, to "publish authors, not just acquire books."

These were what Roger might call "sympathetic noises." The fact that Holtzbrinck had helped produce Nazi propaganda during the war gave Roger pause, but not much. They were "as clean as one could be," he decided, especially in light of the family's postwar friendships with prominent Jews. (Only later did it come out that Georg had joined the Nazi Party.)

Holtzbrinck paid well over FSG's value in order to acquire not a cash cow but a prestigious crown jewel. It still did its due diligence, of course. FSG's greatest asset was its relative health in spite of its under-capitalization and its litany of inefficiencies; imagine what could be done once logical accounting, economies of scale, and some serious capital were brought to bear. Von Holtzbrinck took pains to emphasize that there were no skeletons in FSG's closet, no emergency that led to the sale, and no new mandate for outsize profits. "FSG," Dieter wrote in a press release, "should not be made dependent on a quarterly yield or on the bestseller market chances."

Straus spent late October crafting soothing letters to his authors, of which a note to Isaac Bashevis Singer's widow (he had died in 1991) is typical. "The time has come to ensure the continuity of FSG's traditions and values in the decades to come," Roger wrote. "Dieter von Holtzbrinck and his family have long demonstrated their commitment to the highest standards of our profession, and believe in fostering the independence and integrity of each of the companies in their organization. I want to assure you as a valued collaborator that there will be no change in the way we go about our work."

Reactions ranged widely from knowing congratulations (scout Herbert Lottman: "Your decision to keep away from the New York wolves was a delight for me") to raw laments (Madeleine L'Engle: "While I understand some of the reasons, I'm still deeply sorry"). Richard Seaver, the veteran of the indie publishing trenches who'd left Holt after Holtzbrinck acquired it, sounded a cautionary note: "I remember [Viking head] Tom Guinzburg telling me with absolute assurance about his 'iron-clad contract' that kept him in charge at Viking as long as he chose." Three years after Guinzburg had sold the company his father founded, he was ousted. But Seaver ended well: "You've set an example for all of us, and the quality of your list is unequaled (Sorry, Alfred . . .)."

The staff, Roger's second priority after his writers, also had mixed reactions. One senior editor had seen it coming and lobbied unsuccessfully for shares in the company around the time Rog left. Others were dismayed by the fact that they'd taken salary cuts in exchange for the pride and latitude of independence, only to find themselves conglomerate-owned after all. And some resented the well-known fact that Galassi, having been there only eight years, became a millionaire overnight thanks to his "phantom stock." But they also guessed that the financial disparity with other firms was about to shrink. Ellen Faran, the CFO Rog had hired, wrote her Holtzbrinck counterpart about his ultramodern Stuttgart offices, which she'd visited while brokering the deal. "I did take a few snapshots of 'headquarters' to show the staff here how the parent lives," she wrote. "The result is several requests for a statue in our reception area." Many on staff would settle for a paint job or a toilet-paper dispenser.

Roger's reference to priority number three, the "lousy sharehold-ers," was partly rough humor and partly deflection. His family was the primary beneficiary of the sale. Rog, who held 10 percent of the stock and thus had a windfall of roughly $3 million, used the money to leave publishing once and for all. "I thought, 'If I'm ever gonna take the chance of being a photographer, this is the time,'" he says. His other passion was for road trips—an addiction he developed on those FSG sales journeys in the late fifties, taking inventory and pocketing hotel soap for the office. He's since published seven books of architectural photography. "This is a much more solitary life," he says, "and there are things that I love about it and things that I miss. I did the right thing for me."

Rog, while regretting that his father sold the company, feels it was the right thing for the Strauses, too—that once again, Dad somehow managed to make the right call. "Everyone, including me, thought he was much richer than he was," Rog says. He notes the cost of keeping up servants and maintaining a property at Purchase—"and then they obviously were not buying their clothes at Klein's. So all the surfaces looked very glittering. At the time the Holtzbrincks bought the com-pany—I don't say that the tank was empty, but I think he was probably no longer a rich man." It was another motivation for the sale, and one for which Rog and his family are grateful.

As a young man, Rog once asked his father why he put up such ap-pearances—the silk neck scarves, the Mercedes, the air of an oil baron whose well would never run dry. "Creditors don't hassle me," he said. "If I'm three months late paying a printer's bill, they'd say, 'Oh, you know, he's an eccentric millionaire, but he's good for it.'" And yet it wasn't all surfaces. Straus had paid for the bulk of his granddaugh-ters' college educations, and he wanted to leave them with something more. They each got around $100,000 from the sale. There was also his dream of keeping Sarosca Farm together for future generations, as his father had failed to do.

And so, Straus finally sold the business, forty years after his father, Roger Sr., had suggested he should. Just after the sale, Roger said, "I'm the first person for a number of generations of Guggenheims who made money." His share, fifteen million, wasn't Newhouse money, but it was plenty more than he'd put in. While the Guggenheim mining wealth dissipated into foundations that were often at cross-purposes, the black sheep of his industrialist family turned out to be the most effective capitalist of them all. "It was one of the many things," says Rog, "that made him feel that he'd proved the bastard—the bastard being Roger I—wrong."

Roger didn't have long to brood over the sale. The fiftieth anniversary of Farrar, Straus was fast approaching, and with it a shot at advancing a new narrative: Roger had not capitulated—he had found a way to endure. When he hired a new publicity director, Jeff Seroy, in 1995, Straus told him that one of his first tasks was to organize an anniversary celebration in high style. It was like holding two jobs for a year, but it was a glamorous challenge. Colleagues joked that the openly gay publicist was planning the wedding he'd never have. (In fact, he did eventually get married.)

There would have to be readings, of course. Galassi came up with the idea of dividing them into two nights—not fiction and nonfiction, but poetry and prose. Straus had hoped to hold all major events in the flagship branch of the New York Public Library, which had acquired all the editorial archives in 1991 for $100,000. They asked for at least that amount in return for hosting the whole thing, which was impossible, and so the readings were moved to Town Hall. The library would still host a gala celebration in Astor Hall, its grand, marble-arched entryway.

The final list of poets reading on September 18, 1996, included John Ashbery, Frank Bidart, James Fenton, Thom Gunn, Seamus Heaney, Paul Muldoon, Robert Pinsky, Derek Walcott, C. K. Williams, Charles Wright, and Adam Zagajewski. Bob Giroux, with a wavering voice but precise diction, gave a characteristic stem-winder about the time his old boss, Alfred Harcourt, had rescued Robert Frost from destitution.

Seamus Heaney read a poem called "Keeping Going," about his brother's "stamina and quality," after saying, "I thought it was proper to read it on the fiftieth anniversary of a firm that has stamina and quality and keeps going." Each poet read some of his own work, followed by a poem or two by a departed one, including Giroux's giants—Lowell, Bishop, Berryman, Jarrell.

Joseph Brodsky was included on that second, posthumous list. He'd had heart troubles as far back as his time in Siberia, but he'd seemed preternaturally vital. The Russian Samovar, the shabby-chic restaurant-club in which Brodsky had a stake, had become a midtown haunt for Straus and his trio of beloved foreigners, Walcott, Heaney, and Brodsky. A pre-Soviet Imperial aura prevailed in its smoky bowels, where Joseph and Seamus and Derek conferred with more obscure émigrés under the hazy light of tasseled red lamps, all of them treated by owner Roman Kaplan like royalty in exile. Singers tended to torch songs, balalaika solos, and classic poems set to dirgelike ballads. "It was a scream," says Peggy Miller, "with the white piano, and all the whores at the bar."

At the age of fifty, in 1990, Brodsky married a young student, and you might have thought their wedding was an FSG celebration. Walcott read a poem he'd written for the occasion. It contained more lines serenading his publisher than congratulating Brodsky: "Who let these immigrants through the door / whose finger pushed the elevator / to 19 Union Square, Fourth Floor?"

In the depth of winter in 1996, Brodsky had a fatal heart attack. He was fifty-five. Roger expressed his shock and distress by inviting the public to Brodsky's memorial service—something Brodsky's young widow, Maria, had hoped to avoid. During the planning of the funeral and the settling of Brodsky's estate, Roger clashed with Maria and with Ann Kjellberg, the former FSG assistant whom Brodsky had named as his executor. "There's the cliché of the controlling widow, and this is what I got from Roger," says Kjellberg.

The poetry night at Town Hall was followed by a dinner reception for fifty at the Regency Hotel, where many of the writers were put up for the occasion. The following evening, before the writers of prose read their work, Roger gave a brief introduction, his velvet voice lightly scratched with age. He made a (graciously nameless) reference to Sheila Cudahy's bemoaning all those "wretched authors." Then he blustered—somewhat tautologically—about the firm's continued autonomy: "We publish what we wish to publish, we publish the authors that we wish to publish, and we publish them the way we wish to publish them."

Thursday being more of Roger's night, the tone was a touch lighter and looser. Grace Paley's "Six Days, Some Rememberings," about her imprisonment in Greenwich Village's old Women's House of Detention, made Ian Frazier laugh "the hardest I've ever laughed at a reading." Frazier, Calvin Trillin, Jamaica Kincaid, and John McPhee represented the *New Yorker* delegation. Sontag, regal and standoffish, took twice her allotted time to read a passage from her third novel, *In America,* her follow-up to FSG's surprise bestseller *The Volcano Lover.* Then she left for another engagement. Madeleine L'Engle stood in for the children's book writers. David Grossman, Edna O'Brien, Scott Turow, and Mario Vargas Llosa rounded out the group.

The conspicuous absence of prose night was another writer with heart trouble—Tom Wolfe, who was rapidly convalescing from bypass surgery. Reading a piece of Wolfe's in his place was the artist Richard Merkin. Wolfe had chosen for the occasion his own short profile of Roger, which had just run in *Vanity Fair.* Under the headline ROGER AND ME, it faced a full-page photo of Roger in his aristo-prep glory— unwrinkled linen, thin alligator belt, dark red ascot secured by a jaunty pearl pin, and probably some airbrushing—on the manicured grounds of Sarosca Farm.

Merkin read the story as rendered in Wolfe's accustomed short-hand. There were the status details, including the "North Shore drawl," the Mercedes, and the tan gabardine suits. There was Roger's favorite word, "maaahhhhhhhhhhhhhhhhhhhhhvelous, which he manages to make at least thirty-one letters long." The Holtzbrinck sale was mentioned but quickly set aside: "He remains as publisher." And, as the last speaker of the evening, Merkin closed with a salute. "Tom thanks you, and we all of us thank Roger Straus."

"The whole place just went crazy," Jeff Seroy says. "It was like someone had just hit a game-winning home run." A black-and-white photo commemorates the moment: Roger stands from his front-row seat, his hand resting lightly for balance on the lip of the stage. He smiles broadly. Everyone is applauding enthusiastically except for Jamaica Kincaid, to Roger's right, who keeps a steadying arm just behind his back.

The reading was followed by a mass pilgrimage to the New York Public Library, which resulted in a crush to get in. Eventually the doors flew wide, and as many as 1,500 people, ranging from the literary elite to former employees and freeloading onlookers, partook of the alcohol and the ample food courtesy of Potel et Chabot. From a lectern in front of a flowing curtain and two Grecian arches evoking Raphael's *School of Athens*, Roger told the history of the company in witty, offhand phrases. One former editor, who was standing right beside Dorothea Straus, says neither of them could make out a word.

Roger loved playing host so much that it's hard to believe he had any reservations about throwing a huge, two-day party essentially to honor the great achievement of his life. In the immediate moment, he seemed to eat it up. But some people recall conflicted feelings, at least at a distance. "I don't think he liked it," says his old friend and tennis partner Roger Hirson. "Roger felt that it was a valedictory of some kind, that it had the feeling of 'in memoriam.'" Seroy believes it was more complicated. "He might have got over it when he had the standing ovation," he says. Roger did relish the old-school PR touch delivered by a friend of Peggy Miller's, who knew someone in the mayor's office: September 19 was proclaimed "Farrar, Straus and Giroux Day."

And finally, an anthology was published. But unlike the scuttled twenty-fifth anniversary book, this edition was not for sale. *50 Years: A Farrar, Straus and Giroux Reader* was edited by former Viking publisher Alan Williams and printed privately for friends of the house. Its introduction, so different from Robert Giroux's meaty, self-indulgent preface a quarter century earlier, was a glancing and celebratory foreword. The nettlesome details and the spiky ironies were elided in favor of Roger's oft-told boilerplate. Nonetheless, freed from commercial constraints, the anthology was a real representation of FSG's astonishing range: more than one hundred writers represented on more than six hundred pages, followed by a complete list of awards.

Elisabeth Sifton once asked Williams why there wasn't a richer history. He told her Straus and Giroux could never agree on one story. Nor did either write his memoirs. It wasn't for lack of interest. Warner Books publisher Larry Kirschbaum had a standing offer of $250,000 for Roger's story. Straus took the idea seriously only in the final two years of his life—selecting an editor, buying a little tape recorder, and sketching out his first couple of chapters. And then, he dropped it.

Giroux, having already published long pieces on his writers, got further along. In the mid-nineties he was given a grant from the Rockefeller Foundation to write a book about his Harcourt years, but nothing came of it. As for his much longer time at FSG, he finally confessed to the writer of his *New York Times* obituary that he couldn't find a way to write it without speaking ill of Roger Straus, and he didn't think that would serve anyone well.

Giroux was far too discreet to itemize his gripes, but those who knew him well have cited some resentment over Roger's quick and easy adoption of Jonathan Galassi. Jonathan had also taken over Giroux's office. A few years later, Roger would joke to a reporter, "I'd like it if it were Farrar, Straus & Galassi, but I'm not going to shoot Giroux." Galassi was complicit, too, privately making light of Giroux's pettiness.

It was only in the closing years of his life that Giroux allowed himself a rejoinder to Roger's line about not knowing the difference between an editor and a publisher. "I never wanted to be a publisher," he said then. "I was a damn good editor. There's nothing so great about the word *publisher*, per se, except that one publisher—I think it was the second Nelson Doubleday—said, 'I publish books. I don't read them.' An editor would never say that."

When Holtzbrinck acquired Farrar, Straus, the German company was a small player in American publishing, tiny compared with Bertelsmann or CBS or Advance. But a year later the conglomerate acquired

Macmillan in Britain and, by extension, St. Martin's Press, a commercial house more than five times larger than FSG. "That changed the whole thing," says Galassi, "and I don't think Roger anticipated it." For his part, Galassi says it "provided a lot of opportunities for scale." It was natural for Holtzbrinck to seek parity with its American competitors, and that could be accomplished only by looking for the same economies that other companies enjoyed. With Straus beginning his decline and Galassi more accustomed to playing the company soldier, the timing was right for a tightening of the grip on Farrar, Straus.

In 1998, Roger and selected staff were flown to Gordonsville, Virginia, where, right beside a turkey farm, Holtzbrinck had constructed the country's most advanced book warehouse. There was a laser-guided, computer-controlled scanning system and 430,000 square feet, enough space to store fifty million books at a time (or maybe half of all the copies FSG had ever sold).

Roger got along with the young man who was eventually put in charge of Holtzbrinck's U.S. holdings, John Sargent. One reason was Sargent's publishing lineage: His maternal grandfather was Nelson Doubleday, the publisher who'd allegedly never read books. One of the first things Roger said upon meeting Sargent was, "I had the hots for your grandmother. She was delicious." Sargent loved it. He let the patriarch dote and condescend, all the while growing closer to Jonathan, having separate discussions about the future of the company.

Sargent did have a hard time telling Roger it was necessary to get rid of his commissioned salespeople—those regional reps who'd peddled FSG books ever since the days of Rog's teenaged road trips. "I remember the sales thing was very hard for him," says Sargent. "Some of those commission guys had been around a long time." Roger stalled in his inimitable way. Sargent remembers Dieter accompanying him to what was meant to be the definitive meeting on the issue. "Dieter talked for I would say two or three or five minutes. And Roger just started to talk, and talk, and talk. Dieter occasionally got a word in edgewise, and Roger talked, and we left, and Dieter turned to me and said, 'That went well.' I said to him, 'Dieter? If you think Roger, coming out of that meeting, thinks he agreed to anything you said, I think you're wrong.'" Sargent was right, and months went by before a resolution was reached. When it finally was, several FSG salespeople were brought into the Holtzbrinck fold.

But it was a losing battle, and Roger must have known it. Terms with the new warehouse were, oddly, less friendly than those with the rival firm, Putnam, that FSG had used in the past. What looked like a mundane reorganization marked a radical shift, whereby FSG had to act like a subsidiary rather than a client. Eventually, FSG retained only a skeleton crew of sales staff in charge of chain-store accounts and New York indies. No longer could the house negotiate for its own bookkeeping or insurance. A newly centralized HR office even tried to put up sexual-harrassment flyers—until an FSG exec pointed out that only John Sargent had the clout to tell Roger that he could no longer pat employees on the ass.

The aging boss grumbled, albeit with an undertone of resignation. One day, Sargent showed up to a Farrar, Straus meeting twenty minutes late, huffing and puffing, interrupting Roger in one of his reveries. "Ah, good," said Roger. "There comes my warehouse man." When a new accountant, hired in 1996 to rationalize FSG's finances, presented Roger a sales sheet for Tom Wolfe's *A Man in Full* that held back some money for returned books, Roger became furious and threatened to fire him. Sam Kam, the semiretired former treasurer who'd done the accounting on graph paper, had to be brought in to explain that this was just the modern method of accounting, mandated by their new firm, Ernst & Young. It was hardly a firing offense.

Sometimes Roger was allowed to play with Holtzbrinck money almost as though it were his own. In 1998, his old friend Matthew Evans, head of Faber and Faber—the house T. S. Eliot built—was in deep trouble over his U.S. subsidiary's distribution. Roger made quick, ad hoc arrangements to buy Faber's American branch, negotiating directly with Evans for roughly $1.1 million. From beginning to end, he controlled the process, objecting when one of the von Holtzbrinck auditors visited Faber without Roger's say-so. Faber had a valuable backlist, especially in plays, but it was an inefficient transaction, assuming unnecessary liabilities.

That same year, when Farrar, Straus was vehemently defending its decision to publish an unauthorized *Lolita* sequel, *Lo's Diary*, in the face of a threatened lawsuit from Vladimir Nabokov's estate, Roger suddenly pulled the book out of production. Galassi and the Holtz-brincks disagreed with the reversal, but Roger said some of his writers objected to the book. His decision stayed. In editorial matters, he had final say.

To some extent, Sargent humored Straus, and so did Dieter von Holtzbrinck. The latter once told the story of a typical Farrar, Straus "board meeting." There were not enough seats around Gladys Guggenheim's old table, forcing the billionaire CEO to stand while Roger, without a single piece of paper, extemporized on Pablo Neruda, asked questions about finances instead of answering them, and concluded that everything depended on whether Tom Wolfe would finally deliver his manuscript. "In the end, we always left the meetings happy," Dieter remembered. "And if there's a purpose for board meetings, and for us poor shareholders, it is to leave happy." What he didn't say was that these atmospheric gatherings were often followed by a second meeting, between Phil Zweiger—the CFO brought in to manage the Holtzbrinck transition—and Dieter's financial number two. It was there that the real numbers were hammered out.

If there was a whiff of condescension in the way FSG's overseers chuckled over their incorrigible octogenarian, it was also true that Roger gave up power only gradually and deliberately. He couldn't stop time, and he was realistic. Instead of sowing uncertainty about his succession, Roger cut off speculation during the anniversary festivities. To assorted press, he said plainly (and a little to the editor's surprise), "Jonathan Galassi will follow me."

Galassi has said that Straus "was much mellower and less threatened in his later years." He may well have been, at least with Galassi. But Roger's fights were as fierce as ever. His grudges with Andrew Wylie expanded into months-long spells of enforced silence. Most of the embargoes were triggered by the agent's relentless pursuit of foreign authors and foreign rights. Once, Andrew took over all of journalist Philip Gourevitch's rights retroactively; another time he moved the Turkish novelist Orhan Pamuk to another house. Usually, though, the skirmishes involved Sontag and came in all the permutations of a love triangle. Either she was taking Wylie's side (as when she invited him to dinner with FSG author Péter Nádas behind Roger's back) or Wylie wasn't standing up for her as well as Roger could. When W. W. Norton went ahead with the publication of *Susan Sontag: The Making of an Icon,* a biography Sontag found extremely objectionable, Roger castigated Andrew for not dropping his client Starling Lawrence, a novelist who happened to be the publisher of Norton. Lawrence also happened to be under contract with FSG for his next novel. Roger promptly canceled it. Lawrence responded by saying that Roger "has become a parody or caricature of what he was."

Inevitably, Wylie would wear Roger down with "conceptual flowers" until Roger consented to be taken to lunch before accepting an abject apology. During those silent months, Roger swore off business with Wylie, sometimes in writing, and with a FUCK YOU VERY MUCH stamp. On this and other topics, Galassi told Roger that his grudges could be counterproductive. "Don't give me any of that Christian forgiveness, Galassi," Roger replied. "I'm a vindictive Jew."

But Roger's anger was no longer the cudgel it had been. Even during a six-month embargo on business with the Wylie Agency, conversations about ongoing projects continued among the staff. Once Andrew actually sneaked into the office to have a secret meeting with Galassi. But when he walked into Jonathan's office, Peggy Miller happened to be there, looking for a name in his Rolodex. Knowing her boss's mind, she escorted Wylie firmly out of the office and scolded the younger editor who'd brought him in.

Galassi was left alone, though, and for good reason. Roger's fights were strategically irrational. Each of his scrapes, in its way, made a little more room for his successor. Jonathan could be the reasonable and forward-looking heir apparent: biding his time, expanding his relationships, preparing for the future while the Sun King roared across the hall. In the meantime, Roger's afternoons grew shorter, his naps on the office couch longer, and his fights increasingly tinged with nostalgia.

In late November 1999, a month before his eighty-third birthday and the expiration of his contract with von Holtzbrinck, Roger made good on his promise to Galassi, and passed on to him the title of publisher. Two years after that, he also relinquished the title of president. He wasn't retiring, he insisted. He was becoming an "adviser on future strategy and international issues" to the von Holtzbrinck group. And he reserved one title for himself. It was the title that would have gone to Johnny Farrar in 1946, had Giroux taken that early offer and become Straus's first editor in chief. Farrar did eventually take the title in order to make way for Giroux, and Giroux took it when Robbins succeeded him. It was an emeritus label meant to nudge someone to the side, but without the stigma of retirement, because Roger didn't believe in retirement. And he wasn't retiring, because he was, after all, still the chairman.

15

An Embarrassment of Riches

Among those New Yorkers who made ad hoc plans on September 11, 2001, driven together by emergency and grief, were novelists Jonathan Franzen and Jeffrey Eugenides. Franzen lived on the Upper East Side. Eugenides lived in Berlin but happened to be in town, staying in the West Village. He couldn't make it back downtown that day, so Franzen offered to put him up. They arranged to meet on the steps of the New York Public Library, the site of FSG's glorious anniversary bash five years earlier. It was around the time of that party that their mutual editor, Jonathan Galassi, had set them up. Each had been struggling mightily on his most ambitious project yet—Franzen on a portrait of a fractured midwestern family, Eugenides on the confessions of a hermaphrodite. "Maybe he thought we would be mutually therapeutic," says Eugenides. "It was the closest I've ever been to having a blind date with a man." Since then, the two authors had channeled their competitive urges into literary arguments and tennis matches. And tonight, they and Franzen's girlfriend, Kathryn

Chetkovich, tromped together through streets stunned into silence, found an anonymous Italian restaurant, and commiserated over a changed world.

"Who would have guessed that everything could end so suddenly on a pretty Tuesday morning?" Franzen wrote in a brief essay for the next issue of *The New Yorker.* "In the space of two hours, we left behind a happy era of Game Boy economics and trophy houses and entered a world of fear and vengeance." What he couldn't foresee, but privately hoped, was that America would still need relics of that more complacent age. A precious few of that autumn's artifacts would survive the leap from one era to another. In literature, there was really only one book that did, a novel that had been out for just six days: Jonathan Franzen's *The Corrections.* Farrar, Straus and Giroux made that possible, and Franzen returned the favor, delivering FSG, another proud relic, into an era with a new set of rules. But before that could happen they had other obstacles to confront, among them a talk-show hostess named Oprah Winfrey.

Unlike the first novels of Wolfe and Turow in 1987, Franzen's *The Twenty-Seventh City,* which had led the following year's fall fiction list, was a bargain. A novice agent named Susan Golomb was only twenty-seven, a year older than Franzen, when she took on the challenge of shaping his 1,100-page manuscript about a sinister foreign takeover of St. Louis into a novel she could sell. Her second smart move was to send it to Jonathan Galassi, an editor who not only shared Franzen's goals—to bridge the commercial and the literary—but also had a very thrifty boss. Galassi read the submission raptly, "getting more and more afraid he would ruin it," he remembers, "which is the experience I often have with a book that's really good." He got the pared-down novel for $20,000, and barely changed a word.

"He couldn't believe how clean the manuscript was," Franzen remembers of their first phone call. "He had only one suggestion of any substance and I disregarded it, and it's one of the very few regrets I have." Galassi didn't want Barbara, the sympathetic St. Louis wife, to die at the end. Franzen ignored him. "From where I now stand, the book is kind of inexplicably angry," he says, "and that killing at the end was sort of a symbolic representation of that anger. And this happens in any good editing relationship. The suggestions and questions you're getting have a personal resonance if they're any good. This is your rabbi, this is your shrink in literary matters." Still, Franzen wasn't ready to listen to him. Galassi laid off, establishing the laissez-faire approach that distinguishes him from both Straus and Giroux. "His refrain throughout my years with him had always been, 'It's your book.'"

From the beginning, Franzen was a Jonathan author, and he could never quite get along with the more ebullient Roger Straus. "Some people talk about having dads with whom they just can't find anything to talk about," Franzen says. "That was it with him and me." When *The Corrections* became a bestseller, Roger would half joke, "If Franzen overtakes Wolfe . . . I'll kill him . . . Dump a hundred thousand copies in the East River."

The 1988 catalog touted *The Twenty-Seventh City,* a Book-of-the-Month Club selection, as "one of the most spectacular debuts by an American writer in recent memory." Franzen was described as "ironic and generous in equal measure, and, best of all, he understands suspense." FSG saw the potential for commercial crossover but focused on breaking him out as a literary author first. The reviewers obliged, showering the debut with so many laurels that, years later, a publicist was able to promote its reissue by gathering up "27 Raves for *The Twenty-Seventh City.*" It was rumored to be in line for a National Book Critics Circle nomination. But it was a near miss: certainly a money-maker, given the advance, but it failed to sell out its forty-thousand-copy first printing.

When Galassi saw Franzen's next novel, *Strong Motion,* he told the author, "I can't remember being more disappointed in the ending of a book." Having shelled out roughly $125,000, Galassi wanted more from it, and so would readers. He thought, reasonably, that a science-fiction novel about an earthquake-ridden Boston should end with an earthquake. Franzen listened this time, but it didn't help. Today he blames its abysmal performance partly on FSG blunders. A publicist had decided to tout it as a regional work. "Her plan was, 'Let it take fire in Boston and sweep across the country from there.' And of course the book is saturated with my contempt for Boston. But what did I know? I was leading a very strange and isolated existence at that point. But I think the real mistake was that they put a terrible cover on." It's a gaping black splotch, resembling the marks made by a seismograph during an earthquake, on a field of blood red. Franzen says he "never quite shook the feeling that Jonathan [Galassi] didn't like the book."

Strong Motion's publication was followed by "the worst year of my life," as Franzen later called it. During the mid-nineties he wrote a screenplay and then gave up control over it, divorced his wife, and saw his parents fall ill and die. He worked through the pain in a long, ambivalent *Harper's* essay, venting his various disappointments—over capitalism, over bookstore chains, over a novelist's estrangement, and over the general decline of literature—before seeming to plead with himself for defiant optimism: "The world was ending then, it's ending still, and I'm happy to belong to it again," he concluded. He rejected the kind of social novel for which Tom Wolfe agitated, as well as the postmodern tricks employed by his friend David Foster Wallace. He called instead for a return to the personal, the emotional.

Galassi, Franzen's "shrink," had little to do with his transformation from angry young writer to the great American chronicler of *The Corrections*. He gave Franzen a contract in 1997 for a little less than the *Strong Motion* advance, and then backed off again. "He's like an indulgent older brother," Franzen says. It was Henry Finder, Franzen's editor at *The New Yorker,* who gave him an ultimatum in 2000: Finish your novel or I won't assign you anything. Still, FSG did what it had done for great writers of the past, from Wilson to Wolfe to Sontag: "They stuck with me. They gave me a decent advance. And then they were patient."

Galassi could be inscrutable when it came to writers, especially in contrast to his effusive predecessors at FSG. But that changed for Franzen once *The Corrections* made its way to the office around Election Day 2000. The publisher's praise was unqualified. Other staff members still remember the revelatory moment when they finished the manuscript. Lorin Stein, a very young editor at the time, was given the enviable task of line editing it. "I remember finishing the last page of it and running up two flights of stairs to Jonathan's office," Stein says, "and I remember having tears in my eyes."

Dealing with the author wasn't always so deeply affecting. Franzen had complained vocally about the *Strong Motion* campaign, and publicity head Jeff Seroy got the message. He assigned the book to publicist Peter Miller, who'd grown up, like Franzen, in Webster Groves, the St. Louis suburb fictionalized in *The Corrections*. For that year's BookExpo, publishing's largest bookselling convention, they produced some three thousand giveaway copies with a rare personal note from Galassi. He called the book "a masterpiece, a triumphant fulfillment of everything his earlier work led us to expect. Not only is this his best book to date, it's one of the very best we've published in my fifteen years at FSG." The media dubbed it one of BookExpo's two hot galleys. Rival publishers like Grove/Atlantic's Morgan Entrekin steered buyers to the FSG booth to pick up a copy. "All of us who care about great books are always thrilled to see another one," Entrekin told two of the booksellers, "wherever it's coming from."

It helped that the novel had already been sold robustly abroad. Those sales—and a movie deal with producer Scott Rudin not long after the fair—were the work of his agent, Susan Golomb, whom he'd stuck with despite being courted by Andrew Wylie. His loyalty was rewarded by both Golomb and FSG. Seroy managed to secure almost simultaneous profiles in *Time* and the *New York Times Magazine,* along with a cover ad in *Publishers Weekly.* Agent and publisher worked beautifully in tandem; Galassi, a creature of modern publishing, was happy to share the burden and the credit in a way Roger Straus never could.

FSG was eager to atone for the *Strong Motion* cover. The main idea, they agreed, was to walk the line, as the book often does, between earnest empathy and ironizing intellect. "I wanted to stress the human dimension," Franzen says, "particularly with a title like *The Corrections.*" The echo of William Gaddis's *The Recognitions,* the postmodern triumph that Giroux had published at Harcourt, Brace almost a half century earlier, was intentional.

Franzen says he "tossed out Christmas as a theme" for the cover. The plot moves toward the Lambert family's last Christmas together in fictional St. Jude, as three yuppifying adult children, all long departed, cope with their aging parents. Cover designer Lynn Buckley fretted for weeks over it; then one day she took a walk around a newly gentrified Union Square and skimmed a carousel full of postcards. Among them was a Rockwellian photograph of a Christmas dinner, everyone smiling blandly except for one grumpy kid. She bought the postcard and cropped it so that only the little grump's face was fully shown.

When Buckley called Galassi to share her ideas, Franzen happened to be in the publisher's office. She'd never met him before. "Why don't you come up right now," Galassi said. She was wracked with nerves, expecting the skeptical author to shoot everything down. He did resist the postcard's obvious irony, but eventually decided, "That's the one."

By August 31, the Friday before Labor Day, the novel, set for release the next day, was headed for the bestseller list. Buckley happened to be among the very few people still in the office that holiday afternoon. So was Peter Miller, her boyfriend at the time. Suddenly he called out to her from his office across the hall. He sounded alarmed. She ran out to meet him by the production department's lightboxes. "Oh my god, you won't believe it," he shouted. "The most amazing thing that ever happened for a book just happened for *The Corrections!*"

"What happened?" Buckley asked. "Did it win the Pulitzer Prize?"

"No," he said, "it's an Oprah selection!" *The Corrections* was the forty-fifth pick of Oprah's Book Club, the talk-show host's five-year-old book segment, but it was among only a handful chosen right on publication. Pat Towers, a new editor at *O* magazine, had lent Winfrey one of those advance copies to read on vacation. Miller knew what it meant for the book: hundreds of thousands more copies in sales. It was a boon even to mass-friendly selections like Anna Quindlen and Wally Lamb, never mind what you'd call a "literary" book like *The Corrections*. The excitement failed to register with Buckley. She'd grown up watching Oprah, but thought of her taste as purely mainstream.

This just felt like cognitive dissonance: "I guess it helps a book sell more than a Pulitzer Prize, right? That just seems crazy to me."

Franzen felt much the same way. Around lunchtime, someone called him at home and told him to expect a call from the *New York Times* in forty-five minutes. Would he be home? Sure, he said, befuddled by the cloak-and-dagger routine from a paper he'd already written for. Actually, it was Harpo, Oprah's company, securing the line as though it were one of Roger Straus's CIA contacts. "Everything was bogus from the start," Franzen says. "My first encounter with Harpo Productions was being told a lie." Here's how he remembers the ensuing phone conversation:

"Jonathan?"

"Yes?"

"Oprah Winfrey!"

"Oh. Hi. I recognize your voice from TV."

Awkward silence; deep breath from Oprah.

"Jonathan, I love your book, and we're going to make it our choice for the next book club!"

"That's really great," he remembers answering in an even tone. "My publisher's gonna be really happy."

Franzen believes it was doomed from the start. "I think she was surprised that I wasn't moaning with shock and pleasure," he says. More than a decade later, even after a very public show of reconciliation, he still contrasts his tenuous connection to the queen of all media with his deep ties to Farrar, Straus. "I'd been working nine years on the book and FSG had spent a year trying to make a bestseller of it. It was our thing. She was an interloper, coming late, and with an expectation of slavish gratitude and devotion for the favor she was bestowing."

Later that day, Franzen went up to Tarrytown, New York, to play tennis with his friend the writer David Means, to whom he'd dedicated *The Corrections* (along with Means's wife, Genève Patterson). Though sworn to secrecy, he told him about it. Then he had a few drinks to celebrate. Having only recently bought a cell phone, he wasn't yet accustomed to checking his voice mail. On the train back into the city, he discovered he had seven messages from Peter Miller.

Back at Union Square, Miller had received the fax of a long contract from Harpo, which covered timing, media coordination, and
the important issue of how the Oprah logo could be displayed on the
cover. The contract had to be signed by midnight Chicago time, or
1:00 a.m. Eastern, in the wee hours of Labor Day weekend. Galassi
was already out of town. Jeff Seroy was in the Pyrenees. Spenser Lee,
the director of sales, had left for the day but lived nearby. He came in
to sign the contract in Galassi's place. But no one could sign for Franzen.

The author's train finally eased into the Harlem Metro-North
station around eleven; he and Miller and Buckley met up shortly afterward at Franzen's Upper East Side apartment. With only ninety
minutes to spare, they sat around a table in the galley kitchen of his
rent-stabilized one-bedroom, surrounded by salvaged furniture, and
perused the contract. Buckley had brought along a copy of the Oprah
medallion, which they called the "poker chip," and they tried placing
it over different parts of Buckley's cover. She suggested, half jokingly,
putting it over the Christmas turkey. Could they put it on the back?
Franzen asked. No, they could not.

"Jonathan started talking out loud," Miller remembers. "Saying,
'Why should I do this?' And of course I, being the representative of
the publicity department, said, 'This is an enormous opportunity.'"
Franzen says he never seriously vacillated. "If nothing else, FSG had
stuck with me through a book that hadn't done well, and had been
very patient, and I love what they mean to American literature. The
idea that this was going to add instantly another half million to their
sales—there's no way I wasn't gonna do it for them." What about for
him? "Having gotten there with my own steam, I felt a certain resistance to the boost that [it] would represent." FSG wasn't as eager to
see how the book might do without Oprah's help.

The world would soon know about Franzen's ambivalence, and
would regard it largely as puzzling, foolish, or unforgivably con-
descending. "Snotty, self-absorbed and self-righteous," *Washington
Post* critic Jonathan Yardley would write of his behavior—hardly the
stuff of back-cover blurbs. The backlash against Franzen would only

confirm his prophetic words in that 1996 *Harper's* essay: "In publishing circles, confessions of doubt are commonly referred to as 'whining' . . . However sick with foreboding you feel inside, it's best to radiate confidence and hope that it's infectious." For the moment, however, as Franzen, Buckley, and Miller walked briskly to a nearby Kinko's to fax the contract before 1:00 a.m., those doubts were tossed hurriedly aside. On the way, Franzen muttered, half to himself, "I just realized I'm probably a millionaire."

On September 9, *The Corrections* made the cover of the *New York Times Book Review.* Inside, novelist David Gates raved about "Jonathan Franzen's marvelous new novel." It had conventional appeal but, thankfully, "just enough novel-of-paranoia touches so Oprah won't assign it and ruin Franzen's street cred." The first printing, of 65,000 copies, unfortunately carried two transposed pages. An erratum slip had to be inserted—a correction that's since increased the value of those first editions. It was the first of many awful snags that ironically, perversely, only raised Franzen's stock. Oprah Winfrey was supposed to announce her still-secret pick on her September 13 show. It was postponed, of course, in light of the deadliest terrorist attack on U.S. soil.

Jeff Seroy's team at FSG had drawn up a packed schedule for Franzen's rollout, beginning with a launch party on the roof of a SoHo hotel on September 18. When the staff returned to work on September 13, Seroy struck a defiant pose. "Fuck them," he told Roger, "we should just carry on and do it!" It would be a beat-the-terrorists moment, in the spirit of Mayor Giuliani's order to go shopping. Roger, soon to resign as president, responded with one of his last, and most sensible, judgment calls, as Seroy recalls it: "Are you out of your mind? You want to have everyone at this party standing there staring at the wisps of smoke rising from the ruins of the World Trade Center from the rooftop?" The party was postponed until October 18, after Franzen's tour.

Franzen's next move was to write his essay for that post-9/11 issue of *The New Yorker.* Another contributor to the issue was Susan Sontag, a bomb thrower from a more provocative era. She was sixty-eight and, like her publisher, closer to the end than most people thought. She took the occasion to toss out one last three-paragraph Molotov cocktail. "Where is the acknowledgment," she wrote, "that this was not a 'cowardly' attack on 'civilization' or 'liberty' or 'humanity' or 'the free world' but an attack on the world's self-proclaimed superpower, undertaken as a consequence of specific American alliances and actions? . . . And if the word 'cowardly' is to be used, it might be more aptly applied to those who kill from beyond the range of retaliation, high in the sky, than to those willing to die themselves in order to kill others." It wasn't one of her more popular pieces.

Franzen had a much milder impropriety to share in that issue: "Unless you were a very good person indeed, you were probably, like me, experiencing the collision of several incompatible worlds inside your head. Besides the horror and sadness of what you were watching, you might also have felt a childish disappointment over the disruption of your day, or a selfish worry about the impact on your finances."

Oddly, September 11 seems to have helped *The Corrections*. While Oprah figured out when to announce the selection, FSG had some extra time to print an additional 680,000 copies—ten times more than that first, botched printing—most of them with the Oprah logo on the cover. By the time she did officially announce her selection, on September 24, many stores had already gotten books bearing the logo, exploding Oprah's embargo in a way that only helped build buzz. "A work of art and sheer genius," Oprah told her largely female viewers. "When critics refer to the great American novel, I think, this is it, people!"

The day of the announcement, Franzen was already in St. Louis, two days into his book tour, leading a Harpo Productions camera crew through Webster Groves as they shot background for the future episode in which he would star. Hopping along on his tour itinerary, he'd passed through stringent but sparse airport security lines, stretched out over near-empty airplane rows, alighted in quiet cities, and driven to packed readings. "People were sick of staying home and watching TV," he says. "It was a total embarrassment of riches." Today he blames the ensuing backlash largely on 9/11-abetted Schadenfreude: "I think one of the main reasons that the entire world turned on me during the Oprah thing was that one person had benefited from 9/11, and that was me. Everyone's suffering, and one guy, it all worked for."

Maybe Franzen also felt guilty, because much of the backlash was self-inflicted. The video tour of Webster Groves, which he later wrote about as a thoroughly "bogus" experience, soured him further on the enterprise. A producer demanded to see his old family home, but he refused; he didn't want to see what had become of the place where his family memories were buried. That night, at a reading, Peter Miller gave him a bottle of single-malt Scotch in celebration. He drove off tipsy in his rental car to a late-night flight to O'Hare. In Chicago he shot two long hours with Oprah that would eventually be whittled down to several minutes. Then he proceeded west, where, in interviews with regional press, his ambivalence pushed its way out into the open. "That Oprah selection will probably not sit well with the writers I hang out with and the readers who have been my core audience," he told the *Seattle Post-Intelligencer,* in what could easily be read as a knock on female readers. He told the *Miami Herald* he was "muddled" about the Oprah pick—especially about the "corporate branding" that marred the cover he and his publisher had worked so hard on.

Finally, an article in the Portland *Oregonian,* based on an interview he'd given in midtour, made his reservations the focus of its story: OPRAH'S STAMP OF APPROVAL RUBS WRITER IN CONFLICTED WAYS. He said the pick did as much for Oprah—hitching herself to a book in the "high-art literary tradition"—as it did for him. Maybe it was the headline that finally got Winfrey's attention. On October 12, the day the story ran, Harpo Productions put in a call to Union Square. Peter Miller answered. Oprah wanted to talk to someone in charge, but Galassi was off at the Frankfurt Book Fair. Jeff Seroy, meanwhile, was off on his lunch hour. Miller made a round of Seroy's regular haunts and found him in a trendy restaurant called Coffee Shop. He led his boss back to the office, sat back down to his turkey sandwich, and waited for the fallout. But instead of calling Seroy, Oprah called Miller again. The first thing she said was, "What is this guy's problem?" Then she said it would be very easy to cancel the show. Miller struggled with the bite of turkey sandwich in his mouth as he tried to figure out what to say.

"I felt like I was getting an ulcer," Miller says. "I was terrified that this was going to sink the ship." Oprah might blame them for the mess, jeopardizing their long-term relationship with the arbiter of America's reading taste. Even if Franzen's sales continued, what about Oprah's next pick? Would she take another chance on the publisher that had burned her, however indirectly?

Eventually, Oprah was put through to Seroy, who tried to explain Franzen's phrasing as the unfortunate product of "a very steep learning curve." "I think what I said to her is, 'This is a guy who spent ten years in a cave writing this book,'" he says. But Seroy didn't quite apologize for his author. Today he explains that he never thought it was justified: "He was kind of clumsy, or unpracticed, or graceless in the situation. I don't know whether I would call it a mistake." Seroy's first instinct, and FSG's, is to get the author's back. At the end of the call, Oprah told him she'd let FSG know what she decided to do.

That evening, Franzen officially concluded his reading tour at an Upper West Side Barnes & Noble. Oprah was still undecided. Franzen had dinner with Miller, Seroy, and Susan Golomb, all of whom chided him. But it was Galassi's dressing-down that Franzen remembers most. "He said, 'You've outgrown this,'" Franzen remembers. "I think he was essentially saying, there's no need for you to be so angry anymore. You have a chance to reach lots of people. Don't alienate them." Franzen says Galassi was right.

At FSG's behest, Franzen wrote Oprah a personal letter of apology. In public statements he pleaded guilty to being impolitic, claimed his words had been taken out of context, and offered grudging semi-apologies that, by blending false abjection with unfortunate flashes of honesty, occasionally made things worse. "To find myself being in the position of giving offense to someone who's a hero—not a hero of mine per se, but a hero in general—I feel bad in a public-spirited way," he told USA Today.

By then, everyone at FSG knew it was too late. Oprah had no direct contact with Franzen, but the day after Franzen finally had his SoHo rooftop book launch, she called to inform FSG that he was officially disinvited from appearing on her show. October 23 was hardly a slow news day—anthrax was found in the White House mail facility—but for FSG it was only about one devastating public statement. "Jonathan Franzen will not be on the Oprah Winfrey show," Oprah said, "because he is seemingly uncomfortable and conflicted about being chosen as a book club selection. It is never my intention to make anyone uncomfortable or cause anyone conflict." Mercifully, the corporate logo stayed.

It's possible that airing the show would have sent sales of *The Corrections* into the stratosphere, past a million copies and far beyond anything Roger Straus could dump into the East River. But one clear consequence of the controversy is that it boosted sales by around 150,000 copies. There was still, however, more publicity to do, and Seroy wasn't taking chances. In advance of Franzen's appearances on the *Today* show and *Charlie Rose,* he hired a media coach—typically a $5,000 expense. Over two long sessions, Joyce Newman broke down the author's defenses and taught him to love the idiot box. "I prefer it to print interviews," he says now. Oprah, too, was chastened. After a one-year book-club hiatus, she mostly stuck to classics. Her first selection of a new work after *The Corrections,* in 2005, was James Frey's *A Million Little Pieces.* After coming on her show once, Frey was found to have largely fabricated the addiction tell-all. Frey had taught her the hard way just how wretched authors could be (to paraphrase Sheila Cudahy). Then she went back to classics yet again, and the first one she picked was Elie Wiesel's *Night.* It happened to be on the backlist of FSG imprint Hill & Wang, setting up another great Oprah year for the house.

Both Straus and Galassi had to manage Franzen's trials from afar. After postponing his book party, they had decided to respect tradition and make the rounds of the Frankfurt Book Fair. The convention's doors opened on October 9, three days before Oprah's blistering phone call to Union Square. American traffic was light in the wake of the attacks, but many of Roger's old friends were there, as well as one of more recent vintage. Jeffrey Eugenides, who was living in Berlin and finishing up his would-be masterpiece *Middlesex,* had returned to Germany from his ill-timed stay in New York. He came down to Frankfurt mainly to go over edits with Galassi, but Roger took the opportunity to introduce him to his foreign friends.

The early exposure couldn't hurt. Every year, Frankfurt selected one country as its guest of honor, and this time it was Greece. Not only was Eugenides descended from Greeks, his novel also revolved around a Greek-American family. He and his wife attended the classic FSG dinner in the Parkhotel, where Roberto Calasso and Inge Feltrinelli and the rest gave toasts to New York and to the publisher who'd braved the skies to raise their spirits. "My wife wanted to run off with Roger," Eugenides says. A more gregarious personality than Franzen, Eugenides got along better with Roger. Galassi and Straus were worried about Franzen, wondering what kind of letter he was writing to Oprah. Eugenides wasn't concerned. "It was pretty obvious that the scandal would produce enormous amounts of sales."

Great things were also expected of *Middlesex*. In 1999 Eugenides's first novel, a morbid little tale delivered in the plural third person, had been turned into the gloriously hip debut of filmmaker Sofia Coppola. It was easy to forget that when it first came out seven years earlier, *The Virgin Suicides* was considered the kind of odd, acquired taste that FSG took chances on. It grew out of a story in *The Paris Review,* back when Eugenides was the secretary at the Academy of American Poets, of which Galassi was then the president. The publisher graciously agreed to read Eugenides's novel when it was finished. So did Tom Wolfe's agent, Lynn Nesbit. She took it on in 1992 but told Eugenides that it wasn't "a big money book"—that the story of five sisters in Grosse Pointe, Michigan, committing serial suicide "might be a little macabre." She took the manuscript straight to Galassi, who now says, "I was blown away."

He gave it some light line editing before putting it through production. The undulating layers of blond hair on its cover belonged to Galassi's editorial assistant, Phyllida Burlingame. (Eugenides's third novel, *The Marriage Plot,* would star a woman named Phyllida, whose "hair was where her power resided.") Relying on staff for free modeling is an ongoing FSG tradition. The girl reading on the cover of Franzen's nonfiction collection *How to Be Alone* is its designer, Lynn Buckley, with Peter Miller in the background; the soldiers fronting Scott Turow's *Ordinary Heroes* are artfully muddied assistants; inside the chain-mail suit that decorates Seamus Heaney's translation of *Beowulf* is veteran FSG designer Cynthia Krupat, her graying blonde hair almost visible beneath the armor.

The Virgin Suicides sold out its 25,000-copy first printing, doing well enough for Galassi to call it "a great succès d'estime." Some at the house privately thought another firm might have been more aggressive in selling a darkly hip book about sex and death, with its intriguing narrative voice and sly undercurrent of Motor City American dreams gone to rot. The movie not only changed its fortunes—though it boosted sales only of the paperback, which FSG didn't publish—it also raised expectations on what Galassi already knew was an ambitious, game-changing second novel.

Eugenides prefers to hold off on seeking a contract until a book is finished, but about halfway through *Middlesex,* he ran out of money. He submitted it to Galassi in the late nineties, around the time of Franzen's deal. With the help of a six-figure advance and a couple of grants, he moved to Germany and barreled through two separate versions. One was told largely in the third person, with excursions into fictional anthropology and a subplot wherein his hermaphrodite protagonist, Cal (née Calliope) Stephanides, suffers not just from 5-alpha-reductase deficiency but also from a rare form of cancer. Galassi's instinct, as with *Presumed Innocent,* was to go with the simpler version—to stick with the first person, and cut out the cancer. Franzen also saw both manuscripts, and he preferred the more complicated story. Eugenides went with his editor's advice, and never regretted it.

Even the simpler *Middlesex* goes for broke, depicting the 1922 fall of the Turkish-Greek Smyrna, the sixties Detroit riots, and the sterility of seventies Grosse Pointe from a preternaturally omniscient, androgynous point of view. But it might not have come in for such heavy marketing were it not for Eugenides's successful friend. "We were riding this Franzen thing," says Peter Miller. "We wanted to be able to replicate what we had done"—the high-quality review copies at BookExpo, the plum catalog placement, the carefully structured book tour. "This was more self-conscious, I think," than the Franzen push. The result, though, seemed almost as organic: ample international attention at the London Book Fair; raves from rival publishers at the BookExpo; and the critical consensus that the nine-year wait since *The Virgin Suicides* had been well worth it.

Eugenides was almost as ambivalent as Franzen about modes of promotion. "I hear these horror stories from other writers about the things that these other publishers are making them do—putting duties on them," says Eugenides. Seroy, with whom he became close, honored his desire not to have blurbs on any of his books. Whether or not such conditions dampened sales, the hardcover sold fewer than one hundred thousand copies, according to Bookscan, which covers about three-quarters of total sales.

As it happened, FSG got to test out Buckley's proposition that a Pulitzer meant more than an Oprah pick. *The Corrections* had been a Pulitzer finalist but lost to Richard Russo's *Empire Falls* (though it did win the National Book Award). The following year's prize went to *Middlesex*. The paperback that came out that September, marked not with Oprah's poker chip but with the "corporate branding" of the Pulitzer seal, sold well over a million copies. Eugenides belatedly surpassed his friend. And when Oprah picked *Middlesex* for the book club in 2007, nearly another million were sold. In contrast to *The Virgin Suicides,* this time paperback sales stayed within the company. Thanks to Holtzbrinck's consolidation, FSG fiction hardcovers now went to the company's Picador imprint in paperback. After fifty-plus years of Roger's licensing machinations, Farrar, Straus no longer had its independence, but it finally had a paperback partner.

Within a space of two years, Franzen and Eugenides, Galassi's big discoveries, had become the Wolfe and Turow of the aughts—with better sales and stronger reviews. Just as the reins were being handed over from Straus to Galassi, FSG's new leader proved that he could hold his own doing what had always mattered most at the house:

cultivating the most important writers of the decade and, in so doing, keeping the ship afloat.

In a way, the company's big disappointment the following year, Tom Wolfe's 2004 novel *I Am Charlotte Simmons,* only ratified the changing of the guard. Wolfe's previous novel, *A Man in Full,* had tackled race, wealth, and real estate in Atlanta in grand, panoramic style, earning mixed reviews but robust business. Six years later, *I Am Charlotte Simmons* failed to meet outsize expectations and was being lampooned by critics. Jacob Weisberg, in the *Times,* summarized the problem a little callously in the first sentence of his review: "It's hard to imagine a tougher assignment for an aging journalist than explaining undergraduate life at a big American university." Weisberg gave it a failing grade.

The previous year, Carlos Fuentes had dealt his publisher and friend a grievous blow, defecting to sign a two-book contract with Random House. "I thought that there were other opportunities," Fuentes explained to me before his death, "that perhaps in a very difficult way Roger and I had become too close as friends." Roger had been gracious in public: "I don't blame him. I think he probably needs a shot in the arm and figures he can't get it from us." Privately he told friends, "Carlos wanted something we couldn't give him—his youth." According to Wolfe's harsher critics, he, too, had tried to get his youth back. In failing, he'd cost FSG lots of money. He had moaned for years about bending over backward for Roger; now FSG was the gracious benefactor. The half million copies they sold probably paid off about half of Wolfe's $5 million advance. Roger and Tom's mutual allegiance—two egos beating as one—had overcome resentments on both sides. But someone else was in charge now.

Fittingly, it took another Galassi author, Thomas Friedman, to help FSG recover the following year. The aptly global success of *The World Is Flat* was actually owed largely to Friedman's editor, Paul Elie. Like every publisher who also acquired books, Galassi delegated some of his editing to assistants. When those assistants became editors, they were first in line for the manuscripts he acquired. It soon became a commonplace assumption that, as a typical alum's complaint goes, "the only way you could move up in the company was if you [started out as] Jonathan's assistant. Otherwise, you had to go elsewhere."

To be fair, Galassi's assistants tended to have more experience, and were often hired as assistant editors rather than editorial assistants. Paul Elie seemed fated to become an FSG editor. He wrote a paper on John McPhee in high school, where he also devoured Tom Wolfe's prose and Seamus Heaney's poetry. At Fordham University, a Jesuit priest gave him Flannery O'Connor's *Complete Stories*. "I thought Flannery was a man," says Elie. "But then I read Giroux's introduction and her world was visibly opened to me. Then he compared her to Thomas Merton, and then I was off," following the trail of Giroux's Catholic thinkers. After coming to FSG, he became the company's liaison to the retired Giroux. In 2003 he also became a Farrar, Straus author, with *The Life You Save May Be Your Own*. Informed by chats with Giroux and Straus, and edited by Galassi, the perceptive chronicle of America's midcentury Catholic moment focuses on four writers, three of whom were Giroux authors: Merton, Percy, and O'Connor.

Elie's greatest value to the house, however, lay in his talent as a structural engineer of nonfiction. Like Giroux, he was quiet, tightly wound, and punctilious, but he specialized in the timelier, more journalistic material on which FSG had always been a little soft. Thomas Friedman, a Pulitzer Prize–winning journalist, crafted attractive center-left theories on world affairs, but as a long-running *New York Times* columnist he was prone to the redundancies and rhetorical excesses of the 1,200-word format. "Streamlining the architecture of the book was my role," Elie says, "and figuring out how to integrate all the new material that he hit upon along the way so that it didn't capsize the boat."

No sooner would Friedman submit an argument than he'd think of three more examples that altered its course, deadlines be damned. Unlike Giroux, though, Elie had to worry about timeliness. *The Lexus and the Olive Tree*, Friedman's 1999 book calling for nations to tread carefully on the path to globalization, was taut, accessible, and widely read. *The World Is Flat*, set for 2005, was even more ambitious—and more closely pegged to world events. It was also a less subtle argument, which was probably to its benefit as a popular work in the age of consultant-theorists such as Malcolm Gladwell. Like Giroux, Elie is no number cruncher; he claims to have no idea how many copies Friedman's books have sold. But when he ran into Galassi in the narrow hallways, he ventured a guess. "'I think this will be as big as *The Lexus and the Olive Tree*,'" Elie remembers telling him. "And he said, 'Way bigger.'"

Friedman came down to Union Square the week before his book deadline. In marathon sessions, he and Elie sat side by side with dueling laptops, e-mailing each other chunks of argument and metaphor and aphorisms until they coalesced into one very long but persuasive argument. All other projects gave way when Friedman strode into the office, a latter-day Susan Sontag with a very different sensibility. (In later years, following a backlash against Friedman's breezy swagger and easy conclusions, assistants would mockingly announce his approach, using a popular media nickname: "The Mustache of Understanding is coming!")

The World Is Flat sold more than 1.5 million copies in hardcover alone, without counting two revised editions in subsequent years. It became the Bible of a certain class of businessmen and consultants— and probably the bestselling book in FSG history aside from Elie Wiesel's *Night*. Friedman knew perfectly well that he was top dog among FSG's midlist toilers. Hyperaware of his Amazon sales rank, he demanded that the sales team put an extra focus on shifting books there, even as they struggled to keep brick-and-mortar bookstores freshly supplied. Once, when Galassi was unavailable to take his call, he railed at the publisher's assistant, "Do you know who I am? I'm Tom fucking Friedman, and I pay your fucking salary!" The size of the authorial ego was hardly unprecedented at Farrar, Straus; the source of its inflation, the almighty royalty statement, was more unusual.

Of course, what Friedman said was true. A different former FSG assistant, Charles Battle, remembers involuntarily giving up his workspace so that Friedman could sit there and work. "It was understood that if he was coming into the office you would go work in the conference room. And then *The World Is Flat* came out and it was huge, one of those books that allowed us to do more poetry." If the book's sales were unprecedented, this equation was not. Three decades after Roger Straus had patiently explained to A. J. Heschel's daughter that Gayelord Hauser had subsidized her father's work, Jonathan Galassi understood all too well the value of ministering to a more sophisticated kind of guru, one who hawked windmills and microloans instead of yogurt and blackstrap molasses.

Still, both poetry and bestsellers are harder to publish today than in the days of Hauser. Even with corporate backing, Galassi—whose duties include the position of poetry editor—had to work harder at it. Where Roger had published Harry Truman for peanuts (and barely broken even), Jonathan was forced, in 2000, to bid up to $8 million for Hillary Clinton's memoir. Rebecca Saletan, who headed up the FSG imprint North Point Press, had come over from Simon & Schuster, where she had edited Clinton's It Takes a Village (and also Dear Socks, Dear Buddy: Kids' Letters to the First Pets). Hillary was interested in FSG—for the right price. John Sargent approved the rare sum. Then the first lady used the offer to bid up Simon & Schuster. She preferred their publicity team and (perhaps reasonably) considered it more important than the right editor. Roger's old nemeses at S&S got Living History for just a little over FSG's price.

Even if Galassi didn't want to play on the multimillion-dollar field very often, he could certainly afford to think more commercially. There were genres that FSG could publish well without bankrupting itself: women's fiction, brainy thrillers, popular sociology. If these weren't quite the books Giroux adored, neither did they fit his definition of "ooks" (not quite books). Done well, they could still respect FSG's lofty mission, which had proved key to its survival, while also easing Galassi's concern, expressed to one editor, that the place still felt too "Ivory Towery"—too disconnected from twenty-first-century culture. FSG had never been the "thin Knopf," that phrase Roger had thrown back in Mary McCarthy's face. But now that it was a subsidiary, drawing on a parent company's coffers, couldn't it be the better Knopf? Which was to say, a self-sustaining division that published the best of everything, rather than only the mostly male stars of Franzen's so-called high-art literary tradition?

Galassi had something like this on his mind when he dialed Sarah Crichton's home number in the spring of 2004. As the publisher of Little, Brown in the nineties, Crichton had aggressively acquired intelligent commercial books. She signed up Alice Sebold's *The Lovely Bones* for more than $200,000 and Malcolm Gladwell's *The Tipping Point* for $1.7 million—both purchases that looked silly at the time. "People thought I was crazy," she says. "I don't look so crazy now." Nonetheless, she was pushed out in the heat of the Time Warner merger with AOL, another pawn in the endless corporate chess game. In the intervening four years, she'd been ghostwriting and coauthoring books, most notably *A Mighty Heart*, by the widow of murdered *Wall Street Journal* reporter Daniel Pearl.

Galassi didn't waste any time on the phone. "Do you ever think about going back into publishing?" he asked her. "Only for someone like you," she said. They met a half hour later at Bar Tabac, a restaurant near both of their homes in brownstone Brooklyn. There, he asked her another simple question: "If you had an imprint, what would you do?" She told him she would acquire the books she loved— or at least the ones that could fit in well alongside FSG's main list. A week later they met for lunch near Union Square, she agreed to far less than her asking salary, and they went back to Galassi's office and wrote up a press release.

Galassi didn't give her any marching orders about what to acquire for Sarah Crichton Books—except for telling her once (shades of Alfred Harcourt's advice to Robert Giroux) that she should never buy a book she didn't like just because it would make money. "I felt liberated to turn down things that didn't interest me," she says, adding that she, in turn, "gave FSG a chance to go into certain genres they don't do very comfortably."

Crichton's warmth and extroversion stood out immediately in the rarefied air of Farrar, Straus. "Some of the women—and a lot of the dudes—were soft-spoken and very serious," says a former editor. "Sarah had a different flavor. Instead of writing an e-mail, she would go downstairs and talk face-to-face. It worked because she was totally new." She was also, in the tradition of editors with imprints, as much a publisher as an editor—to some extent her own marketer and jacket designer and advertiser. And she pushed further on all those fronts than the bare-bones marketing team at FSG—Jeff Seroy (who runs both marketing and publicity) and two others.

Crichton began developing thrillers, book club–friendly women's fiction by authors such as Cathleen Schine, and some nonfiction straddling the line between big ideas and big advice. Not too many were hits, but she made one brilliant buy, paying $50,000 for the baggy five-hundred-page diary of a former child soldier from Sierra Leone. Ishmael Beah had been torn from his family at age thirteen and coerced into committing atrocities, before being rescued by UNICEF and placed in a New York foster home, then graduating from Oberlin College. Now an affable twentysomething, he could put an approachable face on a horrific story. Crichton saw its commercial potential from the start. Having started her career as a *Newsweek* editor, she favored the type of book that had what others call "a hook"—something the media could latch on to, turn into news. "I really felt that this was a big story that was about to explode," she says.

Crichton approached it as a marketer would. Breaching the wall between Union Square and Holtzbrinck's headquarters in the Flatiron Building, she put in a call to Peter Janssen, Holtzbrinck's head of academic marketing, to ask how it might fare with students. He advised her to cut the book down to two hundred pages—not to accommodate short attention spans but to ensure it would be assigned in classes. None of this was contrary to Beah's desires. "Often the FSG sensibility is that the book belongs to the author," says Crichton, "and sometimes I think they probably do that too much. In my case, Ishmael wanted a lot of these stories in, but ultimately he wanted the book to be read by kids." Together they whittled it to 240 pages.

Beah was much more resistant to her bold proposal of slapping his photo on the cover. They compromised on a back-cover shot. But it wasn't just Beah she had to deal with; FSG's first cover designs reflected the darkness and sobriety of the subject matter. "The early jackets were all very scary, literary," she says. She rejected them. "I spent money to have him photographed looking very handsome and cheery, because I didn't want a black-and-white scary-looking book . . . It was important that people would feel for him and like him."

It came out looking not very much like an FSG book, a dissonance that only grew after Starbucks decided to sell it nationwide, right alongside its Frappuccinos and Kenny G CDs. It was only the chain's second pick, after Mitch Albom's *For One More Day.* If Starbucks' sales were a drop in the bucket for Albom's book, they made a huge difference for Beah. The friendly packaging helped, of course, as did the slim format. Now the book is read not only in high schools but in some junior high schools. It's closing in, Crichton estimates, on two million copies sold.

Unsurprisingly, another company soon made Crichton a job offer she found hard to refuse. She took it to Galassi, who, in lieu of a decent counteroffer, reminded her of the culture they'd both left behind. "You take that job," she remembers him telling her, "and you can make a lot of money for five years. And in five years, they're gonna really want to see what you've done with that money, and they'll probably let you go. And then you'll wind up in your early sixties looking for another job. I really like working with you, and I can see us working side by side for the next twenty-five years. And you can keep doing the books that you care about." It was the Roger Straus discount, retooled by a new publisher for a new generation. Crichton stayed.

Ishmael Beah's success, and Sarah Crichton's, were roundly cheered in-house. But Farrar, Straus was still largely motivated by those prizes on the wall; by seeking front-page reviews rather than full-page ads; by chasing Nobel medals instead of Oprah poker chips. There was still, in FSG's DNA, a remnant of Roger Straus's notion that the best thing one could do for a book was to get Edmund Wilson to talk about it at a party. Fifty years later, word-of-mouth was still an indispensable currency in book publishing, even—or perhaps especially—during a decade in which "social media" and "discovery" went from buzzwords to full-blown corporate job descriptions at every publishing house.

No one at FSG understood the social side of Roger's publishing instincts better than Lorin Stein. Another former Galassi assistant, Stein was a talented line editor. He worked on the smallest details of Franzen's manuscripts, inserting wry comments such as a warning against dated slang: "The way of the 'dog' is a dangerous one." He convinced Richard Price, a master of the literary thriller, to throw out three hundred meandering pages of his polyphonous novel *Lush Life*. Stein also prized foreign literature, acquiring books on his travels to Paris and sometimes translating them himself. He championed younger writers who were on the verge of breaking through to greater renown, including Sam Lipsyte, Clancy Martin, and John Jeremiah Sullivan.

But in the spirit of Roger Straus, he was known even more, both inside and outside FSG, for his persona. He cut a tapered, aquiline figure, favoring J. Press ties, tailored Lord Willy's shirts, Clarks, and too-tight corduroys. He smoked Nat Shermans and rode a vintage cruising bicycle. He would pause frequently in speech, either to refocus his aperçus or to allow the listener a moment to absorb the full weight of his pensive expression. He melded Roger's flair, Giroux's editorial care, and maybe even a little of Farrar's flushed abstraction. Rumors of sexual indiscretions reinforced the notion that he was a man after Roger's sleazy-chic heart. It almost didn't matter that the books he personally acquired had yet to make a large impact. Resentment of his tender age, his closeness to Galassi, and his tendency to take credit only burnished his image. It wasn't surprising that, when he finally left FSG, it would be to follow in George Plimpton's footsteps as editor of *The Paris Review.* He understood viscerally the soft powers of charisma, flattery, and persuasion.

What this translated to in concrete terms was a talent for building Roger-style literary buzz. His greatest accomplishment in that regard was helping to turn a dead Latin American novelist into a posthumous celebrity. Chilean-born author Roberto Bolaño had been published to wide acclaim in Spain, where he'd eventually settled, before dying of liver disease in 2003. It was around that time that English speakers started catching on. His shorter work was acquired by New Directions, the still-independent literary press that had picked up so many

authors just before Giroux could get to them. But when it came time
to publish his longer fiction, Bolaño's estate approached Farrar, Straus
and Giroux, one of the few houses with both the literary clout and the
corporate dollars to break out an author as wild and challenging—and
as unavailable for interviews—as Bolaño.

Stein had read some of those New Directions translations. Galassi,
on a tip from Susan Sontag, had read *The Savage Detectives* in an Italian
translation and loved it. What wasn't to love about a novel spanning
six hundred pages, twenty years, five dialects, and more than forty nar-
rators, featuring a roving group of Mexican poets calling themselves
Visceral Realists? Stein told the book's translator, Natasha Wimmer,
"I felt more alive reading it than I felt when I went out and lived my
life." Moreover, Bolaño had the international dissident pedigree that
Roger Straus was always after. He'd been arrested by Pinochet in the
same coup that embroiled Pablo Neruda while he was finishing his
memoir for FSG. Bolaño could lay a credible claim to defining the
post-Boom style of Latin American literature, an escape hatch out of
magical realism and into a playful but meaty postmodernism. He was
the perfect Farrar, Straus author, and Stein was determined to make
him a sensation.

From the beginning, the author himself was sold as the story: foreign but approachable, a highbrow outlaw, brimming with punk allure
and snob appeal. The flap copy of *The Savage Detectives* forsook plot
summary for a more general statement about Bolaño's style. Three
thousand advance copies were sent to reviewers along with a lengthy
biographical essay written by the translator. "The basic idea," Stein
explains, "is that the copy had to be more sophisticated, longer, less
about salesmanship and more about giving the press information that
they could use to build articles." In a sense, Stein and the translator
were too successful; so many journalists lifted details from that essay
that Wimmer's erroneous assumption that Bolaño had been a heroin
addict was repeated in *The Economist, The New York Times Book Review,*
and *The New Yorker.*

The Savage Detectives went on to sell roughly 40,000 hardcover copies and 140,000 in paperback. But the next novel looked to be a harder

sell: *2666* was more than nine hundred pages long. It felt even longer, with five loosely connected parts revolving around a series of brutal murders based on an actual crime wave in Juárez, Mexico. Bolaño had not quite smoothed it out before he died. Stein worried that critics would dismiss it as the baggier, less readable stepchild of *The Savage Detectives*. So he wrote a long editor's letter with the galleys, arguing that its value lay precisely in its difficulty. It was a monument, an event. Even the format of the published editions was monumental. Simultaneously with the hardback, whose jacket featured Symbolist painter Gustave Moreau's *Jupiter and Semele*, FSG put out a thirty-dollar set of three paperbacks in a cardboard slipcase.

Following the release of the first Amazon Kindle, publishers had recently begun to take e-books seriously. Would they render the book-as-object obsolete? Some publishers argued that even if they did, there would still be room for the collectible book, an objet d'art akin to the limited-edition vinyl record. That could certainly be said of *2666*. Stein used another new format, Facebook, to promote a very old-fashioned publishing phenomenon, the launch party. The Facebook group "Waiting for *2666*" gained three hundred followers (which was respectable in 2008). It wasn't quite the revival of Herman Melville, but it was still a lot of attention for a dead foreigner. Those fans and more came to the launch in an East Village club, resulting in a mad, chaotic crush inside and a long, snaking line outside—an organizational nightmare. Not since FSG's fiftieth anniversary had the house dealt with so many gate-crashers. The madness was so surprising that Britain's *Economist* wrote a glowing story about it, headlined BOLAÑO-MANIA. Stein credits the article with jump-starting the author's sales in the UK. Back home, the book did even better than *The Savage Detectives*.

The chorus of critical praise was so overwhelming that prizes would have almost been redundant. But awards could still have a big impact on FSG's smaller books. The same year *The Savage Detectives* was published, three novels in which Stein had a hand were nominated for the National Book Award. It was the first time the house scored three fiction nominees since 1967, the year Malamud's *The Fixer* won—and this time there were only five finalists in the category, instead of six. Measured by the numbers Roger cared about most, his house was as successful in the attention-deficient aughts as it had been in the fog and ferment of the late sixties.

One of these finalists was *Tree of Smoke*, by Denis Johnson. Galassi had edited the author's famous collection *Jesus' Son*, eleven linked stories narrated by a drifter named Fuckhead, which spawned a thousand slacker poets and, arguably, a revival of gritty regionalism. FSG had given Johnson a ten-thousand-dollar advance for the collection, just enough to pay off his taxes, but for his next novel, *Already Dead*, he'd gone to HarperCollins. Now he was back at Farrar, Straus with an opus on Vietnam, which went on to take home the National Book Award.

Lydia Davis was another nominee—for her story collection *Varieties of Disturbance*—and another Galassi author. (After his Random House bosses had refused to let him publish Davis in the eighties, he'd sent her to Pat Strachan at FSG.) But the third FSG finalist, Mischa Berlinski's *Fieldwork*, was a Lorin Stein acquisition. A light-footed romp into postmodern storytelling spun by expats in Thailand, it was an in-house favorite that received meticulous editing. It was also awarded a rather backhanded endorsement from Stephen King that highlighted just how much Farrar, Straus's notion of marketing still diverges from the industry standard.

King has a column in *Entertainment Weekly* and often writes about books there. He happened upon *Fieldwork* in a bookstore and loved it, but he couldn't get over how close he'd come to passing it by in the store. So King titled one of his columns "How to Bury a Book." *Fieldwork*, he wrote, was a "great story" hidden behind a "drab title and a drab cover." He went on to say that "publishing houses have two faces. In the case of FSG, Jekyll belongs to the distinguished company that has published such award-winning novels as *Gilead*, *The Great Fire*, and *The Corrections*. Hyde is the side which seems to proclaim 'Don't read this, it's too smart for the likes of you.' Look at the covers. *Gilead*'s is a turquoise smear. *The Great Fire*'s is a red smear. And *Fieldwork*'s cover is a green smear (probably jungle) and a gray smear (probably sky). It communicates nothing."

FSG never responded to the criticism. "In hindsight," Stein says now, "I would agree that we didn't find the right jacket. But it wasn't a matter of being snooty, or trying to make the book look 'literary,' or anything like that. We just didn't quite nail it."

Farrar, Straus's philosophical approach to sales—compounded by its small budgets—is a persistent point of contrast, and often complaint, among those who no longer work there. One former editor recalls his first series of meetings at the conglomerate to which he moved: "The most amazing thing in the world was looking at figures and realizing that, with the same type of book as FSG, we were capable of getting out three times as many copies." Jeff Seroy hotly disputes that impression as "opinion masquerading as fact." But even current staff members regard Farrar, Straus sales head Spenser Lee as incredibly conservative in sales projections. In many cases, that protects the house from dangerously high returns. But sometimes low expectations have a way of fulfilling themselves.

Thomas LeBien, who headed Hill & Wang for much of the aughts, brought to the historical-academic imprint a strong head for numbers and a keen sense of what would and wouldn't work. He realized, for example, that there was a niche for graphic books aimed at schools—the market Peter Janssen knew so well. With Galassi's quick approval, he developed a line of educational comics that grabbed a measure of attention beyond that market—especially an illustrated version of the 9/11 Commission Report that sold close to a hundred thousand copies. But in 2011 LeBien left for Simon & Schuster—partly, he says, because it knows how to sell his style of nonfiction.

"A kind of book that I adore is serious, big-sweep history by an academic author," says LeBien, "and those books are increasingly hard to publish well. The publisher has to have a really robust commitment to marketing, and marketing was always a distant second to publicity at FSG. They still benefit tremendously from a review-driven publishing model, but if you ever discover that that model isn't working for a title, what do you do?"

Jeff Seroy responds to critics with defensive pride. His staff markets plenty, he says; they just don't trumpet it to booksellers the way others do. "I personally feel that an understated approach to marketing is the appropriate one for us," he says. FSG's marketing budget is a comparatively tiny $1 million per year. "We've always published books that bring news to the world, and that's a matter of elbow grease, not a matter of how much we spend," he says. "We do the best we can with the resources we have."

Unlike larger publishers, FSG editors rarely acquire books with marketing already in mind. Galassi remembers Knopf's Bob Gottlieb saying there were two ways of publishing: "You can publish what you think people want to read, and follow public taste, or you can publish what you think is valuable and try to bring readers to it. We're in the second camp, and it involves a different kind of effort."

Sarah Crichton does sometimes think about marketing before she buys a book, and she acknowledges the trade-offs. "Sometimes I will have books that I feel have real potential marketability," she says, "and at another house you might get more financial push behind those books. But then you're trapped in a different system." She prefers the system at FSG. "It's actually moving to be in these meetings where people spend just as much time talking about a thousand-page Hungarian novel as they'll spend talking about some clear bestseller. And they'll assign their best publicists to it."

At FSG, in other words, the world is (relatively) flat. It's been a long time since Stephen King had to compete for a publisher's attention. He should consider the alternative for Mischa Berlinski at a larger house: either not being published at all, or being published and completely ignored. At least at FSG, Berlinski had careful editing and enough of a push to get him on the radar of the National Book Foundation—and Stephen King. Besides, the sales bump from King's column was minuscule. The vast majority of copies were sold in paperback, after the National Book Award nomination.

In any case, if there were editors who truly didn't care about finding readers, the editor of *Fieldwork* wasn't one of them. In response to an article in *Harper's* by Ursula Le Guin arguing that it might be time for highbrow publishers to give up on trying to reach the unreachable, Stein sent in a sharp letter. "When it comes to reading, there is no us or them," he wrote. "Without a critical mass of readers, you don't have a reading culture . . . Fewer readers means lower stakes, lower standards, and more crap getting passed off as the real thing."

For years, Stein toyed with an idea to start a website-cum-book-club that, combined with regular readings, would help form a community of fans for FSG's books. It was a modern version of the age-old dream: to make a publishing house as recognizable a brand as a soda company (or, more aptly, a hip indie record label). Over a drink at a bar near the Flatiron Building, he discussed the idea with Ryan Chapman, a young publishing marketer at Macmillan with a keen interest in online promotion. (Holtzbrinck's U.S. branch was renamed Macmillan in 2007.) Chapman would soon move over to FSG and design a scaled-back version of Stein's dream site. But at this point, he warned Stein that Macmillan would never go for something unless it could be applied across the entire company. "I was so wired to think of scalability," Chapman says now. "At the time, I just didn't get that it would work really well for FSG." Stein eventually dropped the book-club plan. What stymied Stein's experiment wasn't FSG's stinginess or stodginess, but Macmillan's corporate conservatism: a one-size-fits-all culture that shortchanged the power of its own best brand.

But one element of Stein's plan survived, and it went back to what had always worked for FSG: the unique frisson of a smoky, sweaty, overcrowded book party. After that triumphant 2007 National Book Awards ceremony, Lorin Stein and his peers convened at an old haunt freighted with meaning: the Russian Samovar. The former hangout of Joseph Brodsky, Susan Sontag, and Derek Walcott was conveniently close to the Times Square hotel where the awards dinner had taken place. Sitting around and schmoozing with his writers and colleagues, Stein remembered the parties Roger used to throw there. On the day in 2001 when he'd been promoted to assistant editor, there was a party at the Samovar for Susan Sontag's collection *Where the Stress Falls.* (Her second novel, *In America,* had won the previous year's National Book Award—a major fiction prize at last.) Stein was downstairs, "at the kids' table," with the rest of the assistants, when Sontag came down to say hello. She stayed for hours, smoking and drinking vodka with the underlings under a tasseled red lamp. Characteristically, she took credit for Stein's promotion.

Reminiscing about that red-letter day seven years later, Stein got an idea of how to salvage the live part of his book-club scheme. Years ago, there'd been a reading series at the Samovar. Why not revive it, but this time as an all-FSG event? Pair two writers a night, throw in some music, maybe charge five dollars to cover expenses if Macmillan was going to be chintzy about it. It would be fun, it would be enlightening, and it might give readers the idea that FSG was a hip brand, a hot house once more.

The FSG Reading Series was up and running in a matter of weeks. The first event, on January 17, 2008, featured strange bookfellows, Richard Price and comic-slacker Sam Lipsyte. Naturally, Stein invited Peggy Miller. "I said I would only do it if we had something to eat first," says Miller. "So we had dumplings." Owner Roman Kaplan came by and "kissed the hand and we hugged and we kissed and the whole business." Then they went upstairs and found a very familiar scene. Assorted slender literati milled around. In an adjoining dining room whose banquet table would soon groan with black bread and lox, a couple of nostalgic scofflaws defied the ban on indoor smoking. The milieu was unchanged, from the smoke and vodka to the high-flown conversation. But the crowd, to Peggy, was not.

"Lorin is always very sweet," she says. "He made a little speech." Stein introduced his "special guest," the living soul of FSG, and recited Alexander Blok's poem "To Anna Akhmatova" in her honor. Peggy was touched, but it was an awkward evening. "I was older than everybody in the room, as you could imagine. I sat next to someone from Farrar, Straus, whom I didn't know, and who couldn't care less. The room was full of assistants, all these young kids. They move around like gypsies, nobody stays longer than a year at these places." She didn't stay for the lox. "It was a lovely evening and when it was over I left and didn't hang around." What was the point in lingering? Roger was gone.

16

Change

Around the corner from 19 Union Square West, just up 16th Street from the park, is a restaurant as deeply indebted to Roger Straus, and as beloved by him, as FSG itself. The Union Square Cafe had been open only a week or two when Straus and Peggy Miller first strolled in. It was October 1985, and Roger was feeling reborn. He'd recently kicked cancer and his son was back at Farrar, Straus. The Purchase house had been rebuilt, and so had Union Square—bushwhacked and landscaped, drug addicts replaced by the colorful produce of a farmers' market, the subway station (Henry Robbins's last sorry sight) given a face-lift. Klein's, the department store where Rose Wachtel had hunted for pencils, was being replaced by a sleek complex of condos. And here was a promising new bistro on the former site of Brownie's, a health-food store that had once sold Gayelord Hauser's diet books. One lunch break, Roger and Peggy decided to investigate. Inside was the young midwestern owner, Danny Meyer, all smiles and handshakes.

Their lunch that day was the first of thousands Roger would eat at the Union Square Cafe—a record number, by Meyer's reckoning—virtually all of them at table 38, the large corner berth he and Peggy quickly secured. His early patronage turned it gradually into a publishing rite of passage, a lower-key rival to midtown power hubs like Michael's. Every weekday, over seared sea scallops fresh from the farmers' market, the restaurant thrums with kibitzing agents, effusive pitches to book critics, gossipy stage whispers about adulterous novelists. It's soft-power lunch for publishers in their prime, as it was for Roger Straus for so many years.

From the vantage point of that far table, it might as well have been staged for Roger's private entertainment. Lunching on oysters or smoked steak sandwiches and sipping his specially stocked port, Graham's Six Grapes, Roger had his back to the wall and his eyes on the whole room—the better to hail his friends and mutter curses just out of earshot of his enemies. Whenever Meyer was there, which he usually was, Roger would enlist him in the spectacle, as though he were a featured player instead of the owner of the theater. With the clowning gestures of a shadow boxer, Straus would beckon Meyer from across the room. Then he'd "take me by the arm," Meyer says, "and point to some son of a bitch in the dining room and ask me if I knew about him." He'd josh Meyer a little about the menu: "The only reason I'm not here thirty days a month is that you don't make oyster stew, which they do at the Grand Central Oyster Bar." Then he'd pull Meyer close and tell him, just a little too loudly, "how tired I looked, or that I needed a haircut, or that my suit was particularly nice today."

Straus squired Brodsky and Walcott and Sontag into the Cafe as though he were hosting a banquet at the Russian Tea Room or the old '21.' But he was just as solicitous to the awestruck underlings he'd sometimes bring along, teaching them more over their heirloom tomatoes than they ever learned at their desks. He taught Meyer, by example, one of the tenets of his famous hospitality credo: "management by walking around."

Roughly two decades and three thousand Roger Straus lunches

after their first auspicious meeting, Meyer was running a small empire of restaurants, including the fancier Gramercy Tavern and the sleeker Eleven Madison Park. But he usually arranged to walk around his old flagship at noon, imbibing the bookish bonhomie and looking out for Customer Number One. At the beginning of 2004, Jonathan Galassi, by now the usual denizen of table 38, passed along the sad news that his predecessor was in and out of the hospital. Several times, Meyer offered to send over Roger's favorite foods—the *vitello tonnato,* the oyster stew, or even an omelet or a black bean soup. But Roger declined. As Meyer would later write, "His habits were no longer providing him with much comfort, and few of us could conjure fresh ways to bring him pleasure."

Roger had spent his eighty-seventh birthday, January 3, at Lenox Hill Hospital, where he had a hip replaced. "He never really recovered after that," says Roger Straus III. That winter, he focused on staying out of the hospital and visiting the office as often as he could. "He had to walk with a cane, which he hated because he was humiliated—this alpha male," says editor Elisabeth Sifton. "He was always sick." One former assistant remembers seeing him for the second and last time, after a veteran in sales told him he should stop by the big office, tell the old man what a privilege it was to work there. It was March. Roger was at his desk, which was rare in those days when he could hardly rise from the chaise longue. He reared back his head and roared, "When I get better, we'll have a gossipy lunch!" The assistant calls it "one raindrop of an amazing thunderstorm of a personality that I was just lucky to collect."

Roger never did take him out for gossip and Graham's Six Grapes. But as he declined, and as his intermittent hospital stay became permanent, he kept insisting on one more lunch. It took on the flavor of a last request. And so, one day in late April, his wife and son came to the hospital, dressed him in his finery, and ferried him over for what Danny Meyer calls "an ill-advised final trip." Rog's daughters Laura and Rachel joined them there.

Re-creating an authentic Roger Straus lunch proved impossible. There were no editors, no writers, no Peggy. He couldn't even get down the five wooden steps to the usual corner table, so they settled for a café table beside the bar. At table 38, Roger had been protected and all-seeing. Here, beside the entrance and the picture window, he was on display, his family meal a sad tableau for every entering customer to see. Younger editors out for their first pappardelle might have wondered what to make of this elderly man, crisp shirt and sport jacket clashing with the liver spots and bruises that speckled his hands, sitting with people who were trying to overlook his pain and obvious lack of appetite. Older diners, friends and rivals of the elderly man holding quiet court, knew better.

No one at the table was enjoying or even noticing the food. There was a lot of small talk—"everyone trying to be cheerful," says Rog, "and overlook the obvious." Jonathan Galassi happened by, saw them through the window, and came in for a cursory exchange of greetings. It was the last time he would see his once-formidable predecessor and mentor. Rog doesn't remember any grand speeches. "Everyone was hoping for another lunch," he says. But Danny Meyer was also there, and he knew it was their final meeting. Later he recounted it vividly. "He managed a meek smile when I approached the table," Meyer remembered. "No jabbing at the air, without his trademark ascot, and looking gaunt. I leaned over, kissed him on his forehead, and in a voice loud enough that only two or three people at his table could hear it, I told him that he looked tired and was in sore need of a haircut. He looked at me with that wry smile for the last time and said, 'I love you too, baby.'"

Over the next few weeks at Lenox Hill, Rog did the best he could to keep the small talk flowing. "When I'd come over and see him," he says, "what he wanted to know about was publishing gossip." Rog, out of the business for a decade, "was a little out of the loop. So I would make shit up. And he'd be very grateful. Especially if it was about Simon & Schuster." Roger's painful decline ended, officially of pneumonia, on May 25, 2004.

Though his taste for gossip never abated, Roger had turned his attention in those final months to his family, where, as long as he breathed, he was still in charge. It was at the Purchase estate, Sarosca Farm, where they spent the last week of 2003, that Roger had the fall that led eventually to his death, and it was the estate on which he fixated. He had come up with a brilliant idea. Knowing that Rog didn't want the property, he would change his will to pass it straight to his granddaughters.

"There were various problems with that," says Rog, reasoning it out as he did with his father. "Living there together, unless you believe in *The Cherry Orchard,* would have been a sort of difficult proposition. And the expenses of running that place were supersonic."

Rog's daughter Laura says there was a little more to it than that. "There were some powwows about it and my dad was really upset," she remembers. "He said, 'You can't give the three of them that house and skip over me.' I was in complete agreement with my dad. And my sisters were a little less so. More like a lot less so. I didn't want to be part of that." She thought it would have been "a family ender."

It was another example of Roger making the same paternal mistakes that pained him in his youth. Just as Roger Sr. had done, Roger Jr. was threatening to leave his son out of the estate, the only valuable asset he had left. Of course, he was trying to salvage it rather than sell it. Finally, though, the old man relented. "At the very end of his life," says Rog, "he knew it was unrealistic."

Dorothea Straus sold Sarosca Farm three years after her husband died. In one of her last published reflections, addressed to her late husband, she described the property he'd fought so hard to keep in the family. "Our home is standing," she wrote, "where geraniums still beckon from the window boxes, but the demolition crew is approaching, and just as in Rembrandt's painting, *The Anatomy Lesson,* in which a cabal of doctors surround a corpse about to be dissected, with your death our house will be razed, its acres gouged and partitioned when only yesterday it had been alive with the years of our marriage."

During the disposition of Roger's will, the Purchase property was valued at $9.3 million, but developers bought it for roughly $8 million. With Sarosca sold, Dorothea spent her last summer in the 65th Street flat, which is where she died on July 25, 2008, at the age of ninety-one. The money in her estate was worked out to be a little over

$7 million—a figure that might have been impressive when Dorothea's first trust funds were drawn up in the thirties. An assessment of their personal property didn't turn up much. A Picasso once thought to be original turned out to be a copy worth $525. The most valuable effects, counted as a single item, were 1,660 books.

Dorothea was wrong about the manor house. Oscar Straus's pride and joy wasn't demolished; it was renovated. On a recent visit to what is now called Sarosca Farm Estates, the house was surrounded by half-finished custom-built homes for starter millionaires. The old mock Tudor looked almost too finished. The bricks and half timbers were scrubbed bright, the warm russet roof tiles replaced by clean blue slate. A Realtor showing the house pointed out all the "improvements": an open-plan cooking space instead of a cramped kitchen meant only for the help; a large master bath in place of his and hers toilets and sitting rooms. There was no trace of Oscar Straus's spirit in the "ghost room" where Isaac Singer once went lurking. "Can you believe they had the fireplace painted black?" a contractor asked the Realtor, who made a face. (Roger Straus III has a different opinion of the upgrade: "More Tony Soprano than Roger Straus.") But there were no major alterations to the structure. "We didn't touch it," said the contractor. "Except we got rid of the termites."

Over at 19 Union Square West, Jonathan Galassi did some "deferred maintenance" of his own. It was a faster and more thorough transformation than the work at Purchase, though also nobler and more sensitive. Whether it preserved the spirit of its Straus patriarch is an open, perhaps unanswerable question.

On the day Roger died, Jamaica Kincaid told Galassi, "You have to be the dad now." He proved a reluctant father but a swift manager. In late August, he fired his CFO, Philip Zweiger—who had worked ardently to protect FSG's autonomy in the early Holtzbrinck years—and appointed Andrew Mandel to the newly created position of deputy publisher. Whereas Rog, in much the same role, had labored to shore up FSG's self-sufficiency, Mandel's mandate was, as Galassi puts it, "to organize ourselves financially in line" with Holtzbrinck's American properties. "Roger had kept FSG as separate as possible from the group," Galassi says, "not always to the advantage of the company."

Mandel made profit-and-loss projections mandatory for every acquisition—something editors still need to be nagged about today. And he had to approve all but the very smallest purchases. Still, coming from little Workman Publishing, Mandel took seriously the job of defending the taste of the house. "I think he has the values of the company very much at heart," says Lorin Stein, who remembers that when the proposal came their way for *Battle Hymn of the Tiger Mother*, a paean to cartoonishly strict Chinese-style parenting, Mandel joked, "If we publish this, it will be like printing money—and I'll quit."

Galassi had called Sarah Crichton just a couple of days before Roger died, and announced her hiring just two weeks afterward. She and Mandel both started in September, the month of Roger's grand roast of a memorial at the 92nd Street Y. A few months later, Galassi took the Hill & Wang imprint away from Elisabeth Sifton, a once-formidable editor of nonfiction, and gave it to the younger, more numbers-minded Thomas LeBien. And he made another radical decision. He fired FSG's editor in chief.

When Galassi had ascended to publisher in 2002, he'd appointed John Glusman in his place. Over fifteen years at FSG, Glusman had shown a good deal of range—from prestige authors like Jim Crace and Richard Powers to science writer Laurie Garrett and would-be Nobelist Orhan Pamuk (though Pamuk had left for Knopf). Then, three months after Roger's death, Galassi took him to lunch at the Union Square Cafe and told him, "It's time for a change."

"He's a good editor," Galassi says now. "But he was just doing his books. He wasn't thinking globally, that's all"—not attending to books and authors he wasn't personally editing. "I just thought the job of editor in chief wasn't being properly used." Others agree that Glusman was too focused on his own work and not very engaged with the rest of the office—more in the mold of Michael di Capua than Henry Robbins. But they also describe his firing as "unceremonious."

Glusman blames his doomed tenure as editor in chief on Galassi's shortcomings as a boss. He says Galassi failed to delegate authority, hired people behind his back, and created a double line of reporting. "Jonathan essentially wanted to be both publisher and editor in chief," he says. Glusman, now the editor in chief of W. W. Norton, was given three months to wrap up his work—but little insight into why he was let go.

In his place, Galassi promoted Eric Chinski. Chinski was hired away from Houghton Mifflin in 2003; he failed to bring over his star author, Jonathan Safran Foer—both claim it was a contract issue— but he'd developed a promising stable of younger authors, including Rivka Galchen, John Wray, and Chris Adrian. Lately he's also had a run of big-idea nonfiction writers—akin to Malcolm Gladwell but with genuine expertise. Most notably, there was Alex Ross's eloquent, readable survey of classical music, *The Rest Is Noise,* and the recent surprise bestseller *Thinking, Fast and Slow,* by Nobel Prize–winning psychologist Daniel Kahneman. But Chinski is good at "thinking globally," too. One editor describes him as the kind of leader FSG hasn't always been lucky enough to have. "He's quite tough," says the editor. "But it comes naturally to him to be a caregiver and a mother hen."

Galassi's reshuffling served not only to assert his authority but also to build a bridge over the chasm left by Roger Straus. Roger's FSG *was,* in a sense, an antique spinning wheel, as that detractor had called it in the seventies—one that only Roger knew how to operate. Among his outdated devices were those wonderful circulating letters. In the era of cc'd e-mail, all that paperwork seemed unnecessary and wasteful, and shortly after Roger retired, Galassi had justifiably gotten rid of them. Yet they had served a real function, as a way for editors to communicate in the absence of meetings. So had Roger's seemingly casual office walkabouts.

Though she had never worked with Roger, Sarah Crichton noticed his absence from the day she got there. "They didn't really know how to share information," she remembers, "and I realized that's what Roger would do. He would go from office to office, and then, you know, connect the dots. You could see people trying to figure out how to do that . . . Every time you start a new job, people are always saying, 'That's not how we do things here.' And at FSG, it was, 'Well, Roger would say . . .' There was a very big force, being missed."

The memorial service at the 92nd Street Y was the last opportunity for FSG's editors and writers to express their collective sense of that void, right on through the evening afterparty at Roger's throwback hangout, the Lotos Club. Even author non grata Philip Roth attended. Tom Wolfe, in the closing speech of the afternoon, put that absence into keen prose. Roger had always felt, he said, like a "current running at top speed," pulling everyone else along. "I'm still waiting for the current to build up again. I'm waiting for something to give me the feeling of the exhilaration of life, the real joy of life, that Roger did, and quite aside from all his other accomplishments, I think that stands out as one of the greatest."

The current of their friendship had been more turbulent than he let on, but Wolfe's periodic threats to leave FSG had rarely been more than strategic bluffs. With Roger gone, though, nothing was holding him, and for his next novel, he finally did leave. To some observers, his departure for Little, Brown after more than four decades with one publisher was a big surprise. To others it was a foreseeable consequence of Roger's death, combined with the unusually dismal performance of *I Am Charlotte Simmons*. Galassi says that, in the wake of that disappointment, they simply couldn't agree on a price. "We went through a court dance," he says. "Everyone acted their part, and the result could have been predicted from the beginning."

Wolfe's version is, characteristically, magnanimous but slightly aggrieved. "In the Catholic Church you built up your bank account through some good works even if you've had terrible sins," he says. "Making a living as a writer is much more like Protestantism than Catholicism." In other words, FSG was too unforgiving of his great sin, one clunker of a novel, and too eager to overlook all the good work he'd done for the house. Perhaps Wolfe would have stayed with FSG if Galassi had paid the roughly $5 million his agent, Lynn Nesbit, requested. But Galassi's offer didn't even match Roger's in 1988.

According to Nesbit, his leaving had more to do with Wolfe's friend no longer being around. Little, Brown offered not only a $7 million advance and more marketing muscle, but also the services of his long-time editor, Pat Strachan, who'd returned to book publishing in 1992 after four years at *The New Yorker*. It was an utterly logical decision. He wasn't leaving Straus, he was leaving Galassi, whose reaction to the proposal for *Back to Blood,* his 2012 novel about Miami, wasn't exuberant. (Hardcover sales were indeed dismal.) And he was accomplishing something rare in modern publishing, a field in which editors shuttle through publishers and writers shuttle through editors: He was reuniting with an old friend.

Scott Turow had also spoken earnestly at the Y, though he seemed to be mourning the institution as much as the man. "I was Roger Straus's adoring fan," he said. "For me, becoming an FSG author was like making the All-Star Team." Perhaps the awe never quite went both ways, as it did between Roger and Tom. But Turow was forever linked with Wolfe as one of the two writers whose bestsellers transformed FSG in the eighties. So it's fitting that he, too, soon left an FSG transformed by Roger's departure.

Turow says his decision was based on noneditorial concerns. He was still tied to Warner Books for paperbacks, and he thought it made sense to give them the hardcover as well. And, after a couple of books that didn't do too well, he was looking for a reset with more aggressive marketing than FSG could handle. In fact, it was Rog's leadership, not his father's, that Turow missed most of all. "Roger Straus III understood the marketing and sales part of the business as well as anybody," Turow says, "and I don't think anybody has ever gotten Farrar, Straus up to the same level that Rog had them at. I'm sure many can disagree with me on that, but he just brought a lot of marketing savvy that Farrar, Straus had never prized."

Jonathan Galassi took these departures in stride. If anything, they reinforced the sense that a new generation needed new writers—Franzen, Eugenides, Friedman—and new editors—Chinski, Stein, and Sarah Crichton. Nothing could last forever, not even those homely halls of 19 Union Square West.

Early in 2005, CEO John Sargent asked Galassi if he wanted to move FSG into the Flatiron Building, a half mile north at 23rd Street.

There was still some empty space in the landmark flagship that held the other Holtzbrinck publishers. As it turned out, there wasn't quite enough room for FSG, but Sargent says the determining factor was Galassi's belief that the company should remain physically separate. That conviction was a little harder to justify as more and more FSG back-office functions—including much of the sales department—migrated into the Flatiron. Then again, the divide between editorial and sales, between the making and the selling of a book, had always been a point of pride. Why not reinforce it with a few city blocks of distance?

And then, after all that, FSG moved out anyway. When the lease on the old building came up at the end of 2007, the new rent was too high for Macmillan. Thanks to Danny Meyer, the nineties boom, and maybe even Roger Straus, Union Square had gone from a bazaar of bargains (*shmattes,* pencils, heroin) to a shopping hub for the upper-middle class. FSG decided to move into cheaper accommodations five blocks northwest, at 18 West 18th Street. The staff was dragooned into emptying out those navy surplus cabinets, boxing up those first editions, and sending off ancient contracts to the archives. Some departments were sent off to foster homes in the Flatiron Building while they waited for the new office to come online. Others continued to work among the empty shelves and dust bunnies.

Even old-timers smiled at the prospect of permanent hot water, coffee on demand, and bright, whitewashed walls. Galassi was philosophical: "You give up part of your identity, but as Judy Collins said, there is something lost and something gained." Peggy Miller gave it Roger Straus's posthumous seal of approval. "He would have moved," she told Galassi. "He wouldn't have spent money on something inessential, like rent."

If Isaac Bashevis Singer's spirit came around looking for other ghosts, he wouldn't find them at the new Farrar, Straus. As with the Purchase house, the new façade isn't so different from the old: a narrow stone factory loft, still a far cry from the midtown marble-and-glass atria that greet the editors of Random House, HarperCollins, and Simon & Schuster. The interior, though, is all clean lines and blond wood. The lighting is softer than the old blaring fluorescents, the aisles passable by two colleagues walking abreast.

There are nods to the old style, if only in the ersatz way that the sets on nostalgic TV shows like *Mad Men* resemble people's homes in the sixties. Importantly, books still line the halls and the conference rooms, reminding new arrivals of the legacies of Noonday and Sheila Cudahy, of oddball relics like Theodor Reik, Basil Heatter, and Francis the mule. But the shelves that now hold them look more like high-end IKEA constructions than industrial cabinets. Gladys Guggenheim's table is still there, in Galassi's spacious office, though it has a new finish. The rest of Galassi's furniture goes well with it: midcentury reproductions by Knoll—without the termites.

One last, irreplaceable departure was that of Peggy Miller. She visited the hospital on Roger's last day, but after his death, life became, as she might put it, a little awkward. At his funeral service in Temple Emanu-El, Peggy sat separately from the family. It was better, of course, than not being invited at all, especially after missing his last lunch at the Union Square Cafe. At least Roger had made a sort of accommodation. He left Peggy $100,000 in his will.

Galassi could afford to be more openly magnanimous. He recruited Peggy to help coordinate Roger's London memorial, which the two attended together at the end of June. The speakers were publishers Matthew Evans, Christopher MacLehose, and Ivan Nabokov; agent Deborah Rogers; and Seamus Heaney (who quoted Wordsworth: "all that mighty heart is lying still"). All but one of the speakers mentioned Peggy. Galassi told her she could stay at FSG as long as she liked. She was in her late seventies but still poised, sharp, and vital. She decided to remain in London for a couple of weeks, seeing friends, and then she went off to Zurich for a few days. The time away only strengthened her resolve to retire. "I haven't a moment's regret," she says.

When she returned, Galassi insisted that she wait before making it official. She could help with Roger's grand tribute in New York, followed by a service planned for Frankfurt. Galassi wanted her to accompany him to the 2004 book fair, one last time. "It won't be easy," she said, "but I'll go." At the Frankfurt memorial, every speaker mentioned Peggy by name, and Dorotea Bromberg, the Swedish publisher who shared Isaac Singer with FSG, devoted her entire speech to Miller. "I have known Roger for more than twenty-five years," she said, "and for me there has never been any Roger without a Peggy. Ninety-nine percent of the times I saw Roger, he was with Peggy. Of the remaining one percent, when I saw him without her, well, that one percent felt very impoverished."

There was something in Bromberg's words that felt like more than generosity, condolence, or pity. There was the sense that something of Roger survived in his faithful secretary, something that couldn't easily be put in boxes like "assistant," "companion," or "confidante." She complemented and completed the public Straus at least as much as Dorothea did in his private life. Danny Meyer recognized this, which is why there's a rule at the Union Square Cafe. If Peggy calls for a reservation before anyone else, including Jonathan Galassi, she gets table 38.

Now it's Jonathan who presides over the annual Frankfurt dinner at the Parkhotel. He hosted one in 2010, the year of a very pleasant surprise for the house he inherited. The buzz of the fair was multimedia ("Content knows no borders," the director announced), but in the Beaux Arts hotels down the boulevards it could have been 1966. Roger's friend Michael Krüger, who now runs Hanser Verlag, held a dinner in a back room of the Frankfurter Hof. Younger publishers congregated until 4:00 a.m. in the hotel's colonnaded courtyard, but the Hanser soirée was where Roger's sophisticated older peers broke bread and reminisced. There was Inge Feltrinelli, resplendent in an outfit the color of a rich orange sauce, squiring around the previous year's Nobel Prize winner, Herta Müller. And farther back was the publisher-intellectual Roberto Calasso, waxing rhapsodic on Roger's style: "He had a special collection of striped suits in different shades of color. It belonged to him totally. On other people it would be ridiculous." Here was Christopher MacLehose, who loved Roger "without reservation." Gian Arturo Ferrari, the sleek head of Mondadori, was a little cockier. "He was not a great publisher," said Ferrari, "but he was a great man."

The attendees commented on how delighted Roger would have been with that year's Nobel Prize winner. Following the astonishing run of Nobel victories that culminated in Seamus Heaney's award in 1995, FSG had gone fifteen years without a prize. That dry spell was broken on October 7, 2010, when the Peruvian author Mario Vargas Llosa won. The older publishers remembered Roger clearing his schedule so that he could sit by the phone at one in the afternoon, waiting for news from Stockholm. This year, no one had expected an FSG victory. Galassi was at lunch with a British publisher and far from a phone; he didn't know about the announcement for two hours.

One of the first things he did when he heard the news was to e-mail Peggy Miller: "Isn't it wonderful about Mario?" She got the e-mail first thing in the morning, New York time. Having just brushed her teeth, she didn't know "what the hell he was talking about." Then she turned on the television and smiled.

After Roger died, Galassi had managed to walk the line between forceful leadership and accommodation, bringing FSG closer in line with its corporate owners even as he boldly swept out the termites. But in the grim week following Bob Giroux's somber memorial service, it was impossible to deny that he wasn't really in charge—that he lacked not just the charisma of his predecessor but also his free hand.

The collapse of Lehmann Brothers that September had sent the U.S. economy into a tailspin, and in publishing, as in the rest of the country, forecasts and cutbacks were brutal. Just a week after the memorial, on December 15, FSG announced that it was laying off editors Linda Rosenberg and Denise Oswald, subrights director Michael Hathaway, production head Tom Consiglio, and about a dozen others. More drastically, it was also losing independent control over its subrights deals, national sales accounts, and children's imprint. The first two were big structural blows, but the last had symbolic resonance. The department under which Hal Vursell had published *A Wrinkle in Time,* and where Michael di Capua had set Maurice Sendak's drawings to the rhythm of Grimm, was being absorbed into the Flatiron under the direction of Henry Holt. Competing against celebrity kids' books and YA crossovers,

FSG's children's books division had been doing poorly for some time. But that didn't make shedding it any easier. "We were all very proud of our children's department," says Lorin Stein. "It was a moment of very low morale and a feeling of loss."

In a long internal memo, Galassi did his best to emphasize "what stays the same at FSG": its final say over acquisitions. It may have looked like cold consolation, but it was still the key component of the house's DNA. "Stefan von Holtzbrinck, John, Andrew, and I remain committed to ensuring that FSG remains a vitally independent, editorially driven publishing house. Our approach to publishing and what we choose to publish are not going to change."

Implicit in the memo was the fact that it could have been worse. Three years later, Galassi had few regrets about the choices he made. He even implied that the staff cuts were a bit of housecleaning. "I don't think firing people is a bad thing," he said. "I've been fired myself. It was the best thing that ever happened to me. Firing people in a reduction is different. But you have to be able to think of the health of the organism as a whole, and so that's part of responsible leadership."

As far as the consolidation went, Galassi admits to "scratchiness and territoriality at the start," especially with the behemoth Holtzbrinck-owned St. Martin's Press. But he insists that relations have thawed over time: "As everyone got to know each other, things worked themselves out." He declines, however, to talk in depth about losing the children's department. It still feels raw.

The December cuts were the first real crisis of Galassi's tenure, a moment during which Roger Straus's ineffable powers of persuasion and inspiration were sorely missed. Some Roger loyalists, especially those sidelined by Galassi, blame the new president for falling short of Roger's standard. "It's very interesting to those of us who watched the way Roger built up morale and kept everybody's shoulder to the wheel," says one of them. "How can you hang around him and not pick up some pointers on how to do this?" Another says: "People would have come out of their foxholes to do battle for Roger Straus. No one would come out of a foxhole for Jonathan Galassi."

True or not, it's an unfair comparison. First, it's not as though

Roger Straus never laid people off, or pissed people off, or lost big battles. He sold the company, after all. And, most important, Galassi is a very different person. He has charms, but he won't swoop in with a Mercedes convertible and carry you along on a "current at top speed." Pretending otherwise would be ridiculous. A more balanced picture emerges from watching him at work. He can be chilly and hard to read. He communicates well with his favorite authors and editors—Jonathan authors and Jonathan editors—but not as well with those outside his immediate circle. Even on something as basic as meetings or P&Ls, he relies on affable Eric Chinski to hold out the carrots and Andrew Mandel to wield the stick. "Eric made us have editorial meetings," says Lorin Stein. "It was nice having someone around who'd make Jonathan sit through a meeting. Sometimes." Roger hated meetings, of course, but he loved talking, anywhere and everywhere. Between meetings, it's Chinski's office, not Galassi's, that serves as a gathering place and a confessional booth.

Galassi is left to focus on the books he edits and on the thorniest question of all: just how much change to effect, or tolerate, while staying true to Roger's mission. Here, too, his personality dictates his approach, which is adventurous and open-minded, but cautious in the long term. He's a less intrusive editor than Giroux and a less mercurial leader than Roger Straus—but also, ultimately, less indulgent. His philosophy is to let a hundred flowers bloom, and cut down the ugly ones.

When Thomas LeBien pitched his line of graphic history books, he prepared a folder full of numbers to support his proposal. Galassi didn't even open it. "That sounds good," he said. "Go out and prove it." He also let LeBien put out a couple of sports books, one on Tom Brady and another on the University of Michigan football team. They were approved, but with low expectations—which LeBien was able to exceed. He did it, though, largely on his own.

"Jonathan is smart, discerning, and enthusiastic," says LeBien. "He assumed the same was true of anyone acquiring. His starting assumption, I think, was that each editor ought to be the publisher of his or her own books. And it was no different for Jonathan's books, except, of course, Jonathan was the publisher."

Denise Oswald was also given free rein at Faber and Faber—before being sidelined and then laid off. She decided to enliven the imprint with pop crossovers. The poetry of Smashing Pumpkins frontman Billy Corgan sold well enough. But one disastrous result was *Dirty Blonde: The Diaries of Courtney Love,* a book full of the ruined riot grrrl's school-aged jottings superimposed on photos and drawings, produced on very expensive paper and meant to be purchased by Lord knows whom. Permissions took forever to process; marketing cost another $127,000. It was a phenomenal flop, not only because the costs ran high, but also because FSG had almost no experience marketing celebrity books—especially those by unreliable washed-up rock stars. Whether or not it was a factor in Oswald's departure, it wasn't entirely her fault. The book might have failed at any house; at FSG it didn't stand a chance.

Sarah Crichton Books is a happier experiment, both more radical than the Faber relaunch (in the commercial sense) and more sensible. But it also comes up against the limits of FSG's reach. Crichton has been trying, over the past few years, to develop thrillers. FSG had the chance to acquire *The Girl with the Dragon Tattoo.* Galassi rather liked it, but Crichton thought (reasonably) that it started out too slow. Knopf wound up selling tens of millions of copies of it. More recently, Crichton has tried to build another Scandinavian franchise, Lars Kepler (actually the pseudonym of two Swedish writers), beginning with *The Hypnotist.* Despite $100,000 in marketing—more than a tenth of FSG's annual marketing budget—it failed to meet expectations. Crichton is hoping the third book in the series will be the one to take off (they've signed five total).

Another tricky writer is Jason Goodwin, whose chronicles of a Turkish eunuch detective launched in 2006 with *The Janissary Tree.* The British historian's side projects have drawn comparisons to Alexander McCall Smith—the kind of respectable potboilers FSG could publish well. But half-decent sales fell off after the first book, and Goodwin remains obscure. "Thrillers can make good money, good business, and be a very fun part of publishing," Crichton says. "But it takes time to build those careers, and it takes marketing, and it takes a house that's interested in that kind of publishing. I think the biggest challenge right now is to figure out how to do that kind of publishing at a house like FSG." If her boss is really out to build a better Knopf, he isn't there yet.

More of Galassi's attention goes into the house's literary best-sellers, bearing out his somewhat self-fulfilling assertion that at FSG, "quality is commercial." Not only did Jonathan Franzen come out with another blockbuster, *Freedom,* in 2010; this time he did as good a job of promotion as his publisher. When Jeff Seroy told him *Time* was interested in an interview, he said fine—but they should put him on the cover. The gambit worked. And he wrote Oprah a short, personal note offering to reconcile on TV. "I didn't get into it making great TV—I let that be read between the lines," he says. "Everything about publishing *Freedom* and about TV argued for doing it." It was her last year of shows, he reasoned, and she loves a good redemption narrative.

"We had an onstage embrace, and we had a little backstage embrace just to try it out first," Franzen says. To his unpleasant surprise, she brought up the *Corrections* fracas onstage in a casual manner he found "perfectly disingenuous." Franzen's girlfriend had argued against faking redemption with someone he didn't even like, but he retorted that it wasn't real life—it was promotion. On the show, he flattered the audience while just slightly undermining Oprah's questions. "I thought it was one of my weaker performances," he says, betraying his FSG-funded media training. "They had done something to my hair backstage." Still, "it was the right thing to do."

Jeffrey Eugenides published his next book the year after Franzen's—right on schedule. *The Marriage Plot* was a smaller book than *Middlesex,* a more narrowly focused coming-of-age novel, which satirized Brown University's semiotics program but depicted the throes of bipolar disorder with deep sensitivity. FSG pulled out the stops for their favorite son, with a publication party atop the Standard hotel, where Franzen and Eugenides shared a big hug (the latter more exuberantly, as usual).

Shortly before publication, FSG's ad agency called Seroy to tell him there was a last-minute vacancy for a billboard in Times Square. Did he have any ideas? Well, there was this one book they were pushing pretty hard at the moment. "It was not a huge intuitive leap," says Seroy. They had a photo Eugenides's wife had taken, of the author in a billowing black vest, which they half-jokingly called "Marlboro Man." If the original Marlboro Man could have a billboard, why couldn't a slim, balding literary novelist with a jaunty goatee? Above the blown-up portrait Seroy placed the only real blurb they had so far (since Eugenides still doesn't allow back-cover blurbs). An early *Vanity Fair* write-up had called the book "Swoon-worthy," so that's what went above his picture, in all caps. "Well, he kind of is, let's just say it," Seroy says in justification. "He's very charismatic and sexy."

"I was a little shocked," Eugenides says, sounding slightly embarrassed. His wife thought it would be a touch too crass and commercial. He also had reservations: "You have to ask yourself: Would Samuel Beckett do it? But Jeff [Seroy] said, 'I'll take the blame.' I think in the end, everyone was quite happy about it." It scored a lot of tweets and blog hits, including a decent share of snark. "It certainly got a huge amount of attention," says Seroy, "and the book did come on the list at number two, below Nicholas Sparks."

Even allowing for the rare billboard, it's still a lot easier on the FSG budget to advertise literary novels than thrillers. The advances are more reasonable, too, even on the heels of big hits like *The Corrections* and *Middlesex*. Between the two famous authors, Franzen turned out to be the more conservative—and loyal. He didn't even pretend to offer *Freedom* anywhere else, and scored between $1 and $2 million for it. Eugenides drove a much harder bargain; his agent, Lynn Nesbit, "made noises" about leaving, as Eugenides puts it. There was the age-old "court dance," as Galassi calls it, to match the number she demanded. In the end they settled on $4 million, for U.S. rights alone, for *The Marriage Plot* followed by a book of short stories. Hardcover and e-book sales of *The Marriage Plot* were under half a million—not enough to recoup the advance, though it's doing well in paperback. That billboard might not have made much difference. Eugenides had better write some killer short stories.

The new frontier of salesmanship has nothing to do with bill-boards, or anything printed. The less mediated world of the Web might actually play to FSG's strong suit: experimentation on the cheap. One of Eugenides's most interesting bits of hype was an online Q&A with Galassi, discussing the process of editing *The Marriage Plot* more than a year before it was published. It was part of a regular series on FSG's blog and newsletter, "Work in Progress." The site also runs advice from writers and the occasional note from an editor, which, like Lorin Stein's elaborate notes in front of advance copies, do double duty as promotion and critical analysis. Subscribers also get regular offers of free advance copies and chapbooks. The aim is to reach readers through influential fans, and also to build a database of readers loyal not just to the writer but to the whole publisher, as though it were an indie brand. "If you look at Merge Records—that's what I thought it might be," says Ryan Chapman, who developed the site. He found plenty of interest in the interviews and galleys, "a hunger for FSG content—more than we could provide."

It's not too far off from what Stein might have done with his scuttled book-club idea. But Stein is no longer there to offer his help. In 2010, he left to take the unrefusable offer of editing *The Paris Review.* He says he tried to inquire about keeping some of his editing work, but the publishers of the *Review* insisted it was a full-time job. The fact is, he was still a senior editor in a small house with little immediate room for advancement. The *Review,* whose readership is small but very influential, offered him a substantial salary bump. It also gave him the opportunity to expand online without so many corporate fetters. The *Review* now has one of the Web's most vibrant literary hubs.

Last year, Paul Elie left as well, joining the faculty at Georgetown University so that he could focus on teaching and writing. Ryan Chapman is gone, too. All that turnover is enough to lend credence to Peggy's wistful thoughts on young editors "moving around like gypsies." People often came and went at Roger's FSG, and not too many of them heeded his toast of "You'll be back." But you might start to wonder if the FSG lifers who'd sustained its institutional memory and core values are now a thing of the past. Thomas LeBien, another alum, asks an even more important question: "Are they building an author base that will in five or ten years' time be that next round of Franzen, Eugenides, Friedman?"

The latest addition to the editors' ranks, Sean McDonald, is both a cause for and a source of optimism on that front. At Doubleday and then at Riverhead, he published younger writers who would fit comfortably at FSG—Aleksandar Hemon, Junot Díaz, Ellen Ullman, Steven Johnson—and some who might not—Tyler Perry, David Rees, or the RZA, the multifaceted rapper from the Wu Tang Clan. (He also survived editing James Frey's *A Million Little Pieces,* an impressive feat all its own.) His fall list in 2012 was full of new names, would-be Franzens of a grittier, techier ilk. McDonald says that when he met Galassi to discuss the job, one of the writers the publisher was most excited to hear about, after McDonald "started to wax rhapsodic about his brilliance," was the RZA. "His eyes lit up," McDonald remembers, "and there was a distinct sense of 'That's the kind of thing we want to be doing.'"

For the latest in a long, long line of refugees from bigger, wealthier houses—going back to Robert Giroux and John Farrar—the inspiration goes both ways. At first McDonald was stunned by the lack of formal structure at FSG; lately, he finds it refreshing. There's plenty of talk about tablets and Twitter, he says, but not as much panicked hand-wringing as there is in offices where editors spend less time on the books themselves. "There's very little doom and gloom," he says, "which is perhaps unusual in the industry at the moment. I think it's an optimistic place."

A few years ago, Galassi's life changed profoundly, and so did his reputation for being aloof and a little square. Just in time for the 2007 BookExpo, rumors began to spread that Galassi was becoming involved with a talented literary agent named Bill Clegg. Two years earlier, Clegg had briefly disappeared from the business, as a result of what he'd later admit was an epic crack binge. When he'd reemerged, Galassi had become one of his closest confidants. The gossip site Gawker gleefully spread the story of their supposed affair.

It made for a tense atmosphere at the office, no one really knowing how to handle, or avoid, the subject on everyone's mind. Around the same time, Galassi decided to leave his wife and come out quietly as a gay man.

It would be hard to imagine Giroux embroiled in such a crisis, back in an era before Gawker and gay marriage. Even Straus, for all his indiscretions, was careful never to let rumors of his prolific sex life run amok. But Galassi belongs to a different generation. He's much closer in age and outlook to Roger Straus III, who bristled under his father's notion that private longings—for other women, for other jobs—had to be tamped down or kept quiet in the interest of family and reputation. Both Galassi and Rog guard their privacy, but they lack the ability to compartmentalize their secrets as their elders did. Maybe that's why they've managed, despite the obvious obstacles, to remain good friends. Over the past couple of summers, they've made a habit of spending a few weeks vacationing and catching up in Little Compton, Rhode Island. In 2011, Rog's daughter Laura came up to stay with them for four days; it was the first time she'd really spoken with Galassi. "It was very healing," she says. "My dad's really happy. I think the company's exactly where my grandfather would have wanted it to be. I think my father's issues are resolved. After a lifetime of watching this Oedipal struggle, how fantastic."

When Galassi finally decided to come out in public, in 2012, it was through his third poetry collection. *Left-handed* documents his transition from family man to unrequited lover of a man he calls "Jude" and, finally, the serious partner of "Tom." A story in the *New York Times* by former *Book Review* editor Charles McGrath made all the connections explicit (Jude, for example, is Bill Clegg). Finally, the facts were laid out, preempting further speculation, and the gossip was replaced with a smooth narrative of liberation. Calculated or not, it looked like the kind of masterful media management of which Roger Straus might have been proud, despite his probable discomfort with the subject.

One stanza toward the end of *Left-handed,* in the poem "Tom in Rome," nicely encapsulates the conclusion of Galassi's story: "Go ahead and shame us in the Forum / with your ironic fine decorum, do: / Antinous with glasses and umbrella, / deus ex machina of the novella / whose story was that my roads led to you."

Antinous was the young male lover of Emperor Hadrian—the figure to whom, for some reason, all the roads of FSG lead back. Giroux had read the great Roman's deathbed meditation in memory of Henry Robbins and also of Hal Vursell, the gay editor who'd worked so hard on a translation of Marguerite Yourcenar's *Memoirs of Hadrian*. And that novel was, of course, Roger Straus's favorite FSG book. It's probably just a curious coincidence, but as an object of the house's collective fixation, it makes sense. Roger Straus, Robert Giroux, and most of the editors of their day labored in a state of perpetual warfare with the barbarians at the gate. "Catastrophe and ruin will come," Yourcenar had written; the best they could hope for was "intermittent immortality." Rome, and FSG, would one day fall. But it was their duty to fight on, for the good of civilization.

Galassi's role, and his challenge, is vastly different. The barbarians are in the building—or a few blocks north, anyway, in the Flatiron. When it comes to publishing, Galassi prefers a more apt literary-historical analogy. He likes to invoke Giuseppe di Lampedusa's *The Leopard,* "one of the greatest novels of the twentieth century." Among the few midcentury Italian classics that FSG missed out on, the novel follows a line of Sicilian aristocrats struggling with the revolutionary Giuseppe Garibaldi's mission to unify Italy. Galassi finds particular relevance in one important scene: A young noble explains to his uncle, the prince of Salina, why he's siding with the nationalists. If the family doesn't give in to the modernizers, he argues, an even more radical force could destroy everything they've built. "Unless we ourselves take a hand now, they'll foist a republic on us," he says. "If we want things to stay as they are, things will have to change."

"It absolutely applies to publishing," Galassi says. "We need to keep up with the pace of change in the industry, and I think we've been good at doing that, but our core in fact doesn't change—our basic mission and commitment and interest."

The comparison is even more specific to FSG—its history and its future—than Galassi lets on. The old, aristocratic order of Roger

Straus has given way to a world of uniformity and accommodation. No longer do emperors roam the halls of midtown or Union Square, taking their droit du seigneur and yelling, "Fuck the peasants." What few nobles are left serve at the pleasure of powerful technocrats. But they still have their titles, and we still have their books.

Acknowledgments

This book, my first, owes its existence to a handful of lucky breaks and a truckload of generous and insightful people. Thanks first and foremost to my agent, Jane Dystel, for planting the idea in my suggestible brain, and to my editor, Jofie Ferrari-Adler, whose fascination with the culture of publishing is matched by his incredible skill, wit, enthusiasm, and diplomatic application of just the right amount of pressure. Several sources were absolutely essential. The Rosetta Stone of the early chapters was "The Reminiscences of Roger W. Straus, Jr.," a 1,173-page transcript of interviews conducted with Straus between 1977 and 1979, held in the Oral History Collection of Columbia University. Straus's son, Roger W. Straus III, gave me access not only to those records but also to another treasure trove, a dozen hours' worth of conversation featuring his own sharp memories and clever observations. Equally crucial was the patient cooperation of Jonathan Galassi, Roger Straus's successor as publisher of FSG, along with his stalwart marketing director Jeff Seroy and his design director, Rodrigo Corral, who even designed this book's cover. I'm also grateful to Peggy Miller, the living soul of independent FSG, for giving so much of her time.

Another master source was the Farrar, Straus & Giroux, Inc. Records in the Manuscripts and Archives Division of the New York Public Library—invaluable not just for the inner workings of the company but for the heart of the book, the relationships between its staff and its authors. Thanks especially to the division's assistant curator, Thomas Lannon, for guiding me through the work, and to the rest of the staff for their help and forbearance.

Several out-of-town trips contributed to my research, both archival and experiential. At Yale University's Beinecke Library, Eva Guggemos helped make sense of John C. Farrar's professional papers, and at Loyola University of New Orleans, Art Carpenter selflessly extended his hours so that I could spend a week rifling through the Monroe Library's rich collection of Robert Giroux's papers. At the Frankfurt International Book Fair, *Publishing Perspectives* editor in chief Ed Nawotka gave me a chance to earn my keep as well as some sage advice on navigating the festival, the town, and the colorful publishing tribes that have been descending on it for centuries. At Simon & Schuster, Roger's proud nemeses and my saviors, in addition to Mr. Ferrari-Adler I owe effusive thanks to Jonathan Karp, Sarah Nalle, Anne Tate, Tracey Guest, Nina Pajak, Richard Rhorer, Jackie Seow, and Jonathan Evans for making this the book I secretly hoped it might become. Thanks also to Lisa Silverman for her immaculate copyediting and to Jim Kelly for his tireless and clean transcribing. For giving me the time and flexibility to write this, along with countless other opportunities through the years, I'll always be grateful to my eternal employers and editors at *New York* magazine: Adam Moss, Jared Hohlt, David Wallace-Wells, Ann Clarke, and Chris Bonanos—the last, also, for a razor-sharp first read of important chapters.

For patiently wading through half-baked early drafts, and for their friendship and support in spite of these thankless labors, thank you to Sloane Crosley, Logan Hill, Stephen Krieger, and Rose Krieger. And finally, for giving me everything, my family: Aron and Nora and Robin Kachka, and my beloved wife and fellow traveler, Jamie Ehrlich.

Notes

Introduction

2 *Instead he chose:* Richard Merkin, "An Ode to Roger Straus, a Bookmaker with Qualities . . . Even If You've Never Heard of His Favorite Book," *GQ*, September 1988.

2 *"this long and rather beautiful life":* Roger W. Straus, Jr., interview by Louis Sheaffer, "The Reminiscences of Roger W. Straus, Jr." January 27, 1978, in the Columbia Center for Oral History Collection, 448. Hereafter "Reminiscences," CCOHC.

3 *"Life is atrocious":* Marguerite Yourcenar, *Memoirs of Hadrian*, trans. Grace Frick (New York: Farrar, Straus and Giroux, 1963), 293.

5 *"This guy is a hood": Roger W. Straus: A Celebration* (New York: Farrar, Straus and Giroux, 2005), 28.

6 *"If he kept back money":* Ibid., 41–43.

6 *"gave me hope":* Ibid., 82.

6 *"enjoyed thinking about":* Ibid., 87.

7 *"would freeze, the needles in midair":* Ibid., 94.

7 *"He was always doing battle":* Ibid., 89–90.

9 *Aside from editing:* Pat Strachan, written remarks.

10 *"But the fact is that":* Paul Elie, written remarks.

10   *"The guy's crazy"*: Robert Giroux, interview by George Plimpton, *The Paris Review*, no. 155 (Summer 2000), 181.

10   The Trouble with Cinderella: Jonathan Galassi, written remarks.

11   *"The most sobering of all"*: Robert Giroux, *The Education of an Editor: R. R. Bowker Memorial Lectures* (Ann Arbor, MI: R. R. Bowker Co., 1982), 17.

11   *In one fell swoop*: Alan D. Williams, ed., *Fifty Years: A Farrar, Straus and Giroux Reader* (New York: Farrar, Straus and Giroux, 1996), xvii.

13   *"What was so unusual"*: Father Patrick Samway, interview by the author, December 10, 2009.

15   *"The best part of that"*: Al Silverman, *The Time of Their Lives: The Golden Age of Great American Book Publishers, Their Editors, and Authors* (New York: Truman Talley Books, 2008), 37.

Chapter One

17   *"for want of a better"*: "Guggenheim-Straus Marriage Unites Noted Families," *The New York Times*, January 11, 1914.

18   *A pale beauty:* James Reginato, "Literary Lion," *W*, March 1996.

18   *Among the wider circle:* "R. W. Straus Weds Miss Guggenheim," *The New York Times*, January 13, 1914.

18   *"It's an 'Our Crowd' story"*: "Reminiscences," June 29, 1977, 10, CCOHC.

19   *"Broadened by his sojourn"*: Harold Loeb, *The Way It Was* (New York: Criterion Books, 1959), 22–23.

19   *"I am sorry"*: Irwin Unger and Debi Unger, *The Guggenheims: A Family History* (New York: HarperCollins, 2005), 220.

19   *Simon's primary assistant:* Ibid., 175.

20   *Though he lost:* Oscar S. Straus, *Under Four Administrations, From Cleveland to Taft: Recollections of Oscar S. Straus* (Boston: Houghton Mifflin, 1922), 325.

20   *The story became:* Peggy Guggenheim, *Out of This Century: Confessions of an Art Addict* (Garden City, NY: Anchor Books, 1980), 2.

21   *Gladys's father, Daniel:* Roger W. Straus III, interview by author, July 23, 2009.

21   *According to his son:* Reginato, "Literary Lion."

21   *After their honeymoon:* Unger and Unger, *The Guggenheims*, 193.

21   *On the decisive night:* "Dewey Is Up Late Getting Returns," *The New York Times*, November 3, 1948.

21   *In 1949, Dewey:* Unger and Unger, *The Guggenheims*, 193.

21   *Had Dewey indeed defeated:* "Reminiscences," June 29, 1977, 12, CCOHC.

22   *Her second son was born:* Ibid., 14.

22   *When Roger Sr. shipped off:* Unger and Unger, *The Guggenheims*, 192.

22   *The structure was as forbidding:* Ibid., 179.

23   *But up in East Egg:* Florence Straus Hart, interview by author, November 2009.

23   *As "marvelous" as all this:* "Reminiscences," July 6, 1977, 69–78, CCOHC.

23   *A rug embroidered:* Dorothea Straus, *Thresholds* (Boston: Houghton Mifflin, 1971), 177.

24   *"I propose to pay":* Straus, *Under Four Administrations*, 22.

24   *After he died:* "Reminiscences," June 29, 1977, 69–78, CCOHC; Straus, *Thresholds*, 177.

25   *She reminded Dorothea:* Straus, *Thresholds*, 178.

25   *"I was a good athlete":* "Reminiscences," July 29, 1977, 15, CCOHC.

26   *"By the end of the summer":* Florence Straus Hart, interview by author, November 2009.

26   *Roger followed his brother:* "5th Av. Site Is Sold for 36-Story Hotel," *The New York Times*, April 18, 1929.

26   *Never mind that Hitler:* "Roger W. Straus Honored by Club," *The New York Times*, January 19, 1956.

27   *"He was the king":* Andrée Conrad, interview by author, December 28, 2010.

27   *"He didn't have a lot":* Roger Hirson, interview by author, June 18, 2009.

27   *"Whether I would actually":* "Reminiscences," June 29, 1977, 15, CCOHC.

27   *"The teacher said":* Peggy Miller, interview by author, October 23, 2008.

28   *Nor did Mr. and Mrs. Straus:* "Dr. Hamilton Holt, Educator, 78, Dies," *The New York Times*, April 27, 1951.

28   *"heavily to tennis":* "Mr. Ackland's Wills," Education, *Time*, June 30, 1947.

28   *"and this turned me on":* "Executive Memories: My Summer Job," *The New York Times*, June 10, 1979.

28   *"Down under he thirsted":* Norton Mockridge, "The Story That Isn't in the Book," *New York World-Telegram*, November 1, 1965.

29   *Before marrying late in life:* Dorothea Straus, *Virgins and Other Endangered Species: A Memoir* (Wakefield, RI: Moyer Bell, 1993), 9.

30   *"I always maintained":* "Reminiscences," June 29, 1977, 21–22, CCOHC.

30   *Each had a turn:* Hirson, interview by author, June 18, 2009.

30   *"wandered hand in hand":* Straus, *Thresholds*, 176–77.

31   *"She liked the idea":* Straus III, interview by author, July 23, 2009.

31   *After the honeymoon:* Straus, *Thresholds*, 79–80; "Nuptials at Home for Miss Liebmann," *The New York Times*, June 28, 1938.

31   *"I didn't see any future":* "Reminiscences," June 29, 1977, 32, CCOHC.

32   *Given the go-ahead:* Ibid., 24–28.

32   *No doubt the family connections:* Unger and Unger, *The Guggenheims*, 255.

32   *Roger had met Lindbergh:* "Reminiscences," November 16, 1977, 226, CCOHC.

33   *"They are fighting for survival":* Diana Forbes-Robertson and Roger W. Straus, Jr., eds., *War Letters from Britain* (New York: G. P. Putnam's Sons, 1941), vii.

34 *Only recently, Roger:* "Reminiscences," June 29, 1977, 35–36, CCOHC.
34 *He had the angel hood ornament:* Robert H. Boyle, "The Deuce with Love and Advantage," *Sports Illustrated*, August 28, 1972.
34 *"It told you how to salute":* "Reminiscences," June 29, 1977, 38, CCOHC.
35 *"We would all be together":* Ibid., 44.
36 *He was also badly sunburned:* Dorothea Straus, *The Paper Trail: A Recollection of Writers* (Wakefield, RI: Moyer Bell, 1997), 3–6.
36 *Heatter followed her:* "Reminiscences," June 29, 1977, 52–54, CCOHC.
37 *"the few junior officers":* Robert Giroux, unpublished introduction to "Twenty-Five Years: A Retrospective," Box 8, folder 3, Papers of Robert Giroux, Loyola University, New Orleans.
37 *"Rescue from Truk":* Robert Giroux, "Rescue from Truk," *Collier's*, May 13, 1944, 18, 19, 80, 81.
38 *"It's rather a nasty story":* "Reminiscences," June 29, 1977, 58–60, and July 6, 1977, 85, 91, CCOHC.

Chapter Two

40 *"What I'm really talking about":* John Farrar, Manuscripts Box, John Farrar Papers, Beinecke Library, Yale University.
40 *By Farrar's own account:* Al Silverman, *The Time of Their Lives: The Golden Age of Great American Book Publishers, Their Editors, and Authors* (New York: Truman Talley Books, 2008), 22.
40 *"Johnny used to have temper tantrums":* Roger W. Straus, Jr., interview by Louis Sheaffer, "Reminiscences," June 29, 1977, 162, CCOHC.
40 *"a sweet, neurotic, tweedy old man":* Jack Kerouac and Joyce Johnson, *Door Wide Open: A Beat Love Affair in Letters, 1957–1958* (New York: Viking, 2000), 8, 16.
40 *"We were, believe it or not":* Ibid.
41 *She went on to found:* Herbert Mitgang, "Margaret Farrar, 87, Editor of Crossword Puzzles, Dies," *The New York Times*, June 12, 1984.
41 *Stephen Vincent Benét:* C. Gerald Fraser, "John C. Farrar, Publisher, Editor, and Writer, Is Dead," *The New York Times*, November 7, 1974.
41 *"The publisher's greatest luck":* John C. Farrar, "Footnotes to a Publisher's Sunday," Manuscripts Box, John Farrar Papers.
42 *Farrar soon took a leave:* John Farrar Papers.
42 *"many a man has been":* John Farrar, address to Scarsborough School, 21 April 1945, John Farrar Papers.
42 *It was there that:* John Farrar to James Van Toor, 25 September 1944, John Farrar Papers.
42 *"My father was many things":* Curtis Farrar, interview by author, October 23, 2009.
43 *"How can it happen":* Margaret P. Farrar to Hervey Allen, unsent, Family Letters Box, John Farrar Papers.

43   *"He really didn't have"*: "Reminiscences," July 6, 1977, 85–91, CCOHC.

43   *"I'd like to talk to you"*: Ibid., 92.

43   *"The first list"*: FSG internal archives, Farrar, Straus and Giroux, New York. Hereafter "FSG Archives."

44   *"Roger's Raiders"*: Doris Janowitz Huth, interview by author, September 11, 2009.

44   *"Furor, Stress"*: Arthur Orrmont, "Editing in the '40s, or, Flung from the Ivory Tower," *Connecticut Review* VII (October 1973), 6–15.

44   *At the former navy press office*: Box 513, Farrar, Straus & Giroux, Inc. Records, New York Public Library Manuscripts and Archives Division. Hereafter "FSG Records, NYPL."

44   *Beside him was another*: Orrmont, "Editing in the '40s."

44   *Mercifully, Jimmy Van Alen*: Ibid.

45   *An unwieldy adding machine*: John Peck, Papers of Robert Giroux, Box 8, Loyola University, New Orleans.

45   *He and "Mr. Farrar"*: Orrmont, "Editing in the '40s."

45   *"took a poor view of"*: "Reminiscences," July 6, 1977, 93, CCOHC.

45   *Van Alen secured the help*: P. Christiaan Klieger, *The Fleischmann Yeast Family* (Charleston, SC: Arcadia, 2004), 74.

46   *"I would not have tried"*: "Reminiscences," February 15, 1978, 532, 533, CCOHC.

46   *He succeeded*: Farrar, Farrar Publishing Box, John Farrar Papers.

46   *Accordingly, the first list*: Roger W. Straus, Jr., Box 8, FSG Records, NYPL.

46   *"'James Branch Cabell'"*: James Reginato, "Nobel House," *New York*, November 9, 1987, 58.

46   *"for snobbish reasons"*: "Reminiscences," July 6, 1977, 103, CCOHC.

46   *Two years later*: James V. Hatch, *Sorrow Is the Only Faithful One: The Life of Owen Dodson* (Urbana, IL: University of Illinois Press, 1993), 135.

47   *Farrar's catch included*: "Reminiscences," July 6, 1977, 108, CCOHC.

47   *Farrar had met Reik*: Ibid., 112–13.

47   *"The abilities of Roger Straus"*: Orrmont, "Editing in the '40s."

47   *He took them to an East Side*: A. Scott Berg, *Max Perkins, Editor of Genius* (New York: Dutton, 1978), 333.

48   *"I expect to be around"*: "Reminiscences," June 28, 1978, 680–83, CCOHC.

48   *"Farrar, Straus could cut"*: Ian Parker, "Showboat," *The New Yorker*, April 8, 2002.

48   *"Maybe my peanut stand"*: "Reminiscences," July 20, 1977, 135, CCOHC.

49   *"These associations cannot"*: John Farrar to Carlo Levi, 17 April 1946, Box 203, FSG Records, NYPL.

49   *"I wrote a long letter"*: Roger W. Straus, Jr., to Sanford J. Greenburger, 10 April 1946, Box 203, FSG Records, NYPL.

49   *"assure Levi that he has"*: John Farrar to Max Ascoli, 17 April 1946, Box 203, FSG Records, NYPL.

49 *"probably the most conceited man"*: Sanford J. Greenburger to John Farrar and Roger W. Straus, Jr., 17 August 1946, Box 203, FSG Records, NYPL.

49 *"I look a little bit like"*: "Reminiscences," July 20, 1977, 136–38, CCOHC.

50 *"virile, fresh and even exuberant"*: Eleanor Pettinos Blow, "Readers and Writers in Italy," *The New York Times Book Review*, February 9, 1947.

50 *In his oral history*: "Reminiscences," February 9, 1979, 1023–24, CCOHC.

50 *Several sources have identified*: "Senigallia—White," *The New York Times*, December 17, 1949.

51 *By the time Straus met*: Parker, "Showboat."

51 *Straus always thought*: "Reminiscences," June 29, 1977, 13, CCOHC.

51 *The Book-of-the-Month Club*: Box 203, FSG Records, NYPL.

51 *When the lease expired*: "Reminiscences," July 6, 1977, 101, CCOHC.

51 *Stray fabric*: Peck, Box 8, Papers of Robert Giroux.

52 *"I picked up my hat"*: "Reminiscences," July 20, 1977, 143–44, CCOHC.

52 *By his estimate*: Ibid., 1106.

53 *Nothing came of it*: Ibid., 123–26.

53 *It became an office joke*: "Farrar, Straus and Cudahy Celebrates a Tenth Anniversary," *Publishers Weekly*, February 18, 1956.

53 *Lately he'd become*: Box 141, FSG Records, NYPL.

54 *"He is a snob"*: Internal memo, 18 June 1948, Box 141, FSG Records, NYPL.

54 *By the time they met Straus*: Peggy Miller, interview by author, July 2, 2009.

54 *"All of us here"*: Roger W. Straus, Jr., to Frey Brown, 21 June 1948, Box 141, FSG Records, NYPL.

54 *"the female of the species"*: Roger W. Straus, Jr., to Frey Brown, 6 January 1949, Box 141, FSG Records, NYPL.

55 *He wrote back*: Burt Boyar to Roger W. Straus, Jr., 14 December 1970, Box 79, FSG Records, NYPL.

55 *"We are watching"*: Frey Brown to Roger W. Straus, Jr., 20 June 1950, FSG Records, NYPL. Rising sales and Hauser and Brown's nagging documented in Box 141, folder 1; long-term sales total documented in Box 139, folder 8.

55 *"But I trust that you"*: Roger W. Straus, Jr., to Burt Boyar, 8 August 1973, Box 78, FSG Records, NYPL.

55 *Leibowitz had only one thing*: "Reminiscences," January 11, 1977, 341, CCOHC.

56 *It was published*: Ibid., 340–46; supported by Box 301, FSG Records, NYPL.

56 *"a swordless Saracen"*: Orrmont, "Editing in the '40s."

56 *"You blow me"*: Helen Weaver, *The Awakener: A Memoir of Kerouac and the Fifties* (San Francisco: City Lights Books, 2009), 40.

56 *He was the one*: Meyer Berger, "Sutton, Bank Thief, Captured in Street by Brooklyn Police," *The New York Times*, February 19, 1952; Albin Krebs, "Willie Sutton Is Dead at 79," *The New York Times*, November 19, 1980.

57 *A week later he got*: "Reminiscences," January 11, 1978, 348–52, CCOHC.

57 *Quentin Reynolds's advance:* Robert Wohlforth to Frederick Rohlfs, 24 January 1966, Box 301, FSG Records, NYPL; Roger W. Straus, Jr., to Kenneth Littauer, 14 April 1952, Box 302, FSG Records, NYPL.

57 *The damage was limited:* Denial of motion to dismiss amended libel in United States v. 8 Cartons of Molasses, etc., 2 August 1951, Box 141, FSG Records, NYPL; Forbes D. Shaw to Roger W. Straus, Jr., 6 August 1951, Box 141, FSG Records, NYPL.

57 *But the legal fees:* "Reminiscences," July 20, 1977, 154, CCOHC.

57 *Roger eventually buckled:* Internal memo, 20 August 1951, Box 139, FSG Records, NYPL; Roger W. Straus, Jr., to Patrick Sullivan, 8 October 1951, Box 139, FSG Records, NYPL.

57 *Straus and Frey Brown:* Internal memo, 13 August 1952, Box 140, FSG Records, NYPL.

58 *There were boozy dinners:* Donald Porter Geddes to Roger W. Straus, Jr., 21 August 1952, Box 140, FSG Records, NYPL.

58 *The firm had "desperately overspent":* Roger W. Straus, Jr., to Frey Brown, 11 May 1953, Box 140, FSG Records, NYPL.

59 *Only the sale of syndication rights:* "Reminiscences," January 11, 1978, 370–80, CCOHC.

59 *Years later, Straus summed up:* Reginato, "Nobel House."

59 *"dressed in diaphanous":* Dorothea Straus, *The Paper Trail: A Recollection of Writers* (Wakefield, RI: Moyer Bell, 1997), 7–14; "Reminiscences," January 11, 1978, 389–90, CCOHC.

60 *He was also an important:* "Reminiscences," 390–93.

60 *One of the more mystically:* "Psychic Tomorrow," The Press, *Time*, September 16, 1946.

60 *"One of the easier ways":* "Reminiscences," January 11, 1978, 385, CCOHC.

61 *It would be taken:* Ibid., 446–48.

61 *Poaching from them:* Ibid., 396–99.

61 *Along with the physical:* Orrmont, "Editing in the '40s."

61 *Straus met him:* Eric E. Wohlforth, interview by author, December 8, 2010.

62 *"picnic atmosphere":* Helen Weaver, interview by author, January 20, 2011.

62 *Straus asked her how:* John Peck to Mrs. Arthur Peck, 14 February 1955, courtesy of Judy Peck.

63 *The couple returned in May:* News Briefs, *Publishers Weekly*, January 6, 1953, and May 16, 1953.

63 *"an amicable divorce":* "Reminiscences," January 11, 1978, 394, CCOHC.

64 *She was shuffled off:* Edward Pellegrini, interview by author, February 15, 2010.

64 *George (né Giorgio):* Ibid.; "Reminiscences," January 27, 1978, 454, 455, CCOHC.

64   *He hated it:* "Pellegrinis to Publish Ariel Books," *Chicago Daily Tribune*, May 19, 1946.

64   *"I hate the country":* Miller, interview by author, October 23, 2008; Robert Giroux to Matthew Evans, 24 March 1981, Papers of Robert Giroux, Loyola University, New Orleans; Roger W. Straus, Jr., to Susan Sontag, 24 May 1971, Box 342, FSG Records, NYPL.

65   *"The next thing I knew":* "George Pellegrini," *The New York Times*, September 22, 1952.

65   *It's possible he himself:* "Reminiscences," January 27, 1978, 460–61, CCOHC.

65   *Roger's mother came through:* Ibid., 532.

66   *"now assumes a leading role":* "Two Publishing Firms Announce Their Merger," *Chicago Daily Tribune*, April 21, 1953.

66   *"Who is the woman":* "Reminiscences," November 16, 1977, 253, CCOHC.

66   *More than thirty thousand copies:* Roger W. Straus, Jr., to Alberto Moravia, 7 May 1950, Box 257, FSG Records, NYPL; Valentino Bompiani to Betty Winspear, 8 May 1950, Box 257, FSG Records, NYPL.

66   *It met with limited success:* "Reminiscences," November 16, 1977, 258–60, CCOHC.

67   *The critic Irving Howe:* Irving Howe, *A Margin of Hope: An Intellectual Autobiography* (San Diego: Harcourt Brace Jovanovich, 1982), 181.

67   *Dorothea limned the circle's:* Straus, *The Paper Trail*, 61–81.

67   *"the whole theory":* "Reminiscences," 265.

68   *Random House head:* Gallimard's classic series, a way of canonizing France's greatest authors, would become the template for the Library of America series, down to its very similar format. Its establishment was a lifelong dream of Wilson's but only came to fruition in 1982, ten years after his death.

68   *Wilson's story collection:* Jeffrey Meyers, *Edmund Wilson: A Biography* (Boston: Houghton Mifflin, 1995), 313.

68   *Straus recalled being haggled:* Edmund Wilson Worksheet, Box 389, FSG Records, NYPL.

68   *"Mr. Wilson, I understand":* "Reminiscences," November 16, 1977, 278–79, CCOHC.

69   *His first choice:* Publishers Weekly, December 9, 1957. Wilson clipped the second half of the story and sent a copy to Straus—now in the New York Public Library Records—annotating wittily in the margins. Beside this quote he added: "Wouldn't this seem suspicious?"

69   *He later claimed:* Roger W. Straus, Jr., Robert Giroux, Bruce Bliven, Jr., and Naomi Bliven, "Quartet: The Impulse to Publish," *Intellectual Digest* III, no. 3 (November 1972).

69   *"I agree with you":* Frances Kiernan, *Seeing Mary Plain: A Life of Mary McCarthy* (New York: W. W. Norton and Co., 2000), 379.

69 *He had found himself:* Farrar, Farrar Publishing Box, John Farrar Papers.

70 *A doctor did write him:* George Armistead to John Farrar, 19 October 1953, Box 8, John Farrar Papers.

70 *Some veterans of the firm:* Janice Thaddeus to Roger W. Straus, Jr., 10 November 1994, Roger W. Straus Correspondence, Box 3, FSG Records, NYPL.

70 *"The Century and home!":* Dorris Janowitz Huth, interview by author, September 11, 2009.

70 *He was unhappy:* "Reminiscences," January 27, 1978, 472–73, CCOHC.

Chapter Three

71 *One of them clutched:* Robert Giroux, "Remarks by Robert Giroux," *America,* May 28, 1988.

72 *The middle brother:* Katherine Mulvehill, interview by author, January 3, 2010.

72 *One sister, Josephine:* Maclovia Rodriguez, interview by author, February 12, 2010.

73 *He was an obedient student:* Yearbook clipping, Folder 21, Box 7, Papers of Robert Giroux, Loyola University, New Orleans.

73 *"Prohibition and the Crash":* Dorothea Straus, *Thresholds* (Boston: Houghton Mifflin, 1971), 53.

73 *The rest he made up:* Katherine Mulvehill, interview by author, January 3, 2010.

73 *Nonetheless, it was an important:* Robert Giroux, *The Education of an Editor: R. R. Bowker Memorial Lectures* (Ann Arbor, MI: R. R. Bowker Co., 1982), 16.

73 *"I needed one":* Edwin McDowell, "Literary Luminary Gets His Diploma after 57 Years," *The New York Times,* May 12, 1988.

73 *After he finished up:* Giroux, *The Education of an Editor,* 16; Box 512, FSG Archives, New York; Katherine Mulvehill, interview by author, January 3, 2010.

73 *"The times were serious":* Thomas Merton, *The Seven Storey Mountain,* 50th Anniversary ed. (New York: Harcourt Brace, 1998), xii.

74 *Yet they found plenty:* E. M. Halliday, *John Berryman and the Thirties: A Memoir* (Amherst, MA: University of Massachusetts Press, 1987), 18.

74 *They danced scandalously:* Ibid., 16.

74 *"There was a kind of genuine":* Merton, *The Seven Storey Mountain,* 137.

74 *The Spectator was always:* Ibid., 142.

75 *"Come the revolution":* Robert Giroux to the *Columbia Spectator,* 1 May 1934, Box 7, folder 5, Papers of Robert Giroux.

75 *After bartering some cigarettes:* Robert Giroux, interview by George Plimpton, *The Paris Review,* no. 155 (Summer 2000), 162.

75 *"Mark was the great teacher":* Ibid.

75   *He was also:* Mark Van Doren, *Autobiography* (New York: Greenwood Press, 1968), 220.

75   *"For a man to be":* Merton, *The Seven Storey Mountain*, 138.

75   *"Mark's unusual technique":* "Van Doren at 100: Remembering the Quintessential Great Teacher," *Columbia College Today* 21, no. 1 (Winter 1995).

75   *The professor's business:* Van Doren, *Autobiography*, 126–27.

76   *If anyone supposes:* Ibid., 213.

76   *There was also:* Philip Weiss, "Herman-Neutics," *The New York Times*, December 15, 1996.

76   *During his research:* Ibid.

76   *"I thought how great":* McDowell, "Literary Luminary Gets His Diploma after 57 Years."

76   *Berryman exempted Bob:* Paul L. Mariani, *Dream Song: The Life of John Berryman*, 2nd ed. (Amherst, MA: University of Massachusetts Press, 1996), 42.

77   *By the spring of 1935:* Merton, *The Seven Storey Mountain*, 155.

77   *"It was as Mark's student":* Eileen Simpson, *Poets in Their Youth: A Memoir* (New York: Random House, 1982), 23.

77   *Together they advanced:* David Lehman, "Robert Giroux '36," *Columbia College Today* (Fall 1987).

77   *"helped me bridge a gap":* Robert Giroux to Leonard Wallace Robinson, 16 April 1971, Box 507, FSG Records, NYPL.

77   *"more or less the star":* Merton, *The Seven Storey Mountain*, 155.

77   *Giroux was the inside man:* John Haffenden, *The Life of John Berryman* (Boston: Routledge and K. Paul, 1982), 73.

77   *"A Catholic and a person":* Merton, *The Seven Storey Mountain*, 154–55.

78   *He played jazz piano:* Thomas Merton, interview by Robert Giroux, November 23, 1982, transcript, Box 511, FSG Records, NYPL.

78   *He also said Giroux:* Halliday, *John Berryman and the Thirties*, 85.

78   *He had already won:* Mariani, *Dream Song*, 53–55.

78   *Giroux told friends:* Halliday, *John Berryman and the Thirties*, 92n.

78   *After graduating:* Robert Giroux to John Berryman, 10 October 1936, Box 2, Papers of Robert Giroux. "All is forgiven of Giroux by Van Doren. Prodigal son may come home, having squandered his birthright—chance of being *Nation*'s film critic. Van Doren stated he 'didn't know exactly what the trouble was' and decided 'let's forget it,' when he should have been mortally offended and harbored a lasting resentment against the wretch."

78   *But all his interviews:* Robert A. Carter, "Outliving the Bastards," *Publishers Weekly*, November 14, 1986.

79   *"But I am really grateful":* Giroux to Berryman, 10 October 1936, Box 2, Papers of Robert Giroux.

79   *"Here, as the world heard it"*: Crisis–A Report from the Columbia Broadcasting *System* (New York: CBS, 1938), 1.

80   *The founders of the firm*: Giroux, *The Education of an Editor*, 13–15.

80   *"He needed no editing"*: Ibid., 16.

80   *"the silent partner"*: Ibid., 22–23.

80   *Virginia had filled her pockets*: Giroux, interview by Plimpton.

80   *"Bob," Brace said*: Giroux, *The Education of an Editor*, 23.

81   *"You didn't seem to realize"*: Giroux, Box 511, FSG Records, NYPL; Giroux struck the phrase about a book needing a plot from the edited version sent to Merton's archives—probably for economy, though decorum may have played its part.

81   *After Merton's fourth submission*: Robert Giroux to *Columbia College Today*, undated, Box 506, FSG Records, NYPL; letter sent on the occasion of Thomas Merton's death.

81   *Van Doren sent the poetry*: Merton, *The Seven Storey Mountain*, xiii.

81   *But by then Giroux*: Mariani, *Dream Song*, 121.

82   *Nonetheless, he advised*: Haffenden, *The Life of John Berryman*, 217.

82   *"I was so enthralled"*: Robert Giroux, "Hard Years and Scary Days: Remembering Jean Stafford," *The New York Times Book Review*, June 10, 1984.

82   *"it came as a complete"*: Ann Hulbert, *The Interior Castle: The Art and Life of Jean Stafford* (New York: A. A. Knopf, 1992), 140.

83   *"It is well written"*: Giroux, "Hard Years and Scary Days."

84   *But as the day*: Simpson, *Poets in Their Youth*, 22–23, 55–58.

84   *Published in September*: David Roberts, *Jean Stafford: A Biography* (Boston: Little, Brown, 1988), 222.

84   *Straus conceded the fact*: Roger W. Straus, Jr., interview by Louis Sheaffer, "Reminiscences," January 27, 1978, 469–71, CCOHC.

84   *The poet had arrived*: Robert Giroux, "Eliot at 100," draft introduction, City Center Stage II, April 11, 1988, Box 514, folder 6, FSG Records, NYPL.

84   *Giroux later compared*: Giroux the opera fanatic was invoking the graveyard statue of an Italian knight whom Mozart's famous reprobate invites to dinner—the same statue that later drags him to Hell.

85   *He also had a reputation*: Robert Giroux, "A Personal Memoir," *Sewanee Review* 74, no. 1 (Winter 1966), 331.

85   *Henry Volkening had already*: Robert Giroux, draft of speech for Ivan Sandroff/National Book Critics Circle Board Award, January 1988, Box 11, folder 33, Papers of Robert Giroux.

85   *Tiny ducklings wading*: Giroux, "A Personal Memoir," 331.

85   *"There was something about"*: Giroux, interview by Plimpton, 168–69.

85   *Seeing a plaque*: Giroux, "Eliot at 100."

86   *Giroux soon became:* Giroux, interview by Plimpton, 185.

86   *After Giroux settled:* Robert Giroux, draft of speech at Washington University of St. Louis, September 30, 1989, Box 514, folder 7, FSG Records, NYPL.

86   *"a liveliness of spirit":* Giroux, "A Personal Memoir," 337.

86   *One of Eliot's private jokes:* Jason Epstein, interview by author, September 10, 2009.

86   *Giroux visited Eliot:* "Institute for Advanced Study Frees Scholar from Class, Tests, Students," *The Harvard Crimson,* November 7, 1953.

86   *Both stand in profile:* Postcard, Box 3, folder 13, Papers of Robert Giroux.

87   *In March 1946:* Paul L. Mariani, *Lost Puritan: A Life of Robert Lowell* (New York: W. W. Norton, 1994), 133.

87   *He quickly convinced:* Hulbert, *The Interior Castle,* 192; Ian Hamilton, *Robert Lowell: A Biography* (New York: Random House, 1982), 108.

87   *The sales of* Boston Adventure: Simpson, *Poets in Their Youth,* 116.

87   *"The ending comes off":* Hulbert, *The Interior Castle,* 199.

87   *Jealousy boils over:* Jean Stafford, "An Influx of Poets," in *The Collected Stories of Jean Stafford* (New York: Farrar, Straus and Giroux, 2005), 466–88.

88   *Lowell and Gertrude:* Mariani, *Lost Puritan,* 139.

88   *"I fell in love":* Simpson, *Poets in Their Youth,* 144.

88   *By late November:* Hulbert, *The Interior Castle,* 225; Roberts, *Jean Stafford,* 250–53.

89   *He saw Stafford often:* Roberts, *Jean Stafford,* 265.

89   *She wrote Lowell:* Mariani, *Lost Puritan,* 149.

89   *He gave her over:* Frances Kiernan, *Seeing Mary Plain: A Life of Mary McCarthy* (New York: W. W. Norton and Co., 2000), 322.

89   *Lowell eventually turned:* Hamilton, *Robert Lowell,* 124.

89   *If Giroux had had any:* Robert Giroux, "The Poet in the Asylum," *The Atlantic,* August 1, 1988; in various drafts, Box 5, folders 2–8, Papers of Robert Giroux.

90   *"Even people locked up":* Hamilton, *Robert Lowell,* 158–59.

90   *"problem mothers":* Giroux, interview by Plimpton, 165.

91   *"did a very good job":* Robert Giroux, introduction to *The Seven Storey Mountain,* by Thomas Merton, xi–xviii. Two facts—Merton's excision of the illegitimate child and the final quotation noted here—from similar text of lecture given April 2, 2002, St. Joseph's University, and inscribed to Patrick Samway; Box 4, folder 18, Papers of Robert Giroux.

91   *Waugh not only wrote:* Robert Giroux, inscribed lecture, April 2, 2002, St. Joseph University, Box 4, folder 18, Papers of Robert Giroux, 14–16.

91   *The* New York Times: Ibid., 17–18.

91   *"appeared at a time":* Giroux, introduction to Merton, *The Seven Storey Mountain,* xvi.

92   *As Elie emphasizes:* Paul Elie, *The Life You Save May Be Your Own: An American Pilgrimage* (Farrar, Straus and Giroux, 2003), 169.

92 *She arranged benefits:* "Carmen de Arango Engaged to Marry," *The New York Times*, March 6, 1941.

92 *Among the guests:* Kathleen Mulvehill, interview by author, January 3, 2010; Maclovia Rodriguez, interview by author, February 12, 2010; wedding account given in "Carmen de Arango Wed in Greenwich," *The New York Times*, August 31, 1952.

92 *He promised to pray:* Thomas Merton to Robert Giroux, February 1953, Box 4, folder 11, Papers of Robert Giroux.

93 *A* New York Times *notice:* "Paid Notice: Deaths Giroux, Carmen de Arango," *The New York Times*, March 23, 1999.

93 *Some thought O'Connor:* Brad Gooch, *Flannery: A Life of Flannery O'Connor* (New York: Little, Brown, 2009), 159–60.

93 *As was usually the case:* Flannery O'Connor, *The Habit of Being: Letters*, ed. Sally Fitzgerald (New York: Farrar, Straus and Giroux, 1979), 8.

93 *"Lowell was of course":* Gooch, *Flannery*, 172.

93 *Elsewhere Giroux said:* Robert Giroux, draft of speech at Walter Reade Theatre, April 30, 2001, New York, Box 4, folder 30, Papers of Robert Giroux.

93 *They had a firm option:* Gooch, *Flannery*, 135.

94 *Giroux, on receiving them:* O'Connor, *The Habit of Being*, 9: Flannery O'Connor to Elizabeth McKee, 3 February 1949.

94 *"The letter is addressed":* Ibid.: Flannery O'Connor to Elizabeth McKee, 17 February 1949.

94 *"The finished book":* Ibid., 10: Flannery O'Connor to John Selby, 18 February 1949.

94 *He also called O'Connor:* Ibid., 17.

94 *That year, when their daughter:* Giroux, draft of speech at Walter Reade Theatre, Papers of Robert Giroux.

94 *The final corrected galley:* O'Connor, *The Habit of Being*, 29: Flannery O'Connor to Robert Giroux, 3 December 1951.

94 Wise Blood *was:* Gooch, *Flannery*, 206.

95 *Giroux waited too long:* Mariani, *Dream Song*, 203.

95 *"immediately recognized":* Alfred Kazin, *New York Jew* (Syracuse, NY: Syracuse University Press, 1996), 200.

96 *"Malamud wanted success":* Philip Davis, *Bernard Malamud: A Writer's Life* (New York: Oxford University Press, 2007), 113–14.

96 *As they shook hands:* Robert Giroux, draft of Malamud Memorial Service speech, April 20, 1986, 92nd Street Y, New York; Box 4, folder 9, Papers of Robert Giroux.

96 *On its publication:* Davis, *Bernard Malamud*, 111.

96 *After Harcourt, Brace:* "2 Publishing Firms to Merge on Friday," *The New York Times*, December 29, 1947.

96 *"Terrible snob":* Giroux, interview by Plimpton, 182.

96 *"His background was":* Ibid., 176–77.

96 *A few years later:* Robert Giroux to Jessamyn McPherson, 14 April 1977, Box 508, FSG Records, NYPL.

98 *He said he handed:* Giroux, interview by Plimpton, 181–83.

98 *Only Giroux's abject apologies:* Ibid., 176–77.

98 *Van Doren had read:* Ann Charters, *Kerouac: A Biography* (New York: St. Martin's Press, 1994), 107.

98 *Kazin, Kerouac's teacher:* Joyce Johnson, *The Voice Is All: The Lonely Victory of Jack Kerouac* (New York: Viking, 2012), 312, 321–25.

98 *"John Kerouac":* Jack Kerouac, *Selected Letters, 1940–1956*, ed. Ann Charters (New York: Viking, 1995), 184.

98 *Over lunch:* Giroux, interview by Plimpton, 188.

98 *Kerouac, already rejected:* Kerouac, *Selected Letters, 1940–1956*, 185–86: Jack Kerouac to Ed White, 29 March 1949.

99 *"In that period Jack saw":* Robert Giroux to Aaron Latham, 9 February 1972, Box 507, FSG Records, NYPL.

99 *"I don't believe":* Robert Giroux to Robert Calaluce, 7 October 1976, Box 508, FSG Records, NYPL.

99 *"I had put it":* Robert Giroux to Jack Kerouac, 10 May 1950, Jack Kerouac Papers, Berg Collection, New York Public Library.

99 *But he had two special:* Giroux to Calaluce, 7 October 1976, Box 508, FSG Records, NYPL.

99 *"Jack," she told her son:* Giroux, interview by Plimpton, 189.

99 *In July 1949:* Robert Giroux to Jack Kerouac, 8 July 1949, Jack Kerouac Papers, Berg Collection.

99 *In Denver he and Kerouac:* Robert Giroux to Jack Kerouac, 1 August 1950, Jack Kerouac Papers, Berg Collection.

99 *Kerouac bragged:* Kerouac, *Selected Letters, 1940–1956*, 212: Jack Kerouac to Neal Cassady, 28 July 1949; ibid., 210: Jack Kerouac to Allen Ginsberg, 26 July 1949.

100 *But Kerouac reminded him:* Ibid., 208–10: Jack Kerouac to Allen Ginsberg, 26 July 1949.

100 *"I had seen that":* Jack Kerouac, *Windblown World: The Journals of Jack Kerouac, 1947–1954*, ed. Douglas Brinkley (New York: Viking, 2004), 215.

100 *Giroux took Kerouac:* Johnson, *The Voice Is All*, 356–48; Joyce Johnson, interview by author.

101 *Kerouac phoned one day:* Giroux, interview by Plimpton, 189–90.

101 *"All the biographers":* Ibid., 190.

101 *"Giroux says HE likes:* Kerouac, *Selected Letters, 1940–1956*, 318: Jack Kerouac to Neal Cassady, 10 June 1951; Kerouac, *Selected Letters, 1940–1956*, 320: Jack

Kerouac to Neal Cassady, 24 June 1951. A footnote by editor Ann Charters glosses Giroux's conflicting version.

102 *"A lot of people"*: Joyce Johnson, interview by author, February 3, 2011.

102 *He had already declined:* Robert Giroux to Jack Kerouac, 22 June 1950, Jack Kerouac Papers, Berg Collection. Giroux, a vocal critic of the fledgling drug culture, didn't much like Ginsberg, either; he called him "a con artist" in a letter to Aaron Latham, 9 February 1972.

102 *Giroux wrote back:* Robert Giroux to Ellen Lucey, 21 July 1952, Jack Kerouac Papers, Berg Collection.

102 *And near the close:* Jack Kerouac to Robert Giroux, *Selected Letters*, 444–46.

103 *"This isn't the way"*: Randall Jarrell to Jay Laughlin, December 1949, and Jarrell to Robert Giroux, February 1950, *Selected Letters*, 235–37.

103 *"Can nothing be done"*: Alfred Kazin to Robert Giroux, 3 December 1952, Box 1, folder 12, Papers of Robert Giroux.

103 *One of the highest bidders:* Roberts, *Jean Stafford*, 314–15.

104 *"has announced his 'personal' editing"*: Robert Giroux to Alfred Kazin, 15 June 1978, Box 508, FSG Records, NYPL.

104 *Jovanovich's ascension:* Robert Giroux to F. W. Dupee, June 1969, Box 506, FSG Records, NYPL; Ted Morgan, "Feeding the Stream," *Saturday Review*, September 1, 1979.

104 *T. S. Eliot had written:* Robert Giroux, draft of "A Personal Memoir," Box 514, FSG Records, NYPL.

Chapter Four

105 *Giroux named the drawing:* Robert Giroux to Lisa Brower, 13 November 1995, Papers of Robert Giroux, Loyola University, New Orleans; Drawing in Giroux Artifacts, FSG Records, NYPL.

106 *"I feel like a new man"*: Robert Giroux to Anne Ford, 6 April 1955, Box 506, FSG Records, NYPL; "form" letters also located in 1955 folder.

106 *"an endearing and slightly ridiculous figure"*: Edmund Wilson, *The Sixties: The Last Journal, 1960–1972*, ed. Lewis M. Dabney (New York: Farrar, Straus and Giroux, 1993), 425.

106 *Giroux marked up:* Robert Lowell to Robert Giroux, 5 May 1955, Box 506, FSG Records, NYPL.

106 *He wrote to Peter du Sautoy:* Robert Giroux to Peter du Sautoy, 22 April 1955, Box 506, FSG Records, NYPL.

106 *He only found out:* Robert Giroux, "Eliot: A Personal Memoir," *Sewanee Review* 74, no. 1 (Winter 1966).

106 *"I'm not going to let"*: Ted Morgan, "Feeding the Stream," *Saturday Review*, September 1, 1979.

107 *"In terms of your career":* Robert Giroux to Bernard Malamud, 20 November 1953, Box 4, folder 8, Papers of Robert Giroux.

107 *"I see no sales":* J. H. McCallum to Robert Giroux, 31 May 1956, Box 2, Papers of Robert Giroux; Pascal Covici to Robert Giroux, 20 July 1956, Box 2, Papers of Robert Giroux.

107 *Giroux's first reaction:* Robert Giroux to Maarten Asscher, 6 April 1998, Box 2, Papers of Robert Giroux.

107 *Over the next two decades:* Philip Davis, *Bernard Malamud: A Writer's Life* (New York: Oxford University Press, 2007), 114.

107 *He left O'Connor:* Flannery O'Connor, *The Habit of Being: Letters*, ed. Sally Fitzgerald (New York: Farrar, Straus and Giroux, 1979), 76: Flannery O'Connor to Catharine Carver, 2 April 1955.

107 *He advised her to add:* Ibid., 85: Flannery O'Connor to the Fitzgeralds, 10 June 1955.

108 *She made these changes:* Ibid., 120: Flannery O'Connor to Catherine McKee, 5 December 1955.

108 *Lindley's wife:* Elizabeth Bishop and Robert Lowell, *Words in Air: The Complete Correspondence between Elizabeth Bishop and Robert Lowell*, ed. Thomas Travisano with Saskia Hamilton (New York: Farrar, Straus and Giroux, 2008), 266: Robert Lowell to Elizabeth Bishop, 18 September 1958.

108 *Harcourt's editors beat a path:* O'Connor, *Habit of Being*, 276: Flannery O'Connor to the Fitzgeralds, 10 April 1958.

109 *In the summer of 1957:* Bishop and Lowell, *Words in Air*, 207–8: Robert Lowell to Elizabeth Bishop, 3 July 1957; 208n.

109 *"I really think":* Paul L. Mariani, *Dream Song: The Life of John Berryman*, 2nd ed. (Amherst, MA: University of Massachusetts Press, 1996), 295.

109 *"struck again by its power":* Robert Giroux to John Berryman, 13 June 1956, Box 26, FSG Records, NYPL.

109 *Giroux concluded:* Robert Giroux to John Berryman, 19 July 1956, Box 26, FSG Records, NYPL.

110 To Bob: Book dedication draft, Box 2, folder 22, Papers of Robert Giroux.

110 *"Edmund Wilson regrets":* Postcard, Box 806, folder 15, FSG Records, NYPL.

110 *"Inspire Roger!":* Robert Giroux, draft introduction to "Twenty-Five Years: A Retrospective," Box 8, folder 3, Papers of Robert Giroux.

111 *In his fishing lodge:* Roger W. Straus, Jr., interview by Louis Sheaffer, "Reminiscences," February 15, 1978, 538–39, CCOHC.

111 *"He looked much younger":* Helen Weaver, interview by author, January 20, 2011.

111 *"My father was 'the fuck-up'":* Roger W. Straus III, interview by author, July 23, 2009.

112 *"beneath all this crap":* Elisabeth Sifton, interview by author, January 22, 2010.

113 *"At least I'm not at Choate"*: Roger W. Straus III, interview by author, March 11, 2010.

114 *A footnote lists:* Will Herberg, *Protestant, Catholic, Jew: An Essay in American Religious Sociology* (Chicago: University of Chicago Press, 1983), 190, 205.

114 *Not on that list:* "Farrar, Straus and Cudahy Celebrates Tenth Anniversary," press release, 1956, FSG Archives.

114 *Straus's partnership:* Roger W. Straus, Jr., to Lesser Zussman et al., 7 June 1968, Box 150, FSG Records, NYPL. Straus could barely contain his pique after JPS head Lesser Zussman argued that Heschel had been published "all over the lot."

114 *"I suppose as a Jew":* "Reminiscences," March 1, 1978, 646–47, CCOHC.

115 *"found the religious side":* Susannah Heschel, interview by author, January 7, 2010.

115 *"There was this little man":* "Reminiscences," Janurary 18, 1978, 420, CCOHC.

115 *The novelist and story writer:* Based on accounts in: Paul Kresh, *Isaac Bashevis Singer, the Magician of West 86th Street: A Biography* (New York: Dial Press, 1979); Florence Noiville, *Isaac B. Singer: A Life*, trans. Catherine Temerson (New York: Farrar, Straus and Giroux, 2006); Robin Hemley, interview by author, November 22, 2009.

116 *It was right there:* Isaac Bashevis Singer, *The Family Moskat*, trans. A. H. Gross (New York: Farrar, Straus and Giroux, 1965), jacket copy.

117 *He said this while:* Dorothea Straus, *The Paper Trail: A Recollection of Writers* (Wakefield, RI: Moyer Bell, 1997), 198.

117 *"I must hurry to tell you":* Harold Vursell to Isaac Bashevis Singer, 7 January 1965, Box 327, FSG Records, NYPL.

117 *At the end of the session:* Noiville, *Isaac B. Singer*, 106.

117 *"We are like remote cousins":* Straus, *The Paper Trail*, 198.

118 *Giroux agreed and asked:* Robert Blair Kaiser, *Clerical Error: A True Story* (New York: Continuum, 2002), 135n.

118 *In order to boost:* Silvio Senigallia to Roger W. Straus, Jr., 22 May 1963, Box 804, folder 23, FSG Records, NYPL.

118 *"In each of his yarns":* Kaiser, *Clerical Error*, 180.

119 *He persuaded British:* "Reminiscences," January 18, 1978, 421–25, CCOHC.

119 *Heschel's biographer:* Edward K. Kaplan, *Spiritual Radical: Abraham Joshua Heschel in America, 1940–1972* (New Haven, CT: Yale University Press, 2007), 254.

119 *Among its inaccuracies:* Peter Hinzmann to A. J. Heschel et al., 5 January 1970, Box 150, FSG Records, NYPL.

120 *She had one question:* "Reminiscences," January 18, 1978, 431, CCOHC.

120 *"We must have a long talk":* Roger W. Straus, Jr., to Susannah Heschel, 11 February 1977, Box 150, FSG Records, NYPL.

121 *They put together:* "Reminiscences," June 28, 1978, 668–70, CCOHC.

121 Reader's Digest *paid:* Robert Giroux to Viña Delmar, 19 July 1955, Box 506, FSG Records, NYPL; "Talk of the Town: Nautical Party," *The New Yorker*, February 4, 1956, 17–18.

122 *"The thing was up to here":* Richard Merkin, "An Ode to Roger Straus, a Bookmaker with Qualities . . . Even If You've Never Heard of His Favorite Book," *GQ*, September 1988.

122 *Wilson's indictment:* Edmund Wilson, *Memoirs of Hecate County* (New York: Octagon Books, 1979), 250–51.

122 *In 1956 they retained:* Edward de Grazia, *Girls Lean Back Everywhere: The Law of Obscenity and the Assault on Genius* (New York: Random House, 1992), 236.

122 *Straus predicted success:* Roger W. Straus, Jr., to Edmund Wilson, 26 July 1956, Box 389, FSG Records, NYPL.

122 *Wilson's first two books:* Jeffrey Meyers, *Edmund Wilson: A Biography* (Boston: Houghton Mifflin, 1995), 330.

122 *The only Wilson book:* "Reminiscences," November 23, 1977, 312, CCOHC.

122 *Wilson needed a hit:* Lewis M. Dabney, *Edmund Wilson: A Life in Literature* (New York: Farrar, Straus and Giroux, 2005), 454.

123 *The only way Farrar, Straus:* "Reminiscences," March 1, 1978, 633, CCOHC.

123 *It was a costly plan:* Ibid., 633–46.

124 *Straus helped out:* Edmund Wilson to Roger W. Straus, Jr., 8 July 1961, Box 806, folder 15, FSG Records, NYPL.

124 *Roger frequently "prepaid":* Roger W. Straus, Jr., memo, 1 March 1960, Box 389, FSG Records, NYPL.

124 *"You are making a silly":* Roger W. Straus, Jr., to Edmund Wilson, 15 November 1960, Box 389, FSG Records, NYPL.

124 *"You are mistaken":* Edmund Wilson to Roger W. Straus, Jr., 29 March 1960, Box 389, FSG Records, NYPL; reprinted in Meyers, *Edmund Wilson*, 331.

124 *After Straus's key subsidiary:* Roger W. Straus, Jr., to Edmund Wilson, 5 April 1963, Box 389, FSG Records, NYPL.

Chapter Five

126 *The Strauses felt:* Rita Reif, "Versatile Furnishings Ease Art of Entertaining in Town House," *The New York Times*, April 9, 1960.

126 *His face was rather:* Dorothea Straus, *Palaces and Prisons* (Boston: Houghton Mifflin, 1976), 101.

127 *"my mother would be lonely":* Roger W. Straus III, interview by author, June 5, 2009.

128 *"The three of us":* Ibid.

128 *"a Virginia Woolf type book":* Roger W. Straus, Jr., interview by Louis Sheaffer, "Reminiscences," February 15, 1978, 534, CCOHC.

128 *Heschel was not:* Roger W. Straus, Jr., to Robert Giroux, memo, 17 March 1977, Box 150, FSG Records, NYPL. He added, in reference to a collection of essays, "[Dorothea] tells me they are first rate."

129 *Later he came to regret:* "Reminiscences," February 15, 1978, 549, CCOHC.

130 *He wrote many letters:* Dorothea Straus, *The Paper Trail: A Recollection of Writers* (Wakefield, RI: Moyer Bell, 1997), 99.

131 *"There is a certain":* N. R. Kleinfield, "Roger Straus: Making It as an Independent," *The New York Times Book Review,* March 2, 1980.

131 *"Is it a move":* Mary McCarthy to Roger W. Straus, Jr., 8 June 1960, Straus Papers, Box 5, FSG Records, NYPL.

132 *"And now a bit of news":* Roger W. Straus, Jr., to Mary McCarthy, 14 June 1960, Straus Papers, Box 5, FSG Records, NYPL. The next sentence in the letter reads: "It also reminds me, dear Mary, that we have sort of a contract for a book of essays." Her *Theater Chronicles* would be collected under Noonday in 1963.

132 *When I became a publisher:* Jason Epstein, *Book Business: Publishing Past, Present, and Future* (New York: W. W. Norton, 2001), 56.

133 *Roger called him:* Roger W. Straus, Jr., to Mary McCarthy, 14 June 1960, Box 802, folder 23, FSG Records, NYPL.

134 *But by the late fifties:* Robin Hemley, "The Moment Juste," courtesy of Robin Hemley.

134 *Straus made the usual:* "Reminiscences," June 28, 1978, 676, CCOHC, for the cost of Noonday.

134 *One potential stockholder:* Correspondence between Roger W. Straus, Jr., and Harvey Breit, Box 789, folder 21, FSG Records, NYPL.

135 *Around that time:* Roger Straus, Jr., letter to the editor, *The Bookseller,* November 3, 1973.

135 *"The new address":* Roger W. Straus, Jr., to Chanler Chapman, 28 September 1960, Box 799, folder 5, FSG Records, NYPL.

137 *"the poorest publisher":* N. R. Kleinfield, "A Success Story at Farrar, Straus," *The New York Times,* December 1, 1978.

137 *Hemley's son Robin:* Hemley, "The Moment Juste."

137 *FSC's Paris scout:* Herbert Lottman to Paula Diamond, 1 December 1961, Box 321, FSG Records, NYPL.

137 *"Of course he's a Yiddish writer":* Paula Diamond to Herbert Lottman, 5 December 1961, Box 327, FSG Records, NYPL.

137 *Soon afterward:* Roger W. Straus, Jr., to Herbert Lottman, 14 January 1965, Box 327, FSG Records, NYPL.

138 *Within three years:* Paul Kresh, *Isaac Bashevis Singer, the Magician of West 86th Street: A Biography* (New York: Dial Press, 1979), 331; Memo, 8 May 1961, Box 327, FSG Records, NYPL Contract, 4 June 1963, Box 327, FSG Records,

NYPL; Heinrich Ledig-Rowohlt to Roger W. Straus, Jr., 23 February 1967, Box 327, FSG Records, NYPL.

138 *"Mr. Straus":* Isaac Bashevis Singer to Roger W. Straus, Jr., 31 May 1963, Box 327, FSG Records, NYPL.

138 *One worrying hour later:* Robin Hemley, interview by author, November 22, 2009.

138 *He pleaded for fair pay:* Roger W. Straus, Jr., memo, 25 July 1963, Box 327, FSG Records, NYPL.

138 *In return, he demanded:* Hemley, "The Moment Juste."

139 *"a clean Malachi Martin":* "Reminiscences," January 27, 1978, 463, CCOHC.

139 *She was to receive:* Roger W. Straus, Jr., to Sheila Cudahy, 13 July 1962, Box 327, FSG Records, NYPL.

139 *She would portray Straus:* Edward Pellegrini, interview by author, February 15, 2010.

139 *"All those things":* "Reminiscences," January 27, 1978, 463, CCOHC.

139 *Giroux, surprised to see:* Helen Weaver, *The Awakener: A Memoir of Kerouac and the Fifties* (San Francisco: City Lights Books, 2009), 60.

140 *In a handwritten postscript:* Robert Giroux to Jack Kerouac, 18 April 1962, Jack Kerouac Papers, Berg Collection, New York Public Library.

140 *"pretended to dislike Joyce":* Weaver, *The Awakener,* 99.

140 *"In my last two years":* Ibid., 117.

140 *Of all the manuscripts:* Helen Weaver, interview by author, January 20, 2011.

141 *Published in 1962:* Farrar, Straus and Giroux report to United States Trust, 24 September 1973, Box 513, FSG Records, NYPL.

141 *"I drink and drink":* Jack Kerouac to Robert Giroux, 31 March 1962, Jack Kerouac Papers, Berg Collection.

141 *"Mr. Giroux":* Robert Giroux, interview by George Plimpton, *The Paris Review,* no. 155 (Summer 2000), 180.

141 *On Emerald Beach:* Robert Giroux, "T. S. Eliot: A Personal Memoir," draft, Box 514, folder 7, FSG Records, NYPL.

141 *But the first book:* Announcement for *Publishers Weekly,* 28 September 1964, Box 506, FSG Records, NYPL.

142 *"Let's make an end":* John Berryman to Robert Giroux, 18 February 1963, Box 26, FSG Records, NYPL.

142 *Giroux wrote that:* Robert Giroux to John Berryman, 8 March 1963, Box 26, FSG Records, NYPL.

142 *Giroux tried to cheer him:* John Berryman to Robert Giroux, 16 July 1965, Box 26, FSG Records, NYPL; Robert Giroux to John Berryman, 19 July 1965, Box 26, FSG Records, NYPL.

142 *He rarely expressed it:* Elizabeth Bishop and Robert Lowell, *Words in Air: The Complete Correspondence between Elizabeth Bishop and Robert Lowell,* ed.

Thomas Travisano with Saskia Hamilton (New York: Farrar, Straus and Giroux, 2008), 288.

Chapter Six

144 *"Jason Epstein told me"*: Robert Giroux to Susan Sontag, 1 June 1981, Box 509, FSG Records, NYPL.

144 *She had told friends:* Ibid.

144 *Straus separately confirmed:* Roger W. Straus, Jr., interview by Louis Sheaffer, "Reminiscences," July 12, 1978, 775, CCOHC.

145 *"He absolutely flipped"*: Robert Giroux to Susan Sontag, 1 June 1981, Box 509, FSG Records, NYPL.

145 *Straus probably met:* Carl Rollyson and Lisa Paddock, *Susan Sontag: The Making of an Icon* (New York: W. W. Norton, 2000), 76.

145 *On April 30, 1962:* Roger W. Straus, Jr., to Susan Sontag, 30 April 1962, Box 344, FSG Records, NYPL.

145 *Phillips recalled:* William Phillips, *A Partisan View: Five Decades in the Politics of Literature* (Piscataway, NJ: Transaction Publishers, 2003), 255–56.

146 *Placing the book within:* Susan Sontag, "Demons and Dreams," *Partisan Review* 29 (Summer 1962), 460–63.

146 *Years later:* Edmund Wilson, *The Sixties: The Last Journal, 1960–1972*, ed. Lewis M. Dabney (New York: Farrar, Straus and Giroux, 1993), 202.

146 *The first time they met:* Ibid., 179.

147 *Though he would have:* Frances Kiernan, *Seeing Mary Plain: A Life of Mary McCarthy* (New York: W. W. Norton and Co., 2000), 538.

147 *Just after* The Benefactor: Lila Karpf to Catharine Meyer, 28 August 1963, Box 346, FSG Records, NYPL.

147 *Published in 1966:* Roger W. Straus, Jr., to Monique Nathan, 18 September 1963, Box 344, FSG Records, NYPL.

147 *He wrote to a friend:* Roger W. Straus, Jr., to Candida Donadio, memo attached to letter, 2 February 1968, Box 342, FSG Records, NYPL.

147 *"And that was that"*: Roger W. Straus, Jr., to Alexander S. Frere, 3 February 1966, Box 800, folder 9, FSG Records, NYPL.

147 *"You're the only person"*: Sigrid Nunez, *Sempre Susan: A Memoir of Susan Sontag* (New York: Atlas & Co., 2011), 40.

148 *She also received:* Checks and attached memos: 14 March 1963, 1 August 1963, and 4 August 1964, Box 344, folder 1, FSG Records, NYPL.

148 *Straus touted her:* Roger W. Straus, Jr., to Arthur M. Schlesinger, Jr., 2 July 1963, Box 344, FSG Records, NYPL.

148 *She answered:* Susan Sontag to Gladys Carr, cc'd to Roger W. Straus, Jr., 13 April 1965, Box 342, FSG Records, NYPL.

148 *Another time:* Susan Sontag to Roger W. Straus, Jr., 7 February 1974, Box 342, FSG Records, NYPL.

148 *From the start:* Roger W. Straus, Jr., memo, 17 September 1963, Box 342, FSG Records, NYPL.

148 *"regularly employed":* Robert Wohlforth to "Whom It May Concern," 18 May 1966, Box 342, FSG Records, NYPL.

149 *But then she would:* Susan Sontag to Roger W. Straus, Jr., 25 February 1971, Straus Papers, Box 8, FSG Records, NYPL.

149 *On this occasion:* Roger W. Straus, Jr., to Susan Sontag, 1 March 1971, Straus Papers, Box 8, FSG Records, NYPL.

149 *She added a highly:* Susan Sontag to Roger W. Straus, Jr., 5 July 1972, Box 344, FSG Records, NYPL.

149 *"Your mail isn't as interesting":* Roger W. Straus, Jr., to Susan Sontag, 9 June 1966, Box 805, folder 9, FSG Records, NYPL.

150 *"As I get older":* Roger W. Straus, Jr., to Alexander S. Frere, 23 December 1964, Box 800, folder 9, FSG Records, NYPL.

150 *It says something:* Ibid.

150 *As Sigrid Nunez wrote:* Nunez, *Sempre Susan*, 71.

151 *"That was his idea of Heaven":* Peggy Miller, interviews by author, October 23, 2008, and July 2, 2009—as are quotes below. For Leo K. Miller: "Deaths," *The New York Times*, March 20, 1944.

153 *Farrar Straus intends:* Roger W. Straus, Jr., to Alexander S. Frere, 9 June 1964, Box 800, folder 9, FSG Records, NYPL.

155 *"It was soon clear":* Robert Giroux, "Henry Robbins: In Memoriam," printed remarks, Box 509, FSG Records, NYPL.

155 *"Henry had his eye":* Christopher Lehmann-Haupt, interview by author, September 17, 2009.

155 *The Catholic satirist:* Roger W. Straus, Jr., to Alexander S. Frere, 25 June 1964, Box 800, folder 9, FSG Records, NYPL.

156 *"soft-spoken":* "Henry Robbins, Editor in Chief of Trade Books at Dutton, Dies," *The New York Times*, August 1, 1979.

156 *At the same time:* Giroux, "Henry Robbins: In Memoriam."

156 *Straus would apologize:* Lehmann-Haupt, interview by author.

156 *"a man who took himself":* Michael Korda, *Another Life: A Memoir of Other People* (New York: Random House, 1999), 368.

156 *"Henry was hot-headed":* Tracy Daugherty, *Hiding Man: A Biography of Donald Barthelme* (New York: St. Martin's Press, 2009), 306.

156 *Robbins expressed:* Henry Robbins to Jessamyn West, 17 June 1965, Box 397, FSG Records, NYPL.

156 *The title of his first book:* Tom Wolfe, "There Goes (Varoom! Varoom!) That

Kandy-Kolored (Thphhhhhh!) Tangerine-Flake Streamline Baby . . . ," *Esquire*, November 1963.

157 *The "Ruler" in question:* Tom Wolfe, "Tiny Mummies! The True Story of the Ruler of 43rd Street's Land of the Walking Dead!" *New York*, April 11, 1965, 7–27; Tom Wolfe, "Lost in the Whichy Thicket," *New York*, April 18, 1965, 18–25.

157 *Wolfe's piece:* "Reminiscences," July 26, 1978, 845, CCOHC.

158 *Wolfe made the final decision:* Ibid., 847. For Wolfe on taking it out, see Gabriel Snyder, "Tom Wolfe Disinters 'Tiny Mummies!' after 35 Years," *The New York Observer*, February 14, 2000.

158 *It was divisive enough:* Dwight Macdonald, "Parajournalism II: Wolfe and The New Yorker," *The New York Review of Books*, February 3, 1966, 24.

158 *He also wrote:* Dwight Macdonald, "Parajournalism, or Tom Wolfe & His Magic Writing Machine," *The New York Review of Books*, August 26, 1965, 4.

158 *The writer had very recently:* "Reminiscences," July 26, 1978, 845, CCOHC.

158 *"the first literary mob scene":* Giroux, "Henry Robbins: In Memoriam."

158 *He wrote Roger:* Tom Wolfe to Roger W. Straus, Jr., undated (replied to by Straus 12 July 1965), Box 806, folder 17, FSG Records, NYPL.

159 *He envisioned: Roger W. Straus: A Celebration* (New York: Farrar, Straus and Giroux, 2005), 92.

159 *Your splendid dinner:* Tom Wolfe to Roger W. Straus, Jr., 21 February 1965, Box 806, folder 17, FSG Records, NYPL; Roger W. Straus, Jr., to Tom Wolfe, 26 February 1965, Box 806, folder 17, FSG Records, NYPL.

159 *"He transmitted":* Roger W. Straus III, interview by author, June 5, 2009.

159 *"Excellent book":* Kurt Vonnegut, Jr., review of *The Kandy-Kolored Tangerine-Flake Streamline Baby*, by Tom Wolfe, *The New York Times*, June 27, 1965.

160 *"I can't bring myself":* Tom Wolfe to Henry Robbins, 26 April 1967, Box 397, FSG Records, NYPL.

160 *She closed:* Lila Karpf to Irv Goodman, 12 May 1967, Box 397, FSG Records, NYPL.

161 *"It just made me laugh":* Carl Brandt, interview by author, February 7, 2011.

161 *"Harcourt, Brace":* Burt Boyar, interview by author, January 7, 2010.

162 *What Roger really felt:* "Reminiscences," July 26, 1978, 823, CCOHC.

162 *"We learned a lot":* Burt Boyar to Roger W. Straus, Jr., 14 December 1970, Box 79, FSG Records, NYPL.

162 *"Every editor would say":* Peggy Miller, interview by author, October 23, 2008.

164 *Unfortunately, a massive:* These strikes had a profound impact on the media that overlapped with Farrar, Straus's writers in several ways. In 1963 Bob Silvers, Elizabeth Hardwick, and Barbara Epstein (Jason's wife) founded *The

New York Review of Books in part to fill the gap created by the on-strike *Times Book Review*—and became for a time Susan Sontag's steadiest publisher after Roger Straus. The successive strikes also felled the *Herald Tribune*, Wolfe's great champions, though *New York* magazine emerged from its ashes.

164 *"Since when?":* Silvio Senigallia to Roger W. Straus, Jr., 8 November 1965, Box 804, folder 23, FSG Records, NYPL.

165 *When Percy won:* Patrick H. Samway, *Walker Percy: A Life* (New York: Farrar, Straus and Giroux, 1997), 219.

165 *Naturally, Percy began:* Ibid., 233.

165 *Robbins followed up:* Ibid., 237.

165 *"The three of us":* Joan Didion, *After Henry* (New York: Simon & Schuster, 1992), 16.

165 *"He enabled me":* Joan Didion, interview by author, August 5, 2011.

165 *Two years after:* Tracy Daugherty, *Hiding Man*, 299.

166 *"is not criticism at all":* Susan Sontag, *Against Interpretation, and Other Essays* (New York: Farrar, Straus and Giroux, 1966), viii.

Chapter Seven

168 *As their romance:* Quotations in this and following paragraphs: Nina Straus, interview by author, July 28, 2011.

170 *He let his son:* Much of the previous section from Roger W. Straus III, interview by author, June 5, 2009. Peter Clark material from Susan Bergholz, interview by author, February 9, 2011.

170 *FSG bought Hill & Wang:* Straus III, interview by author, October 29, 2009. Henry Raymont, "Farrar, Straus Gets Hill & Wang," *The New York Times*, September 29, 1971.

172 *"with Truman Capote":* Inge Feltrinelli, interview by author, September 7, 2009.

172 *"We have been singularly":* Roger W. Straus, Jr., to Allan Maclean, 3 August 1966, Box 804, folder 23, FSG Records, NYPL.

173 *Roloff brought FSG:* Michael Roloff, interview by author, September 9, 2009.

173 *Roger came to his:* Roger W. Straus, Jr., to Carlos Fuentes, 31 August 1966, Box 109, FSG Records, NYPL.

174 *There were about ten:* Inge Feltrinelli, interview by author, September 7, 2009.

175 *"Publishing in the sixties":* Matthew Evans, interview by author, October 11, 2010.

175 *He invited his scout:* Roger W. Straus, Jr., to Silvio Senigallia, 25 July 1967, Box 804, folder 23, FSG Records, NYPL.

175 *Roloff saw him:* Michael Roloff, interview by author, September 9, 2009.

176 *They usually stayed:* Michael Krüger, interview by author, February 18, 2010; also in *Roger W. Straus: A Celebration* (New York: Farrar, Straus and Giroux, 2005); confirmed by Peggy Miller.

176 *Take 1968:* Spring and Fall 1968 catalogs, Box 535, FSG Records, NYPL.

177 *He pleaded repeatedly:* "Roger Straus" entry, *Current Biography Illustrated,* 1980, FSG Archives.

177 *He put out a puff:* Isaac Frederick Marcosson, *Metal Magic: The Story of the American Smelting & Refining Company* (New York: Farrar, Straus, 1949); Frank J. Manheim, *A Garland of Weights: Some Notes on Collecting Antique French Glass Paperweights for Those Who Don't* (New York: Farrar, Straus and Giroux, 1967).

177 *The book:* "USIA Hit for Sponsoring Book Published in U.S.," *Publishers Weekly* 185, no. 31 (May 11, 1964).

178 *The problem:* Hedrick Smith, "U.S.I.A. Attacked on Anti-Red Book," *The New York Times,* May 3, 1964.

178 *"I said to this young man":* "Reminiscences," February 9, 1979, 1024–25, CCOHC.

178 *"That was my last":* Ian Parker, "Showboat," *The New Yorker,* April 8, 2002.

178 *"I have such an inexact":* Straus III, interview by author, October 29, 2009.

178 *He opposed:* Roger W. Straus, Jr., to Alexander S. Frere, 25 September 1964, Box 800, folder 9, FSG Records, NYPL: "I don't think Goldwater has a ghost of a chance, but having said that, I am doing something I have never done before, and that is to get an absentee ballot just to make sure I am right."

178 *"Lord knows":* Roger W. Straus, Jr., to Arthur M. Schlesinger, 19 March 1963, Box 800, folder 9, FSG Records, NYPL.

178 *In letters and cables:* Roger W. Straus, Jr., to Henry Kissinger, cable, 28 February 1969, Box 109, FSG Records, NYPL; Roger W. Straus, Jr., to John Mitchell, 28 February 1969, Box 109, FSG Records, NYPL.

179 *Before he died:* Carlos Fuentes, interview by author, September 22, 2009.

179 *"There is no ray":* Eduardo Cardenas to Sylvia Dudley, 6 July 1964, Box 109, FSG Records, NYPL.

180 *"It ain't exactly the way":* Roger W. Straus, Jr., to Carl Brandt, 7 November 1966, Box 261, FSG Records, NYPL.

180 *He spoke to Neruda:* Carlos Fuentes to Roger W. Straus, Jr., 2 November 1966, Box 261, FSG Records, NYPL.

180 *"I'm a meddler":* Paul Kresh, *Isaac Bashevis Singer, the Magician of West 86th Street: A Biography* (New York: Dial Press, 1979), 229.

181 *"This is the way":* "Reminiscences," January 24, 1979, 915, CCOHC.

181 *In the meantime:* Roger W. Straus, Jr., to Ernest Hecht, 17 April 1973, Box 261, FSG Records, NYPL; Roger W. Straus, Jr., to Carmen Balcells, 8 May 1973, Box 261, FSG Records, NYPL.

181 *Eventually, Roger threw in:* Carmen Balcells to Roger W. Straus, Jr., 16 April 1973, Box 263, FSG Records, NYPL; Roger W. Straus, Jr., to Balcells, 20 April 1973, Box 263, FSG Records, NYPL; Balcells to Roger W. Straus, Jr., 13 June 1973, Box 263, FSG Records, NYPL; Roger W. Straus, Jr., to Balcells, 20

June 1973, Box 263, FSG Records, NYPL; Balcells to Roger W. Straus, Jr., 24 August 1973, Box 263, FSG Records, NYPL; Roger W. Straus, Jr., to Balcells, 29 August 1973, Box 263, FSG Records, NYPL; Balcells to Roger W. Straus, Jr., 7 September 1973, Box 263, FSG Records, NYPL.

181 *"The North Americans"*: Herbert Mitgang, "Publishing: Neruda Speaks," *The New York Times*, January 7, 1977.

181 *Questioned about:* Adam Feinstein, *Pablo Neruda: A Passion for Life* (New York: Bloomsbury, 2004), 412–13.

182 *But Neruda died:* Ibid., 414.

182 *Neruda's widow, Matilde:* "Reminiscences," 917–19; Mitgang, "Publishing: Neruda Speaks."

182 *"no intention of becoming"*: Frank MacShane, "Neruda in New York," *The New York Times*, March 13, 1977.

183 *Roger called him:* Roger W. Straus, Jr., to Max Reinhardt, 22 July 1970, Box 340, FSG Records, NYPL.

184 *"You are wrong"*: Max Reinhardt, *Memories* (Biddles Limited, 1998), 74.

184 *A negative* New York Times *review:* Patricia Blake, "A Diseased Body Politic," *The New York Times*, October 27, 1968.

184 *"We were dealing"*: "Reminiscences," January 31, 1979, 987, CCOHC.

184 *By his own admission:* Henry Raymont, interview by author, March 10, 2010.

185 *He made a preemptive:* Roger W. Straus, Jr., to Max Reinhardt, 16 June 1971, Box 140, FSG Records, NYPL.

185 *If it would help:* Roger W. Straus, Jr., to Otto Walter, 23 June 1971, Box 140, FSG Records, NYPL.

186 *"I had had no conversation"*: "Reminiscences," 1000–1006, 1011–12.

186 *Over two hours:* Roger W. Straus, Jr., to Otto Walter, 1 July 1971, Box 340, FSG Records, NYPL.

186 *It later came out:* Henry Raymont, "Farrar Straus Gets Solzhenitsyn Book," *The New York Times*, July 6, 1971.

186 *"I am glad to say"*: Ibid.

Chapter Eight

187 *"Viking had purged"*: Roger W. Straus, Jr., to Henry Raymont, 21 December 1970, Box 804, folder 13, FSG Records, NYPL.

187 *"I didn't know"*: Roger W. Straus, Jr., to Henry Raymont, 17 February 1971, Box 804, folder 13, FSG Records, NYPL.

188 *As of late 1973:* Report to the bank, 24 September 1973, Box 515, FSG Records, NYPL.

188 *"No one has dared"*: Roger Jellinek, "The Last Word: August 1972," *The New York Times Book Review*, September 24, 1972.

188 *Straus canceled part:* Roger W. Straus, Jr., to Max Reinhardt, 14 September 1972, Box 340, FSG Records, NYPL; Roger W. Straus, Jr., to Max Reinhardt, 18 September 1972, Box 340, FSG Records, NYPL.

189 *Roger gave up on:* Roger W. Straus, Jr., to Claude Durand, 14 April 1976, Box 342, FSG Records, NYPL.

189 *After a contracted work:* Roger W. Straus, Jr., memo, 4 November 1974, Box 346, FSG Records, NYPL.

189 *Knowing the type:* Roger W. Straus, Jr., to Henry Carter Carnegie, series of letters, 1973–74, Box 346, folder 2, FSG Records, NYPL.

189 *The twenty-thousand-word:* Tom Stewart, interview by author, January 7, 2011; Stewart was Tom Wolfe's editor at the time.

189 *In March 1973:* Contract request, 2 March 1973, Box 397, FSG Records, NYPL; advance check receipt, 20 March 1973, Box 397, FSG Records, NYPL.

190 *"I stopped believing":* Julian Scheer to Tom Wolfe, 30 August 1978, Box 397, FSG Records, NYPL.

190 *Faced with the prospect:* Roger W. Straus, Jr., interview by Louis Sheaffer (1981), "Reminiscences," February 28, 1979, 1124, CCOHC.

190 *"But he is not the kind":* Ibid., 1122–27.

191 *"A thank-you note":* Andrée Conrad, interview by author, December 28, 2010.

191 *"I read the manuscript":* Robert Giroux to William Maxwell, 14 May 1968, Box 396, FSG Records, NYPL.

191 *"I thought you at least knew":* Michael di Capua to Larry Woiwode, 23 October 1970, Box 396, FSG Records, NYPL.

191 *Di Capua would wire money:* Michael di Capua to Candida Donadio et al., 9 January 1975, Box 396, FSG Records, NYPL.

191 *leading Wilfrid Sheed to quip:* Wilfrid Sheed, "The Good Word: Since I Went Away," *The New York Times*, November 3, 1974.

192 *the advance swelled:* Interoffice memo, 27 March 1975, Box 396, FSG Records, NYPL.

192 *Roger insisted:* Larry Woiwode, interview by author, November 27, 2010.

192 *"During the last year":* Larry Woiwode to Roger W. Straus, Jr., 16 November 1972, Box 396, FSG Records, NYPL.

192 *"sentimental in the best sense":* Christopher Lehmann-Haupt, "Books of the Times: Beyond, but Not Much Further," *The New York Times*, October 14, 1975.

192 *It sold almost:* Larry Woiwode, interview by author, November 27, 2010.

193 *Straus blamed it on:* "Reminiscences," March 7, 1979, 1159, CCOHC.

193 *the book came to be known:* Dinitia Smith, "The Genius," *New York*, September 19, 1988, 61.

193 *Eventually he switched:* Ibid., 62.

193 *Hauser wrote to Roger:* Gaylord Hauser to Roger W. Straus, Jr., 15 December 1972, Box 139, FSG Records, NYPL.

193 *It almost made Giroux:* Robert Giroux to John Berryman, 16 February 1965, Box 26, FSG Records, NYPL.

193 *The beautifully presented:* In 2009, the National Book Foundation polled its members on their favorite National Book Award winner of the last sixty years. Among six nominees, they chose Flannery O'Connor's *Complete Stories.*

194 *It was Berryman:* Pat Strachan, interview by author, November 6, 2008.

194 *"What a waste":* Robert Giroux to Catharine Carver, 8 March 1972, Box 507, FSG Records, NYPL.

195 *Wilson's journals:* Edmund Wilson, *The Sixties: The Last Journal, 1960–1972,* ed. Lewis M. Dabney (New York: Farrar, Straus and Giroux, 1993), 569.

195 *Giroux used it:* Robert Giroux to Jean Stafford, 23 June 1966, Box 5, Papers of Robert Giroux, Loyola University, New Orleans; Jean Stafford to Robert Giroux, ca. June 1966, Box 5, Papers of Robert Giroux. Also, regarding 21st Anniversary Edition: Roger W. Straus, Jr., to Carlos Fuentes, 31 August 1966, Box 109, FSG Records, NYPL.

195 *Its only legacy:* Christopher Lehmann-Haupt, "Robert Giroux, Editor, Publisher and Nurturer of Literary Giants, Is Dead at 94," *The New York Times,* September 6, 2008.

195 *Convinced this was really:* Ibid.

196 *When we met:* Draft introduction to "Twenty-Five Years: A Retrospective": Box 8, folder 3, Papers of Robert Giroux.

196 *There, Giroux recounted:* Alternate draft, Box 8, folder 4, Papers of Robert Giroux.

196 *"Bob—I must admit":* Ibid., Box 8, folder 6, Papers of Robert Giroux.

197 *He would have preferred:* Ibid., Box 8, folder 2, Papers of Robert Giroux.

197 *Another, presumably later:* Box 517, "Twenty-Five Years: A Retrospective" folder, FSG Records, NYPL.

197 *"Fights were something":* Conrad, interview by author, December 28, 2010.

198 *"When I look back":* Philip Robbins, interview by author, February 23, 2012.

198 *In this latest chapter:* Lynn Warshow, interview by author, January 21, 2011; "Harlem 4: Singing a Different Tune," editorial, *The New York Times,* July 9, 1972.

198 *Warshow's first thought:* Warshow, interview by author, January 21, 2011.

198 *Robbins later told:* Robert Giroux, "Henry Robbins: In Memoriam," printed remarks, Box 509, FSG Records, NYPL.

198 *Its upshot was that:* Report to the bank, 24 September 1973, FSG Records, NYPL.

199 *He liked working:* Giroux, "Henry Robbins: In Memoriam."

199 *"He positively glowed"*: Michael Korda, *Another Life: A Memoir of Other People* (New York: Random House, 1999), 166.

200 *"decided to go through"*: Victoria Meyer, interview by author, September 3, 2009.

200 *Robbins would say:* Tom Buckley, "Portrait of an Editor," *The New York Times,* June 3, 1979.

200 *Straus crafted:* Eric Pace, "Simon & Schuster Elated Over Editorial Coup," *The New York Times,* December 24, 1973.

200 *"No announcement has been made":* Ibid.

201 *"There was a series":* Deborah Rogers, interview by author, October 13, 2010.

201 *"authors are large":* Donald Barthelme to Lewis Lapham (probably), cc'd to Robert Giroux, undated, Box 21, FSG Records, NYPL.

201 *"I would have much preferred":* Donald Barthelme to Roger W. Straus, Jr., 9 January 1974, Box 21, FSG Records, NYPL.

201 *Roger explained why:* Roger W. Straus, Jr., to Donald Barthelme, 11 November 1974, Box 21, FSG Records, NYPL; Donald Barthelme to Roger W. Straus, Jr., 16 January 1974, Box 21, FSG Records, NYPL; Roger W. Straus, Jr., to Donald Barthelme, 18 January 1974, Box 21, FSG Records, NYPL.

202 *Joan Didion was more:* Lois Wallace to Roger W. Straus, Jr., 3 January 1974, Box 89, FSG Records, NYPL; Roger W. Straus, Jr., to Wallace, 9 January 1974, Box 89, FSG Records, NYPL; Joan Didion to Roger W. Straus, Jr., 17 January 1974, Box 89, FSG Records, NYPL; Roger W. Straus, Jr., to Wallace, 29 January 1974, Box 89, FSG Records, NYPL.

202 *"Now I also find":* Roger W. Straus, Jr., to Lois Wallace, 25 July 1974, Box 86, FSG Records, NYPL; Wallace to Roger W. Straus, Jr., 31 July 1974, Box 86, FSG Records, NYPL; Roger W. Straus, Jr., to Wallace, 1 August 1974, Box 86, FSG Records, NYPL.

203 *The suit was dismissed:* John Carey, *William Golding: The Man Who Wrote Lord of the Flies: A Life* (New York: Free Press, 2010), 386–87.

203 *In a letter to:* Gillon Aitkin to Roger W. Straus, Jr., 7 August 1974, Box 798, folder 3, FSG Records, NYPL; Roger W. Straus, Jr., to Aitkin, 12 August 1974, FSG Records, NYPL.

203 *Some were only* assigned: Both Patrick Samway's *Walker Percy: A Life* and Paul Elie's *The Life You Save May Be Your Own* describe numerous instances of editorial intervention into Percy's work—particularly his overlong sermonizing epilogues.

203 *"That list of authors":* "Reminiscences," February 28, 1979, 118–19, CCOHC.

204 *Even Michael Korda admitted:* Korda, *Another Life,* 367.

204 *Robbins got it worse:* Buckley, "Portrait of an Editor."

204 *"I'm not going to sit here":* Korda, *Another Life,* 368–69.

205   *In the title essay:* Joan Didion, *After Henry* (New York: Simon & Schuster, 1992), 19.

206   *Giroux couched it:* Amendments to Deferred Compensation Agreement, 15 February 1974, Box 1, folder 22, Papers of Robert Giroux.

206   *Roger signed a revised:* Deferred Compensation Agreement, 1 March 1974, Box 507, FSG Records, NYPL.

Chapter Nine

207   *"Everybody was fucking":* Leslie Sharpe, interview by author, July 24, 2010.

209   *"Farout, Strut and Xerox":* Maurice Sendak to Roger W. Straus, Jr., two cards, December 1973, Box 806, folder 20, FSG Records, NYPL.

211   *"It did boost sales":* Roger W. Straus III, interview by author, September 10, 2011.

212   *"These were dreams":* Nina Straus, interview by author, July 28, 2011.

212   *Rog called his father:* "Roger W. Straus, Jr., President of Farrar, Straus and Giroux, Reflects on His Firm's 30-Year Pursuit of Literary Excellence," *Publishers Weekly*, February 7, 1977.

212   *"At that point":* Straus III, interview by author, July 23, 2009.

212   *Straus responded:* Roger W. Straus, Jr., to Jackson Ream, 2 April 1976, Box 1, folder 22, Papers of Robert Giroux.

212   *"It may be":* Ibid.

213   *"My problem":* Roger W. Straus, Jr., to Colin Draper, 27 June 1977, Box 805, FSG Records, NYPL; Thomas Tilling folder (no. 22) contains full correspondence on the deal.

213   *But a few months after:* Frank J. Prial, "Macmillan General Editor Quits 4 Months After Joining Publisher," *The New York Times*, November 15, 1974.

213   *"an absolutely passionate":* Margalit Fox, "Aaron Asher, Editor of Literary Heavyweights, Dies at 78," *The New York Times*, March 22, 2008; Prial, "Macmillan General Editor Quits 4 Months After Joining Publisher"; Paul L. Montgomery, "N.L.R.B. Studies Macmillan Ousters," *The New York Times*, October 22, 1974.

213   *They always had:* Linda Asher, interview by author, January 13, 2010.

214   *"Where the fuck":* Tom Stewart, interview by author, January 7, 2011.

214   *He must have appreciated:* Christopher Lehmann-Haupt, interview by author, September 17, 2009.

214   *"care and feeding":* Aaron Asher to Philip Roth, 14 September 1976, Box 677, FSG Records, NYPL.

214   *"I too am sad":* Roger W. Straus, Jr., to Heinrich Ledig-Rowohlt, 25 October 1976, Box 677, FSG Records, NYPL.

214   *"We did a hell of a job":* Roger W. Straus, Jr., interview by Louis Sheaffer "Reminiscences," February 28, 1979, 1128–30, CCOHC.

214 *"There was personal"*: Aaron Asher, interview by Carl E. Rollyson, transcript, Carl E. Rollyson Papers, University of Tulsa, Tulsa, Oklahoma; by permission of interviewer.

214 *Roth would repay:* N. R. Kleinfield, "Roger Straus: Making It as an Independent," *The New York Times Book Review*, March 2, 1980.

214 *As she had no health:* "An Appeal," ca. 1976, Box 342, FSG Records, NYPL.

214 *Carlos Fuentes donated:* Carlos Fuentes to Roger W. Straus, Jr., 10 February 1976, Box 806, folder 17, FSG Records, NYPL.

215 *Straus brainstormed deals:* Roger W. Straus to F. W. Roberts, 29 October 1975, Box 342, FSG Records, NYPL.

215 *Soon after that:* Sigrid Nunez, interview by author, March 1, 2011; Sigrid Nunez, *Sempre Susan: A Memoir of Susan Sontag* (New York: Atlas & Co., 2011), 94.

216 *Reviews, Roger wrote:* Roger W. Straus, Jr., to Peter Carson, 30 November 1977, Box 346, FSG Records, NYPL.

216 *The issues of* The New York Review: Mary Sonnichsen to Martha Kinney, 30 January 1978, Box 346, FSG Records, NYPL.

216 *Three Sontag books:* N. R. Kleinfield, "A Success Story at Farrar, Straus," *The New York Times*, December 1, 1978.

217 *"He would start talking":* John McPhee, interview by author, January 20, 2010.

217 *"That surprised him":* Ibid.

217 *"I went to a dinner party":* "Reminiscences," July 26, 1978, 845, CCOHC.

218 *Frankfurt was elegant:* Ibid., 857–85, for many details of Roger's time in Stockholm.

218 *"not only a place":* John Vinocur, "Singer, in His Nobel Lecture, Hails Yiddish," *The New York Times*, December 9, 1978.

218 *Someone told Giroux:* Robert Giroux, interview by George Plimpton, *The Paris Review*, no. 155 (Summer 2000), 180.

219 *"They could just as well":* Kleinfield, "A Success Story at Farrar, Straus."

219 *"I think his opinion":* Ibid.

220 *"an object of great curiosity":* Ibid.

220 *"I just used to giggle":* Kleinfield, "Roger Straus: Making It as an Independent."

221 *His life had been:* Donald Hall, "Robert Giroux: Looking for Masterpieces," *The New York Times*, January 6, 1980.

221 *On the record:* Kleinfield, "Roger Straus: Making It as an Independent."

221 *Giroux, drafting the award proposal:* Statement for the Harold T. Vursell Memorial Award, 30 March 1978, Box 517, FSG Records, NYPL.

222 *standing up in Giroux's box:* Ian Hamilton, *Robert Lowell: A Biography* (New York: Random House, 1982), 341.

222 *passing out from excess lithium:* Paul L. Mariani, *Lost Puritan: A Life of Robert Lowell* (New York: W. W. Norton, 1994), 432.

222 *Now he was one of ten:* Richard F. Shepard, "Majestic Service Marks Farewell to Robert Lowell," *The New York Times,* September 17, 1977.

222 *"For one of America's most expressive":* Robert Giroux, "Hard Years and Scary Days: Remembering Jean Stafford," *The New York Times Book Review,* June 10, 1984.

222 *"a brilliant and disturbing story":* Robert Giroux to William Shawn, 12 August 1978, Box 5, Papers of Robert Giroux, Loyola University, New Orleans.

222 *"how sad and arduous":* Giroux, "Hard Years and Scary Days."

223 *Robbins still lived near:* "Henry Robbins, Editor in Chief of Trade Books at Dutton, Dies," *The New York Times,* August 1, 1979.

223 *"come home again":* Roger W. Straus, Jr., to Joan Didion, 8 August 1979, Box 86, FSG Records, NYPL.

223 *Little soul, gentle and drifting:* Robert Giroux, "Henry Robbins: In Memoriam," printed remarks, Box 509, FSG Records, NYPL.

Chapter Ten

224 *His "illegitimate son":* Michael D'Antonio, "Little David, Happy at Last," *Esquire* 113, no. 3 (March 1990); David Rieff, interview by author, June 26, 2011.

224 *"friends" abroad:* Roger W. Straus, Jr., to Matthew Evans, 18 July 1984, Box 799, folder 25, FSG Records, NYPL.

224 *He'd already ruined:* Ian Frazier, interview by author, June 16, 2011.

225 *"It turns out":* Roger W. Straus III, interview by author, July 23, 2009.

225 *It was, on the one hand:* Full list of Nobel laureates during this period: Isaac Bashevis Singer, 1978; Czesław Miłosz, 1980; Elias Canetti, 1981; William Golding, 1983; Wole Soyinka, 1986; Joseph Brodsky, 1987; Camilo José Cela, 1989; Nadine Gordimer, 1989; Derek Walcott, 1992; Seamus Heaney, 1995. Per www.nobelprize.org.

226 *When Brodsky moved:* Joseph Brodsky to Nancy Meiselas, 8 November 1977, Box 41, FSG Records, NYPL.

226 *He landed for a year:* Nancy Meiselas to John Hollander, 23 March 1978, Box 41, FSG Records, NYPL.

226 *Sometimes his suggestions:* Kushner: David Rieff, interview by author, June 26, 2011; Zagajewski: editorial meeting minutes, 8 November 1983, Box 797, FSG Records, NYPL: "DR considering Adam Zagajewski's poems, submitted through Brodsky."

226 *Asher had avidly pursued:* Editorial meeting minutes, 15 February 1977, Box 796, FSG Records, NYPL.

226 *Peggy Miller says:* Peggy Miller, interview by author, October 23, 2008.

226 *Alas, the following year's winner:* See Chapter 6.

227 *Across from the park:* Kristin Kliemann, interview by author, January 8, 2010.

227 *"If you're concerned":* Stephen Roxburgh, interview by author, February 19, 2010.

228 *"Like everyone else":* Clipping of Hillary Mills, "Changes at Farrar, Straus," *The Washington Star*, February 1, 1981, Box 509, FSG Records, NYPL.

229 *So Dorothea Straus explained:* James Reginato, "Nobel House," *New York*, November 9, 1987.

229 *He'd opined in 1964:* Roger W. Straus, Jr., to Alexander S. Frere, Box 800, folder 9, FSG Records, NYPL.

229 *Nine years later:* Tracy Daugherty, *Hiding Man: A Biography of Donald Barthelme* (New York: St. Martin's Press, 2009), 448–49.

229 *So intent was Barthelme:* Ibid., 449.

229 *"interest and paper clips":* Dinitia Smith, "The Genius: Harold Brodkey and His Great (Unpublished) Novel," *New York* 21, no. 37 (September 19, 1988).

230 *"Between the fact":* Sigrid Nunez, interview by author, March 3, 2011.

230 *I do not understand:* Roger W. Straus, Jr., to Lynn Nesbit, 13 May 1980, Box 806, folder 17, FSG Records, NYPL.

231 *Instead, Nesbit and Straus:* Roger W. Straus, Jr., to Lynn Nesbit, 20 May 1980, Box 806, folder 17, FSG Records, NYPL; Roger W. Straus, Jr., to Lynn Nesbit, 6 June 1980, Box 806, folder 17, FSG Records, NYPL; Roger W. Straus, Jr., to Lynn Nesbit, memo, 31 December 1981, Box 713, FSG Records, NYPL.

231 *He later told Sontag's biographers:* Aaron Asher, interview by Carl Rollyson, Carl E. Rollyson Papers, University of Tulsa, with permission of the interviewer.

231 *"Maybe [the Barbato firing]":* David Rieff, interview by author, June 26, 2011.

231 *"I thought he was":* Straus III, interview by author, October 29, 2009.

231 *"It's probably amusing":* Edwin McDowell, "A New Air of Confidence Pervades Harper & Rowe [sic]," *The New York Times*, April 4, 1981.

232 *FSG sold most of his foreign:* Roger W. Straus, Jr., to Philip Roth, 11 February 1981, Box 676, FSG Records, NYPL.

232 *"My plan is to stay":* McDowell, "A New Air of Confidence Pervades Harper & Rowe."

232 *Two years later:* Contract request for *Zuckerman Unbound*, Box 676, FSG Records, NYPL; Roger W. Straus, Jr., to Deborah Rogers, 15 March 1983, Box 676, FSG Records, NYPL.

232 *For* The Counterlife: Memo on *Counterlife*, by Evgenia Citkowitz, 24 March 1986, Box 676, FSG Records, NYPL.

232 *Zuckerman Unbound sold:* Roger W. Straus, Jr., to Andrew Wylie, worksheet, 22 September 1989, Box 677, FSG Records, NYPL.

233 *"was interested in the prestige"*: Rieff, interview by author, June 26, 2011.

233 *Roth was cranky:* Philip Roth to Roger W. Straus, Jr., 4 October 1980, Box 676, FSG Records, NYPL: "I would like you to play Pepler in the movie. Think about it." Philip Roth to Roger W. Straus, Jr., 25 February 1981, Box 676, FSG Records, NYPL: "Will you play Andre Schevitz?"

234 *"Michael was a grown-up"*: Rieff, interview by author, June 26, 2011.

234 *"I barely noticed"*: Pat Strachan, interview by author, November 6, 2008.

235 *Sontag was the first reader:* Editorial meeting minutes, 27 January 1981, Box 797, FSG Records, NYPL.

235 *"Come on, how many Wops"*: Ian Parker, "Showboat," *The New Yorker*, April 8, 2002.

235 *In 1982, while considering:* Roger W. Straus, Jr., to Philip Roth, 11 January 1983, Box 676, FSG Records, NYPL.

235 *Had Farrar, Straus published Eco:* Roger W. Straus, Jr., to staff, memo, 11 January 1983, Box 799, folder 25, FSG Records, NYPL.

236 *"Knights are for sleeping in"*: Christopher MacLehose, interview by author, October 13, 2010.

236 *"I'd like to comment"*: Larry Woiwode, interview by author, November 27, 2010.

236 *"I found him at once"*: D'Antonio, "Little David, Happy at Last."

236 *"He was very bright"*: Aaron Asher, interview by Carl E. Rollyson, transcript, Carl E. Rollyson Papers, University of Tulsa, Tulsa, Oklahoma; by permission of interviewer.

236 *"Seven Thousand Days"*: D'Antonio, "Little David, Happy at Last."

236 *After the end of an affair:* Ibid., confirmed in interview with Rieff by author, June 26, 2011.

236 *"During that period"*: Rieff, interview by author, June 26, 2011.

236 *He gave a more general apology:* D'Antonio, "Little David, Happy at Last."

236 *"One day I woke"*: Rieff, interview by author, June 26, 2011.

237 *"the only home I'd ever had"*: D'Antonio, "Little David, Happy at Last."

237 *"I remember thinking"*: Straus III, interview by author, March 11, 2010.

237 *No one had been there:* Ibid.; Peggy Miller, interview by author, July 2, 2009.

237 *Only a couple:* Nina Straus, interview by author, July 28, 2011.

238 *"Shall we say"*: Peggy Miller, interview by author, July 2, 2009.

238 *But after he returned:* Roger W. Straus, Jr., to S. I. Newhouse, 30 October 1984, Box 799, folder 4, FSG Records, NYPL.

238 *There was no such takeover:* Straus III, interview by author, July 23, 2009; news accounts include Thomas J. Maier, "The Ins and Outs of Random House," *Newsday*, February 24, 1991.

239 *"Roger was very proud"*: Joy Isenberg, interview by author, May 1, 2011.

239 *Fittingly, Giroux:* Robert Giroux, *The Book Known as Q: A Consideration of Shakespeare's Sonnets* (New York: Vintage Books, 1983).

240 *"If I'm not careful"*: Robert Giroux to Matthew Evans, 24 March 1981, Box 509, FSG Records, NYPL.

240 *"As you are a pro"*: Matthew Evans to Robert Giroux, 9 June 1981, Box 6, Papers of Robert Giroux, Loyola University, New Orleans; subsequent letters with Weidenfeld editors.

240 *Straus and Faber's*: Matthew Evans to Roger W. Straus, Jr., 17 July 1984, Box 799, folder 25, FSG Records, NYPL; Roger W. Straus, Jr., to Matthew Evans, 18 July 1984, Box 799, folder 25, FSG Records, NYPL.

240 *"It must be wonderfully convenient"*: Robert Giroux to Valerie Eliot, 1 August 1984, Box 510, FSG Records, NYPL.

240 *"Far from having withdrawn"*: Robert Giroux to Valerie Eliot, 18 September 1984, Box 510, FSG Records, NYPL.

241 *"That never happened"*: Straus III, interviews by author, to end of section (except where noted).

241 PUBLISHER NAMES AIDE: "Publisher Names Aide," *The New York Times*, August 17, 1985.

Chapter Eleven

242 *"class-mass"*: Robert S. Boynton, "The Burden of Profit," *Manhattan, Inc.*, September 1990.

242 *"You got a guy"*: David Rieff, interview by author. In fact, Galassi did both simultaneously. When, in the late seventies, Galassi got a fellowship to do his Montale translations in Paris and Rome, Conroy followed him to Europe so that they could work on his novel, *The Lords of Discipline*, together. Pat Conroy, "On Paris, Writing, Food, and Friendship," *Gourmet*, August 2006.

243 *Galassi's father*: Jonathan Galassi, interviews by author; among other stories, Janny Scott, "How to Persuade With a Feather (Or a Quill)," *The New York Times*, January 20, 1999.

243 *Already a translator*: Jofie Ferrari-Adler, "Agents & Editors: A Q&A with Jonathan Galassi," *Poets & Writers*, July/August 2009.

243 *A journalist later wrote*: Boynton, "The Burden of Profit."

243 *But before they could meet*: Jonathan Galassi to Robert Giroux, 23 July 1973, Box 507, FSG Records, NYPL; Jonathan Galassi to Robert Giroux, 24 August 1973, Box 507, FSG Records, NYPL.

243 *"I was very interested"*: Ferrari-Adler, "Agents & Editors."

243 *"It turned out that"*: Craig Lambert, "Editor Extraordinaire Jonathan Galassi '71 and the Risky Art of Publishing Books," *Harvard Magazine*, November–December 1997.

244 *"didn't have any books"*: Ibid.

244 *"I almost left the business"*: Jonathan Galassi, interview by author, October 22, 2010.

244 *"I think Rog was looking"*: Ibid.

244 *"It's a business"*: Ferrari-Adler, "Agents & Editors."

245 *Unsurprisingly, it was Rog's:* Catalogs courtesy of Farrar, Straus and Giroux.

245 *"I have just hired"*: Robert A. Carter, "Outliving the Bastards," *Publishers Weekly*, November 14, 1986.

245 *Galassi would share:* Ibid.; Pat Strachan and Jonathan Galassi, interviews by author.

246 *Rog and Jonathan wouldn't:* Figures per Scott Turow.

246 *"Jonathan gave me"*: Scott Turow, interview by author, February 11, 2010.

246 *He wanted to accelerate:* Jonathan Galassi to Scott Turow, 11 November 1986, Box 816, FSG Records, NYPL; also Scott Turow, interview by author, February 11, 2010.

246 *Of all the rejection letters:* Scott Turow, interview by author, February 11, 2010.

246 *"the least money"*: Jamaica Kincaid, interview by author, August 8, 2009.

247 *"in the same way that people"*: Ian Frazier, interview by author, June 16, 2009.

247 *"you're engaged in a truth"*: Kincaid, interview by author, August 8, 2009.

247 *"Dear God, you must think"*: Scott Turow to Roger W. Straus III, 30 April 1990, Box 816, FSG Records, NYPL.

248 *I combed the book:* Jonathan Galassi, "The Furniture! Another Toast for Scott Turow, Chicago, June 26, 1990," courtesy of Jonathan Galassi.

249 *Then they had a paperback:* Jeff Shear, "A Lawyer Courts Best-Sellerdom," *The New York Times*, June 7, 1987.

249 *Joseph Brodsky would take:* "Adult New York Times Best Seller Listings," Hawes Publications, www.hawes.com/pastlist.htm.

249 *For three glorious winter weeks:* Ibid.

250 *While the company's growth:* R. Z. Sheppard, "Winning the Old-Fashioned Way," Books, *Time*, February 8, 1988.

250 *The list of adult titles:* Edwin McDowell, "An Independent Publisher Slowly Changes Its Ways," *The New York Times*, February 18, 1987.

Chapter Twelve

252 *"a moisturized fist"*: Gideon Lewis-Kraus, "The Last Book Party: Publishing Drinks to a Life After Death," *Harper's*, March 2009.

252 THE NAUGHTY SCHOOLBOY: Priscilla Painton, "The Naughty Schoolboy," *Time*, June 12, 1989.

252 *"You could anticipate"*: Andrew Wylie, interview by author, November 11, 2009.

253 *"the intimacy of underprivilege"*: Lynn Barber, "Paying with Words," *The Observer*, February 7, 1999.

253   *return with anecdotes:* Aram Saroyan, *Friends in the World: The Education of a Writer: A Memoir* (Minneapolis, MN: Coffee House Press, 1992), 92.

253   *He was dismissed in 1965:* Craig Lambert, "Fifteen Percent of Immortality," *Harvard Magazine,* July–August 2010.

253   *He later used the same tactic:* Ibid.

253   *For all of Wylie's promise:* Saroyan, *Friends in the World,* 107.

253   *poetry that would have made:* Elizabeth Schambelan, "He Is Curious (Yellow)," *Bookforum,* April/May 2007.

253   *"When an author earns out":* Robert McCrum, "The Numbers Game," *The Observer,* April 8, 2001.

254   *"I needed documentary evidence":* Saroyan, *Friends in the World,* 117.

254   *Wylie blames his decision:* Andrew Wylie, interview by author, November 11, 2009.

254   *As Wylie has pointed out:* Lambert, "Fifteen Percent of Immortality."

255   *"Neither of them was":* Roger W. Straus III, interview by author, March 11, 2010.

256   *"I'm lucky to be alive":* Ken Adachi, "Here Comes Sontag, Radiantly Literate," *The Toronto Star,* March 28, 1987.

256   *"Roger was simply unresponsive":* David Rieff, interview by author, June 26, 2011.

257   *He signed Pakistani:* Emma Brockes, "Agent Provocateur," *The Guardian,* November 24, 2003.

257   *"What I persuaded David":* Andrew Wylie, interview by author, November 11, 2009.

257   *"It is because of his":* David Rieff, interview by author, June 26, 2011.

257   *"I'm bursting to write it":* Carl Rollyson and Lisa Paddock, *Susan Sontag: The Making of an Icon* (New York: W. W. Norton, 2000), 260.

257   *Before signing with Wylie:* Margaria Fichtner, "Susan Sontag's Train of Thought Rolls into Town," *Miami Herald,* February 19, 1989.

258   *"You're a rich man":* David Rieff, interview by author, June 26, 2011.

258   *"As you have gathered":* Roger W. Straus, Jr., to Andrew Wylie, 6 February 1989, Box 805, folder 9, FSG Records, NYPL.

258   *"I don't think it was":* David Rieff, interview by author, June 26, 2011.

258   *Jonathan Galassi pushes back:* Jonathan Galassi, interview by author, July 28, 2011.

259   *"I realized that he":* Ian Frazier, interview by author, June 16, 2011.

259   *"Flushed with that success":* Edwin McDowell, "Farrar, Straus Thrives on Success of 2 Novels," *The New York Times,* May 17, 1988.

260   *"In 1980 I leaned":* Tom Wolfe to Lynn Nesbit, forwarded to Roger W. Straus, Jr., 7 July 1988, Box 806, folder 17, FSG Records, NYPL.

261   *"But from that day forward":* Lynn Nesbit, interview by author, August 30, 2010.

261 *Nesbit broke off:* James Reginato, "Literary Lion," *W*, March 1996.

261 *In the same interview:* Ibid.

261 *The reality is simpler:* David Rieff, interview by author, June 26, 2011.

262 *Wylie told Roth:* Andrew Wylie, interview by author, November 11, 2009.

262 *Wylie came to Straus:* Roger Cohen, "Roth's Publishers: The Spurned and the Spender," *The New York Times*, April 9, 1990; also, Andrew Wylie, interview by author, November 11, 2009.

262 *Wolfe had written five:* The number of bestsellers is per Wolfe's accounting, in Lynn Nesbit to Roger W. Straus, Jr., 7 July 1988, Box 806, folder 17, FSG Records, NYPL.

262 *Roger also said he bet:* Reginato, "Literary Lion."

262 *Elsewhere he said:* Edwin McDowell, "Book Notes: Roth Changes Houses," *The New York Times*, August 16, 1989.

262 *According to him:* Andrew Wylie, interview by author, November 11, 2009.

263 *"Roth liked Roger well enough":* David Rieff, interview by author, June 26, 2011.

263 *That summer, Roth:* Hermione Lee, "Essentially Indiscreet," *The Independent*, September 2, 1990.

263 Dear Roger: Andrew Wylie to Roger W. Straus, Jr., 15 August 1989, Box 676, FSG Records, NYPL.

264 *He gladly provided Wylie:* Roger W. Straus, Jr., to Andrew Wylie, 22 September 1989, Box 676, FSG Records, NYPL.

264 *He sent back a note:* Roger W. Straus, Jr., to Deborah Karl, undated, reply to Karl's letter to Straus of 3 October 1989, Box 676, FSG Records, NYPL; Deborah Karl to Roger W. Straus, Jr., 17 October 1989, Box 676, FSG Records, NYPL.

264 *"I could have bought this":* David Streitfeld, "Grapes of Roth," *The Washington Post*, August 27, 1989.

264 *He predicted Simon & Schuster:* Cohen, "Roth's Publishers."

264 *And yet again:* Sales figures: Roger W. Straus, Jr., to Andrew Wylie, 22 September 1989, Box 676, FSG Records, NYPL; bestseller list, "Adult New York Times Best Seller Listings," Hawes Publications, www.hawes.com/pastlist.htm.

264 *"stop analyzing his imagination":* Cohen, "Roth's Publishers."

265 *"Roger said publicly":* Jonathan Galassi, interview by author, May 7, 2010.

Chapter Thirteen

266 *As Scott Turow:* Roger W. Straus III and Jonathan Galassi, interviews by author.

267 *Turow's third book:* Farrar, Straus and Giroux catalog, Spring–Summer 1993, courtesy of Farrar, Straus and Giroux, New York.

267 *Rog has a different spin:* Roger W. Straus III, interview by author, July 23, 2009.

269 *"No one thought":* Helene Atwan, interview by author, July 31, 2009.

270 *In any event:* D. T. Max, "Straus Dad Turns Page after Son Exits Farrar," *The New York Observer*, November 15, 1993.

270 *"As usual":* Roger W. Straus III, interview by author, July 23, 2009.

270 *"genteel family tiff":* Sarah Lyall, "Farrar, Straus Heir Apparent Quits in a Genteel Family Tiff," *The New York Times*, September 23, 1993.

271 *"He felt, and I think":* Roger W. Straus III, interview by author, July 23, 2009.

271 *"I think Roger was totally":* David Rieff, interview by author, June 26, 2011.

272 *"He wants to try":* Lyall, "Farrar, Straus Heir Apparent Quits in a Genteel Family Tiff."

272 *"We're too small for that":* Max, "Straus Dad Turns Page after Son Exits Farrar."

273 *Among his early acquisitions:* Farrar, Straus and Giroux catalogs, 1988–93, courtesy of Farrar, Straus and Giroux.

274 *"You do not think":* Elisabeth Sifton, interview by author, August 11, 2010.

274 *Turow has another word:* Scott Turow, interview by author, February 11, 2010.

274 *"Roger always needed":* Jonathan Galassi, interview by author, October 22, 2010.

274 *By this point:* Roger W. Straus III, interview by author, July 23, 2009.

Chapter Fourteen

276 *"He didn't look like":* Ethan Nosowsky, interview by author, August 31, 2011. He lists his priorities in various letters related to the Holtzbrinck sale, Box 800, folders 1–5, FSG Records, NYPL.

277 *He and his lousy shareholders:* Confirmed with Roger W. Straus III.

277 *More recently:* Von Holtzbrinck and S. Fischer Verlag company histories via www.vonholtzbrinck.com.

278 *Not long before:* Sarah Lyall, "Book Notes," *The New York Times*, January 19, 1994.

278 *Only later did it come out:* Mark Landler, "Another German Publisher Mulls Its Wartime Past," *The New York Times*, October 14, 2002.

278 *"FSG," Dieter wrote:* Rough translation of German press release, late October 1994, Box 800, folder 5, FSG Records, NYPL.

279 *"The time has come":* Roger W. Straus, Jr., to Alma Singer, 28 October 1994, Box 800, folder 5, FSG Records, NYPL.

279 *"Your decision to keep":* Herbert Lottman to Roger W. Straus, Jr., 15 November 1994, Box 800, folder 5, FSG Records, NYPL.

279 *"While I understand":* Madeleine L'Engle to Roger W. Straus, Jr., undated, Box 800, folder 5, FSG Records, NYPL.

279 *But Seaver ended well:* Dick and Jeanette Seaver to Roger W. Straus, Jr., 28 October 1994, Box 800, folder 5, FSG Records, NYPL.

279 *"I did take a few":* Ellen Faran to Dr. Arno Mahlert, fax, courtesy of Ellen Faran.

280 *"This is a much more solitary life":* Roger W. Straus III, interview by author, June 5, 2009.

280 *They each got:* Laura Straus, interview by author, September 9, 2011.

281 *"It was one of the many things":* Roger W. Straus III, interview by author, October 29, 2009.

282 *Walcott read a poem:* FSG Archives, Farrar, Straus and Giroux, New York.

282 *"There's the cliché":* Ann Kjellberg, interview by author, February 25, 2010.

283 *"We publish what we wish":* Tape recordings of readings courtesy of Farrar, Straus and Giroux; some details from Nosowsky, interview by author, August 31, 2011, and Jeff Seroy, interview by author, August 18, 2009.

283 *"the hardest I've ever laughed":* Ian Frazier, interview by author, June 16, 2011.

283 *David Grossman . . . rounded out the group:* Programs and recordings courtesy of Farrar, Straus and Giroux.

284 *Everyone is applauding:* Photo and recording courtesy of Farrar, Straus and Giroux; Seroy, interview by author, August 29, 2011.

284 *"I don't think":* Roger Hirson, interview by author, June 18, 2009.

285 *Warner Books publisher:* John Glusman, interview by author, July 16, 2009; confirmed by Kirschbaum.

285 *In the mid-nineties:* Robert Giroux to Monika Schoeller, 28 December 1994, Box 2, Papers of Robert Giroux, Loyola University, New Orleans.

285 *As for his much longer time:* Christopher Lehmann-Haupt, interview by author, September 17, 2009.

285 *"I'd like it if it were":* Ian Parker, "Showboat," *The New Yorker,* April 8, 2002.

285 *"I never wanted to be":* Al Silverman, *The Time of Their Lives: The Golden Age of Great American Book Publishers, Their Editors, and Authors* (New York: Truman Talley Books, 2008), 33–34.

286 *"That changed the whole thing":* Jonathan Galassi, interview by author, July 23, 2011.

286 *There was a laser-guided:* Christine Neuberger, "Book Nook," *Richmond Times Dispatch,* March 8, 1998.

286 *One of the first things:* John Sargent, interview by author, November 5, 2010.

287 *When it finally was:* Ibid.

287 *"Ah, good":* Ibid.

287 *Roger made quick:* Matthew Evans to Roger W. Straus, Jr., 6 April 1998, Box 800, folder 2, FSG Records, NYPL.

287 *From beginning to end:* John Rogers to Roger W. Straus, Jr., 29 April 1998, Box

800, folder 2, FSG Records, NYPL; Roger W. Straus, Jr., to John Rogers, 30 April 1998, Box 800, folder 2, FSG Records, NYPL.

288 *"In the end": Roger W. Straus: A Celebration* (New York: Farrar, Straus and Giroux, 2004), 119–22.

288 *To assorted press:* Galassi, interview by author.

288 *"was much mellower":* Jofie Ferrari-Adler, "Agents & Editors: A Q&A with Jonathan Galassi," *Poets & Writers,* July / August 2009.

289 *Lawrence responded by saying:* Parker, "Showboat."

289 *Inevitably, Wylie would:* Andrew Wylie, interview by author, November 11, 2009.

289 *"Don't give me any of that": Roger W. Straus: A Celebration,* 28.

290 *He wasn't retiring:* Tom Holman, "Straus Gives Way to Galassi," *The Bookseller,* February 1, 2002.

Chapter Fifteen

291 *"Maybe he thought":* Jeffrey Eugenides, interview by author, April 30, 2012.

292 *"In the space":* "The Talk of the Town," *The New Yorker,* September 24, 2001.

292 *Galassi read the submission:* Jonathan Galassi, interview by author, July 28, 2011.

292 *"He couldn't believe":* Jonathan Franzen, interview by author, July 23, 2012; subsequent quotes and details are from this interview, unless otherwise indicated.

293 *"If Franzen overtakes Wolfe":* Ian Parker, "Showboat," *The New Yorker,* April 8, 2002.

293 *The 1988 catalog:* Farrar, Straus and Giroux catalog, Fall 1988, courtesy of Farrar, Straus and Giroux, New York.

293 *The reviewers obliged:* Peter Miller, interview by author, June 28, 2012.

293 *It was rumored:* Franzen, interview by author.

294 *"the worst year of my life":* Karen Heller, "A People Book," *Philadelphia Inquirer,* September 26, 2001.

294 *He called instead:* Jonathan Franzen, "Why Bother?" *Harper's,* April 1996.

295 *He called the book:* Catalog copy courtesy of Farrar, Straus and Giroux.

295 *"All of us who care":* Hillel Italie, "Look Out This Fall for the Four 'T's," *Associated Press,* August 27, 2001.

296 *When Buckley called Galassi:* Lynn Buckley, interview by author, July 24, 2012; Franzen, interview by author.

298 *"Snotty, self-absorbed":* Jonathan Yardley, "The Story of O," *The Washington Post,* October 29, 2001.

299 *"In publishing circles":* Franzen, "Why Bother?"

299 *"Jonathan Franzen's marvelous new novel":* David Gates, "American Gothic," *The New York Times Book Review,* September 9, 2001.

299 *An erratum slip:* Franzen, interview by author; basic online book-collecting search.

299 *"Are you out of your mind?":* Jeff Seroy, interview by author, August 11, 2009; dates per Peter Miller.

300 *"Unless you were a very good person indeed":* "The Talk of the Town."

301 *The video tour:* Jonathan Franzen, "Meet Me in St. Louis," *The New Yorker,* December 24, 2001. The rest of the St. Louis account corroborated by Peter Miller.

301 *"That Oprah selection":* John Marshall, "Suddenly into the Heat of the Light: Meteoric Success a Novel Experience for Author Jonathan Franzen," *Seattle Post-Intelligencer,* October 6, 2001.

301 *He told the* Miami Herald: Margaria Fichtner, "Author Uses Family Saga to Comment on Society," *Miami Herald,* October 9, 2001.

301 *He said the pick:* Jeff Baker, "Oprah's Stamp of Approval Rubs Writer in Conflicted Ways," *Portland Oregonian,* October 12, 2001.

302 *At the end of the call:* Seroy, interview by author.

302 *Franzen says Galassi was right:* Franzen, interview by author.

302 *"To find myself":* Ann Oldenburg, "Franzen Says He Feels 'Awful' About Feud," *USA Today,* October 25, 2001.

303 *"Jonathan Franzen will not":* David D. Kirkpatrick, "Winfrey Rescinds Offer to Author of Guest Appearance," *The New York Times,* October 24, 2001.

303 *one clear consequence:* Alexandra Jacobs, "Clench Buttocks and Talk!" *The New York Observer,* April 29, 2002.

303 *Over two long sessions:* Miller, interview by author; Franzen, interview by author.

304 *"It was pretty obvious":* Eugenides, interview by author.

304 *"might be a little macabre":* Ibid.

304 *"I was blown away":* Galassi, interview by author.

305 *The girl reading on the cover:* Buckley, interview by author. Cynthia Krupat has not responded to interview requests.

305 *Eugenides went with his editor's:* Eugenides, interview by author.

306 *The paperback:* Per BookScan, 1,063,978 copies of the 2003 paperback.

306 *And when Oprah picked:* BookScan lists 667,571 copies of the 2007 release, representing 75 percent of sales.

307 *"It's hard to imagine":* Jacob Weisberg, "'I Am Charlotte Simmons': Peeping Tom," *The New York Times,* November 28, 2004.

307 *"I thought that there":* Carlos Fuentes, interview by author, December 20, 2010.

307 *"I don't blame him":* Hillel Italie, "Carlos Fuentes Drops Publisher," *Associated Press,* July 8, 2003.

308 *Informed by chats:* Published September 18, 2012.

308 The World Is Flat: BookScan hardcover sales: 1,357,702, again accounting for roughly 80 percent of sales.

311 *"People thought I was crazy"*: Sarah Crichton, interview by author, July 23, 2012; account of Galassi's hire per Crichton.

313 *"You take that job"*: Crichton, interview by author.

314 *He worked on the smallest details:* Franzen, interview by author.

314 *He convinced Richard Price:* Charles McGrath, "Sleepy-Eyed Writer, Wandering Byzantium," *The New York Times*, March 2, 2008.

315 *"I felt more alive"*: Bob Thompson, "A Writer Crosses Over," *The Washington Post*, April 8, 2007.

315 *"The basic idea"*: Lorin Stein, interview by author, July 14, 2012.

316 *Those fans and more:* "Meet the Media Mensches, 2009," *The New York Observer*, January 6, 2009.

316 *The madness was so surprising:* "Bolaño-mania: Hymn to a Dead Chilean," *The Economist*, November 20, 2008.

317 *FSG had given Johnson:* Michael Scott Moore, "Poet of the Fallen World," *SF Weekly*, February 19, 2003.

317 *He happened upon:* Stephen King, "How to Bury a Book," *Entertainment Weekly*, April 15, 2007.

318 *"In hindsight"*: Stein, interview by author.

318 *a hundred thousand copies:* Per Farrar, Straus and Giroux, in all editions; BookScan lists 54,280.

318 *"A kind of book"*: Thomas LeBien, interview by author, July 13, 2012.

319 *"We've always published books"*: Seroy, interview by author.

319 *Galassi remembers:* Galassi, interview by author.

319 *The vast majority:* According to BookScan, 35,588 paperback copies in 2008 versus 6,995 hardcover in 2007.

319 *"When it comes to reading"*: "Letters," *Harper's*, April 2008.

320 *Sitting around and schmoozing:* Stein, interview by author.

321 *"I said I would"*: Peggy Miller, interview by author.

Chapter Sixteen

323 *"The only reason"*: Preceding page based on Peggy Miller, interview by author, October 23, 2008, and Danny Meyer, interview by author, May 26, 2011.

323 *Then he'd pull Meyer close: Roger W. Straus: A Celebration* (New York: Farrar, Straus and Giroux, 2004), 73.

325 *"He managed a meek smile"*: Ibid., 76.

325 *"When I'd come over"*: Roger W. Straus III, interview by author, June 5, 2009.

326 *"There were various problems"*: Laura Straus, interview by author, September 9, 2011; Straus III, interview by author, September 10, 2011.

326 *"There were some powwows"*: Laura Straus, interview by author.

326 *"Our home is standing"*: Dorothea Straus, "Real Estate," *Fiction* 20, no. 1 (2006).

326 *During the disposition*: Per Roger W. Straus III.

327 *A Picasso once thought*: Per Roger W. Straus III and Dorothea Straus, Last Will and Testament, Room 311, New York County Surrogate's Court, 31 Chambers Street, New York, NY.

327 *But there were no major*: Personal visit, October 2009.

327 *On the day Roger died*: *Roger W. Straus: A Celebration*, 45.

328 *"Roger had kept FSG"*: Jonathan Galassi, interview by author, October 22, 2010.

328 *"I think he has the values"*: Stein, interview by author, July 14, 2012.

329 *But Chinski is good*: Galassi, interview by author.

329 *"He's quite tough"*: Stein, interview by author.

330 *Roger had always felt*: *Roger W. Straus: A Celebration*, 95.

330 *"We went through"*: Galassi, interview by author, August 2008.

330 *Wolfe's version is*: Tom Wolfe, interview by author, August 2008. After an early interview on a related story, Wolfe—busy on his latest overdue novel—repeatedly parried efforts to schedule an interview about Straus.

331 *He was reuniting*: Motoko Rich, "Tom Wolfe Leaves Longtime Publisher, Taking His New Book," *The New York Times*, January 3, 2008.

331 *"I was Roger Straus's"*: *Roger W. Straus: A Celebration*, 80.

331 *"Roger Straus III"*: Scott Turow, interview by author, January 11, 2010; for disappointing *Ordinary Heroes* sales, see Michael Coffey, "House of Galassi," *Publishers Weekly*, July 31, 2006.

332 *"He would have moved"*: Rebecca Mead, "Dislodging F.S.G.," *The New Yorker*, March 3, 2008.

333 *At least Roger*: Roger W. Straus, Jr., Last Will and Testament, Room 311, New York County Surrogate's Court, 31 Chambers Street, New York, NY.

333 *The speakers were publishers*: *Roger W. Straus: A Celebration*, 8.

333 *"I haven't a moment's regret"*: Miller, interview by author (as is much of this final account, confirmed with Jonathan Galassi).

334 *If Peggy calls*: Galassi, interview by author; Meyer, interview by author; Miller, interview by author.

334 *"He was not a great publisher"*: In-person interviews, October 7, 2010, Frankfurt Book Fair, Frankfurt, Germany.

336 *In a long internal memo*: Leon Neyfakh, "Farrar, Straus Publisher Jonathan Galassi Carefully Assures Staff: 'We Are Not Going to Change,'" *The New York Observer*, December 17, 2008.

336 *"I don't think firing people"*: Galassi, interview by author.

338 *Permissions took forever*: Per BookScan, 21,781 copies.

338   *Another tricky writer:* Per BookScan: 45,555 copies for *Janissary Tree* in all editions; 9,211 for *The Bellini Card.*

338   *"Thrillers can make good money":* Sarah Crichton, interview by author, July 23, 2012.

339   *"They had done something":* Jonathan Franzen, interview by author, July 23, 2012.

339   *FSG pulled out the stops:* Personally attended.

340   *"Well, he kind of is":* Jeff Seroy, interview by author, August 3, 2012.

340   *Hardcover and e-book:* Per BookScan, 150,346.

341   *One of Eugenides's:* "Editor & Author: Jonathan Galassi and Jeffrey Eugenides," *Work in Progress,* July 14, 2010, www.fsgworkinprogress.com.

341   *"If you look at Merge Records":* Ryan Chapman, interview by author, June 23, 2012.

342   *"There's very little doom":* Sean McDonald, interview by author, July 10, 2012.

343   *"It was very healing":* Laura Straus, interview by author, September 9, 2011.

343   *A story in the* New York Times: Charles McGrath, "Contradictions of the Heart," *The New York Times,* January 27, 2012.

343   *One stanza toward the end:* Jonathan Galassi, *Left-handed: Poems* (New York: Alfred A. Knopf, 2012), 100.

344   *"Unless we ourselves":* Giuseppe di Lampedusa, *The Leopard,* trans. Archibald Colquhoun and Guido Waldman (New York: Random House, 2007), 28.

Bibliography

Collections Consulted and Referenced

Farrar, Straus & Giroux, Inc. Records 1899–2003. New York Public Library Manuscripts and Archives Division.

Jack Kerouac Papers. Henry W. and Albert A. Berg Collection of English and American Literature, New York Public Library.

John Chipman Farrar Papers. Beinecke Rare Book and Manuscript Library, Yale Collection of American Literature.

Robert Giroux Collection. Loyola University, New Orleans, Special Collections and Archives.

The Reminiscences of Roger W. Straus, Jr., Columbia Center for Oral History Collection.

Books

Berg, A. Scott. *Max Perkins: Editor of Genius*. New York: Dutton, 1978.

Berryman, John. *Homage to Mistress Bradstreet*. New York: Farrar, Straus and Giroux, 1956.

Birmingham, Stephen. *"Our Crowd": The Great Jewish Families of New York*. Syracuse, NY: Syracuse University Press, 1967.

Bolaño, Roberto. *2666*. Translated by Natasha Wimmer. New York: Farrar, Straus and Giroux, 2008.

Bonn, Thomas L. *Heavy Traffic and High Culture, New American Library as Literary Gatekeeper in the Paperback Revolution*. Carbondale, IL: Southern Illinois University Press, 1989.

Brinkley, Douglas, ed. *Windblown World: The Journals of Jack Kerouac, 1947–1954*. New York: Viking, 2004.

Carey, John. *William Golding: The Man Who Wrote* Lord of the Flies. New York: Free Press, 2010.

Charters, Ann. *Kerouac: A Biography*. New York: St. Martin's Griffin, 1994.

———, ed. *Kerouac: Selected Letters: 1940–1956*. New York: Penguin, 1995.

Crisis: A Report from the Columbia Broadcasting System. New York: CBS, 1938.

Dabney, Lewis M. *Edmund Wilson: A Life in Literature*. New York: Farrar, Straus and Giroux, 2005.

Daugherty, Tracey. *Hiding Man: A Biography of Donald Barthelme*. New York: St. Martin's Press, 2009.

Davis, Philip. *Bernard Malamud: A Writer's Life*. Oxford: Oxford University Press, 2007.

Davis, Sammy, Jr., Jane Boyar, and Burt Boyar. *Yes I Can*. New York: Farrar, Straus and Giroux, 1965.

Didion, Joan. *After Henry*. New York: Vintage, 1993.

———. *Slouching Towards Bethlehem*. New York: Farrar, Straus and Giroux, 1968.

Elie, Paul. *The Life You Save May Be Your Own*. New York: Farrar, Straus and Giroux, 2003.

Epstein, Jason. *Book Business: Publishing Past, Present, and Future*. New York: W. W. Norton and Company, 2002.

Eugenides, Jeffrey. *The Marriage Plot*. New York: Farrar, Straus and Giroux, 2011.

———. *Middlesex*. New York: Farrar, Straus and Giroux, 2002.

———. *The Virgin Suicides*. New York: Farrar, Straus and Giroux, 1993.

Feinstein, Adam. *Pablo Neruda: A Passion for Life*. New York: Bloomsbury, 2004.

Fitzgerald, Sally, ed. *The Habit of Being: The Letters of Flannery O'Connor*. New York: Farrar, Straus and Giroux, 1979.

Forbes-Robertson, Diana, and Roger W. Straus, Jr., eds. *War Letters from Britain*. New York: G. P. Putnam's Sons, 1941.

Franzen, Jonathan. *The Corrections*. New York: Farrar, Straus and Giroux, 2001.

———. *Freedom*. New York: Farrar, Straus and Giroux, 2010.

Galassi, Jonathan. *Left-handed: Poems*. New York: Alfred A. Knopf, 2012.

Giroux, Robert. *The Book Known as Q: A Consideration of Shakespeare's Sonnets*. New York: Vintage, 1983.

———. *A Deed of Death*. New York: Alfred A. Knopf, 1990.

———. *The Education of an Editor*. R. R. Bowker Memorial Lecture, 1982.

Gooch, Brad. *Flannery: A Life of Flannery O'Connor*. New York: Little, Brown and Company, 2009.

Grazia, Edward de. *Girls Lean Back Everywhere: The Law of Obscenity and the Assault on Genius*. New York: Vintage, 1993.

Grimm, Wilhelm, and Maurice Sendak. *Dear Mili*. New York: Farrar, Straus and Giroux, 1988.

Guggenheim, Peggy. *Out of this Century*. New York: Chameleon, 1980.

Haffenden, John. *The Life of John Berryman*. London: Routledge, 1982.

Halliday, E. M. *John Berryman and the Thirties: A Memoir*. Amherst, MA: University of Massachusetts, 1998.

Hamilton, Ian. *Robert Lowell: A Biography*. New York: Random House, 1982.

Hatch, James V. *Sorrow Is the Only Faithful One: The Life of Owen Dodson*. Champaign: University of Illinois Press, 1995.

Hemley, Cecil, and Dwight W. Webb, eds. *Noonday 2: Stories, Articles, Poetry*. New York: Noonday Press, 1959.

Herberg, Will. *Protestant, Catholic, Jew*. Chicago: University of Chicago Press, 1983.

Howe, Irving. *A Margin of Hope: An Intellectual Autobiography*. San Diego: Harcourt Brace Jovanovich, 1984.

Hulbert, Ann. *The Interior Castle: The Art and Life of Jean Stafford*. New York: Alfred A. Knopf, 1992.

Kaiser, Robert Blair. *Clerical Error*. New York: Continuum, 2004.

Kaplan, Edward K. *Spiritual Radical: Abraham Joshua Heschel in America*. New Haven, CT: Yale University Press, 2009.

Kazin, Alfred. *New York Jew*. Syracuse, NY: Syracuse University Press, 1996.

Kerouac, Jack, and Joyce Johnson. *Door Wide Open: A Beat Love Affair in Letters, 1957–1958*. New York: Viking, 2000.

Kiernan, Frances. *Seeing Mary Plain*. New York: W. W. Norton & Company, 2002.

Klieger, Christiaan. *The Fleischmann Yeast Family*. Mount Pleasant, SC: Arcadia, 2004.

Korda, Michael. *Another Life*. New York: Random House, 1999.

Kresh, Paul. *Isaac Bashevis Singer: The Magician of West 86th Street*. New York: The Dial Press, 1979.

Lampedusa, Giuseppi di. *The Leopard*. Translated by Archibald Colquhoun and Guido Waldman. New York: Random House, 2007.

Lewis, Jeffrey. *Edmund Wilson: A Biography*. Boston: Houghton Mifflin, 1995.

Loeb, Harold. *The Way It Was*. Vancouver: Criterion Books, 1959.

Malamud, Bernard. *The Assistant*. New York: Farrar, Straus and Giroux, 1957.

———. *The Natural*. New York: Farrar, Straus and Giroux, 1952.

Manheim, Frank J. *A Garland of Weights: Some Notes on Collecting Antique French Glass Paperweights for Those Who Don't*. London: Bodley Head Ltd., 1968.

Marcosson, Isaac F. *Metal Magic: The Story of the American Smelting & Refining Co.* New York: Farrar, Straus and Giroux, 1949.

Mariani, Paul L. *Dream Song: The Life of John Berryman.* Amherst, MA: University of Massachusetts Press, 1996.

———. *Lost Puritan: A Life of Robert Lowell.* New York: W. W. Norton and Company, 1994.

Merton, Thomas. *The Seven Storey Mountain.* San Diego: Harcourt Brace & Company, 1999.

Meyers, Jeffrey. *Edmund Wilson: A Biography.* Boston: Houghton Mifflin Harcourt, 1995.

Noiville, Florence. *Isaac B. Singer: A Life.* Translated by Catherine Termerson. Evanston, IL: Northwestern University Press, 2006.

Nunez, Sigrid. *Sempre Susan: A Memoir of Susan Sontag.* New York: Atlas & Co., 2011.

O'Connor, Flannery. *The Complete Stories.* New York: Farrar, Straus and Giroux, 1972.

———. *Wise Blood.* New York: Farrar, Straus and Giroux, 1990.

Phillips, William. *A Partisan View: Five Decades in the Politics of Literature.* Piscataway, NJ: Transaction Publishers, 2004.

Reinhardt, Max. *Memories.* Biddles Limited Private Edition, 1998.

Reynolds, Quentin. *I, Willie Sutton.* New York: Farrar, Straus and Giroux, 1952.

Roberts, David. *Jean Stafford: A Biography.* New York: Little, Brown and Company, 1988.

Roger W. Straus: A Celebration. New York: Farrar, Straus and Giroux, 2004.

Rollyson, Carl, and Lisa Paddock. *Susan Sontag: The Making of an Icon.* New York: W. W. Norton and Company, 2000.

Saroyan, Aram. *Friends of the World: The Education of a Writer.* Minneapolis, MN: Coffee House Press, 1992.

Silverman, Al. *The Time of Their Lives: The Golden Age of Great American Book Publishers.* New York: Truman Talley Books / St. Martin's Press, 2008.

Simpson, Eileen. *Poets in Their Youth.* New York: Random House, 1982.

Singer, Isaac Bashevis. *The Family Moskat.* New York: Farrar, Straus and Giroux, 1965.

Solzhenitsyn, Aleksandr. *August 1914.* Translated by Michael Glenny. New York: Farrar, Straus and Giroux, 1972.

Sontag, Susan. *Against Interpretation.* New York: Farrar, Straus and Giroux, 1966.

———. *The Benefactor.* New York: Farrar, Straus and Giroux, 1963.

———. *Illness as Metaphor.* New York: Farrar, Straus and Giroux, 1978.

———. *On Photography.* New York: Farrar, Straus and Giroux, 1977.

Stafford, Jean. *The Collected Stories of Jean Stafford.* New York: Farrar, Straus and Giroux, 2005.

————. *The Mountain Lion.* Albuquerque: University of New Mexico Press, 1972.

Straus, Dorothea. *Palaces and Prisons.* Boston: Houghton Mifflin, 1976.

————. *The Paper Trail: A Recollection of Writers.* New York: Moyer Bell, 1997.

————. *Thresholds.* Boston: Houghton Mifflin, 1971.

————. *Virgins and Other Endangered Spirits.* New York: Moyer Bell, 1994.

Straus, Oscar S. *Under Four Administrations.* Boston: Houghton Mifflin, 1922.

Thompson, John B. *Merchants of Culture: The Publishing Business in the Twenty-First Century.* Cambridge: Polity, 2010.

Travisano, Thomas, and Saskia Hamilton, eds. *Words in Air: The Complete Correspondence of Robert Lowell and Elizabeth Bishop.* New York: Farrar, Straus and Giroux, 2008.

Turow, Scott. *Presumed Innocent.* New York: Farrar, Straus and Giroux, 1987.

Unger, Irwin, and Debi Unger. *The Guggenheims: A Family History.* New York: HarperCollins, 2005.

Van Doren, Mark. *The Autobiography of Mark Van Doren.* San Diego: Harcourt Brace & Company, 1958. Greenwood Press reprint, 1968.

Weaver, Helen. *The Awakener: A Memoir of Kerouac in the Fifties.* San Francisco: City Lights, 2009.

Williams, Alan D., ed. *Fifty Years: A Farrar, Straus and Giroux Reader.* New York: Farrar, Straus and Giroux, 1996.

Wilson, Edmund. *Memoirs of Hecate County.* New York: Farrar, Straus and Giroux, 1980.

————. *The Sixties.* Edited by Lewis M. Dabney. New York: Farrar, Straus and Giroux, 1993.

Yourcenar, Marguerite. *Memoirs of Hadrian.* Translated by Grace Frick. New York: Farrar, Straus and Giroux, 1963.

Articles

Adachi, Ken. "Here Comes Sontag, Radiantly Literate." *The Toronto Star,* March 28, 1987.

Berger, Meyer. "Sutton, Bank Thief, Captured in Street by Brooklyn Police." *New York Times,* February 19, 1952.

Blake, Patricia. "A Diseased Body Politic." *New York Times,* October 27, 1968.

Bliven, Bruce, and Naomi Bliven. "Quartet: The Impulse to Publish." *Intellectual Digest,* November 1972.

Blow, Eleanor Pettinos. "Readers and Writers and Italy; A Report from Italy." *New York Times Book Review,* February 9, 1947.

Boyle, Robert H. "The Deuce with Love and Advantage." *Sports Illustrated,* August 28, 1972.

Boynton, Robert S. "The Burden of Profit." *Manhattan, Inc.,* September 1990.

Brockes, Emma. "Agent Provocateur." *The Guardian,* November 24, 2003.

Buckley, Tom. "Portrait of an Editor." *New York Times*, June 3, 1979.

Carter, Robert A. "Outliving the Bastards." *Publishers Weekly*, November 14, 1986.

Chicago Daily Tribune. "Pellegrinis to Publish Ariel Books." May 19, 1946.

———. "Two Publishing Firms Announce Their Merger." April 21, 1953.

Coffey, Michael. "House of Galassi." *Publishers Weekly*, July 31, 2006.

Cohen, Roger. "Roth's Publishers: The Spurned and the Spender." *New York Times*, April 9, 1990.

Columbia College Today. "Van Doren at 100." Winter 1995.

Conroy, Pat. "The Lords of Discipline, Together, 'On Paris, Writing, Food and Friendship.'" *Gourmet*, August 2006.

D'Antonio, Michael. "Little David, Happy at Last." *Esquire*, March 1990.

The Economist. "Bolaño-mania: Hymn to a Dead Chilean." November 20, 2008.

Ferrari-Adler, Jofie. "Agent & Editors: A Q&A with Jonathan Galassi." *Poets & Writers*, July 1, 2009.

Fichtner, Margaria. "Author Uses Family Saga to Comment on Society." *Miami Herald*, October 9, 2001.

———. "Susan Sontag's Train of Thought Rolls into Town." *Miami Herald*, February 19, 1989.

Fox, Margalit. "Aaron Asher, 78, Editor of Literary Heavyweights." *New York Times*, March 22, 2008.

Franzen, Jonathan. "Meet Me in St. Louis." *The New Yorker*, December 24, 2001.

———. "Why Bother?" *Harper's*, April 1996.

Fraser, C. Gerald. "John Farrar, Publisher, Editor, and Writer, Is Dead." *New York Times*, November 7, 1974.

Gates, David. "American Gothic." *New York Times Book Review*, September 9, 2001.

Giroux, Robert. "Hard Years and Scary Days: Remembering Jean Stafford." *New York Times Book Review*, June 10, 1984.

———. "A Personal Memoir." *Sewanee Review*, Vol. 74, No. 1 (Winter 1966).

———. "Rescue at Truk." *Collier's*, May 13, 1944.

———. "Robert Giroux: The Art of Publishing III." George Plimpton. *Paris Review* 155 (Summer 2000).

Hall, Donald. "Robert Giroux: Looking for Masterpieces." *New York Times*, January 6, 1980.

The Harvard Crimson. "Institute for Advanced Study Frees Scholar from Class, Tests, Students." November 7, 1953.

Heller, Karen. "A People Book." *Philadelphia Inquirer*, September 26, 2001.

Holman, Tom. "Straus Gives Way to Galassi." *The Bookseller*, February 1, 2002.

Italie, Hillel. "Carlos Fuentes Drops Publisher." *Associated Press*, July 8, 2003.

———. "Look Out This Fall for the Four 'T's.'" *Associated Press*, August 27, 2001.

Jacobs, Alexandra. "Clench Buttocks and Talk!" *New York Observer*, April 29, 2002.

Jellinek, Roger. "The Last Word: August 1972." *New York Times Book Review*, September 24, 1972.

King, Stephen. "How to Bury a Book." *Entertainment Weekly*, April 15, 2007.

Kirkpatrick, David D. "Winfrey Rescinds Offer to Author of Guest Appearance." *New York Times*, October 24, 2001.

Kleinfield, N. R. "Roger Straus: Making It as an Independent." *New York Times*, March 2, 1980.

———. "A Success Story at Farrar, Straus." *New York Times*, December 1, 1978.

Krebs, Albin. "Willie Sutton Is Dead at 79." *New York Times*, November 19, 1980.

Lambert, Craig. "Editor Extraordinaire Jonathan Galassi on the Risky Art of Publishing Books." *Harvard Magazine*, November–December 1997.

———. "Fifteen Percent of Immortality." *Harvard Magazine*, July–August 2010.

Landler, Mark. "Another German Publisher Mulls Its Wartime Past." *New York Times*, October 14, 2002.

Lee, Hermione. "Essentially Indiscreet." *The Independent*, September 2, 1990.

Lehman, David. "Robert Giroux '36." *Columbia College Today*, Fall 1987.

Lehmann-Haupt, Christopher. "Beyond, but Not Much Further." *New York Times*, October 14, 1975.

———. "Robert Giroux, Editor, Publisher and Nurturer of Literary Giants, Is Dead at 94." *New York Times*, September 6, 2008.

Lewis-Kraus, Gideon. "The Last Book Party." *Harper's*, March 2009.

Lyall, Sarah. "Farrar, Straus Heir Apparent Quits in a Genteel Family Tiff." *New York Times*, September 23, 1993.

Macdonald, Dwight. "Parajournalism, or Tom Wolfe & His Magic Writing Machine." *New York Review of Books*, August 26, 1965.

———. "Parajournalism II: Wolfe and The New Yorker." *New York Review of Books*, February 3, 1966.

Maier, Thomas J. "The Ins and Outs of Random House." *Newsday Magazine*, February 24, 1991.

Marshall, John. "Suddenly Into the Heat of the Light: Meteoric Success a Novel Experience for Author Jonathan Franzen." *Seattle Post-Intelligencer*, October 6, 2001.

Max, D. T. "Straus Dad Turns Page After Son Exits Farrar." *New York Observer*, November 15, 1993.

McCrum, Robert. "The Numbers Game." *The Observer*, April 8, 2001.

McDowell, Edwin. "Farrar, Straus Thrives on Success of 2 Novels." *New York Times*, May 17, 1988.

———. "An Independent Publisher Slowly Changes Its Ways." *New York Times*, February 18, 1987.

———. "Literary Lion Gets His Diploma After 57 Years." *New York Times*, May 12, 1988.

———. "A New Air of Confidence Pervades Harper & Rowe." *New York Times*, April 4, 1981.

———. "Roth Changes Houses." *New York Times*, August 16, 1989.

McGrath, Charles. "Contradictions of the Heart." *New York Times*, January 27, 2012.

———. "Sleepy-Eyed Writer, Wandering Byzantium." *New York Times*, March 2, 2008.

McShane, Frank. "Neruda in New York." *New York Times*, March 13, 1977.

Mead, Rebecca. "Dislodging F.S.G." *The New Yorker*, March 3, 2008.

Medchill, Lisa. "Meet the Media Mensches, 2009." *New York Observer*, January 6, 2009.

Merkin, Richard. "An Ode to Roger Straus, a Bookmaker with Qualities . . . Even if You've Never Heard of His Favorite Book." *GQ*, September 1988.

Mitgang, Herbert. "Margaret Farrar, 87, Editor of Crossword Puzzles, Dies." *New York Times*, June 12, 1984.

———. "Publishing: Neruda Speaks." *New York Times*, January 7, 1977.

Mockridge, Morton. "The Story That Isn't in the Book." *New York World Telegram*, November 1, 1965.

Moore, Michael Scott. "Poet of the Fallen World." *SF Weekly*, February 19, 2003.

Neuberger, Christine. "Book Nook." *Richmond Times Dispatch*, March 8, 1998.

The New Yorker. "The Talk of the Town." September 24, 2001.

New York Times. "Carmen de Arango Engaged to Marry." March 6, 1941.

———. "Dewey Up Late Getting Returns." November 3, 1948.

———. "Dr. Hamilton Holt, Educator, 78, Dies." April 27, 1951.

———. "Executive Memories: My Summer Job." June 10, 1979.

———. "5th Ave. Site Is Sold for 36-Story Hotel." April 18, 1929.

———. "Guggenheim-Straus Marriage Unites Noted Families." January 11, 1914.

———. "Harlem 4: Singing a Different Tune." July 9, 1972.

———. "Henry Robbins, Editor in Chief of Trade Books at Dutton, Dies." August 1, 1979.

———. "Nuptials at Home for Miss Liebmann." June 28, 1938.

———. "Paid Notice: Deaths: Giroux, Carmen de Arango." March 23, 1999.

———. "Roger W. Straus Honored by Club." January 19, 1956.

———. "R. W. Straus Weds Miss Guggenheim." January 13, 1914.

———. "Senigallia—White." December 17, 1949.

———. "2 Publishing Firms to Merge on Friday." December 29, 1947.

———. "U.S.I.A. Attacked on Anti-Red Book." May 3, 1964.

Neyfakh, Leon. "Farrar, Straus Publisher Jonathan Galassi Carefully Assures Staff: 'We Are Not Going to Change.'" *New York Observer*, December 17, 2008.

Oldenburg, Ann. "Franzen Says He Feels 'Awful' About Feud." *USA Today*, October 25, 2001.

Orrmont, Arthur. "Editing in the '40s; or, Flung from the Ivory Tower." *Connecticut Review* VII, October 1973.

Pace, Eric. "Simon & Schuster Elated Over Editorial Coup." *New York Times*, December 24, 1973.

Painton, Priscilla. "The Naughty Schoolboy." *Time*, June 12, 1989.

Parker, Ian. "Showboat." *The New Yorker*, April 8, 2002.

Partisan Review. "Demons and Dreams." Vol. 29, Summer 1962.

Plimpton, George. "The Poet in the Asylum." *Atlantic Monthly*, August 1988.

Prial, Frank J. "Macmillan General Editor Quits 4 Months after Joining Publisher." *New York Times*, November 15, 1974.

Publishers Weekly. "Farrar, Straus and Cudahy Celebrates a Tenth Anniversary." February 18, 1956.

———. "Roger W. Straus, Jr., President of Farrar, Straus and Giroux, Reflects on His Firm's 30-Year Pursuit of Literary Excellence." February 7, 1977.

———. "USIA Hit for Sponsoring Book Publishing in U.S." May 11, 1964.

Raymont, Henry. "Farrar, Straus Gets Hill & Wang." *New York Times*, September 29, 1971.

———. "Farrar Straus Gets Solzhenitsyn Book." *New York Times*, July 6, 1971.

Reginato, James. "Literary Lion." *W*, March 1996.

———. "Nobel House." *New York Magazine*, November 9, 1987.

Reif, Rita. "Versatile Furnishings Ease Art of Entertaining in Town House." *New York Times*, April 9, 1960.

Scott, Janny. "How to Persuade With a Feather (and a Quill)." *New York Times*, January 20, 1999.

Shambelain, Elizabeth. "He Is Curious (Yellow)." *Bookforum*, April–May 2007.

Shear, Jeff. "A Lawyer Courts Best-Sellerdom." *New York Times*, June 7, 1987.

Sheed, Wilfrid. "The Good Word: Since I Went Away." *New York Times*, November 3, 1974.

Shepard, Richard F. "Majestic Service Marks Farewell to Robert Lowell." *New York Times*, September 17, 1977.

Sheppard, R. Z. "Winning the Old-Fashioned Way." *Time*, February 8, 1988.

Smith, Dinitia. "The Genius: Harold Brodkey and His Great (Unpublished) Novel." *New York Magazine*, September 19, 1988.

Snyder, Gabriel. "Wolfe Disinters 'Tiny Mummies' after 35 Years." *New York Observer*, February 13, 2000.

Straus, Dorothea. "Real Estate." *Fiction*, vol. 20, no. 1 (2006).

Streitfeld, David. "Grapes of Roth." *Washington Post*, August 27, 1989.

Thompson, Bob. "A Writer Crosses Over." *Washington Post*, April 8, 2007.

Time. "Mr. Ackland's Wills." June 30, 1947.

———. "The Press: Psychic Tomorrow." September 16, 1946.

Vincur, John. "Singer, in His Nobel Lecture, Hails Yiddish." *New York Times*, December 9, 1978.

Vonnegut, Kurt, Jr. "The Kandy-Kolored Tangerine-Flake Streamline Baby." *New York Times*, June 27, 1965.

Weisberg, Jacob. "'I Am Charlotte Simmons': Peeping Tom." *New York Times*, November 28, 2004.

Weiss, Philip. "Herman-Neutics." *New York Times*, December 15, 1996.

Wolfe, Tom. "Lost in the Whichy Thicket." *New York Herald-Tribune*, April 18, 1965.

———. "Tiny Mummies! The True Story of the Ruler of 43rd Street's Land of the Walking Dead!" *New York Herald-Tribune*, April 11, 1965.

Yardley, Jonathan. "The Story of O." *The Washington Post*, October 29, 2001.

Index

Photo Credits

New Orleans. Bottom: Courtesy of Hugh J. McKenna and the Monroe Library at Loyola University New Orleans.

Page Five

Top: Copyright © Mondadori/Getty Images. Middle: Copyright © Bettmann/CORBIS. Bottom: Copyright © Mondadori/Getty Images.

Page Six

Top: Courtesy of Farrar, Straus and Giroux. Middle: Copyright © Nancy Crampton. Bottom: Copyright © Julian Wasser.

Page Seven

Sammy Davis: Copyright © Al Levine, by courtesy of Farrar, Straus and Giroux. Wilson and Sontag: Courtesy of Farrar, Straus and Giroux. Brodsky: Copyright © 2000 by Nancy Crampton.

Page Eleven

Top: Courtesy of Laura Straus. Bottom: Copyright © 2000 Nancy Crampton.

Page Twelve

Top: From *My World and Welcome To It*. Copyright © 1937 by Rosemary A. Thurber. Reprinted by arrangement with Rosemary A. Thurber and The Barbara Hogenson Agency. All rights reserved. Bottom: Courtesy of FSG.

Page Thirteen

Top: Copyright © Gasper Tringale, courtesy of Farrar, Straus and Giroux. Bottom: Copyright © Nancy Crampton.

Page Fourteen

Franzen: Copyright © 2011 Greg Martin. Eugenides: Copyright © Ricardo Barros. Bolaño: Copyright © the heirs of Roberto Bolaño, used by permission of The Wylie Agency LLC.

Page Fifteen

Both photos: Courtesy of Farrar, Straus and Giroux.

Page Sixteen

Top: Copyright © Abigayle Tarsches, courtesy of Farrar, Straus and Giroux. Bottom: Courtesy of Farrar, Straus and Giroux.

About the Author

Boris Kachka is a contributing editor at *New York* magazine, where he has written and edited pieces on literature, publishing, and theater for more than a decade. He also writes about culture and travel for *Condé Nast Traveler, GQ, Elle,* and other magazines. Born in the former Soviet Union, he was raised in Brooklyn, where he lives today with his wife.